Therapeutic

COMMUNICATION

By Jurgen Ruesch, M.D.

The Norton Library

W · W · NORTON & COMPANY · INC ·

NEW YORK

COPYRIGHT © 1973, 1961 BY W. W. NORTON & COMPANY, INC.

First published in the Norton Library 1973

ALL RIGHTS RESERVED
Published simultaneously in Canada by
George J. McLeod Limited, Toronto

W. W. Norton & Company, Inc. is also the publisher of the
works of Erik H. Erikson, Otto Fenichel, Karen Horney, Harry Stack
Sullivan, and The Standard Edition of the Complete Psychological
Works of Sigmund Freud.

Library of Congress Cataloging in Publication Data

Ruesch, Jurgen, 1909–
    Therapeutic communication.

    (The Norton library)
    1. Psychotherapy.   I.   Title.
[RC480.R8   1973]   616.8'914   72-10275
ISBN 0-393-00672-7

PRINTED IN THE UNITED STATES OF AMERICA

    4 5 6 7 8 9 0

Contents

Part One
The Framework

Part Two

The Recognition of Disturbed Communicative Behavior

Part Three

The Doctor's Therapeutic Operations

Part Four
Long-Term Therapeutic Goals

Part Five

Therapy with the Disturbed Individual

Part Six

The Disturbed Individual and his Surroundings

Preface to the 1973 Edition

GREAT CHANGES HAVE occurred since the first appearance of this book in 1961. For one, our commitment to the technological civilization has accelerated; but unfortunately we have not as yet fully understood, much less accepted, the psychological and social changes associated with the new sources of energy, the exploration of space, and the computer revolution. All we are certain of is that these changes have influenced human communication, as mentioned in the Preface to the 1968 Edition of *Communication, the Social Matrix of Psychiatry*, and our views of abnormal behavior, as sketched in the Preface to the 1972 Edition of *Disturbed Communication.*

Many of the conflicts existing between people can be traced to a discrepancy between the social order required by technology and the one needed by the individual. Characteristic of the old order is the person orientation that has dominated western civilization since the beginning of history. Characteristic of the new order is the system orientation that has come into being since the advent of the atomic age. If the world of the past was structured around people, its technology was subservient to immediate human needs; space was organized to satisfy the sense of territoriality; history was written around the personalities of the leaders; laws defined personal responsibility; tradition and informal organization regulated human relations; and communication was personal and mostly private. The new world is structured around systems made up of man, machine, and the surrounding environment. Concern with the human being as the center of the social order has given way to a concern with man-machine interaction. The individual thus has become anonymous; space and property are shared rather than owned; responsibility is collective; personal communication has given way to group communication; and privacy is rapidly disappearing.

The changing social order and the politicization of daily life are reflected in man's expectations about communication with others. Skillful, elegant, and deeply felt interpersonal exchanges are on the wane, and personally motivated communication and action intended to help another person are being replaced by third party sponsored professional procedures. And while the informal methods of yesteryear usually were voluntary and based on intimate knowledge of persons and situations, the new procedures are proscribed and carried out by interchangeably trained staff members who have little familiarity with patient or client. Mechanization and third party control of mental health procedures, whereby man is viewed as an entity that can be tuned and overhauled like a machine in the workshop, require that therapeutic communication and action be subject to peer review. Today, psychotherapy no longer is patient oriented; it is method oriented and those features that lend themselves for measurement or objective rating predominate. As the state assumed responsibility for the nation's health, maintenance and care procedures tendered by others became more important than the self-help devices of individual or family.

But no form of society can exist for long without mature, responsible individuals who are self-sufficient and self-reliant. Interpersonal communication has always been a tool of maturation and individuation, strengthening an individual's ability to cope with others, adding to his joy of life, enabling him to overcome limitations of space and time and to share with others the culture of which he is a part. Therapeutic communication as described in this book thus is not meant to be a collective procedure capable of producing a systematic effect or to change behavior in a desirable direction; rather it is intended to help the individual to overcome anxious and stressful periods, to tolerate some particularly disturbing forms of pathology, and to go on with the process of individuation and self-realization. Only if people can pursue the paths that fit their backgrounds and preparation, seeking individually meaningful goals, and coping with others in a non-disruptive way will they be able to become useful members of a community and a society. Communication, and particularly therapeutic communication, is a way of discovering the true self and gaining the courage to resist the pressures and temptations of a conformist environment. In that sense, social communication, particularly in a one-to-one setting, has been for thousands of years the force that elaborated a person's awareness of his identity. And we must presume that it will remain that way for a long time to come. That's what this book is all about.

JURGEN RUESCH

July, 1972

Preface

THE IDEAS advanced in this book rest upon foundations which were laid more than twenty years ago when I, like many others, began to investigate the psychiatric procedures of rehabilitation. It soon became apparent that all therapists, regardless of training or background, establish personal contact with the patient. From these observations there emerged the idea that inasmuch as this person-to-person element is common to all psychotherapeutic procedures it might contain the agent responsible for the improvement of the patient. However, the notion of "human relation" or "doctor-patient relationship" was too broad a concept to work with, and the need arose to isolate more specific elements in the psychological and social approaches to the patient. Inevitably the attention turned to the empirical observation of the processes of communication.

The results of the inquiries into human communication have been presented in several steps. The relation of communication theory to the field of mental health I have discussed, together with Gregory Bateson, in a volume entitled *Communication, the Social Matrix of Psychiatry* (Norton, 1951). The roles of action, gesture, and the material environment I treated pictorially, with Weldon Kees, in a volume entitled *Nonverbal Communication* (University of California Press, 1956). In *Disturbed Communication* (Norton, 1957), I drew attention to the fact that what we call social or psychological pathology is embedded in communicative behavior. When considering psychopathology, therefore, it seems more appropriate to deal with empirical observations and generalizations of the communicative process itself than to speculate about hypothetical causes inside the organism. Also, behavioral pathology cannot be treated like tissue pathology. It is neither static nor unalterable, and its phenomenology depends to a large measure upon the responses of other people.

Human experience is not an end state, and at each moment it alters its configurations, never to become the same again. Unlike the physical scientist who assumes that truth is valid unto eternity, the therapist knows of another kind of truth that is valid for brief moments only. Not as a casual observer but as a participant in an ongoing exchange, the therapist may, at some rare moments, observe that both the style and the content of a message correspond to the existing naked reality. He can also appreciate the fleeting fit of words to nonverbal components of expression; and through the combination of observation with the subjective experience of effective or ineffective communication, he can arrive at an appraisal of the disturbances of communication that prevail at a given moment.

If what we perceive as psychopathology is in essence a disturbance of communicative behavior, then our therapeutic efforts should be directed at correcting faulty communication. The present volume deals with therapeutic communication, which term covers whatever exchange goes on between people who have a therapeutic intent. The study does not emphasize one type of therapy to the exclusion of another; it does not signal the founding of a new therapeutic school or a new philosophy of life. It merely focuses on some processes that seem to be rather universal. Therapeutic communication is an activity which is probably as old as human language. As a matter of fact, one can state without exaggeration that whenever a priest, nurse, doctor, or lay person helps another human being, some elements of therapeutic communication are used, regardless of the external situation.

The trouble with most learned discussions about therapy is that the experts act like certain cooks who exhibit their spice cabinets and their utensils and let everybody taste the meal they have prepared but rarely let anybody watch them work. The tables of contents of books about therapy reflect this state of affairs. On the one hand, we find statements about theory on a high level of abstraction, and on the other hand we find case studies that tell about the personality of the patient, but rarely do we get any idea about the

workings of therapy. Everyone has to learn this the tedious way—
in the role of patient and in the role of therapist. This volume, of
course, is no exception to the rule. What is different from the
customary approach, however, is the emphasis upon the empirical
observation of the communicative process. Obscure theoretical
language has been avoided as much as possible and no global theory
of therapy has been advanced. Instead, an attempt has been made
to describe and illustrate the mediating process of mental healing—
therapeutic communication.

Acknowledgments

WHEN A MANUSCRIPT is based upon ideas and observations that have been collected over decades, it is unavoidable that some of these appear in speeches and writings before the volume is completed. Grateful acknowledgment is due to S. Karger, A. G., for permission to reproduce in part an article entitled "Transference Reformulated" which appeared originally in the Transactions of the International Congress of Psychotherapy, Zurich, 1954. I wish to thank Prof. Dr. F. Gonseth for permission to reprint parts of an article entitled "Principles of Human Communication," which appeared in Dialectica, 1957. To the two publishers of my previous works on human communication, W. W. Norton & Company and the University of California Press, I wish to express my appreciation for their unfailing support. And to Miss Susan West, who with patience and skill has assisted me with my work over the years, go my thanks for typing, editing, and bibliographical research.

THERAPEUTIC COMMUNICATION

The Argument

DEATH, DISABILITY, and anxiety remain among man's greatest concerns. Human history illustrates the diversified ways in which people have attempted to face their biological limitations. Attempts to arrest the wheels of time range from eulogies on the immortality of the soul to the accusation of sexual functions as the cause of all evil. While the dialectic materialist suggests that the establishment of a rational society will push the boundaries of the unknown farther away and therewith obviate people's insecurity, the religious fanatic insists that our existence should be devoted to a preparation for the life hereafter. Having witnessed all the solutions proposed and believed in by the great system builders of antiquity, the Renaissance, and the nineteenth century, mankind finally arrived at the propositions advanced today—namely, the scientific ones. But unfortunately it looks as utopian to alleviate inner anxiety and outer threats by collecting facts, carrying out controlled experiments, and improving comfort as it was to believe in magic (1, 3).

If we look at the achievement of science, we find that it has contributed towards the improvement of human standards of living; it has abolished many epidemic diseases; it has made possible better transportation, more rapid communication, more efficient distribution of food, and better heating and refrigeration. But so far, none of the machines that have been constructed, none of the chemicals that have been synthesized, and none of the social theories that have been advanced have fundamentally changed human nature. Neither reason nor technology has substituted for the alarm reaction which helps man to master the dangers of living. Man has remained a carnivorous animal, and whenever his aggressive tendencies are interfered with he develops rage, fear, or anxiety. In the past as well as now, aggressiveness and anxiety have been both the prime movers of behavior and the curse of mankind.

The removal of many vital threats and the improvement of standards of living did not abolish human suffering. In the past, people feared the catastrophes of nature such as plague, drought, and famine and they dreaded human aggression with weapons such as the sword, poison, and fire. Modern man does not fear nature as much as he does enervation through mechanical devices, destruction through bombs, and slow torture through radioactive substances and bacteriological warfare. Although the objects of our apprehensions have changed, the basic theme has remained the same. The age-old proposition that fear and anxiety have to be mastered individually still stands. No scientific invention and no scientific knowledge has averted the irreversible changes which biological systems are destined to undergo. In the course of centuries, our scientific knowledge about death has not increased. Death can be experienced only once, and because those who are dead are not in a position to make a scientific report about the process of dying, the event of dying is and will remain a unique first and last experience for every human being.

Many people question whether any form of psychotherapy is worth the effort, time, and money expended. To answer such a question one might turn to science to see whether there exist any research studies which would tell whether psychotherapy is as efficient as surgical or pharmaceutical intervention. The answer could be found if psychotherapy could be limited to a short span of time; but when a process takes many months or years, it is impossible to exclude other contributing factors. Therefore it is unlikely that one can decide whether psychotherapy is better or worse than another method, or just what it accomplishes (4). Therapy is a learning process, and learning requires involvement with other people. That such cannot be replaced by drugs or by electrical or chemical procedures is quite obvious. The only question is whether such a learning process can be carried out more advantageously in one setting as opposed to another. Just as there are different accommodations in hotels, so there are different arrangements to carry out therapy: in the private office, at home, or in the hospital.

Just as we have no way of comparing psychotherapy to other treatment methods, we have no way of comparing one method of psychotherapy to another. Nobody can be subjected to the same course of psychotherapy twice, and nobody can specify the state of the patient who begins therapy or the state of the patient who terminates therapy. All we can say is that many years later either the patient seems to fill his place in society or else he is permanently hospitalized. And if the patient is functioning satisfactorily, can we ascribe the improvement to therapy? Nobody can answer this question with certainty. Educators face somewhat the same difficulty. Can the graduates of Sandhurst be compared to those of West Point? In all educational and communicative procedures, we have to accept the fact that validation is usually impossible. We educate and do therapy the best we can, and in the course of centuries a cumulative body of knowledge evolves which seems to set a style. And although this procedure sounds highly unscientific, this is the way the world has lived and existed up to now and in all probability is going to exist for a long time to come.

In raising the question of the validity of therapy, one might just as well question the justification for living or inquire whether man would be better off without a nose. But inasmuch as life exists and people have noses, we had better accept these facts as given; and this applies to people's need for therapy and counsel as well. Whether an individual is happier under one set of circumstances as opposed to another cannot be answered by scientific methods because the feeling of gratification and the sense of worthwhileness are appraisals which each individual has to carry out for himself. Psychotherapy has not been designed to make people more successful or more efficient but happier, adjusted, and contented. When medical men or surgeons validate a treatment method, they use as a criterion the survival of the organism or the functioning of an organ system (2). But mental diseases and neuroses are not fatal, nor do they produce blindness, deafness, or limitation of movement. Psychiatric conditions are the result of a multitude of forces which impinge upon the inner experience of man and are expressed in the patient's communicative behavior. If, as therapists, we can reestablish contact and help the patient towards a subjectively more rewarding way of communication, we know that the patient ceases to be in trouble. He still may have some of his symptoms; he still may be incapacitated; but he feels happier. The task of psychotherapy thus is not to achieve "objective improvement"—a condition which is defined by the value system of the observer—but "subjective improvement," which is defined by the experience of growth and satisfaction of the patient.

From the viewpoint of the external observer, psychotherapy hardly changes the character of people in a radical way. Instead, through continuous exchange the patient is helped to accept the physical, psychological, and social limitations of his existence, and he learns not to deplore what he is or what he has but to make the best of it. If through social interaction the patient thus can come nearer to the realization of his potentialities while at the same time respecting, within limits, the conventions imposed by the group, and if he can find within this framework a new meaning in life, then the therapist has accomplished his task. This indeed is but a definition of goals which can be achieved my many different means. There exist many methods of psychotherapy, and the term "therapeutic communication" perhaps best does justice to these multitudes of approaches.

There are those who feel that therapy can only be experienced and not assessed. There are even a few who believe that it cannot be reasonably discussed—particularly not in writing. To arrange verbal symbols one after the other and to read line after line in no way correspond to the impact of simultaneous impressions experienced in live interaction. The reader compensates for this deficiency by combining the meaning of what he reads with his own past experiences in order to have the printed word come to life. Although therapeutic communication is a skill learned by practice and applied in action, it has components which are based upon scientific propositions that can be reported in writing. It is obvious that actions and words are accessible to a neutral observer, that their impact upon others can be studied, and that, within limitations, people's reactions can be predicted. Then there are those aspects of therapeutic communication that have to be experienced by a participant who in turn can give us a personal report. The aspects of therapeutic communication that are based upon existential propositions involve scanning of evidence, decision-making, timing, and all the affective components that accompany these processes. It goes without saying that some of the sensations experienced by the participants actually cannot be talked about because there are no words which would do them justice.

Thus therapeutic communication remains a mixture of observable facts, reportable experiences, and non-reportable emotions. Art, craft, and science are combined to help the individual maintain his own identity and sanity against the pressures of mass communication and the collective state. Therapeutic communication is a skill practiced by professionals in order to help people overcome temporary stress, to get along with other people, to adjust to the unalterable, and to overcome psychological blocks which stand in the path of self-realization.

References

1. Polanyi, M.: *Personal Knowledge.* 428 p. Chicago: University of Chicago Press, 1958.
2. Ruesch, J.: Science, behavior, and psychotherapy. In *Modern Concepts of Psychoanalysis* (L. Salzman and J. H. Masserman, editors.) New York: Philosophical Library, 1961.
3. Siu, R. G. H.: *The Tao of Science.* 180 p. Cambridge and New York: Technology Press and Wiley, 1957.
4. U. S. National Advisory Mental Health Council, Community Services Committee: *Evaluation in Mental Health.* Report of the Sub-committee on Evaluation of Mental Health Activities. 292 p. Washington: U. S. Public Health Service Publication #413, 1955.

Part One

The Framework

Chapter One

The Development of Therapeutic Communication

THE CULTURAL MATRIX OF PSYCHOTHERAPY

The Judaeo-Christian tradition · The Greco-Roman tradition · The Anglo-Saxon tradition · The Judaeo-Christian tradition in psychoanalysis · Greco-Roman tradition and classical psychiatry · Anglo-Saxon tradition and group psychology · American psychiatry and Western tradition

THREE SIGNIFICANT traditions have influenced psychotherapeutic practices in Western Civilization: the Judaeo-Christian, the Greco-Roman, and the Anglo-Saxon.

The Judaeo-Christian tradition is characterized by an emphasis on moral and abstract principles. The Jewish culture contributed to Western civilization the ten commandments at the time of Moses, the turning of the cheek at the time of Christ, the restrictions on private property at the time of Marx, and the knowledge of the unconscious at the time of Freud. All of these contributions have in common the fact that the individual has to master a moral principle which may go against his nature. The ten commandments are anti-instinctual; the turning of the cheek is anti-aggressive; the Marxian idea is anti-retentive; and the Freudian idea is anti-conscious.

The Greco-Roman tradition evolved on the eastern shores of the Mediterranean and later extended westward. It began with the Phoenicians, enveloped the Greeks and Romans, and ended in Western Europe. Unlike the Semitic tradition which prohibited the reproduction of pictures of God, the Mediterranean tradition emphasized imagery. In the thousands of years of Jewish history, contributions which require analogic codification have been few and far between, and those that require digital or verbal codification have been plentiful. As a matter of fact, in the Jewish culture the analogic was practically suppressed. In the Greco-Roman tradition, however, two- and three-dimensional models of deities and of people are embodied in countless temples, statues, and murals. The Greco-Roman solution to human problems was not to establish morality in the individual but to create a man-made social order, which culminated in the codification of Roman Law. From the attempts of City Republics like Athens to the proposals of French Revolutionaries, the aim was to establish the supremacy of an order administered by the church or the state which would transcend individual morality. "Liberté, egalité, fraternité" is the slogan of the French Revolution that established a new order in the Western world.

Finally we have in the north the Anglo-Saxon tradition which was neither moralistic nor legal. The common law is a history of past decisions, made by human beings about human beings, in which few abstract principles are involved and expediency predominates. The Anglo-Saxon solution to human affairs is to meet in groups, to talk about the issues involved, to find a compromise, or, if this is impossible, to fight.

These three traditions are exemplifed in many of the psychiatric therapies. The Judaeo-Christian tradition is upheld by psychoanalysts, who check upon one another and upon their trainees to see that each person faithfully upholds psychoanalytic principles. Purity of belief, exclusion of dissenters, adherence to an established methodology, and dogmatic defense of the established theory thus become prime concerns. The goal of psychoanalysis is the understanding of intrapsychic conflicts which is arrived at by exploration of the unconscious. Working through of conflicts in the transference situation brings about greater understanding of self, which in turn may or may not be accompanied by an improvement of the patient. The psychoanalytic method has taken over many features from

Judaism and Catholicism. Introspection, interpersonalization of inner conflicts, interpretation, ritualization, and redemption of the morally guilty sinner by the Savior are but a few examples in question.

The Greco-Roman influence led to the development of a different kind of tradition. Men such as Kraepelin, Bleuler, Charcot, and Janet began to study natural phenomena and tried to derive laws which would do justice to nature-made order. Kraepelin's prognostic types, Kretschmer's constitutional types, Jung's work on the introvert and the extrovert, and finally the contributions of the phenomenological psychiatrists and the existentialists all are built upon the assumption that there are some unalterable facts in behavior which have to be accepted. While the Judaeo-Christian tradition implies that man triumphs over nature through moral or otherwise appropriate behavior, the Greco-Roman tradition assumes that man is in nature, subject to its laws, and that adaptation to the unavoidable is the best solution.

Finally we have the Anglo-Saxon influence with its belief that man triumphs over nature by daring, exploitation, resourcefulness, and industrial production. It is the extrovert's solution to life. He believes that as long as he does, and does right, nothing can happen to him. He depends upon the support of his peers; and as a result of this attitude group therapy, interpersonal schools of psychiatry, and the study of communication have emerged.

All three traditions are found in American psychiatry. The orthodox psychoanalysts represent the Judaic tradition of moral triumph; the existential psychoanalysts and the traditional psychiatrists represent the man-in-nature principle of the Greco-Roman tradition; and finally the group therapists, the child psychiatrists, and the interaction therapists represent the Anglo-Saxon tradition. It goes without saying that these three basic trends intermingle with one another and eventually will be amalgamated, but many of the controversies and the bitter feuds in psychiatry and psychoanalysis can be traced to these different value systems and views of nature which go deeper than the individual dares to think (48).

PSYCHOTHERAPEUTIC METHODS

Magic and faith healing · Rational healing methods · The humane approach · Hypnotism · Sigmund Freud · The psychoanalytic method · Educational methods · Authoritative methods · Other Psychotherapeutic schools · Psychotherapy in America

Since time immemorial the art of healing has been rooted in empirical observation on the one hand and in magic on the other. As people learned to make medicines out of herbs, roots, leaves, animal tissues, and minerals and as they concocted liniments, mixed ointments, and acquired the skill to set fractures and to treat wounds, the empirical foundations of medicine were laid. In later centuries, progress became intimately tied to science and technology, which developed instruments and methods to explore bodily functions and to combat disease.

The magic component of the art of healing originated in people's emotional make-up. In the face of adversity, when they could neither understand nor manage threatening experiences, they developed certain explanations, beliefs, and rituals which would assuage anxiety and uncertainty. Since supernatural experiences are closely related to magic beliefs, healing became intimately tied to religion. Psychotherapy thus is founded not only on early oriental or western magic beliefs but also on religious practices as laid down in the sacred books of the East—the Upanishads, the Bhagavad-Gita, and Buddha's Fire Sermon—and the holy books of the West—from the Old and New Testaments all the way to Mary Baker Eddy's *Science and Health* (14). In ancient times, therefore, priests frequently engaged in the art of healing and, depending upon their culture, they may have engaged in magic healing, practiced therapy by amulet or they may have relied upon faith healing. Although the dividing line between magic and faith healing cannot be drawn with any accuracy, one can usually distinguish one from the other. Magic healing is based upon extremely improbable assumptions which are not founded in experience; faith healing, in contrast, relies upon observable psychological phenomena and its underlying assumptions are much more probable and are the outgrowth of concrete experiences.

In the history of mental healing, the naturalistic, magical, and faith components all have had their day. During the enlightened Hellenic period of civilization, the teachings and writings of Plato, Epicurus, and Hippocrates did much to introduce rational healing methods. At the time of Rome's domination of the ancient world, the naturalistic approach, which prescribed diet, diversion, and rest and advocated the overcoming of fear, existed side by side with logical persuasion and belief in miracle cures. With the decline of the Roman Empire and the advent of Christianity, rational and naturalistic approaches disappeared and reliance upon pure faith healing predominated. This state of affairs continued in the western world until the rise of scientific psychology in the eighteenth century (7).

In the age of enlightenment, the intellectual approach to life advocated by such men as Voltaire, Hobbes, and Locke prepared the way for later scientific psychotherapy, and many of their notions have survived to the present day. The rational trends of the eighteenth century did not significantly alter earlier Greek formulations, inasmuch as both were intellectual and naturalistic and both represented to some extent a reaction against demonology, magic, and ignorance (41). The rational approach was of course intimately tied to the development of logic. From the days of Aristotle to the nineteenth century, hardly any important innovations were made, inasmuch as logic was treated as a closed system similar to Euclidian geometry. It was taught in western universities in the same way as Aristotle had taught it about 330 B.C. (45). Actually, the great turn of events came in the nineteenth century when Pinel in France, Tuke in England, and Rush in America advocated respect for the integrity of the mentally ill. Pinel took off the iron anklets and handcuffs of his wards, he talked to his patients, and he treated them with kindness (14). Tuke stood for moral therapy, encouragement, and judicious kindness. At that time, the foundations were laid for the basic attitudes prevailing in modern psychiatry: first, that the patient is a human being; second, that he is approachable and treatable; and, third, that the human relationship is of the essence.

In the middle of the nineteenth century, psychotherapy began to develop along technical lines. In 1843, Braid introduced the term "hypnotism" to contrast his procedure and theory with Mesmerism and animal magnetism, which, after over sixty years of existence, finally disappeared. Braid observed the recovery of memories, he postulated the existence of a double consciousness, and he described the suggestibility of his patients which made them anxious to comply with the requests of others. But the greatest boost hypnosis received was from the scientific work of Charcot, Liébeault, and Bernheim, whose investigations paved the way for the discovery of the psychoneuroses (62).

Freud, born in 1856, was able to partake of and to learn from the work of the French psychiatrists. He saw hypnotism practiced in the Salpêtrière in Paris and heard of the work done in Nancy. His studies of hysteria (6), particularly, are deeply affected by these experiences, although his later works progressed beyond the phenomena of suggestibility and hypnosis. Freud's contributions to psychotherapy were mainly of a theoretical nature and aimed at a better understanding of the psychological forces within the individual. Introducing the concept of mechanism, he postulated that the force of repression blots out unpleasant memories or motives that are bound to have painful consequences. Thoughts which are removed by repression from awareness are supposed to continue their existence in the unconscious, from where they exert a powerful influence upon the conscious strata of the mind. Following this line of thought, Freud then judged that if unconscious memories were brought into consciousness they would cease to exert their subversive influence. He conceived of psychoanalysis as a process devoted to the undoing of the patient's mechanisms of defense and an exposure of his unconscious conflicts by means of free association and contextual inference of the therapist. He realized that the patient's biography is the proper object of medical study and insisted that the patient's emotional relationship to the physician is central to all therapy (44).

Although a fair degree of agreement exists with regard to the choice of therapeutic methods in clearly diagnosed cases, dispute exists as to the merit of each method in borderland conditions. The opinions seem to be especially divided when psychoanalysis, psychotherapy, and group therapy are compared. In psychoanalysis, for example, the patient is seen from four to five times a week. He reclines on a couch, does not face the therapist, and engages in free association. The patient is supposed to become aware of his unconscious fantasies and conflicts as the therapist, through interpretations, tries to act like a mirror. The whole procedure is based upon the assumption that a rational individual who faces "reality" and has insight lives more successfully and more gratifyingly than does the person who engages in magic thinking. The analytic method has been applied with good results to patients who have character neuroses or psychoneuroses. But inadvertently a generalization crept in, and all the assumptions which apply to a well-defined analytic situation were transferred without modification to differently structured therapeutic contexts. By implication, the belief became widespread that only an analytically trained person would make a good psychotherapist (11). Although psychoanalytic training may help an individual to understand himself, a great many other factors enter into the making of a psychotherapist. As a matter of fact, psychoanalytic training may in some persons obliterate those features which make for good therapy—namely, flexibility. By insisting upon the existence of a method, it offered a crutch to those whose rigidity of character did not allow flexible adaptation.

Everybody is familiar with the need to adapt methods to circumstances and patients rather than to squeeze patients into the mold of therapeutic methods for which they are not fitted. The failures of the psychoanalytic method, for example, are found in therapy with schizophrenics, psychopaths, immature people, and persons suffering from brain disease. These types of patients comprise well over ninety per cent of the psychiatric case material. These patients cannot be treated by means of free association and interpretation because they either have an underdeveloped symbolization system or have suffered through disease. In these cases, the patients' significant expressions fall into the realm of action, gesture, or exhibition of body parts (47) rather than into the field of verbal expression. The therapists who specialize in education and re-education fare somewhat better with immature persons and psychopathic personalities than the psychoanalysts. Since infantile patients cannot be controlled through verbal communication, they have to be taught through the compelling nature of personal contact, action, and group experience. The psychosomatic or psychopathic patient who is not well versed in the digital-verbal methods of communication improves when nonverbal-analogic methods of communication are employed. Conversely, it is worth noting that the educational and re-educational methods seem to fail in the field of the psychoneuroses proper, where the word exerts a more controlling influence.

A correctly functioning individual is able to integrate the most diversified experiences. Such integration is not possible, however, if some information is missing. Educational and re-educational methods aim at compensating for this deficiency. In one instance, a person may lack technical information; or the emphasis may be more in the direction of feelings rather than thoughts or actions. The depressed patient who maximizes feelings minimizes action; the psychopath who maximizes actions tends to minimize feelings. Only if these components of existence are well balanced can the individual operate with information and interpolate, extrapolate, and predict events. The more authoritative approaches of therapy, which advocate the establishment of strict discipline not only for action behavior but also for the management of thoughts and feelings, are useful in therapy with certain labile and undisciplined personalities. Sometimes people can organize their thoughts and feelings if new ways of solving problems are offered them by a benevolent parent substitute. Dubious of authoritative methods, such patients discover, sometimes as a first experience, the supportive function of a person in authority, which enables them to learn.

But in addition to these happenings on Main Street, a few other contributors have to be remembered (34, 52, 53). Dubois (13) advocated powerful autosuggestion as well as suggestion induced by another person as a method of therapy, and he called his procedure "moral orthopedics." This idea, which later was accepted by Janet (32), was also propagated by Coué, an apothecary of Nancy. In America, Adolf Meyer, who had rejected the Kraepelinian notion of different mental diseases, postulated that psychological illness is a reaction to internal and external stress. His therapeutic method, later called "distributive analysis," emphasized not so much the abnormal features in the patient's personality as those aspects which could improve the patient's life situation. The doing was put ahead of the being, and the conscious over the unconscious. His theoretical position did much to pave the way towards a therapeutic attitude which postulates that psychotic patients can be treated by means of psychotherapy. Without minimizing the psychotherapeutic contributions of Jung, Adler, Reich, Stekel, and many others, one can in all fairness state that their work did not fundamentally alter the picture of psychotherapeutic practices in the United States.

When psychoanalysis slowly spread from Europe to America, it met entirely different conditions from those that were prevalent on the continent. Behaviorism, psychobiology, and the group oriented attitude of the people were foundations on which a more socially and action-oriented form of therapy could grow. The Anglo-Saxon-dominated scene was a paradise for extroverts, where doing was put before being and where the introverts were for all practical purposes considered misfits. Here the essentially introspective character of psychoanalysis changed; it became a standardized method, taught in a standardized way. And the heretofore therapeutically oriented body of theory was applied to a great many different fields. Psychology, anthropology, child development, social work, and nursing thus were deeply influenced by psychoanalytic thinking, which fact in turn helped to create a mental hygiene atmosphere which radically differs from that of other countries. Sullivan (56), Horney (28), Fromm (19), and others combined knowledge gained from psychoanalysis and human development with the findings of social science and the much older body of knowledge of psychotherapy which has been handed down to us since antiquity. That this rephrasing and reintegration has influenced the psychiatric scene at large is evident in the contributions of such diversified authors as

Alexander and French (2), Cameron (8), Diethelm (12), Fromm-
Reichmann (20), Masserman (36), Wolberg (61), and many others
(29, 30, 40). After including culture and society in their therapeutic
considerations, the therapists naturally turned their attention to
the group phenomena. That therapy no longer is limited to two-
person situations is evident in the writings of group therapists (16,
25, 33, 37, 55) who have much to offer to the student of therapeutic
communication. After focusing upon the patient's inner conflicts,
his social relations, and the society and culture in which he lives,
the cycle would not be complete without study of the therapist
himself. In recent years, the endowment, training, and natural
qualifications of the therapist and his choice of patients have occupied more of the limelight than before (15, 27). The yearly reviews of psychotherapy (42) reflect both the range and the gradual
shift of interest within the field that is taking place in America and
abroad today.

COMMUNICATION AND THERAPY MERGE

*The individual in isolation · The individual in the group · Communica-
tion as a therapeutic tool · Culturally and socially oriented therapists ·
Theory of communication · Thought reform · Brainwashing · Reintegration after reform · Differences between brainwashing and therapy ·
Convergence of science and therapy · Consolidation of theory with practice*

At the turn of the nineteenth century, Freud presented us with
what was then the most sophisticated model of intra-individual
functioning; and today, almost sixty years later, it is still the most
suitable model for the understanding of intrapsychic phenomena.
Freud's great advances were made possible because he changed
some fundamental assumptions in his scientific approach and hence
could raise questions which were new and different. Significantly
he turned from the study of organic to organismic events, from
neurology to psychology, and from part functions to whole functions.
Being a scientist, he was familiar with the advances made in neurology and neurophysiology; and being a thinker, he was capable

of abstracting some of the principles he saw operating in other fields. He then applied these principles to psychological thinking and developed the psychoanalytic model of psychic functioning (18). However, we cannot rest on the laurels that our forefathers earned. Now, in the middle of the twentieth century, we have come to recognize that the study of individuals in isolation from one another and from their surroundings does not explain satisfactorily abnormal behavior. Thus we have gradually included in our observations aggregates of human beings—groups and society—as being equally significant in the investigation of mental disease (23).

Every person living at a given historical period is both a contributor to and a victim of the cultural climate of his time (57). Scientists thus cannot escape the intellectual heritage passed on to them by their predecessors or the contemporary influence exerted by neighboring fields. Nor are they immune to the changing economic structure of their time. Today, people are specialized, manufacturing in one region one kind of product—for example, automobiles—and relying on another region for food. Today it is possible to have breakfast on one continent and lunch on another, while ideas travel around the globe in a matter of seconds. This quickening tempo of technological advances makes people more interdependent upon one another. Gone are the days of self-sufficiency; and even psychotherapists cannot shield themselves against these trends of collectivism, automation, diffusion of information, and encounters with members of an out-group. Gone are the times when people strove for mastery, stability, and universality. The age of the individual has passed and we have entered the corporate era of existence—a new form of feudal dependency, with the difference that the overlord is the corporation, the union, the university, or the government (58). As early as high school, the up-and-coming youngster has to cast his lot with an industrial concern. Retirement, security, and promotion possibilities are tied to seniority, and if the individual should change his mind around the age of forty he becomes an "out" and has no possibility of becoming an "in" again. That in such an atmosphere the emphasis of therapeutic practice shifts from the individual to the group is not surprising. And instead of engaging in introspection and speculation about intra-psychic processes, the modern psychotherapist by necessity has to concern himself with interpersonal communication (38, 39). This shift in emphasis is, furthermore, accompanied by a shift in the role of the psychotherapist. Formerly an alienist and concerned with the insane, he now has become the guardian and educator of marginal people. Some of these stand with one foot in the cesspool of glory and the other in the grave, while hypertension, ulcers, or alcoholism slowly but surely gnaws away at their insides. Others may have barely made the grade and floated along until they discovered that they were nobodies, going nowhere. In middle age, then, despera-tion may have induced them to seek psychiatric help. Finally, there are those who for a variety of reasons never did make it; often with-out kin or family to take care of them, they have to be woven back into the structure of society.

In this group-oriented, "quick flux" cultural matrix, psychotherapy has to be group-oriented and communication-minded (1, 24). The psychotherapist, like his younger cousin, the psychoanalyst, and his nephew, the group therapist, relies upon communication to ap-proach his patient. Scorning drugs and shying away from surgical procedures, he makes his living by observing and exchanging signals. The communication engineer, the semanticist, the linguist, the propagandist, the anthropologist, and even the neurophysiologist come along and provide him with facts and theories about sym-bolic behavior. And having been exposed, in all likelihood, to psy-choanalysis, the psychotherapist cannot help but discover that psy-choanalytic theory is, and has been right along, nothing but another theory of communication in disguise. Burdened by older formula-tions which date back to the time when scientists loved to dissect the individual, psychoanalytic theory is swamped with constructs such as "mechanism" or "resistance," and the student often cannot see the forest for the trees. And then all of a sudden it strikes home: the notions of transference, countertransference, transference neurosis, and working through represent nothing else but attempts to intro-duce notions of communication into a rather mechanical and linear theory of behavior. There is really no cogent reason why in therapy the patient's free associations, his coherent accounts, dreams, and nonverbal statements should be reduced to terms such as energy or instinct. We observe communication; we respond through communication; so let us stick to empirical generalizations of communication. The closer our theoretical thinking remains to our empirical operations, the better off we are; otherwise the relationship between theory and practice may become purely coincidental.

Many modern therapists are aware of these difficulties. If Fromm, Sullivan, and Horney often have been lumped together as culturalists (14), it seems but fair to point out that by including culture in their formulations they did indeed move a step closer to communicative reality; they recognized that abnormalities of behavior are defined by cultural norms and that their expression occurs through verbal and nonverbal language. Sullivan pioneered such notions as the participant-observer in which he states that the experience of the individual is dependent upon his role and function in a particular communication system. He also called attention to the interpersonal infectiousness of anxiety and dared to make such a basic human experience as loneliness—which was later elaborated by Fromm-Reichmann (21)—the subject of study (56). In a way, Sullivan's interpersonal emphasis is much closer to the existential and phenomenological orientations of contemporary European therapists (3, 4, 5) than to the nineteenth century thinking of orthodox Freudians. Unlike Freud, who was caught in the straitjacket of natural science with its Cartesian subject-object split, Sullivan was more familiar with the social sciences. In paying more attention to the total experience of an individual at a given moment, he is more present- than past-oriented and less deductive and deterministic. He is mainly responsible for a revival of a more optimistic attitude towards the treatment of schizophrenics which much earlier was initiated by Bleuler and Jung and in recent years found expression in the work of Fromm-Reichmann (20).

In the last fifteen years, many psychotherapists (50) and psychoanalysts (10) have become fascinated with communication theory, which offers enough flexibility to take care of all psychotherapeutic exigencies. The introduction of modern notions of feedback and correction (59) into therapeutic theory represents a significant advance over older theoretical models. In dealing with information about action rather than with action itself, the system has attained flexibility and complexity suitable for the study of complicated psychic and social events. In emphasizing the exchange of material elements and information within the system and with the surroundings, the theory has the characteristics of an open system. And being a theory concerned with the inter-relatedness of parts with other parts and the whole, it has become a theory of theories (46). Communication theory is not particularly concerned with those processes which deal with the structure of constituent parts but leaves this task to the various technical disciplines which, with their own methods and theories, can do a better job. Instead, it treats parts of the system as "black boxes" which are characterized by input and output and a device to retain information. While the organ or the individual may be analyzed in terms of neurophysiology or psychoanalysis, the relationship of one part to another can be explained better in terms of communication theory than by any other theory.

In recent years there has arisen another type of behavioral reform which did not have its origin in the psychiatric community. The Russians and Chinese subjected their prisoners to "thought reform" and dealt at great length with the problems of anxiety, anger, fear, guilt, shame, and depression. Lifton (35) described the brainwashing procedures as follows: After the prisoner is brought in, repeated interrogation leads to a kind of emotional assault in which all the ideas the prisoner believed in and all the things he did are condemned. In this phase, the prisoner is gradually deprived of his old value system and he suffers a symbolic death. His identity herewith is wiped out, and it is clearly established that he is guilty of a crime. The breakdown is hastened by feeding the prisoner a poor diet, by separating him from others, or by not giving him hygienic facilities. After the morale of the prisoner has been systematically undermined, he is faced with an acute conflict: his jailers present him with a new view and a new system of values which deride the old ones, while at the same time the new system is so inflexibly presented that the prisoner cannot master the relevant cues even if he is willing to do so. As a result, the prisoner experiences complete despair and feels utterly helpless.

After the prisoner has broken down, a period of leniency is interposed. Here the prisoner is given hope and he begins to see a way out of his heretofore insoluble confusion. This leniency is combined with a suggestion to confess, and as time progresses the prisoner is told to denounce his former beliefs, to expose his associations, and to purge himself of the past. This process is hastened by interposing periods of silence and isolation.

As the breakdown progresses, the prisoner is helped, in a third stage, to channel his guilt and to pin it onto specific actions of the past. The concretization of the feeling of having done wrong is the first step towards acquiring a new identity.

In a fourth stage, the prisoner learns that his personal wrongdoings are not isolated phenomena. He is told that he has been a victim of imperialist warmongers, and by now he is ready to express his need for personal reform. This declaration is rewarded by group acceptance, by sharing ideas with others, and by better physical treatment. And as he has suffered sufficient punishment for his guilt, he acquires a different perspective of the world in which the new political regime offers him an additional lease on life (26).

The reader will immediately see that many parallels exist between psychotherapy and thought reform (51), with the exception that psychotherapy does not use physical stress to weaken the individual. In brainwashing, some of the interview procedures such as interrogation, conversation, and accusation are liberally employed. Catharsis and confession—the tools of the psychiatrist and the priest—are likewise represented. Repetition is prominent—that is, the restating of desirable goals, which is a method familiar to the advertiser. Thought reform thus has welded the methods of the clergy, the psychiatrists, the advertisers, and the police into a new method. While brainwashing showed some striking short-term results, the long-term effect has been poor. Eventually many of the brainwashed prisoners either resisted or returned home, to adopt once more their original system of values. Destruction of existing attitudes, beliefs, and values forces the victim to embrace whatever is offered; but unless hope, belief, faith, and trust are present to direct the individual's anticipatory behavior, the results will be poor. Apparently improvement of a lasting nature is always accompanied by faith in the person who acts as a therapist (17), and this was not present in the case of brainwashing.

In summary, then, one might say that therapeutic communication is the get of four grandparents known as psychoanalysis, reeducation, logical reasoning, and authoritative suggestion. Not being concerned with purity of origin, loyalty to forefathers, or other mythological aspects of art and science, the communication therapist is free to use any source to accomplish his ends. To understand the exchange of messages between people, he borrows from social psychology and cybernetics (46, 50); to appraise what goes on inside the individual, he utilizes the psychoanalytic scheme; to assess pathology (49) and some of the therapeutic processes, he draws heavily from clinical psychiatry; and to assess the cultural and social milieu, he turns to the social scientist (60). In terms of technology, we are but at the beginning of the experimental exploitation of therapy. In terms of experience, however, we have a cumulative body of knowledge which recounts the beneficial results of human communication over several thousand years.

At present we are in a phase of consolidation. The differences of opinion of the various schools of therapy seem to be giving way to a more tolerant and constructive attitude (42). Similarities are emphasized more than differences, and therapists have discovered that their practices are more alike than their theories (48). Interdisciplinary research at the theoretical and practical levels (22) as well as international meetings have yielded promising results (29, 30). To the outsider, these steps are perhaps not spectacular; but the insider knows that concepts of social psychiatry and communication engineering have been introduced into the theory of therapy (9, 31, 50, 54) and therapeutic and psychoanalytic concepts have found their way into social science (43); and so goes the process of diffusion. As the development of social science and therapy progresses, the theoretical structure of psychiatry is likely to become more operational and therefore more connected with the empirical procedures of the therapist.

References

1. Ackerman, N. W.: *The Psychodynamics of Family Life*. 379 p. New York; Basic Books, 1958.

2. Alexander, F., and French, T. M.: *Psychoanalytic Therapy*. 353 p. New York: Ronald Press, 1946.

3. Berg, J. H. van den: *The Phenomenological Approach to Psychiatry*. 105 p. Springfield: Thomas, 1955.

4. Blauner, J.: Existential analysis: L. Binswanger's *Daseinsanalyse*. Psychoanal. Rev., 44, 51–64, 1957.

5. Boss, M.: *Psychoanalyse und Daseinsanalytik*. 155 p. Bern and Stuttgart: Hans Huber, 1957.

6. Breuer, J. and Freud, S.: *Studies in Hysteria*. (Tr. by A. A. Brill). 241 p. New York: Nervous and Mental Disease Publishing Co., 1936.

7. Bromberg, W.: *Man above Humanity: A History of Psychotherapy*. 342 p. Philadelphia: Lippincott, 1954.

8. Cameron, D. E.: *General Psychotherapy*. 304 p. New York: Grune & Stratton, 1950.

9. Caudill, W.: Applied anthropology in medicine. Pp. 771–806 in *Anthropology Today* (A. L. Kroeber, editor). Chicago: University of Chicago Press, 1953.

10. Colby, K. M.: *Energy and Structure in Psychoanalysis*. 154 p. New York: Ronald Press, 1955.

11. Conference on Psychiatric Education: *The Psychiatrist; his Training and Development*. 214 p. Report of the 1952 Conference. Washington: American Psychiatric Association, 1953.

12. Diethelm, O.: *Treatment in Psychiatry*. (3rd ed.) 545 p. Springfield: Thomas, 1955.

13. Dubois, P.: *The Psychic Treatment of Nervous Disorders*. 466 p. New York: Funk & Wagnalls, 1906.

14. Ehrenwald, J. (Editor): *From Medicine Man to Freud*. 416 p. New York: Dell, 1956.

15. Ekstein, R. and Wallerstein, R. S.: *The Teaching and Learning of Psychotherapy*. 334 p. New York: Basic Books, 1958.

16. Foulkes, S. H.: *Introduction to Group-Analytic Psychotherapy*. 181 p. New York: Grune & Stratton, 1948.

17. Frank, J. D.: *Persuasion and Healing*. 282 p. Baltimore: Johns Hopkins Press, 1961.

18. Freud, S.: *An Outline of Psychoanalysis*. 127 p. New York: Norton, 1949.

19. Fromm, E.: *The Sane Society*. 370 p. New York: Rinehart, 1955.

20. Fromm-Reichmann, F.: *Principles of Intensive Psychotherapy*. 246 p. Chicago: University of Chicago Press, 1950.

21. Fromm-Reichmann, F.: Loneliness. Psychiatry, 22, 1–16, 1959.

22. Grinker, R. R.: *Psychosomatic Research*. 208 p. New York: Norton, 1953.

23. Grinker, R. R. (Editor): *Toward a Unified Theory of Human Behavior*. 375 p. New York: Basic Books, 1956.

24. Grotjahn, M.: *Psychoanalysis and the Family Neurosis*. 320 p. New York: Norton, 1960.

25. Hinckley, R. G. and Hermann, L.: *Group Treatment in Psychotherapy*. 136 p. Minneapolis: University of Minnesota Press, 1951.

26. Hinkle, L. E., Jr., and Wolff, H. G.: Communist interrogation and indoctrination of "enemies of the states." Arch. Neurol. Psychiat., 76, 115–174, 1956.

27. Holt, R. R. and Luborsky, L.: *Personality Patterns of Psychiatrists*. 2 v. New York: Basic Books, 1958.

28. Horney, K.: *The Neurotic Personality of our Time*. 299 p. New York: Norton, 1937.

29. International Congress for Psychotherapy: *Proceedings*, Zurich, July, 1954. 742 p. Basel: S. Karger, 1955.

30. International Congress for Psychotherapy: *Proceedings*, Barcelona, July, 1958. (In press.)

31. Jaco, E. G. (Editor): *Patients, Physicians, and Illness*. 600 p. Glencoe: Free Press, 1958.

32. Janet, P.: *Principles of Psychotherapy*. 322 p. New York: Macmillan, 1924.

33. Klapman, J. W.: *Group Psychotherapy; Theory and Practice* (2nd ed.). 301 p. New York: Grune & Stratton, 1959.

34. Kronfeld, A.: *Perspectiven der Seelenheilkunde*. 384 p. Leipzig: Thieme: 1930.

35. Lifton, R. J.: "Thought reform" of Western civilians in Chinese communist prisons. Psychiatry, 19, 173–195, 1956.

36. Masserman, J. H.: *The Practice of Dynamic Psychiatry*. 790 p. Philadelphia: Saunders, 1955.

37. Moreno, J. L. (Editor): *Group Psychotherapy: A Symposium*. 305 p. New York: Beacon House, 1946.

38. Moreno, J. L.: *Psychodrama*. First Vol. 429 p. New York: Beacon House, 1946.

39. Moreno, J. L.: *Sociometry*. 220 p. New York: Beacon House, 1951.

40. Mullahy, P. (Editor): *A Study of Interpersonal Relations*. 507 p. New York: Hermitage Press, 1949.

41. Murphy, G.: *Historical Introduction to Modern Psychology*. 466 p. New York: Harcourt Brace, 1949.

42. *Progress in Psychotherapy.* Vols. 1–4. (J. L. Moreno, coordinating editor). New York: Grune & Stratton, 1956–1959.

43. *Psychoanalysis and the Social Sciences.* Vols. 1–5. New York: International Universities Press, 1947, 1950, 1951, 1955, 1958.

44. Rado, S.: The contribution of psychoanalysis to the medical study of behavior. J. nerv. ment. Dis., 123, 421–427, 1956.

45. Rapoport, A.: The aims and tasks of mathematical biology. ETC., 8, 254–269, 1951.

46. Ruesch, J.: Synopsis of the theory of human communication. Psychiatry, 16, 215–243, 1953.

47. Ruesch, J.: Nonverbal language and therapy. Psychiatry, 18, 323–330, 1955.

48. Ruesch, J.: Communication difficulties among psychiatrists. Amer. J. Psychother., 10, 432–447, 1956.

49. Ruesch, J.: *Disturbed Communication.* 337 p. New York: Norton, 1957.

50. Ruesch, J. and Bateson, G.: *Communication, the Social Matrix of Psychiatry.* 314 p. New York: Norton, 1951.

51. Sargant, W.: *Battle for the Mind.* 263 p. New York: Doubleday, 1957.

52. Schilder, P.: *Psychotherapy.* 396 p. (enlarged and revised ed.). New York: Norton, 1951.

53. Schultz, J. H.: *Die seelische Krankenbehandlung* (4th ed.). 404 p. Jena: Gustav Fischer, 1930.

54. Simmons, L. W. and Wolff, H. G.: *Social Science in Medicine.* 254 p. New York: Russell Sage Foundation, 1954.

55. Slavson, S. R.: *Analytic Group Psychotherapy with Children, Adolescents, and Adults.* 275 p. New York: Columbia University Press, 1950.

56. Sullivan, H. S.: *The Interpersonal Theory of Psychiatry.* 393 p. New York: Norton, 1953.

57. Szasz, T. S., Knoff, W. F., and Hollender, M. H.: The doctor-patient relationship and its historical context. Amer. J. Psychiat., 115, 522–528, 1958.

58. Whyte, W. H., Jr.: *The Organization Man.* 429 p. New York: Simon & Schuster, 1956.

59. Wiener, N.: *Cybernetics, or Control and Communication in the Animal and the Machine.* 194 p. New York: Wiley, 1948.

60. Wilmer, H. A.: *Social Psychiatry in Action.* 373 p. Springfield: Thomas, 1958.

61. Wolberg, L. R.: *The Technique of Psychotherapy.* 869 p. New York: Grune & Stratton, 1954.

62. Zilboorg, G.: *A History of Medical Psychology.* 606 p. New York: Norton, 1941.

Chapter Two

The Ingredients of Therapeutic
Communication

THERAPEUTIC communication is experienced by both doctor and patient. To report such an experience, we have to use language; but let us beware of the fallacious belief that because a word has been found it does justice to the total experience itself. Language forces us to dissect in order to talk, and only if the one who reads or hears words puts them together again can he hope to get an idea of what the other one is talking or writing about. It is the task of the therapist to choose words and gestures which, when combined in the head of the patient, will produce something that is alive. Unlike the scientific expert who chooses his words in such a way that the dictionary definitions correspond to the state of affairs to be described, the therapist cares for the impact words have upon people. To produce an effect and to interpret messages are the immediate tasks of the therapist.

THERAPEUTIC COMMUNICATION
TAKES PLACE ANYWHERE

Ubiquity of communication · *Therapeutic effect of communication*
Therapeutic and ordinary communication compared

Communication is a universal function of man that is not tied to any particular place, time, or context; and basically communication which produces a therapeutic effect in no way differs from what happens in ordinary exchanges. Therapeutic communication, therefore, is not confined to an appointed hour in the doctor's office. On the contrary, it occurs almost anywhere—on the playfield, in battle, on the ward, at home, or at work. Neither is it bound to the use of certain props such as couch or chair, nor does it run off according to a special formula. Generally therapeutic communication involves more than just the therapist and the patient. A child can be therapeutic for the mother and a boss can be therapeutic for his employee; therapy is done all day long by many people who do not know that they act as therapists, and many people benefit from such experiences without knowing it. Therapeutic communication is not a method invented by physicians to combat illness; it is simply something that occurs spontaneously everywhere in daily life, and the physician is challenged to make these naturally occuring events happen more frequently.

Therapeutic communication is remedial in that a person who has learned to relate effectively will be able to accept the inevitable while steering his existence in matters where he has some choice. Therapeutic communication thus presupposes the presence of several people, one of whom must be wiser, more mature, and more skilled in communication than the others; and if this more able person uses his skills to develop the communicative functions of the immature, young, or seriously disturbed individual, then he is engaging in therapeutic communication. At times, this process is referred to as therapy; at other times as education; some call it counselling; others simply friendship. But regardless of the label given, the criterion of whether an exchange becomes therapeutic or not is tied to the perception that the other person has a certain readiness to understand, to acknowledge, and to reply. This has been aptly referred to as the therapeutic milieu (28).

But if therapeutic communication is similar to other forms of communication, what is the nature of the doctor's skill in practicing psychotherapy? Mutual influence and transmission of information are characteristic of all communication; the difference, therefore, between therapeutic communication and the kind that is carried on between people under ordinary circumstances is found in the doctor's motivation. The therapist consciously intends to influence the patient for his own good, without misusing his power to achieve personal advantages. His only reward is the fee paid by the patient or the salary he receives. While in ordinary life the salesman influences the customer to get a signature on a contract, the political candidate vies for votes, and the lawyer wishes to sway the jury, the therapist, in contrast, attempts to improve the method of communication of the patient. He focuses upon the breakdown of feedback functions, on deviant application of language, on non-integrated feelings and thoughts, and on all those processes which prevent the patient from further growth and development.

CERTAIN HOURS MAY BE SET ASIDE
FOR THERAPEUTIC COMMUNICATION

Improvement brought about by different means · Ritualization is superfluous · Appointments

The aim of therapeutic communication is to improve the patient's ability to function alone, with one other person, and in groups. This can be achieved by different means. In some instances, the internist or the neurosurgeon restores the patient's ability to communicate by medical or surgical intervention. In some cases, the clinical psychiatrist improves the patient's communication system by means of shock therapy or drug therapy. On other occasions, it may be the psychotherapist who, through social interaction, helps the patient to handle his human relations. But to achieve this end, a person must be able to perceive, to evaluate, and to express himself so that through interaction with others correction and self-correction can take place. Any event that corrects information and compels re-evaluation of the information on hand is beneficial. In formal therapeutic sessions, a given time and a given place may be reserved for the study of the patient's communicative behavior. In so doing, the doctor deliberately announces that the patient's ways of communication will be under scrutiny. In ordinary life, in contrast, talk about communication is avoided. It is impolite to make remarks about how somebody expresses himself, and messages are to be taken at face value—or so the rule says.

Most of the principles governing the management of patients have been invented for the convenience of the therapist rather than for the benefit of the patient. The rituals attached to the use of the couch, the chair, the playground, the stage, or the meeting room have developed because they increase the well-being of the therapist, and a secure therapist, of course, is more successful with his patients than an insecure one. The location of the office or the props used, therefore, are not characteristic of psychotherapy. The feature which characterizes planned therapy is the setting apart of a period of time when people convene for the purpose of communicating about communication. In such a situation, one person—the therapist —is willing to observe the processes of communication and go through the tedious work of responding in such a way that eventually the other person—the patient—will become aware of both the form and the content of his communications. This may happen in the evening or in the morning, on the playfield or in the office; but after the set time is over, the therapist is delighted to relinquish his position of therapist because anybody who has ever engaged in this activity knows how hard the work is.

Therapy does not need to be an ordeal; nor does it need to be a visionary or inspirational sort of experience. On the contrary, it is a realistically defined procedure consisting of an exchange of messages according to certain rules which have to be taught to the patient. In psychoanalysis, for example, there is a rule which indicates that the therapist should not see the patient in any other place than in his office. This rule was created for the convenience of the therapist, who has difficulty in switching from the role of therapist vis-à-vis his patient to the role of host or guest at a cocktail party. Such a rule protects both the therapist and the patient from using information gained in the course of the inquiry for the achievement of social position, power, or other private interests. However, the communication therapist has learned that it is of advantage to see a patient in different contexts with different people (20). One or several home visits are always indicated, and the therapist should have more than a fleeting acquaintance with the children and the husband or wife of the patient. In order to indicate to the patient that encounters outside the office should not be interpreted as social calls, the doctor makes an appointment beforehand. If he indicates that he would like to make a home visit on a certain day at a certain time, the patient knows that this means work.

THERAPEUTIC COMMUNICATION IS NOT A METHOD

Natural functions of man · The notion of methodology is false · Hypnosis and psychoanalysis

With the progressive development of the arts of healing, many human functions have become the subject of methodological regimentation. In formulating rules and procedures for breathing, sleeping, eating, relaxing, or walking, physicians have concentrated upon intraorganismic processes under the control of the person. Inasmuch as the ability to use these functions is built into the organism, all that regimentation can do is to create optimal conditions under which such functions can be exercised. In the case of communication, we deal with a more complex function, that is dependent upon the presence of several people. In part, it is learned spontaneously, like walking; in part it has to be taught as in the case of speaking. We know that speech and language develop fully only if another person is willing to be present and to fully participate.

There is no one method or practice that produces better communicative development than another. The most diversified childraising practices produce mature individuals; in the East, the Japanese and the Chinese, and in the West the French, the Germans, the Italians, and the English produce erudite individuals in spite of the fact that they were raised under different conditions. In any culture, educational and therapeutic practices merely attempt to utilize naturally existing conditions and practices. One can truly speak of a method only where the nature of a tool determines the technique; to be used, a screwdriver has to be inserted into the slot in the head of the screw; and screwdrivers make notoriously poor hammers. But the psychiatrist does not introduce extraneous substances or penetrate surgically under the skin. He is not limited in his procedure by the nature of the gadget. The skill of the therapist is characterized by appropriately fitting, spacing, timing, and selecting his own statements in reply to the statements of the patient. The analogy between physical and psychological "method" is thus out of place.

The rejection of the notion of methodology as applied to the natural functions of man does not bar anybody from studying earlier systematizers who had hoped to find psychological treatment methods which would introduce something that radically differs from what man experiences in daily life. Perhaps the oldest school of methodologists from whom much can be learned about communication are the hypnotists (4). Indeed, hypnosis is a method because it does not occur naturally in daily life. The hypnotists not only developed a cunning skill in selecting suitable patients for their art but they also formulated the do's and don't's of procedure and described props for the pursuit of their practice (16, 21, 33). Another source containing information about therapeutic communication is the psychoanalytic literature. Again, psychoanalysis can be called a method because people in daily life are not in the habit of free associating. The technical writings of Freud (13), Fenichel (7), Ferenczi (8), Glover (17), Reich (26), Sharpe (31), Stekel (32), Braatøy (3), and others are rich in scattered comments about communicative behavior.

THERAPEUTIC COMMUNICATION RELIES UPON SPONTANEOUS EXPRESSION

Empirical vs. hypothetical generalizations · Spontaneous expression and spontaneous reply

One of the fundamental differences between therapeutic communication as outlined in this book and the varied methods of psychotherapy and psychoanalysis described elsewhere is found in the manner in which communication is controlled. In psychoanalysis, for example, the patient has to be trained in free association and the patient's messages to the therapist may be disguised in his dreams and fantasies. The psychoanalyst, who is used to thinking in terms of such hypothetical entities as motivation, transference, defense, resistance, or fixation, also has been taught not to reply directly to the messages of the patient. And if he does reply, he usually offers an interpretation at a higher level of abstraction which may have no direct counterpart in the patient's experience. As the existential therapists and phenomenologists have pointed out (2), emphasis upon hypothetical constructs and concern with certain abstract aspects of the process of free association may interfere with the understanding of the patient and certainly disrupt the direct process of communication. Closer to the patient's empirical experiences are those therapists who emphasize overt behavior such as overprotection (23) and rivalry (22) or distinct experiences such as despair (6) or loneliness (15).

The inner experience of a patient cannot be approached by means of free association but only by studying the spontaneous expressions of the patient. The therapist who relies upon the patient's habitual ways of communicating will quickly detect whether the patient's means of expression are inadequate, in which case he will attempt to gradually change these by judicious use of replies. The closer the understanding, acknowledgment, and reply of the therapist match the empirical experience of the patient, the more effective therapy becomes. This working hypothesis is based upon the following observations:

–That understanding is based upon the mutual appreciation of actions and words.

–That verbal or action signals, if they are to be mutually understood, have to be coded in ways that are intelligible to all.

–That a reply amplifies, connects, or alters the initial statement of the patient.

–That such a reply is the more effective the more it is phrased in the language of the patient.

Therapeutic communication thus requires adaptive behavior on the part of the therapist. Not only has he to understand the messages of the patient but he has to phrase his reply in a way that is comprehensible to the patient and effective in its impact. The control measures that are necessary to maintain free association in psychoanalysis are here replaced by adaptive measures on the part of the therapist. By selectively replying or not replying, the therapist steers communication in a direction which is beneficial to the patient.

SELF-REALIZATION IS MORE IMPORTANT THAN ADJUSTMENT

Self-realization does not imply acting out · Limited adjustment

Therapeutic communication is not geared towards making a superman out of the patient; it is designed to enable the patient to experience fully, to accept what he has experienced, and to share these experiences with others. Once he is capable of doing so, he will find an equilibrium which will provide for more basic satisfactions. Therapeutic communication strives not towards conformity or adjustment but towards self-realization of the patient. This does not mean that lawlessness, acting out, complete withdrawal, or other forms of social or antisocial behavior are silently tolerated. No, on the contrary, this kind of behavior has to be corrected. But instead of judging and condemning, the therapist tries to understand the message that is coded in the patient's action behavior. A careful review usually reveals that whatever the message may be, more appropriate forms of expression and action can be worked out. This brings the patient closer to self-realization and does not conflict with law, tradition, or custom.

The word "adjustment" has an ominous flavor. It implies surrender to the values of the group, agreement with what goes on, and denial of self-determination. In Nazi Germany, many a person was well adjusted because he went along with the group and passively agreed to the terror regime. To give up individuality means moral suicide. Instead, we urge the patient towards active participation in the group, mobilizing his self-determining tendencies in an attempt to settle with others whatever differences he might have. Self-realization (30) thus requires from people the acceptance of differences and the recognition that interpersonal difficulties are settled not by violence or withdrawal but by means of communication. A person who is happy with what he is doing and is satisfied that his characteristics have been accepted has more to offer to others and is more cooperative than one who surrenders and acquiesces; on the surface, of course, adjustment may look like self-realization, but under stress, when the group disintegrates, adjustment crumbles. Only the man who has achieved a degree of self-realization can withstand adversity.

THE PRESENT MATTERS MORE THAN THE PAST OR THE FUTURE

Handling current events · What happens in the interview is the starting point

Therapeutic communication deals with the inner experiences of people as they occur at the moment. The purpose of therapeutic communication therefore is not to recall the past and to discuss endlessly events in which the doctor did not participate. Instead it is geared to the understanding of the present, and only insofar as the past helps in the understanding of the present is it called upon to help. This orientation makes demands upon the participants—acuity of observation of self and of others, ability to react openly and without reservation to the communications of the other person, and a good memory. Since many patients are incapable of observing others, of relating what they experience, and of remembering what happened, much time has to be spent in preparing the individual for communication. Once the patient has accepted the fact that he has to handle each current event on the spot, his thinking will become geared to problem-solving. The unfaltering acceptance of what exists at the moment leads to the acceptance of memories that bear upon painful events of the past. Acceptance means, of course, that the individual believes that, right now, things cannot be different than they are; it means elimination of anticipatory feelings and fantasies which detract from consideration of the status quo.

In the pursuit of effective communication, both the patient and the psychiatrist must learn to respond. Any statement of the patient produces an effect in the therapist, regardless of whether it is phrased in terms of words, gestures, or action. Statement and reply thus constitute the point of departure for any discussion that patient and doctor might have in the therapeutic situation. From the reply the patient gives, the doctor can infer whether his statement was understood in the way he had intended it. Any deviation can be analyzed and traced to its sources. Eventually the patient learns about all the factors, past and present, which influence his behavior. But the starting point is always in the present.

RECONSTRUCTION OF CHILDHOOD EVENTS HELPS IN THE UNDERSTANDING OF CURRENT AFFAIRS

Indirect influence of childhood events · The patient charts his own course

Freud's greatest contribution to psychiatry, perhaps, consisted in his calling attention to the importance of earlier events for the shaping of future events (11). Today, it is generally accepted that childhood events shape the character of the growing human being and are responsible for most of his views in adult life. But acceptance of this genetic principle does not imply that the adult's recollection of childhood events is therapeutically effective. Although we have to acknowledge that in hysterical characters the lifting of repressions is of benefit, we also must grant that the remembering of vital childhood events rarely changes the character of psychopathic personalities or schizophrenics. Patients who have read and heard about psychiatry and psychoanalysis very often seem to believe that the recovery of childhood memories has a magic effect upon a person's behavior. The belief that lost memories are responsible for psychopathology and that awareness changes behavior overnight reflects an attitude held some thirty or forty years ago. For purposes of therapeutic communication, one might reformulate this concept and state that an understanding of childhood events helps in the appraisal of contemporary affairs. By accepting the past as unalterable and by viewing life as a sequence of events which are interconnected, the patient can examine whether his values and views which derive from his childhood are still suitable in his present circumstances.

Understanding of his development helps the patient to make wise choices, to pursue a long-term plan of living, to become aware of the conditions needed for his existence, to substitute his own experience for the decisions and values taken over from others, to avoid errors, and to perfect skills which were acquired earlier. Once the main directions of his development have become clearer, the patient loses some of his feelings of helplessness; he becomes aware that others are not all-powerful and that he is not entirely powerless; and he discovers that he can, to a certain extent, steer his own affairs. But the course he chooses must somehow represent a continuation and modification of what he has experienced before. Without full utilization of past experiences, a human being cannot function appropriately.

MOBILIZATION OF LATENT MEMORIES
AND SKILLS IS ATTEMPTED

Subliminal perception · Repressed memories · Interpersonal elaboration · Revival of skills

Frequently human beings perceive events without being aware of the traces these experiences have left inside of them. This fact has been demonstrated experimentally by Poetzl (25) and Fisher (9), who worked in the field of preconscious perception, and by others who experimented with unconscious conditioning (19). Human beings may also suppress consciously perceived impressions. Both of these occurrences result in information which is inaccessible to the patient. Under stress, the organism rearranges established patterns of thought; lost information may become available, and previously available information may become inaccessible. After the emergency is over, information about failure in action is rerouted in such a way that it can pass through conscious inspection over and over again until contradictory pieces of evidence can be properly understood. However, the field of consciousness is limited and only a few items can be scrutinized at any one time. Therefore any piece of information which appears in consciousness represents but an infinitesimal part of the information we possess as a whole. Consciousness thus can be conceived of as a special feedback device in which information deriving either from memory or from recent exteroception is subjected to special scrutiny because immediate understanding was impossible (18).

In rotating pieces of information through consciousness, we are primarily aware of the information we are focusing upon. The background information which we do not focus upon also permeates our field of awareness, but it is less distinct than the subject of concern. But the preconscious pool of memory traces should not be confused with the items of information which have difficulty to rise to consciousness. This difficulty may be due to several causes: first, the experience may have occurred a long time ago so that the memories have been condensed and fused with later memories; second, the experience may have occurred recently and the corresponding information has not yet been properly arranged and catalogued; third, the cognitive aspects of an experience may have been discrepant with the emotional aspects and one of the components is repressed.

Due to the repetitive character of traumatic events, it is probable that repressed elements will be triggered into consciousness. But the productive utilization of unconscious memories that have risen into consciousness is contingent upon a favorable situation. When children can relive traumatic experiences and can elaborate discordant pieces of information, memories can be detraumatized. Accordingly, when a patient recounts painful experiences it indicates that he is expecting help and assistance from the therapist. The human brain apparently can cope with moderately contradictory pieces of information by conscious inspection, but highly contradictory and painful memories have to be elaborated with the help of at least one other person. Since neurotic and psychotic patients either never possessed or have lost their ability to utilize interpersonal feedback for elaboration of experiences, they usually fall back upon a variety of control devices. In therapeutic communication, the task of the therapist is clear. By a variety of communicative procedures he can help the patient to recover lost information. Only in an interpersonal feedback situation can the patient afford to consciously inspect painful memories and to relive conflictual situations.

The same applies to the revival of latent skills. A girl who danced in the ballet or painted with water colors, a boy who was a good marksman or tinkered with his bicycle have acquired skills that with some additional learning can usually be employed in a productive way. Dancing as a libidinized activity of the legs may be converted into hiking, running, or tennis. Painting can be changed into an interest in wall colors, textiles, or other materials. Marksmanship may be transformed into other pursuits that require eyehand coordination. The principle is always the same. First the therapist inquires which kind of activity is libidinized; this involves specific body parts, organ systems, and movements on the one hand and certain perceptions and evaluations on the other. The combination of input, output, and evaluative functions forms a pattern which in the past may have been pleasurable. Usually these patterns were experienced as pleasurable because they formed an important link to another person. Perhaps it was father who went shooting with the son, or mother who painted with the daughter. Out of this combination of psycho-motor pattern, human relation, environmental situation, and sense of gratification, the patient developed a motivation which can be revived and employed anew. Of course, the reason for losing a skill is found in the fact that when people move to another place, get older, or live under different economic conditions, one or several of the factors in the pattern may get changed and render it obsolete or unpleasurable.

DISSECTION OF BEHAVIOR IS AVOIDED

Awareness of theory results in dissection of messages · Words should not be classified

In psychoanalytic theory, the various devices which the organism uses to avoid danger, anxiety, and unpleasantness are called mechanisms of defense (10). The psychoanalytic observer of human behavior, therefore, has to separate actions which are defensive in purpose from those which satisfy a basic instinct. In learning theory, a similar choice has to be made in distinguishing between drive, cue, implementation, and reward (5). The use of any theoretical model thus forces the therapist to sort, label, and classify. In his preoccupation, he frequently loses the opportunity to experience subjectively the impact of a patient's message, such as any other person would in daily life. By depriving himself of such an experience, he loses the chance to learn from his own reply as well as from the patient's counter-reply. Whenever somebody is engaged in communication, the exchange becomes distorted if he attempts to dissect the messages according to a prearranged scheme.

To understand the danger of dissection, one might consider what happens to language when it is analyzed according to the rules of grammar or syntax. If a scientist, instead of evaluating and replying to a message, were to concern himself with classifying the other person's words in terms of nouns, adjectives, adverbs, and verbs, or subdivide the sentence into its subject and predicate, he probably would miss entirely the meaning of the sentence and would therefore be unable to understand what the patient said. Apparently the successful communicator immerses himself in the ongoing communication process—much as he would listen to a piano concerto—without isolating certain detailed aspects in favor of others. If he is unable to immerse himself, he has little aptitude for therapeutic communication. But this in no way precludes a scientist from analyzing at a later date parts of the exchange in whatever terms he chooses. For example, in practice the therapist may have the chance to witness repeat performances on the part of the patient. After having understood the pattern of a self-accusatory performance, he may use later repetitions for purposes of breaking down the pattern into its component parts (27). All he has to remember is that when he is actively engaged in the process of communication, either as speaker or as listener, dissection is detrimental to understanding.

OBSERVATION OF EFFECTS REPLACES
INFERENCE OF MOTIVATIONS

Cause and effect · "Why" and "how" · Feedback · Effect orientation

The use of a lineal system necessitates that a cause be assigned to an effect. In the behavioral sciences, the concept of motive, therefore, is a theoretical construct to explain behavior by means of a lineal system. Motives as such are not accessible to direct observation; they can only be inferred. Motives are said to be inborn or learned. Among the inborn motives we find the various instincts, which Freud (14) defines as the forces which we assume to exist behind the tensions caused by the needs of the id. This province of the organism contains everything that is inherited, that is present at birth, and that is fixed in the constitution. Let us now examine what corresponds to the concept of the id in communication theory.

The ancient question as to the "why" of things has in modern science been replaced by an inquiry into the "how." The modern operationalist is more interested in observing the impact which behavior produces upon self, others, and the material world than in speculating about hypothetical causes. Effects can be observed and verified; motives never can. Furthermore, a motive can be assigned to a behavioral act only after its effect has been observed. In communication theory, therefore, the scientist is content with the observation of effects and he abstains from the assignment of motivations. All that is subsumed under such terms as constitution is embodied in the characteristics of the instruments of communication. Inasmuch as the vital forces of existence can manifest themselves only in a concrete behavioral act there is no need to assume the existence of a separate hypothetical force.

The older theories of behavior assumed an intermittent, repetitive, or continuous existence of forces labeled drives, instincts, or motives. Communication theory, which is circular rather than lineal, explains the repetitiveness of certain behavioral acts by the absence of negative feedback and the presence of positive feedback which maximizes a certain kind of behavior. What is called neurotic behavior recurs over and over again because within the patient, as well as between the patient and others, corrective feedback operates unsatisfactorily while pathology-supporting feedback contributes towards stabilization of the abnormality.

The modern operational attitude of the scientist has rubbed off on the therapist, who focuses on the question of the "how," conveying to the patient the notion that the sequence of "action—observation of effects—correction" is of the essence. Instead of asking "Why did I do that?" the patient is taught to ask "What can I do about it?" Instead of searching for speculative explanations of his present behavior, he learns to accept the effect he produces upon self and others. Within the therapeutic hour, he experiences the impact of the therapist's actions upon himself and he is taught to observe the effects of his own behavior upon the therapist. In emphasizing effect orientation, the patient has to face his own behavior. This in turn furnishes the foundations upon which correction is based and growth can be resumed.

REGRESSIVE BEHAVIOR MENDS
BROKEN DOWN COMMUNICATION

Fixation · Regressive language · Emotional response of the therapist

The concept of fixation refers to a state of arrested development whereby an individual retains in adulthood the aims and means of gratification characteristic of an earlier phase of development (11). Inasmuch as fixation is the result of unsatisfactory human relations in childhood, these incomplete, abnormal, or infantile ways of communication are likewise present in adulthood. The infantile person's way of communication appeals emotionally to the parental attitudes in the other person.

Closely related to fixation is the concept of regression, indicating that when an individual is subjected to internal or external stress he reverts not only to earlier means of gratification but also to primitive modes of expression (12). Whenever communication fails on a higher level of symbolization, the patient attempts to reestablish human contact by means of more primitive methods.

When, in the course of an argument, people cannot agree and one of the participants loses his temper, his anger expressed by a pounding on the table is universally understood regardless of language, culture, or age. By switching the focus of discourse, agreement can be reached because the participants are forced to react to the angry man. Regression, therefore, implies the use of a language the emotional impact of which is universally understood—often even by animals. Once people have established contact on this basis, the foundations have been laid for later return to a more rational form of communication. People who regress are therefore people who have experienced a breakdown in communication and who, in order to re-establish contact, resort to primitive emotional language (29).

Therapeutically, therefore, it is of the greatest importance that the therapist acknowledge the emotional language of the regressed patient so that he can establish contact and overcome his feelings of isolation and loneliness. Because if the patient is left to his own devices and is cut off from communication with others, his behavior will become more and more disorganized. Once contact on a primitive emotional level has been established, the pleasure experienced will induce the patient to seek more gratification of the same sort; and in order to secure this pleasure, he will adapt to the more complex means of communication of the therapist.

THE COMPELLING INFLUENCE OF CONSCIENCE AND IDEALS CAN BE MODIFIED

Superego and ego · Strengthening the ego

Freud (14) defined the superego as an agency within the ego in which the parental influence is prolonged beyond the time it can exert a direct influence. Insofar as the superego is different from or opposed to the ego, it creates an intrapsychic conflict. In communication theory, the superego can be viewed as stored information which exerts a mandatory influence upon the individual. That portion of the body of information which corresponds to the superego largely derives from verbal admonitions of parents and authority figures. The body of information which corresponds to the ego has its roots in action. If verbal admonitions and actions are well synchronized and integrated, no conflict exists. If, however, the two kinds of information—superego- and ego-derived—point to different solutions, decision-making becomes difficult. The superego and the ego ideal are formed at a time when the individual does not possess a sufficient range of experiences to make his own decisions. The youngster, therefore, is guided by the experiences of others, and these do not necessarily correspond to his own. Experiences pertaining to actions initiated by others are in some ways more difficult to integrate than experiences derived from self-initiated actions. Traces left by self-initiated action do not exert the same mandatory influence as traces derived from actions forced upon the child.

In order to cope with the superego forces therapeutically, we must help the patient to make decisions which are based upon probabilities derived from his own experiences. In some instances, the values taken over from the parents may prevent the patient from exposing himself to vital experiences which are necessary for his own development. In this case, the bonds between therapist and patient are utilized to induce the patient to temporarily disregard the pressures exerted by his own compelling values. With a few authoritative gestures, the therapist can assume a controlling position which enables the patient to make the therapist the administrator of his conscience and ideals. Under these circumstances, the patient can gain first-hand experience and can attempt to make more decisions of his own; as the strength of the ego increases, superego pressures diminish.

AN APPROPRIATE VIEW OF SELF AND OF THE WORLD IS ESSENTIAL

Types of learning · Small-scale model · Improbable assumptions

The need for an accurate model of self and of the world and the processes necessary to acquire and maintain such a model are considered in both learning theory and psychoanalytic theory. In psychoanalytic theory, the ego is considered the executive agency of the organism, regulating internal tensions and mediating the contact with the outside world. Its special functions are perception, evaluation, action, adaptation, control, and the regulation of pleasure and unpleasure. If the ego discharges these functions satisfactorily so that the organism utilizes all its potentialities in a near optimal way, the ego is characterized by strength (14). In learning theory, we have two kinds of learning: solution learning, which is action oriented, problem-solving, and tension reducing; and sign learning, or conditioning, which is problem producing and only in the long run tension reducing (24). Communication theory has some advantages over both psychoanalytic theory and learning theory. In assuming that all information controls action, it does away with distinctions among sources of information, id force versus superego force, or instinctual versus learned. Once information exists, either inborn or acquired, it steers human behavior, and this steering process is the focus of interest for therapeutic communication.

The therapist who is familiar with communication theory believes that when a person possesses a satisfactory small-scale model of the world such information will enable him to adapt to the surroundings or control the environment in a satisfactory manner. Such a model, of course, cannot accurately reproduce all aspects of existence. But it suffices if in some general way the principal features are adequately represented. In order to acquire an accurate small-scale model of the world, a person has to engage in:

–Appropriate perception, evaluation, and self-expression, the lack of which may result in somatic, mental, or interpersonal symptoms;

–Learning of the language, symbolic, and metacommunicative systems which prevail in his culture;

–Acquisition and correction of information in order to maintain an appropriate view of self and of the world. This requires a certain degree of self-awareness;

– Integration of separate experiences into a whole, and resolution of contradictions within self;

–Learning, either by trial and error or by imitation, of the skills necessary for the implementation of wishes and decisions;

–Elimination of interferences on the part of others, organization of the environment, or adjustment to the unalterable. Both control and adaptation must be mastered.

Finally, in order to survive, any individual must make a number of highly improbable assumptions. Faith in the impossible or improbable has to be balanced with realistic attitudes in order to maintain a constructive attitude towards life. This means that awareness of the world and of self as it exists dóes not preclude some thought of how to improve upon it or even pretending that the situation is different. Depending upon the age of people and their circumstances, a factual appraisal of the world may be highly unrealistic. After careful examination, the doctor may discover that an erroneous picture of the world safeguards the patient and insures his survival. The combat soldier, the sick patient, or the aerial acrobat, if realistically aware of the danger of death, might become so anxious that he would omit ordinary life-saving precautions. Ignoring some danger therefore may be life-saving. The goal of treatment, therefore, particularly in the older age groups, on occasions may differ from the requirements of a realistic appraisal of the world.

THERAPEUTIC COMMUNICATION ALWAYS INVOLVES SEVERAL PEOPLE

The group is the unit that is ill · *Treatment of the group*

Neuroses and psychoses are group phenomena and the disturbances of communication affect not only the patient but also the group in which the patient lives. Traditionally, therapists tend to avoid treating members of the same family; this practice, of course, prevents them from recognizing, studying, and treating the disturbances of communication between people. The doctor will be more successful in bringing about improvement if he studies the communication system of the family, of the husband-wife team, of the mother-child team, or of any other role combination that seems pertinent (1). If, in a family, all concerned know that they are actively participating in the disturbances of the patient, an atmosphere develops which is conducive to improvement and correction. The patient's "in-laws" have to become aware that although one member only may have the symptoms, the whole family is sick.

Inasmuch as a psychoṣis or neurosis can be viewed as a mode of adaptation to an existing social situation, it does not make sense to treat a patient in complete isolation from the people and conditions with which he has lived. However, treatment of all the patient's family members may be impossible, for practical reasons. The choice of procedure then has to be guided by an estimate of what can be achieved with the patient alone. If he improves, the better. By improvement is meant an increase in the ability of the patient to gratify his individual wishes while at the same time maintaining social interaction with others and respecting, within limits, the conventions of his time. The therapist, therefore, is justified in treating the single patient only if the social network in which he lives is functioning passably well; but if it is not operative, the patient has to be brought into a milieu which at first is therapeutic and later will maintain the healthy functioning of the patient. No sick patient is capable of reorganizing or creating a social environment for himself. Correction and self-correction can operate only if other people help the patient in meeting his goals. One of the tasks of the therapeutic session, therefore, is a thorough discussion of where and how the patient is going to establish himself in a human network.

References

1. Ackerman, N. W.: Interlocking pathology in family relationships. Pp. 135–150 in *Changing Concepts of Psychoanalytic Medicine* (S. Rado and G. E. Daniels, Editors). New York: Grune & Stratton, 1956.

2. Berg, J. H. van den: *The Phenomenological Approach to Psychiatry.* 105 p. Springfield: Thomas, 1955.

3. Braatøy, T.: *Fundamentals of Psychoanalytic Technique.* 404 p. New York: Wiley, 1954.

4. Bramwell, J. M.: *Hypnotism: Its History, Practice, and Theory.* (1903) 480 p. New York: Institute for Research in Hypnosis and Julian Press, 1956.

5. Dollard, J. and Miller, N. E.: *Personality and Psychotherapy.* 488 p.

New York: McGraw-Hill, 1950.

6. Farber, L. H.: The therapeutic despair. Psychiatry, 21, 7–20, 1958.

7. Fenichel, O.: *Problems of Psychoanalytic Technique.* 130 p. Albany, N. Y.: The Psychoanalytic Quarterly, 1941.

8. Ferenczi, S.: *Further Contributions to the Theory and Technique of Psycho-Analysis.* (Compiled by J. Rickman). 480 p. London: Hogarth Press, 1950.

9. Fisher, C.: Dreams and perception: the role of preconscious and primary modes of perception in dream formation. J. Amer. Psychoanal. Assoc., 2, 389–445, 1954.

10. Freud, A.: *The Ego and the Mechanisms of Defense.* 196 p. London: Hogarth Press, 1942.

11. Freud, S.: *A General Introduction to Psycho-Analysis.* (Tr. of rev. ed. by J. Riviere.) Garden City: Garden City Publishing Co., 1943.

12. Freud, S.: *The Interpretation of Dreams.* (3rd ed.) 600 p. New York: Macmillan, 1945.

13. Freud, S.: Papers on Technique. Pp. 285–402 in *Collected Papers,* Vol. 2. London: Hogarth Press, 1946.

14. Freud, S.: *An Outline of Psychoanalysis.* 127 p. New York: Norton, 1949.

15. Fromm-Reichmann, F.: Loneliness. Psychiatry, 22, 1–16, 1959.

16. Gill, M. M. and Brenman, M.: *Hypnosis and Related States.* 405 p. New York: International Universities Press, 1959.

17. Glover, E.: *The Technique of Psycho-Analysis.* 404 p. New York: International Universities Press, 1955.

18. Grinker, R. R. (Editor): *Toward a Unified Theory of Human Behavior.* 375 p. New York: Basic Books, 1956.

19. Klein, G. S.: On subliminal activation. J. nerv. ment. Dis., 128, 293–301, 1959.

20. Kolb, L. C. and Montgomery, J.: An explanation for transference cure: its occurrence in psychoanalysis and psychotherapy. Amer. J. Psychiat., 115, 414–421, 1958.

21. Lecron, L. M. and Bordeaux, J.: *Hypnotism Today.* 278 p. New York: Grune & Stratton, 1947.

22. Levy, D. M.: *Studies in Sibling Rivalry.* 96 p. Amer. Orthopsychiat. Assoc. Res. Monogr. No. 2, 1937.

23. Levy, D. M.: *Maternal Overprotection.* 417 p. New York: Columbia University Press, 1943.

24. Mowrer, O. H.: *Learning Theory and Personality Dynamics.* 776 p. New York: Ronald Press, 1950.

25. Poetzl, O.: Experimentell erregte Traumbilder in ihren Beziehungen zum indirekten Sehen. Ztschr. f. Neurol. & Psychiat., 37, 278–349, 1917.

26. Reich, W.: Technique. Pp. 3–140 in *Character-Analysis*. (3rd ed.) New York: Orgone Institute Press, 1949.

27. Reik, T.: *Listening with the Third Ear*. 514 p. New York: Farrar, Straus; 1948.

28. Rioch, D. McK. and Stanton, A. H.: Milieu therapy. Psychiatry, 16, 65–72, 1953.

29. Ruesch, J.: *Disturbed Communication*. 337 p. New York: Norton, 1957.

30. Sechehaye, M. A.: *Symbolic Realization*. 184 p. New York: International Universities Press, 1951.

31. Sharpe, E. F.: Papers on technique. Pp. 3–122 in *Collected Papers on Psycho-Analysis*. London: Hogarth Press, 1950.

32. Stekel, W.: *Technique of Analytical Psychotherapy*. (Tr. by E. and C. Paul.) 408 p. New York: Norton, 1940.

33. Wolberg, L. R.: *Medical Hypnosis*. 2 v. New York: Grune & Stratton, 1948.

Part Two

The Recognition of Disturbed
Communicative Behavior

Part Two

The Recognition of Deictic
Communicative Ability

Whether medical or psychiatric diagnosis matters at all in the practice of psychotherapy is a question which has not been answered satisfactorily. Diagnoses are short-hand terms that the physician uses to describe the etiology of the condition, the deviation in structure, and the disturbance in function. Since with few exceptions no single factor can be held responsible for any psychiatric condition, the etiological approach has proven of little value. Deviations in anatomical structure, except for conditions associated with brain disease, do not show a one-to-one correlation with disturbed behavior. The attempts to relate personality structure to physical pathology and specific psychodynamic constellations have on the whole remained unsatisfactory. Whatever conflict was thought to be specific for a given condition also was found in many other diseases, and the only valid conclusion that could be reached indicated that emotional conflicts, immaturity, and difficulties in human relations frequently are associated with psychosomatic disease. The symptomatologically defined diagnostic entities such as schizophrenia or manic depressive psychosis are much less pure or stable than previously assumed. Many patients first diagnosed in one category later turn up in another, so that the efforts of Kraepelin and Bleuler to establish a prognostic and symptomatological classification likewise have not proven useful for therapy. None of the existing classifications inform the therapist about the severity of the condition, the likelihood of success in therapy, or the duration of treatment. A schizophrenic with an acute episode may recover faster and later on function better than a compulsion neurotic; and the latter may survive better than an oral character with depressive episodes. Today, the only system that is useful to the psychotherapist is the psychoanalytic classification of the psychoneuroses and character disorders. But the psychoanalytic formulations have proven less appropriate for the use of the hospital administrators who have to decide about the availability of beds and personnel and who have to treat psychotic patients. Therefore we have to conclude that most classifications in existence today either are valid only for a specific segment of behavioral pathology or are suitable for purposes other than therapy.

But what, then, can the therapist use for the assessment of therapeutic possibilities of his patient? Well, he actually deals with at least four viewpoints which he amalgamates in his head. Before beginning any psychological exploration, the therapist has to know of the presence of physical disease, regardless of whether it may be treatable or not. Therefore the doctor has to carefully examine the patient, or, if he wishes, he may delegate this task to an internist or a general practitioner. If a diagnosed disease is present, a specialist should be consulted. If the patient has no evidence of disease, the psychotherapist must be constantly on the lookout for conditions which may develop while the patient is under treatment. If he encounters symptoms which he believes to fall outside the province of his competence, he has to refer the patient to the proper specialist. When the therapist deals with hospitals, courts, referring physicians, or departments of mental hygiene, it is important to designate the patient's condition in terms of the prevailing diagnostic terminology. Such a classification usually implies the severity of the condition, its probable duration, and the type of facility needed for its treatment.

Age, sex, occupation, nationality, social class, and many other aspects referring to the patient as a social being have to be considered. The patient comes with his constitutional endowment and lives in a social reality which may determine the type of illness he contracts, the duration of recovery, and the treatment method used. The age of the patient may, in certain circumstances, be more compelling in the choice of treatment than the nature of the disease.

Living produces permanent traces in the individual which are generally described under the heading of personality. Experiences that happened over the years and at different places are telescoped and condensed; they are then described in terms of attitudes, traits, talents, or processes without specific references to people or places. In spite of this distortion, the study of personality gives the therapist valuable information. For therapeutic purposes, the psychoanalytic personality scheme is the most suitable one, although promising attempts have also been made with schemes employing learning theory as their basis.

If personality assessment is based on an appraisal of the patient's past behavior, the study of his communicative behavior refers to actually observed events at the moment. The way the patient perceives, expresses, and evaluates; the kind of knowledge he possesses; the way he considers his own impact upon others; the language he uses; his metalinguistic and manipulative devices—this all is duly considered. Such an appraisal gives the therapist an inventory of those functions he can use in approaching the patient, those that are disturbed, and those that have to be developed.

Chapter Three

The Patient's Social Characteristics

Difference of value systems · Cultural differences between doctor and patient

EVALUATION of the cultural background of the patient determines in part the therapist's decision as to whether or not the patient would profit from any of the known communication therapies (62). If patient and doctor do not speak the same language, or if the patient comes from a background which is totally unknown to the doctor, communication will meet with tremendous difficulties. Furthermore, when the therapist encounters a patient with a moderately different cultural background, he has to decide whether he can understand the values of the patient and whether these clash with his own value system, because only under circumstances of tolerance can therapy proceed without becoming an indoctrination course. Therefore both patient and doctor have to ascertain whether their communications are favorably received by the other; if they conclude that they can only treat each other as enemies or foreigners, it might be more economical to introduce physical treatment methods and to abandon the psychological approach.

The cultural background of the patient is explored along three different dimensions (9). First, the doctor determines the national or ethnic background of the patient. Secondly, he explores the social status or class membership of the patient. And third, he examines the ecological patterns which govern the patient's living. He then compares these data to those that apply to himself. The treatment of members of different social, ethnic, and ecological groups is characterized by the fact that differences of values exist between the therapist and the patient. When the patient and the therapist are too much alike, improvement seems to be slow or absent; and if the doctor and the patient belong to groups which are too different, improvement is likewise slow or absent. There seems to exist an optimal degree of difference in the views and the values of patient and doctor under which therapy seems to prosper (44).

ETHNIC ORIGIN

Minorities · Native and foreign borns · Immigrant depression · Displaced persons · Acculturation · Character difficulties camouflaged · Therapy with members of other cultures · Collective attitudes · Metacommunication

The ethnic background of the patient is the most important determinant of the patient's value system (47). Similarity or dissimilarity of the values held by the patient as compared with his social surroundings furnishes an index of the difficulties to be encountered. The likelihood is great that the therapist will meet patients with such conflicts, inasmuch as one third of the people at large are engaged in some kind of culture change. Thus, according to the 1950 census, 6.7 per cent of the population of the United States were foreign born whites, 15.7 per cent were native born whites of foreign or mixed parentage, and 10.4 per cent were non-white people comprising primarily Negroes and to a lesser degree Indians, Japanese, Chinese, and members of other races. It is safe to assume that the majority of these people have problems in acculturation, inasmuch as immigrants and colored minorities in the United States tend to strive towards a legendary American core culture most clearly represented by Anglo-Saxon middle-class Protestants.

The stress encountered in the process of culture change is clearly revealed in the comparison of morbidity and mortality of the immigrant population with that of the native population (37). Foreign born persons are more susceptible to physical and mental disease than natives. They are usually married, have many children, and are law-abiding citizens; and as a protection against the impact of new values, they tend to live within the family circle and avoid outside contacts. Among the native borns, those of foreign or mixed parentage are exposed to conflicting value systems; the opinions of the parents frequently clash with those of the surroundings and the subsequent conflict is undoubtedly related to the higher rate of delinquency, crime, and susceptibility to mental and physical disease found in this group. The non-white man belongs to a caste (36); conflicting value systems and poor economic conditions make for rebellion and crime, and the strain of being a member of a subjugated group as well as poor hygienic conditions is probably associated with the higher morbidity and mortality from tuberculosis and venereal disease. Non-white minorities also have a greater infant mortality rate than white people.

In the psychiatric care of immigrants, the therapist frequently meets reactive depressions which occur at the end of the first year or perhaps at the beginning of the second year after immigration (17, 27). The same also happens to natives who migrate from the east to the west coast. If ties with the old surroundings are severed at a time when identification with the new surroundings has not been accomplished as yet, the migrants are neither members of their old groups nor members of a new group. They feel unloved and isolated and develop all the symptoms of a minor depression.

The various ethnic groups differ in their particular problems (7). While the immigrant who belongs to one of the well-established national groups has the advantage of being able to live among fellow countrymen, the displaced person (40), who has either gone through years of imprisonment or experienced many cultural changes, is somewhat of a stray dog. He fits everywhere and nowhere. In therapy, the displaced person's first task is to face the realities of his new surroundings. The patient has to be helped to handle the red tape connected with immigration and citizenship for which purpose he may be referred to a social agency (24, 56, 58). If the immigrant has family members who were left abroad, he may be helped to secure their immigration. Ethnic groups in the United States may assist the immigrant to establish relationships with his compatriots in the American community and to become aware and tolerant of other ethnic groups on the local scene, even if these may have been his former enemies.

While this step is relatively easy, the second step meets with more opposition. It consists of teaching the immigrant to get in contact with natives, and efforts are made to interpret the American culture to the newcomer. Information about the American value systems, customs, and traditions can be conveyed to the patient by urging him to participate in language and citizenship classes and in artistically and socially oriented group activities. Finally, after having been made familiar with the basic principles and the language of the new culture, the immigrant is helped in obtaining employment and proper housing and in learning to use the outlets which the community and the government provide for health, education, and recreation.

The adjustment difficulties of immigrants are not exclusively related to adaptation to changed conditions. If the motive which makes a person leave the old country is related to hardships of a physical or social nature, he usually can easily be settled in another country. But persons who were unable to get along in their group of origin will tend to show the same difficulties in the new country. Often personality difficulties are blamed on culture change when the individual's character is the source of trouble. In these cases, psychotherapy is directed at correcting the basic disturbance which prevents the patient from relating satisfactorily to other individuals.

The literature on mental illness in primitive societies (4, 60) and on therapy or psycholanalysis of white men with members of other races is scarce. Adams (2), Bernard (5), Hillpern (21), Kennedy (26), Kardiner (25), McLean (35), and St. Clair (48) have been concerned with the problems of Negroes; Devereux (11) and Leighton (31) with American Indians. Babcock and Caudill (3) and Handley (19) comment upon casework and therapy with Japanese; Eaton and Weil (12) report their experiences with the Hutterites; and Ruesch (44) reports about therapy with Japanese, Chinese, Negroes, and Parsis. Therapists agree that it is easier to treat Chinese, Japanese, and Indians who are not Americanized and who retain their old cultural endowment than it is to treat people of the same nationalities who want to Americanize themselves. In the latter case, the therapist is looked upon as a teacher and as an arbiter of acculturation; such a procedure may as a matter of fact increase the patient's maladjustment so that he fits neither into the American core group nor into his own ethnic group; he then is destined to live among displaced persons of both cultures. Marginal people with heterogeneous values and means of communication show behavior patterns which derive from different cultures, classes, and castes. Colonies of displaced people exist—as on the Riviera, in Hong Kong, or in any large metropolitan center—where life for the marginal person may not be too unpleasant.

The white, upper-middle-class psychiatrist who undertakes therapy with Indians, Negroes, Japanese, or Chinese runs head on into institutionalized attitudes; as a white person, he has been assigned a role, in the mind of the patient, which expresses the attitude of the non-white vis-à-vis the white man. The psychiatrist likewise sees in the patient a representative of a race against which many white people have prejudices. Collective attitudes of nations and races have to be taken seriously; they influence therapy and the choice of a method. Actually, it is easier for a white doctor to communicate with a white member of Western civilization who does not speak the language than to do therapy with a person who speaks English but belongs to an African or an Asian type of civilization.

Difficulties in cross-cultural therapy are essentially related to a mutual lack of familiarity with interpretative schemes. The cues pertaining to familiarity and distance, to approval and disapproval, are not shared in common; the basic assumptions about communication and the nonverbal modifiers of messages are different; the social approaches vary; and in this confusion it is difficult to interpret messages correctly. And if the white psychiatrist gets the patient to accept some of the means of communication that he uses, he imperceptibly imparts to the patient some of the Western values. Ultimately, however, the patient will live among Chinese, Japanese, Negroes, or Indians rather than among whites, and the new values will hardly help him to adjust to his own group.

MEMBERSHIP IN SOCIAL GROUPS

Status differences · Social class and disease · Social mobility and personal isolation · Therapy with upper-class persons · Therapy with lower-class persons · Language determines type of therapy · Duration of psychotherapy · Therapy with members of different religions · Change of religion · Therapy with political radicals · Therapy with unidentified people · Therapy with criminals

Within a social system mutual relationships are determined among other things by who looks up to whom and who looks down upon whom. This social judgment, based on features actually held or merely attributed, does not necessarily bother people as long as social mobility functions adequately. Difficulties arise when talented people are unable to move out of a low status position because they do not possess the techniques to engineer a change, or when successful climbers move repeatedly into new territories without ever mastering the new situation. The subtle cues that indicate status or prestige are more easily detected in group gatherings; here the astute observer will discover that certain key figures direct the conversation, make value judgments, and initiate action; such persons usually are given the preferred positions at the dinner table, have first choice when it comes to the distribution of spoils, and in general seem to be in the number one or two position in the pecking order.

If differences in ethnic background may constitute gross obstacles to communication therapy, social class differences may give rise to more subtle troubles. First, a word about social class and disease. Middle-class persons, with their tendency to conform and to minimize emotional expression, have a predilection for tension syndromes involving the gastro-intestinal and the vascular systems (45, 46). Lower-class people, in turn, are more likely to be afflicted by conditions which are the result of exposure to machines, violence, crowded conditions, and unsatisfactory hygiene. The lower the income, the higher the incidence of serious mental disease (37). Actually, the commitment rates by occupational groups seem to decline with higher income and prestige (10). It is remarkable that the schizothymic personality occurs more often in the lower classes, the cyclothymic personality in the upper classes (22).

To improve their social position, people frequently attempt to move from one social class to another. These mobile people are more liable to contract tension disorders than those who are satisfied with their social position. That social mobility is widespread can be seen from the fact that probably more than thirty per cent of the United States population are involved in change of social status (42). The stress involved in social change is related to the unlearning of old approaches and the mastery of new ones at an advanced age. But in spite of all efforts on the part of the individual, the new group may not necessarily accept the newcomer socially as an equal, and the old group is likely to be envious and resentful of his success. This rejection by two groups may lead to social isolation.

Social class membership determines in part the mode and place of treatment (52). In our culture, the private practitioner fulfills the function of individual adviser to the upper classes and our clinics serve the lower classes. Patients of the higher social classes rely mostly upon trusted family members, friends, and physicians for referral to a competent professional man. For the prominent, the doctor is frequently nothing but a skilled employee, and certain ambitious doctors overadapt to the whims of their wealthy patients to improve their social status and to make further contacts. If both parties utilize each other for their own secret purposes, therapy may become a failure.

If patients are members of the lower social classes, treatment is rarely adapted to the individual patient. Instead, therapy is then viewed as a procedure which has to help the majority of patients, and the treatment tends to become impersonal. Patients of the lower classes rely more upon social institutions and the facilities provided by government, state, and community. These practices, of course, do not apply only to psychiatric problems but pertain to legal, architectural, financial, and other advice as well. Therapy dispensed by institutions is geared to the achievement of tangible external results. The methods by necessity involve drugs, shock, and physical rehabilitation procedures.

In the upper classes, the prerequisite for personalized contact is, of course, based on the existence of a common language and a common system of interpretation. Since we know that the middle-class physician speaks a somewhat different language and has different value systems from the lower-class patient, it is but natural that under such circumstances intimate communication can rarely occur at the verbal level. If one cannot speak the language, if one has no experiences in common, if one does not possess the same means of expression or similar devices of interpretation, then of course one resorts more and more to nonverbal means of communication. When we travel in a foreign country and do not speak the language, we cannot engage in sophisticated discussions with the natives; instead we confine our transactions to the exchange of goods, which we can accomplish with the help of changes in facial expression, gesticulation, and other nonverbal devices such as counting, pointing, or display of money.

These conditions find their repercussions in the intensity and duration of treatment (54). If one cannot communicate well, there is no sense in prolonging contact unduly or in having frequent interviews. Members of the lower classes thus experience shorter treatment and fewer interviews (23). And if the patient's language is completely unknown to us, any kind of therapy relying upon communication is out of the question. In these instances, we can provide food, shelter, nursing care, and rest; and we can add drugs, surgery, and other physical therapies. Therefore, with an increasing gap between the status of the physician and that of the patient, progressively more physical forms of therapy are introduced and less reliance is put upon the therapies utilizing communication.

Psychotherapy undertaken with members of religious groups who either implicitly or explicitly adhere to the values dictated by their church presents similar difficulties. Though therapy can in part be successful without touching upon theological matters (63), most religions prescribe practices which bear upon physical and mental hygiene, eating habits, sexual mores, and the like. Resistances which a patient may have in facing the realities of his situation may be blamed upon the teachings of his church (16), but as the patient handles his daily problems, these tend to disappear. Religious differences thus are often a smokescreen for severe pathology.

People who change their religious affiliation (30, 49, 51) usually express rebellion against their family or in-group. Such a person hurts the relatives by letting them know that what is dear to them is not dear to him. Therapy usually is more successful if the rebellion originated in adolescence than if the rebellion dates back to early childhood. A person who has not learned to accept the values of his group and who has made an incomplete or hostile identification has difficulty in accepting any kind of values later in life. To be in opposition thus is the only kind of identity such people know, and removal of the rebellious pattern merely increases the chances that such patients will become more maladjusted or depressed. In many ways it is better that they remain unaware of their hostile identification and their deep-seated conflicts and compensate for their problem by changing their religious denominations (32, 61), which enables them to be or remain in opposition. With such cases, therapy is successful only if the patient can be given a chance to convert his negative and hostile attitude into a positive and cooperative attitude.

Therapy with political radicals is not very different from therapy with members of other social or religious groups (29). To the naive observer, it seems but natural that different opinions exist about political systems. Upon closer scrutiny, however, it may become evident that rebellion against an existing political system is related to personality problems rather than to the political issues at stake (28, 34, 50). Persecution and oppression may enable the revolutionary to function, but once he is unopposed he may not know how to act judiciously. Psychotherapy with this type of person shows that revolutionary interests tend to disappear as the authority problem is managed.

There are people who, either because of repeated change of environment in their early childhood or through inconsistency and lack of continuity in their human relations, never acquired an identity (14). These persons do not know who they are; they do not know what they want; they are in doubt whether they belong and where; they possess so many conflicting and controversial values that their inner existence is really chaotic. To clarify their inner confusion, they may join all sorts of groups and activities, only to discover that what they chose really is not what they wanted. Therapy with these non-identified people may stretch over a period of many years. The acquisition of an identity is achieved through a consistent and continuous contact with one and the same person—the therapist. Through this contact, the patient is enabled to mature (43).

Therapy with the criminal remains difficult (33) because the therapist is a representative of the group which prosecutes and condemns him for his actions. This basic reality cannot be ignored, particularly when the offender is serving a sentence. Except in the case of anxiety states and acute depressions, psychotherapy under duress is ineffective. Furthermore, life in prison is so sheltered and the freedom of the prisoners is so restricted that therapy is not supported by a concomitant progress in life experience. While the magnitude of the crime has little relation to the success of therapy (53), the date of treatment is of relevance. The best time is the period immediately following discharge from the penal institution. But unfortunately there are few institutions which provide for the treatment of discharged prisoners (1). No therapy with criminals can be successful unless the climate of opinion that surrounds the man on parole is favorable. Some advances in this direction have been made in the treatment of juvenile delinquents (8, 13, 55, 41), and the responsible authorities show a growing understanding for the viewpoint that youthful offenders should not be punished but rehabilitated. The same, though on a smaller scale, is happening in the management of sex offenders (6, 18).

ECOLOGICAL BACKGROUND

Climate and geography · *Early imprinting* · *Urban centers* · *Rural areas* · *Ecological change* · *The feeling of belonging*

If horizontal and vertical stratification of groups and their characteristics constitute two determinants of the patient's cultural background, the nature of the physical environment is the third. After all, man's social relations, his values, his beliefs, and his habits are shaped by his physical surroundings. Whether a person is a country or a city dweller, nomad or permanent settler, maritime or mountain man determines his outlook on life, nature, and people. Some love the sea, other hate it; some prefer to live on hillsides, others prefer the plains. Some abhor what one might call the "asphalt culture" of the big cities—the lack of green, the impersonal attitude of people, their cynicism, and their mobility; others love it. Some disintegrate when left in the country with animals, fields, and forests; others thrive on it.

The experiences that set the individual's style of living occur early (20). The baby who lies in his crib under a high oak tree, whose early companions were dog and cat, whose first contact with nature's sound was the singing of birds and the rustling of leaves is imprinted in a different way than is the baby whose crib is shaken every seven minutes by the rattling of the subway, whose contact with sound is dominated by the honking of automobile horns, and whose nostrils get accustomed to the stench of the sidewalk and the smog of the city.

Perhaps it is not accidental that people in the process of culture change, displaced persons, neurotics, and psychotics tend to settle in large cities. Mental disorders concentrate in urban centers, declining in all directions towards the periphery (15). Good housing, of course, is found at the periphery of modern cities, and the mentally sick usually have to be content with the undesirable sections of town. But perhaps the significance is deeper than that. In the cities are found all those people who are unrelated to man and nature. Their slogan is "let us be alone together." Herded in masses on subways, streetcars, and in housing projects, these people cannot love one another. Every other person takes away space, fresh air, and accommodations. In order to live in such surroundings, symbol and word manipulation have to be practiced and mastered early— but not for the purpose of pleasure but for sheer survival. In the city are found those who talk excessively, who promote and advertise, as well as those who are disillusioned, disgusted, or resigned.

In the more sparsely populated areas, conditions are different. Here people communicate because they want contact and news. The world is more stable and the liar and cheater are not so frequent. People are known by name; they have plenty of space around them; their tempo is unhurried. They are less polished, less verbal, but they know the pleasure of physical action, the proximity to nature, and peace with self.

If a person of upper or lower class origin moves from the country to the city, he may experience serious difficulties. Raised in the non-verbal tradition of the country, he may balk at adapting to the relativistic values of an urban culture. The whole world is different, and even though he may adapt superficially he feels lonely and loses self-respect. And the man who moves from the city to the country becomes a suburbanite (38) but not a country boy. And the suburbanite, the exurbanite, and the ex-suburbanite are too well known in caricature to dwell on them any longer (57). But it is significant that with the ever-growing mental health problem goes a significant decrease in the farm population of the United States. In 1910, the farm population comprised about thirty-five per cent of the total; in 1950 it was only sixteen per cent. And with the shift from country to city, we also have a significant interstate migration. Approximately twelve per cent of the population migrates from one state to another, and among these people the intercity migrant is especially prone to be disturbed (59).

The frustrations encountered by the immigrant to the United States and the socially mobile person within our society likewise are shared by the geographic migrants within the United States. Whenever a geographically or socially mobile person moves to another place and into another group, he at first occupies a marginal status (39). Therapeutic communication can help such persons to overcome the tension produced by change, and the therapist can be instrumental in helping the patient to acquire a communication system which will enable him to relate to his new surroundings. In some cases, the surroundings will be composed of other marginal people; in other cases, the psychiatrist will be capable of integrating the patient into a core group. But the therapist has to face the fact that therapeutic communication with people of other races, nationalities, social classes, and religious and political beliefs remains limited. Basic differences of assumptions cannot be changed in therapy unless accompanied by an actual change in the patient's physical and social environment. But what can be done in therapy is to teach the patient to acquire tolerance for other value systems, helping him to derive gratification from communicating with different kinds of people.

References

1. Abrahamsen, D.: Evaluation of the treatment of criminals. Pp. 58–77 in *Failures in Psychiatric Treatment*. (P. H. Hoch, Editor). New York: Grune & Statton, 1948.

2. Adams, W. A.: The Negro patient in psychiatric treatment. Amer. J. Orthopsychiat., 20, 305–310, 1950.

3. Babcock, C. G. and Caudill, W.: Personal and cultural factors in treating a Nisei man. Pp. 409–448 in *Clinical Studies in Culture Conflict* (G. Seward, editor.) New York: Ronald Press, 1958.

4. Benedict, P. K. and Jacks, I.: Mental illness in primitive societies. Psychiatry, 17, 377–389, 1954.

5. Bernard, V. W.: Psychoanalysis and members of minority groups. J. Amer. Psychoanal. Assoc., 1, 256–267, 1953.

6. Bowman, K. M. and Engle, B.: The problem of homosexuality. J. soc. Hyg., January, 1953.

7. Brown, F. J. and Roucek, J. S.: *One America*. 717 p. New York: Prentice-Hall, 1945.

8. Cabot, P. S. deQ.: *Juvenile Delinquency: A Critical Annotated Bibliography*. 166 p. New York: H. W. Wilson, 1946.

9. Caudill, W.: *Effects of Social and Cultural Systems in Reactions to Stress*. 34 p. New York: Soc. Sci. Res. Counc. Pamphlet 14, 1958.

10. Clark, R. E.: Psychoses, income, and occupational prestige. Amer. J. Sociol., 54, 433–440, 1949.

11. Devereux, G.: *Reality and Dream: Psychotherapy of a Plains Indian*. 438 p. New York: International Universities Press, 1951.

12. Eaton, J. W. and Weil, R. J.: *Culture and Mental Disorders*. 254 p. Glencoe: Free Press, 1955.

13. Eissler, K. R.: Some problems of delinquency. Pp. 3–25 in *Searchlights on Delinquency* (Edited by K. R. Eissler). New York: International Universities Press, 1949.

14. Erikson, E. H.: The problem of ego identity. J. Amer. Psychoanal. Assoc., 4, 56–121, 1956.

15. Faris, R. E. L. and Dunham, H. W.: *Mental Disorders in Urban Areas*. 270 p. Chicago: University of Chicago Press, 1939.

16. Fromm, E.: *Psychoanalysis and Religion*. 119 p. New Haven: Yale University Press, 1950.

17. Frost, I.: Home-sickness and immigrant psychoses. J. ment. Sci., 84, 801–847, 1938.

18. Guttmacher, M. S. and Weihofen, H.: *Psychiatry and the Law*. 476 p. New York: Norton, 1952.

19. Handley, K. N.: Social casework and intercultural problems. J. soc. Caswk., 28, 43–50, 1947.

20. Hess, E. H.: Imprinting. Science, 130, 133–141, 1959.

21. Hillpern, E. P., Spaulding, I. A., and Hillpern, E. P.: *Bristow Rogers: American Negro; A Psychoanalytic Case History*. 184 p. New York: Hermitage House, 1949.

22. Hollingshead, A. B. and Redlich, F. C.: Social class and psychiatric disorders. Pp. 195–208 in *Interrelations between the Social Environment and Psychiatric Disorders*. New York: Milbank Memorial Fund, 1953.

23. Hollingshead, A. B. and Redlich, F. C.: *Social Class and Mental Illness*. 442 p. New York: Wiley, 1958.

24. Kage, J.: Ego-supportive therapy with displaced persons. Soc. Casewk., 31, 65–70, 1950.

25. Kardiner, A. and Ovesey, L.: *The Mark of Oppression*. 396 p. New York: Norton, 1951.

26. Kennedy, J. A.: Problems posed in the analysis of Negro patients. Psychiatry, 15, 313–327, 1952.

27. Kino, F. F.: Alien's paranoid reaction. J. ment. Sci., 97, 589–594, 1951.

28. Krout, M. H. and Stagner, R.: Personality development in radicals. Sociometry, 11, 31–46, 1939.

29. Krugman, H. E.: The role of hostility in the appeal of communism in the United States. Psychiatry, 16, 253–261, 1953.

30. Kupper, W. H. and Rubin, B. G.: A case study of a proselyte from Catholicism to Judaism. J. nerv. ment. Dis., 107, 575–578, 1948.

31. Leighton, A. H. and Leighton, D. C.: *The Navaho Door*. 149 p. Cambridge: Harvard University Press, 1945.

32. Liebman, J. L. (Editor): *Psychiatry and Religion*. 202 p. Boston: Beacon Press, 1948.

33. Lindner, R. M.: *Rebel Without a Cause*. 296 p. New York: Grune & Stratton, 1944.

34. McCormack, T. H.: The motivation of radicals. Amer. J. Sociol., 56, 17–24, 1950.

35. McLean, H. V.: Psychodynamic factors in racial relations. Ann. Amer. Acad. polit. soc. Sci., 244, 159–166, 1946.

36. McLean, H. V.: The emotional health of Negroes. J. Negro Educ., 18, 283–290, 1949.

37. Malzberg, B.: *Social and Biological Aspects of Mental Disease.* 360 p. Utica: State Hospital Press, 1940.

38. Mills, C. W.: *White Collar: The American Middle Classes.* 378 p. New York: Oxford, 1951.

39. Park, R. E.: *Race and Culture.* 403 p. Glencoe: Free Press, 1950.

40. Rawley, C.: The adjustment of Jewish displaced persons. J. soc. Casewk., 29, 316–321, 1948.

41. Redl, F. and Wineman, D.: *Controls from Within.* 332 p. Glencoe: Free Press, 1952.

42. Ruesch, J.: Social technique, social status, and social change in illness. (1948) Pp. 123–136 in *Personality in Nature, Society and Culture* (2nd ed.). Edited by C. Kluckhohn, H. A. Murray, and D. M. Schneider. New York: Knopf, 1953.

43. Ruesch, J.: The infantile personality: the core problem of psychosomatic medicine. Psychosom. Med., 10, 134–144, 1948.

44. Ruesch, J.: Social factors in therapy. Pp. 59–93 in *Psychiatric Treatment* (ARNMD #31). Baltimore: Williams & Wilkins, 1953.

45. Ruesch, J., Harris, R. E., Loeb, M. B., Christiansen, C., Dewees, S., Heller, S. H., and Jacobson, A.: *Chronic Disease and Psychological Invalidism.* 191 p. New York: Amer. Soc. Res. Psychosom. Probl., 1946. 2nd printing, Berkeley and Los Angeles: University of California Press, 1951.

46. Ruesch, J., Harris, R. E., Christiansen, C., Loeb, M. B., Dewees, S., and Jacobson, A.: *Duodenal Ulcer.* 118 p. Berkeley and Los Angeles: University of California Press, 1948.

47. Ruesch, J., Jacobson, A., and Loeb, M. B.: Acculturation and illness. Psychol. Monogr., 62(5), 1–40, 1948.

48. St. Clair, H. R.: Psychiatric interview experiences with Negroes. Amer. J. Psychiat., 108, 113–119, 1951.

49. Salzman, L.: The psychology of religious and ideological conversion. Psychiatry, 16, 177–187, 1953.

50. Sanai, M. and Pickard, P. M.: The relation between politico-economic radicalism and certain traits of personality. J. soc. Psychol., 30, 217–227, 1949.

51. de Sanctis, S.: *Religious Conversion.* 324 p. New York: Harcourt Brace, 1927.

52. Schaffer, L. and Myers, J. K.: Psychotherapy and social stratification. Psychiatry, 17, 83–93, 1954.

53. Schmideberg, M.: The analytic treatment of major criminals: therapeutic results and technical problems. Pp. 174–189 in *Searchlights on Delinquency* (Edited by K. R. Eissler). New York: International

Universities Press, 1949.

54. Simmons, O. G.: *Social Status and Public Health*. 34 p. New York: Soc. Sci. Res. Counc. Pamphlet 13, 1958.

55. Solomon, J. C.: *A Synthesis of Human Behavior*. 265 p. New York: Grune & Stratton, 1954.

56. Spaulding, R. G.: Techniques in casework with displaced persons. Soc. Casewk., 31, 70–77, 1950.

57. Spectorski, A. C.: *The Exurbanites*. 278 p. Philadelphia: Lippincott, 1955.

58. Tannenbaum, D. E.: The family agency as a community resource for the adjustment of displaced persons. Soc. Serv. Rev., 25, 14–18, 1951.

59. Tietze, C., Lemkau, P., and Cooper, M.: Personality disorder and spatial mobility. Amer. J. Sociol., 48, 29–39, 1942.

60. Tsung-yi Lin: A study of the incidence of mental disorder in Chinese and other cultures. Psychiatry, 16, 313–336, 1953.

61. VanderVeldt, J. H. and Odenwald, R. P.: *Psychiatry and Catholicism*. 433 p. New York: McGraw-Hill, 1952.

62. Wittkower, E. D. and Fried, J.: A cross-cultural approach to mental health problems. Amer. J. Psychiat., 116, 423–428, 1959.

63. Zilboorg, G.: Psychoanalysis and religion. Atlantic Monthly, January, 1949.

Chapter Four

The Diagnosis of Disturbed Communication

Therapeutic diagnosis · *Psychosis* · *Neurosis* · *Breakdown of feedback* ·
Self-consciousness · *Poor health* · *Lack of growth* · *Inappropriacy of
response*

THE STUDY of communicative behavior is relevant for the therapist
because it tells him how to use his own communicative behavior to
influence the patient. Up to now, different vocabularies and theories
have been employed to describe personality, social events, pathology,
and therapeutic procedures. For example, most personality theories
emphasize repetitive, intense, and unusual features whereby successive events which occur over the course of years are telescoped into
such constructs as preferences, attitudes, or traits. Psychoanalytic
theories emphasize intrapsychic events and processes that are inferred to exist within the individual. But only when we learn to
diagnose the difficulties of our patients in terms of the same scientific
universe in which we explain our therapeutic methods will we be
able to evaluate therapy in a meaningful way. As long as the diagnosis
is made in terms of one system and therapy is explained in terms
of another system we cannot match therapy to pathology. Therefore
it seems feasible that patients be diagnosed in terms of their ability
to communicate and the disturbances that interfere with it. The therapeutic diagnosis thus is principally based upon the evaluation of the
communicative behavior of the patient, and therapeutic communication is designed to overcome the difficulties.

In all the psychoses, the perceptive-evaluative processes are seriously disturbed. This criterion can be used to separate the psychoses

from the neuroses and the personality disorders, in which perception is not grossly disturbed. A patient who is confused and disoriented and who hallucinates is obviously not in a position to communicate effectively, regardless of the nature of his disease. Disturbed perception and evaluation may be brought on by toxic, infectious, or degenerative processes in the brain, with the result that the patient has to curtail his contact with others; or it may be brought on by a voluntary withdrawal of the patient from social contact with subsequent signs of sensory deprivation. Missing outside stimulation is supplanted by imagined interactions (6, 10), or, in brief, output is adapted to input and vice versa (7). In the psychoses, then, the therapeutic task is to widen the feedback circuits to include other people so that the organism can again be steered by the exchange of information with the outside world.

The patient who suffers from a personality disorder or a psychoneurosis is characterized by a basically different disturbance of communication. Rarely does such a patient show disturbances of perception, disorientation, or confusion, although social perception may be somewhat distorted. His processes of evaluation are not globally disturbed, and the disability is confined to a topic, an activity, a situation, or a person. In the neurotic we find side by side some functions which are undisturbed and some that are seriously impaired. The neurotic disturbance consists of defective feedback in the area of the conflict, while correction and self-correction outside this area may be quite appropriate.

The initial breakdown of feedback functions may occur for either of two reasons. The patient may not have learned to function in a human network because he was reared in an inadequate group, or his organs of communication are affected in such a way that the demands of the wider network cannot be met. The result is more or less the same. In the rehabilitation of the mentally ill patient, then, the psychiatrist has to tackle the problem in two places: restoration of the organs of communication, which may be diseased or may have suffered from disuse, and rehabilitation of the functions of communication within a given social network. For both purposes, the psychiatrist has to appraise the disturbances of communication so that he can arrange for proper rehabilitation.

Perhaps the most significant sign of disturbed communication is the patient's subjective feeling of being ill at ease, of being dissatisfied, and of not being up to his task. The therapist may interpret this phenomenon as indicative of inappropriate gratification—particularly the gratification that is available through the act of communication. Missing gratification, of course, prevents the acquisition of skills in communication.

A second sign of disturbed communication is poor physical health. Loss of weight, loss of appetite, sleeplessness, symptoms of anxiety and tension, restlessness, and specific syndromes affecting the vascular, intestinal, muscular, or respiratory system may be in the foreground. Although these subjective and objective signs of ill health may indicate the presence of a physical disease such as tuberculosis or cancer, they may on the other hand be the prodromal signs of a psychosis.

To differentiate the signs of ill health due to physical disease from those due to mental disease or personality disorder we have to consider a third aspect: the patient's growth and development. When information cannot be corrected through appropriate exchange, when skills are not learned, practiced, and maintained, then lack of growth becomes quite evident. The patient is stuck. He may or may not be aware of this stagnation, but a carefully elicited history will show that patterns of living have not been modified and adapted to present circumstances. Retarded growth is often accompanied by poor human relations. If an individual does not distribute his time appropriately between being alone, being in two-person situations, and being in groups, then difficulties develop and lack of growth and even regression may result. Although the introvert will spend greater amounts of time alone than in the group and the extrovert more time with others, one can state flatly that a person cannot grow if he spends no time alone or if he is never to be found in a group.

A fourth and last sign of disturbed communication bears upon quantitative aspects of the exchange. An intense reaction, far out of proportion to the circumstances, may betray a difficulty of communication. For example, children who do not obtain an appropriate response often become noisy and destructive. Conversely, if news that commonly elicits intense emotions falls flat, the psychiatrist knows that in all probability there is a disturbance hidden beneath the apparent calm. Inappropriacy of response in terms of timing and intensity is the secret of disturbed communication. A little verse sums it up quite nicely (11):

> Too much,
> Too little,
> Too early,
> Too late,
> At the wrong place,
> Is the disturbed message's fate.

THE EMERGENT DISTURBANCE: *DE MINIMIS MAXIMA*

Over-reaction · Undigested experience · Reconstruction and elaboration · Withdrawal symptoms · Symbolic and actual loss · Substitution therapy · Dependency upon partners · Interference with neurotic behavior · Developing new ways of communication · Omissions · Prevention and rectification

In observing communicative behavior, both verbal and nonverbal, we occasionally encounter disturbances which seem to arise suddenly out of a clear sky. These emergent events usually can be traced to interactions in which a harmless stimulus sets in motion an overpowering reaction.

TRIGGER SIGNAL

The trigger of a gun or the push-button of an elevator is set in motion by a relatively small movement of one finger, but the effect of this movement may be colossal. In clinical practice, a patient may report that when someone called him "dirty nigger," "white trash," "kike," or "wop," he flew into a rage and practically killed the other person. Another patient may mention that his boss announced the possibility of a lay-off, and he went home and took an overdose of sleeping pills. Or a doctor may inform a patient that he has to operate to explore a tumorous growth and the patient thinks that he has cancer and shoots himself. The trigger signal apparently sets in motion some preset patterns of behavior whereby the significant sign is interpreted as a real or physical danger. Over-reaction to the symbol may mean that careful assessment of the actual danger is neglected.

When the psychiatrist works through the connotations of the trigger signal, it becomes evident that the patient connects the symbol with some experience out of his past. The over-reaction actually is not an over-reaction at all. It is the kind of reaction anybody might have when he first gets in contact with a new situation—the first ride on a horse, the first appearance on the stage, the first contact with death, and so on. Actually the organism provides for a massive response to all new situations because the individual has not as yet learned to choose the muscles and sense organs and the patterns of expression that are most effective. The reaction persists because learning did not eliminate superfluous motions. The stimulus word or the stimulus action stands for a signal that in the past produced over-excitation and massive response. In the original context, such powerful response may have been the response of a child who could not cope with the situation. But now, many years later, the pattern is out of place. People who react to trigger phenomena have unresolved conflicts which prevent them from appropriately coping with the present situation.

Therapeutic communication can be helpful in coping with this kind of reaction. A stimulus that produced an over-excitation can be isolated and verbally elaborated. The reconstruction of original events helps the individual to understand the present situation. Then the therapist discusses the reaction most appropriate to the moment. The discussion and the support of the therapist on repeated occasions may induce the patient to react less violently. Each time the patient experiences the same reaction, verbal elaboration and emotional support given by the therapist help him to handle one or the other facet better, until in the long run the reaction assumes normal proportions.

STIMULUS WITHDRAWAL

The opposite of the trigger phenomenon is exemplified in the sudden removal of a habitual stimulus to which an individual could respond, or a habitual target which he could abuse. Loss of a beloved or hated person, loss of membership in a group to which the patient belonged, or the loss of a forum in which he could express himself may be reacted to with a sudden disturbance. The ensuing withdrawal symptoms are similar to those observed after withdrawal of alcohol, morphine, or barbiturates. The loss leaves a void, creates tension, craving, and loss of self-respect. These behavior patterns are variously referred to as mourning, grief reactions (12), or reactive depressions.

There are two components to this process. A man may grieve when he receives news of the death of his wife whom he has not seen in five years, or he may grieve because he loses a companion with whom he lived and talked every day. The former is a symbolic death which requires the rearrangement of images, thoughts, and feelings in the patient's fantasy; the latter is an actual loss, and action that has gone on for years ceases to exist. Under the heading of symbolic rearrangement, we also have to include those situations in which a patient has to rearrange his ideals, give up hopes, or change his faith because of sudden or unexpected circumstances. Stimulus withdrawal may also occur after loss of hearing or sight—that is, loss of the organ that makes perception possible.

The internal reasons for a depression have been well formulated by Abraham (1), Freud (2), Lewis (4, 5), and others. These formulations have taught the therapist to intervene in situations in which there is an actual loss. Knowing that a sudden withdrawal of stimulation or activity will be compensated for by the organism through increased internal stimulation (6), the doctor has to see that the patient does not become severely depressed or develop delusions or hallucinations. Although with most people a period of solitary meditation is beneficial, there are patients who react unfavorably. If a grieved person is left alone, self-destructive behavior is likely to increase and the danger of suicide may become imminent.

An acute loss may reawaken old conflicts or it may, as in the case of symbiotic relations, actually mean the loss of the connecting link with the outside world. It is important that the physician provide another person—for example, a nurse—to be with the patient for twenty-four hours a day. Therapy is of little help because the patient can see the doctor only for a limited period of time, and what he needs is constant, benevolent, affectionate, and respectful company. That human stimulation is needed has been recognized since time immemorial. In most cultures it is customary that those afflicted by illness, death, or misfortune are supported by relatives or friends. Helpful neighbors or even strangers may stay with the afflicted person until he can find his bearings. At times of emotional stress, some cultures demand self-discipline while others prescribe emotive behavior of an expressive nature. On such occasions, special rituals may be prescribed so that the survivors are kept busy and, through the ritual, experience alleviation from feelings of guilt.

HABIT INTERFERENCE

There are patients who are addicted to certain forms of expression, perception, or more complex communicative transactions. Some cannot abstain from being sarcastic, submissive, or seductive, and others cannot refrain from judging or disapproving. They seem to use this form of approach regardless of person or situation. Fixation to a preferred mode of communication may explain why certain people are so intimately tied to their partners who reciprocate in specific ways. The exhibitionist may have a voyeuristic partner; the doer may team up with a thinker. Whenever separation threatens such patients, they are drawn into a tailspin and try desperately to re-establish the lost relationship.

There are two ways to cope therapeutically with such an addiction. The first is to use the prevalent mode and satisfy it in a non-human context. The voyeur may acquire a hobby like photography, collect pictures, or go to the theatre; the nurturant person may become a nurse, a social worker, or seek work in a hospital. The sarcast may learn to become a theatre critic or review books; the efficiency addict may become an industrial efficiency expert. In this way the preferred mode of expression or action can be elevated to the level of a professional performance. This can be achieved if the patient, through understanding of his motives, is helped to realign his strivings, first by involving the therapist and then by using his activity to earn a living.

Another way of dealing with habit repetition is to render other activities more rewarding and the prevalent habits more ineffective. In implementing this goal, the therapist should not respond to any attempt of the patient to communicate in his preferred mode but reply only when he employs new ways. Although the doctor should beware of being punitive, lest he reinforce the existing patterns, he can bank on the fact that the patient's hunger for communication will induce him to try out different approaches. When these are well received by the therapist, the patient is stimulated to continue his experiments with communication. It goes without saying that in the acute phases of the condition the therapist tries as much as possible to gratify the patient's needs until he has regained his balance. The sarcast has to be allowed to be sarcastic; the dependent person has to be nurtured; the oppositionist has to be permitted to oppose. Only after the acute phase is over does the therapist attempt to cover new ground.

AVOIDANT EXCLUSION

Some patients communicate in such a way that they carefully exclude certain topics, persons, words, or ideas or avoid using certain body areas or systems. And should another person bring up the crucial topic, they manage not to hear, on occasions they do not reply, or they gloss over the issue. Avoidant exclusion may be associated with a compensatory preoccupation with another topic. In therapy, for example, a patient may systematically avoid talking about his mother but report extensively about his father. The experienced therapist considers verbal avoidance a signal that indicates a shift of expression to nonverbal action, just as loud words may cover up some omission in action. A more subtle form of exclusion is the wording given to certain sentences which indicates that the speaker does not include himself or that the other person is excluded. A mother, for example, might say, "Father and I are going to the movies," leaving it open whether the child is going with them or remains at home. Another person may say, "You have to go to the party," indicating that he himself is not counting on going.

The therapist discovers avoidant exclusion by considering that which is said and done as a unit; if lacunae recur consistently, the therapist can be pretty sure that the patient has a problem. What the therapist perceives are the boundary lines that the patient sets around certain types of information; he has, as it were, barbed wire fences in his brain. By showing that one can talk about almost everything at varying levels of abstraction and that one can mention forbidden topics by switching from verbal to nonverbal forms of communication, the therapist can retrain the patient. Many exclusions deal with conflictual material, part of which is repressed, and many patients do not possess the communicative means to solve such conflicts by themselves. By gaining versatility in communication, the patient learns to elaborate the conflictual material in a way that is acceptable. After all, avoidant exclusion evolved less because of the nature of the original events and more because of inadequate symbolic elaboration following the traumatic events. While therapeutic communication has no power to change the original events, it can successfully prevent learning blocks and lacunae in the awareness of the individual and help to resolve fixations.

THE DOCTOR'S SUBJECTIVE EXPERIENCE OF THE PATIENT AS A DIAGNOSTIC TOOL

Frustration of the therapist · The voice of the patient · Blank minds · Daily chores · The calculating person · Learning to be human · Intrusive possessiveness · Controlled incorporation · The therapist's nonparticipation in the destructive game · Communication with equals · Projection and attack · Exhibition and defeat · Appeal to omnipotence

If formal inspection does not reveal signs of inadequate communication, then the therapist has to rely upon a much finer instrument —his own reactions. This more subtle exploration of the patient is not exhausted after one session but may become rewarding only after twenty or thirty interviews. As time goes on, the doctor will notice that the patient has a certain stereotyped impact upon him. These effects, commonly referred to as transference and transference neurosis, are produced by certain repetitive messages that the patient addresses to the doctor. If the therapist studies the feedback patterns and communicative characteristics of these repetitive messages, he may discover certain formal deviations (11); but more often than not the first clue is not cognitive but is found in the psychiatrist's sense of frustration. He experiences that he cannot get things across to the patient; he becomes the scapegoat, or then again the victim of criticism, ridicule, or admiration of the patient. The frustrated efforts of the psychiatrist therefore become a diagnostic sign of the disability of the patient. Naturally they vary from doctor to doctor and from patient to patient, but each therapist gains experience of how he is met by certain types of patients.

THE PATIENT'S ACOUSTIC IMPACT

The "five R's"—Respiration, Range, Register, Resonance, and Rhythm—determine the principal acoustic dimensions of the human voice, although it may be further modified by such features as melody, intensity of sound, speed, accent, emphasis, pathos, and exactness in phonation (8). The healthy voice is deep and sonorous; the individual relaxes his diaphragm and phonates on expiration. Every normal person, when excited, talks with varying intensity and produces a wider range in pitch. But the pathologically excited person shows in addition a contraction of pharyngeal and neck muscles, an absence of the lower tones, variation in intensity toward soft or loud, or even an inflection of the voice which may distort the meaning of the sentence. The quarrelsome, plaintive voice is familiar to the psychiatrist; the patient gradually glides into a lower pitch with a marked decrease in intensity. The voice of anxiety or fear, which is characterized by inspiratory phonation, whispering, or aphonia, has a rough or quavering tone which indicates a respiratory pressure which is weaker than that of the glottis.

Acoustic scanning is informative because the healthy individual has harmonious tones and agreeable rhythm, produces a pleasant impact, and employs agreeable transitions. If a patient has a voice which arouses suspicion or alarm, the foundations for a subsequent disturbance of communication have been laid. The listener then becomes defensive and is more preoccupied with safeguarding himself than with responding to the speaker. On occasions, an increase in pitch and loudness of the whole voice and a hissing sound similar to snorting, sneezing, or violent exhalation may arouse the listener. In this case, the windpipe presses upon the vocal cords and this occurs when the individual is disturbed. The opposite can also be observed when the tone of the voice fades and the patient becomes aphonic, due to constriction of the vocal cords. But both changes indicate that the person is under internal or external pressure which changes the contraction of the muscles and the rhythmical patterns of breathing and interferes with the functions of the vocal cords.

The psychiatrist obviously does not consciously analyze these features (11), but he reacts to the patient's vocal behavior as a whole. His ear, accustomed to scan the sounds, connects certain voices with patients he has seen. These acoustic associations influence his diagnostic formulations and guide his therapeutic interventions. Tonal cues reveal emotionally loaded topics that have to be searched for and brought into the open. Minute by minute the therapist is guided by these acoustic cues, and he himself can use his own voice to influence the patient to relax. Imperceptibly he reduces anxiety by movements of his speech apparatus; he does not mirror the disturbance of the patient but tells him that he, the therapist, is not disturbed. Through negative acoustic feedback, the patient begins to quiet down.

THE PATIENT WHO ISN'T THERE

The vacuum phenomenon is characterized by the peculiar feeling that the other person does not respond. But it is not a hostile non-responding, nor is it an avoidant non-responding. One plainly gets the feeling that the other person is not there. Upon inspection, one might detect a blank stare, as in people who do not understand the language, are in shock, or suffer from aphasia. But these people do not suffer from an organic lesion of the central nervous system.

They even reply and observe the amenities of social intercourse, but their facial expressions seem to be non-participating, their posture does not acknowledge, and they have nothing pertinent to contribute.

Patients who produce this effect are often immature people who hide primitive rages and other infantile desires behind this nothingness. Sometimes such patients vacillate, and during a conversation they may disappear, as it were. Bodily they are sitting there, but their thoughts and feelings seem to be directed towards objects and persons that are not present; hence the therapist obtains the feeling that he cannot reach them. We also meet this phenomenon in people who feel that they are unworthy, untalented, or nonentities; they differ from the acutely depressed and the unhappy ones in that they feel that nothing can be done to change their condition. They have a somewhat beaten appearance which is similar to the hopelessness that one sees in prisoners of war or inmates of concentration camps. Some of these features are found in the bohemian members of the "beat generation" who bemoan their inability to contribute— San Francisco's own "beatniks" (9).

The therapist who encounters such a communicative vacuum has to give the individual time to develop confidence and trust; eventually the more primitive emotions of hatred, concern with bodily functions, and the sense that no activity is pleasurable may be expressed. But more often than not the patient has such an amorphous experience that he cannot pinpoint his difficulties. He wallows in unpleasant sensations and he avoids human contact because he wishes to hide his internal chaos. Whenever the therapist encounters such a person, he knows that he is dealing with a rather sick patient, and that only prolonged contact will bring some amelioration and growth. This is achieved by clarifying little incidents that happen under the therapist's eyes. A gesture that expresses fear, or a posture that denotes anger may be commented upon. Events that happened that morning or the evening before may be discussed; concrete plans for daily programs are made; menus are discussed, budgets made, expenditures analyzed, and week ends planned. Only on such a concrete level can the patient be helped to emphasize work, play, and participation rather than amorphous trepidation.

THE PATIENT WHO KEEPS HIS DISTANCE

There are some patients to whom the therapist can never get close. Such a person is polite, cooperative, and punctual; but the fact that he never dispenses with social amenities, that his fantasies do not reveal the animal that is hidden in every human being, makes him into something of an automaton. Man, after all, is half animal and half calculating machine. And what makes him human is the ability to engage in reasonable discourse while maintaining all the same those qualities that make animals lovable and fearful. But the distant patient lacks these mammalian qualities. To describe to the patient that which he does not have is no easy task. It is simpler to point to something that happens than to describe something that is not there; and it takes all of the therapist's resources to point up this lack of expressive functions and the patient's inability to respond to stimulations other than intellectual. The trouble with the intellectual, rational, and distant person is that although he maintains his clear vision, he forfeits the support and appreciation that a group has to give.

In therapy, the distant person has to be trained in a threefold way: first, to perceive and evaluate patterns and Gestalten instead of analyzing their component parts; second, to perceive and appreciate analogically coded events—movements, color, forms, sounds —instead of sticking to verbal and digital symbols; and third, to utilize emotions arising in self as a source of information instead of discarding them as artifacts or complications. A decontamination from intellectualism is achieved by pointing to those events for which words do not exist, which can be experienced rather than be described. Finally, the patient can be induced to use his nose, his tongue, and his fingers more than his eyes and ears. The distant person has to relearn the use of the proximity receivers, and eventually he will become a warmer person (11).

THE UNDULY FAMILIAR PATIENT

Some patients are unduly familiar and behave as if they had been brought up with the therapist from early childhood. Amenities are omitted, intimacies are discussed too soon, and the patient assumes closeness where none exists. Some patients may pry into the private life of their doctors by asking questions and commenting about other patients, or members of the doctor's family. The patient's appetite seems to increase with every defensive move of the physician until such time as the doctor confronts the patient with his behavior. At this point, the doctor usually experiences frustration because his efforts at correction are of no avail. Either the patient withdraws with the feeling of rejection or he renews his relentless efforts.

Therapy with incorporative or communal patients has to be directed at supporting them without being "eaten up." Stricter rules, firm discarding of comments that do not bear upon the discussion, and warm encouragement to deal with problems of self instead of those of others have their effects. The distortion of familiarity usually sets in at once, perhaps in the first interview, and gradually dissolves as the patient becomes stronger. But escaping the whale's mouth is an art which is time-consuming to learn. The best way to describe it is to say that the therapist permits controlled incorporation. At first the patient always hopes for more, and this expectation keeps him going. The doctor has to allow this anticipation to exist; otherwise the patient quits therapy and seeks another doctor.

THE PATIENT WHO SPOILS THE THERAPIST'S EFFORTS

The patient who gracefully accepts all that the doctor has to say but somehow manages to indicate that his therapeutic efforts are in vain spoils the efforts of the therapist. He may accuse the doctor of not producing quick results; he may point to the fact that other physicians use different methods, prefer to put the patient on a couch, or belong to another school of thought. The patient may allude to the doctor's intellectual or emotional shortcomings, to his deficiencies in status, skill, or wealth. All this is done with great subtlety so that the physician cannot refer to something that has been said overtly; instead he has to rely upon the impact that such statements have made upon him. The patient then, especially if he is dialectically well trained, will reply that the effect produced is due to the personality of the doctor and that his own conflicts and idiosyncrasies induce him to make such interpretations. If the doctor is healthy, he is not particularly impressed with these acrobatics. The discussion then does not center around what the impression is that was created but upon the fact that the impact cannot be changed. He will point out that the patient should double his effort to change the impression that he creates, and that his inability to do so is a sign of neurosis. The therapist then points out that if the patient's major aim is the defeat of the therapist, this aim is unrealistic, irrelevant, and a sign of transference neurosis.

The therapist will experience some difficulty with such a competitive, self-destructive patient. The patient, being a dependent sort of a character, assumes that, overtly, the doctor will do everything in his power to prevent him from being destructive, while at a covert level—as with the parent in his past—he is out to defeat him. In response to this attitude, the therapist can support the patient gently and consistently, giving him an opportunity to discover that he will neither prevent the patient from being destructive nor push him into it. Soon the patient discovers that the doctor does not play his game and then of course the tension increases. Not being able to relate except through this game, the patient is at a loss and needs more support. But from this point on, a new relationship can evolve.

THE PATIENT WHO SETS THE DOCTOR ON A PEDESTAL

There are people who specialize in communication with superiors and inferiors. Because of their vertical specialization, they may have difficulties with horizontal communication—that is, with their peers. Therefore, when they meet equals, they structure the situation by putting the other person on a pedestal and attributing to him superior features. The therapist, for example, may become something of a Greek god—beautiful, ideal, and superior. All those little features that make a person human—the fact that fleas bite him or that he has to blow his nose or that he is late for the appointment—are overlooked. Soon the therapist notices that he has difficulty in living up to the ideal in the patient's head, and eventually the patient expresses resentment because the psychiatrist does not behave like an ideal person. The subsequent development may take two directions: either the therapist is slowly undermined and torn down or attempts are made to keep up his legendary position.

In these circumstances, the therapist has to aim at making himself appear as a human being. To achieve this end, the psychiatrist sometimes has to resort to a change in procedure. As long as the patient is seen in the office and the interaction is stereotyped, the patient has few if any incentives to correct his assumptions. But if the therapist is seen in different social contexts, the likelihood of maintaining the fiction diminishes (3). It helps if the patient sees the doctor eat a hot dog or play with a child or talk to a member of the family. The therapist therefore might schedule a home visit, invite the husband or wife to sit in on the interview, change the seating arrangement, or talk about problems of the world instead of those concerning the patient. The more factual impression the patient can gain, the less the distortion.

THE PATIENT WHO USES THE DOCTOR AS AN ANVIL

Between hammer and anvil, iron is wrought. On many occasions, the patient treats the psychiatrist as an anvil which has to receive his blows. The world, people, and society are blamed and the psychiatrist is made responsible. He becomes the target for the patient's ill temper, his hatred, and his sadistic procedures. Such antagonism exists because the patient projects many of his own features upon the therapist, giving himself an opportunity to attack what he does not like about himself. The psychiatrist becomes aware of the patient's disturbance when he discovers that these accusations are not related to his own behavior. In the case of the schizophrenic, the distortions are obvious to everybody; in neurotic patients, the attacks may be disguised. The doctor is treated as if he had an undesirable character and whatever happens is blamed upon the method, the school, or the circumstances, or upon the doctor personally. At first the patient does not realize his own projections, and the first step of therapy consists of making the patient aware of the fact that he excludes himself from this troubled world. The doctor's good natured acceptance of the patient's attacks helps in making him aware of his distortions; eventually he may begin to use the pronouns *I* and *me* instead of *they* and *them*, and this signals the inclusion of self in the world.

Almost the reverse situation exists when the patient reduces himself to an anvil. Helpless, faulty, loaded with pathology, and undesirable, the patient presents himself to the doctor as a target. With great skill, the critical, sarcastic, and even sadistic features in the doctor's personality are tantalized. If the doctor gets seduced, blow after blow is absorbed with masochistic delight. With each visit, more undesirable features are exhibited to give the therapist a better opportunity to condemn, criticize, and dissect. The punishment received relieves some of the patient's feelings of guilt, and often the patient improves. However, the therapist has to be aware that the improvement will last only as long as the blows continue to fall. In the treatment of the patient, the therapist has to attempt not to respond. With his non-participating attitude, the doctor indicates that he stays out of the game; the lack of response attenuates the patient's behavior and avoids further stimulation. Gently and firmly the original circumstances that brought on this behavior are recalled and the patient is reminded of the present reality situation. The appropriate behavior for the therapeutic session then is discussed.

THE PATIENT WHO OFFERS HIMSELF AS A MOLDABLE SUBJECT

The patient who indicates, "I am in competent hands; I do as you say; I am your creation; I shall contribute to your glory; I am willing to do anything you say" is a dangerous patient. When the patient implies "I have no will of my own; I am an empty person; you mean everything to me and therefore I do as you say; I surrender," he really does not offer true cooperation but a denial of self. This passive resignation is designed to stimulate the omnipotent features of the therapist. And for fear of being discovered, of having his own inferiority revealed, the patient yields to the superior conqueror. The patient forfeits his own development in favor of a pleasing symbiosis in which the other person makes the decisions and the patient becomes the executor. The therapist has to oppose this division of the functions of communication. He has to indicate to the patient that he does not enjoy his assigned position as omnipotent ruler because to carry the patient in his arms, as it were, or to drag him along, is no fun. Once the patient has understood that the only way to get along with the therapist is to develop himself, he may abandon his attitude in due time.

References

1. Abraham, K.: *Selected Papers.* 527 p. London: Hogarth Press, 1942.
2. Freud, S.: Mourning and melancholia. Pp. 152–170 in *Collected Papers,* Vol. 4. London: Hogarth Press, 1946.
3. Kolb, L. C. and Montgomery, J.: An explanation for transference cure: its occurrence in psychoanalysis and psychotherapy. Amer. J. Psychiat., 115, 414–421, 1958.
4. Lewis, A. J.: Melancholia: Clinical survey of depressive states. J. ment. Sci., 80, 277–378, 1934.
5. Lewis, A. J.: Melancholia: A historical review. J. ment. Sci., 80, 1–42, 1934.
6. Lilly, J. C.: Mental effects of reduction of ordinary levels of physical stimuli on intact, healthy persons. Pp. 1–9 in *Research Techniques in Schizophrenia.* Psychiatric Research Reports #5. Washington: American Psychiatric Association, 1956.
7. McCulloch, W. S. and Pitts, W.: The statistical organization of nervous activity. J. Amer. statistical Assoc., 4, 91–99, 1948.
8. Moses, P. J.: *The Voice of Neurosis.* 131 p. New York: Grune & Stratton, 1954.
9. Rigney, F. J. and Smith L. D.: *The Real Bohemia.* 250 p. New York: Basic Books, 1961.
10. Rosenzweig, N.: Sensory deprivation and schizophrenia: some clinical and theoretical similarities. Amer. J. Psychiat., 116, 326–329, 1959.
11. Ruesch, J.: *Disturbed Communication.* 337 p. New York: Norton, 1957.
12. Volkart, E. H.: Bereavement and mental health. Pp. 281–307 in *Explorations in Social Psychiatry* (A. H. Leighton, J. A. Clausen, and R. N. Wilson, editors). New York: Basic Books, 1957.

Chapter Five

Distorted Social Orientations

THE VALUES that govern an individual's relations to superiors and inferiors, to intimates and casual acquaintances, and to the group in which he lives can be subsumed under the term "social orientation." These values, which form the backbone of a person's conscious and unconscious attitudes, have to be rather stable if any consistency in behavior is to be achieved. But if an individual becomes either too flexible, shedding his values at a moment's notice, or extremely rigid in his orientation, then we are dealing with pathology. Once his behavior has become fixed, the patient usually strives to achieve or maintain a certain social role regardless of circumstances and personal sacrifice. Such an attitude prevents the patient from adapting reasonably to other people. Strivings such as social climbing, or repeated change of human relations, may become all-consuming preoccupations which so disturb the patient's life that he can no longer go about satisfying other vital needs. The task of the psychiatrist is to correct some of the distortions that result from rigidity or over-flexibility and to help the individual to regain a sense of balance.

THE VERTICAL ORIENTATION:
STATUS AND DEPENDENCY

Specialists in perception of status · Adjusting life to the vertical orientation · Socially mobile individuals · Social climbers · Social decliners · Coping with status change · Acquiring a more solid identity · Socially static individuals

Some life experiences sensitize an individual to perceive and evaluate the other person's status. Perception of status superiority in terms of age, seniority, skill, achievement, success, affection, or wealth is essentially a duplication of the child's view of his parents; after all, they have more power than he has and they can help when need arises. This vertical orientation is particularly prominent in youngest children in the family (13, 14) who have to protect themselves against the transgressions of the older siblings. Oldest borns, conversely, are prone to perceive status inferiority. They have younger siblings; and if the parent of the same sex dies, the oldest child has to replace the parent vis-à-vis the younger siblings. In the oldest daughter who has to take the place of her deceased mother, for example (12), the vertical orientation consists of a nurturant attitude towards the younger siblings. A similar attitude is found among many teachers, nurses, social workers, and all the other people who work in the caretaking disciplines. The vertical orientation thus stems from two character features: dominance-submission on the one hand, and nurturance-dependency on the other.

When people are driven to dominance or submission, they sooner or later maneuver themselves into a position in which their favorite social approach can be utilized (8). By necessity, then, they will get together with others who show a complementary constellation in their social behavior; and they will avoid those that do not respond. People with a vertical orientation rarely fit into groups that are made up of peers because they lack the ways of communication suitable for coping with equals. People with vertical orientation of course suffer frequently from authority problems. Either they attach themselves to a powerful authority and at the same time rebel against it, or they surround themselves with inferiors and at the same time reject them.

Therapy with this kind of disorder is difficult. The best that the psychiatrist can do is to incorporate the patient into a social structure in which the vertical orientation can be usefully applied. He can guide young people into professions in which this orientation is useful: teaching; care of the sick, the young, the old, and the deviant. And the person who feels helpless and has to rely upon others can be guided into a position of subservience, in which there will always be someone else to tell him what to do. Simultaneously the psychiatrist can work on the conflicts which prevent the patient from successfully occupying such a position. He can make him aware of his resentment, further the expression of hostility, and help him to accept the consequences of his character. The principle, therefore, is clear. Dependent people are not made independent; they are merely guided into situations in which their dependency can be successfully gratified by an institution, by an organization, or by an older and status-carrying person. Nurturant people, conversely, can be steered into those organizations and situations that concern themselves with the underprivileged.

A particular form of vertical orientation is found in the socially mobile individual. Unlike the dependent person who yearns for approval the socially mobile person transforms his dependency into an impersonal social problem. To him, every individual is but the bearer of status who can help or deter him in getting where he wishes to go. In the group of socially mobile patients, there are three types. First, there are those who identify with their parents' social mobility; they climb or decline in conformance with the trend established by the family. These persons are actually well-adjusted because they have been equipped by their parents with all the attitudes and techniques necessary to be on the move. However, maladjustments can occur if such patients are caught in extraordinary circumstances where mobility is precluded. Many enlisted men and officers broke down during the war because their ambitions were frustrated and they were denied promotion. A second type of socially mobile patient, the rebel, rejects the ideals of the parents and reverses their social trend. In reversing the parents' decline, for example, he may be seen to recoup the family fortune or to abandon an unprofitable family business. To reverse the upward trend of the parents, the patient may engage in assorted antisocial behavior. To embarrass his people, he may become involved in religious, political, intellectual, or artistic radicalism. It is remarkable that a person's change of the family's social trend is unconsciously motivated by a disapproval of the parents and the intent of hurting their pride. This is particularly true of adolescents, who have a need to demonstrate their independence and to reject the parents' ideals. At a more mature age, such adolescent rebellion may revert to compliance with the ideals and status of the parents. A third type is characterized by a mixture of status gains and status losses. This type of social mobility may be seen in people whose parents advanced in the economic field. The children then have to make up the lag in the social and ideological spheres in final fulfillment of the aspirations of the parents. But in making an intellectual or artistic effort, they may lose some of the economic ground that the parents had already gained.

Improvement in status per se is not a pathological feature if it coincides with mastery and achievement (5). However, if social climbing becomes a way of life at the expense of learning, it is an expression of inner conflict and usually is accompanied by a lack of identification with the group of origin (9). The social climber abuses every human relationship, every position, and every recreational activity for social betterment. He learns to manipulate symbols and gestures of status but fails to master any particular skill. His human relations are of a passing character, and deep attachments are rarely formed unless these be to another social climber who travels in the same direction. Eventually a mobile individual finds himself in groups that are entirely strange to him, whose language he does not know, and whose rules he has not mastered. Since old and well-established groups rarely accept the newcomer fully, the climber then joins a group of his own—a group of socially mobile people or displaced persons who lead a make-believe life. These groups are heavily represented among suburban socialites, café society, and the semi-bohemian circles of our metropolitan centers. Groups with real power and well-entrenched influence prefer to stay out of the limelight in order to retain their freedom of movement. It is out of this group of highly mobile people that many psychotherapists recruit their clientele. The established groups, in contrast, seek the psychiatrist only when the condition of the patient is rather serious.

The social decliner is seen less often in a psychiatrist's office than

the climber. He shuns therapy and seems to take pride in falling
to pieces all by himself. He may be brought to the doctor because
police, practicing physicians, or relatives believe that something
should be done about him; he may be a drifter who has been accidentally picked up or an alcoholic who is admitted to a hospital
because of delirium tremens. These patients are very difficult to
treat because they have dedicated their lives to social self-destruction. The only thing that seems to hold them is group membership
in an informal society that respects idiosyncrasies and converts the
tendency towards self-destruction into a tendency to help others.
Alcoholics Anonymous has done more in this respect than all psychiatrists put together (2, 7). But there are others who are content
to lead the life of hoboes, who live alone, drift, and shun the group
—and who are not alcoholics.

Therapy with a socially mobile individual begins with an exploration of feelings. Since he tends to pay attention to other people's
reactions, he now has to be taught to focus upon what he himself
thinks and feels. And to his great amazement, he may discover that
what he himself thinks and feels in no way coincides with what
others feel and think, and that he simply disregards his own thoughts
and feelings in order to avoid conflict. While such disavowal of
self is frequently found among prominent people who manage to
hide their real selves until they have reached the top, our patients
usually have such a flexible self that it is hard to discern what their
real self is. In the second phase of therapy, then, and after the
relationship with the therapist has been thoroughly established, a
discussion of the patient's phoniness frequently leads to his rather
complete deflation. What he strove for turns out to be empty, and
what he learned—the manipulation of symbols—did not yield any
satisfaction for him. Now, when he is faced with failure, the therapist
can intervene and demonstrate to him that as a social climber he
possesses a great deal of knowledge of people and situations and
that this social knowledge can be employed for both occupational
and recreational purposes.

Phase three of therapy can be thought of as a reconstruction
period in which an inventory is taken, the experiences and talents

of the patient are realigned, and a new approach to life is started. After the patient has accepted the fact that he has not mastered many skills, he must be given hope that it is never too late to go through boot camp. Perhaps he can become interested in an organization and acquire administrative skills; or he can develop along professional or semi-professional lines; or he might use his social skills in some sort of service function. The fourth phase, which partly overlaps the third, is devoted to an understanding of how the patient became a social climber. The parents' contentment with mere gestures or symbols of effort and their lack of insistence on mastery may then become quite apparent. If the patient's parents were social climbers like himself, he will have a hard time finding a new identity, and learning with and from the therapist may represent a first experience. But if he became a climber out of rebellion against rigorous parents, the resolution of the conflict may unravel the fact that the patient really possesses some solidity. Therefore therapy with social climbers is rather drawn out because it involves either a return to and acceptance of earlier attitudes which had been rejected or a learning anew, which may take many years.

Persons with a stable social status usually have parents who are satisfied and who tend to accept their social status. Feeling quite secure, such parents do not push their children towards social achievement. Unfortunately, such a stable person can automatically lose status if he does not attain the increases in power that come with age and seniority. For example, an extremely capable scientist may find himself relatively retarded in advancement because all of his colleagues spent their time to butter up their superiors while he simply did his work. Therapy with such an individual is geared to make him overcome his social inhibitions. He has to learn to undertake certain actions which those in power consider desirable; he has to demonstrate that he is a good boy, willing to play the game, being hungry for advancement, and eventually those in power will give him his well-deserved promotion. Such a patient has to be convinced that in a socially mobile culture personal propaganda is necessary and that he is not a cheater and not dishonest if he attends to his own welfare. He has to recognize that a moderate amount of politicking does not harm him in any way and that he has to accept this as part of social reality.

THE HORIZONTAL ORIENTATION: INTIMACY AND DISTANCE

The biological roots of intimacy · The social determinants of intimacy · The forcibly intimate or distant · Therapy with the intimate patient · Therapy with the distant person

Man's experience of closeness and distance is related to his progressive detachment from mother after birth. First in utero, then in close proximity with the breast, later somewhat detached when bottle fed, then away from mother for longer periods until geographical separation occurs, the individual's orientation is shaped along a scale of lessening contact with mother. Those who experience difficulties with this gradual detachment, either because of early deprivation or because of over-protection, struggle with these problems well into adult life. Intimacy is thus related to several fundamental biological facts: being born, crawling out of the shell, and maintaining autonomy through incorporation of food and information. In terms of body systems, the experience of intimacy is related to hand-mouth coordination while the experience of distance is related to eye-leg coordination. Since locomotion and leg coordination develop only after sucking, biting, and hand coordination have been mastered, the experience of distance develops considerably later than the experience of closeness. In adult life, women who bear children and attend to the oral needs of their children are more concerned with intimacy than are men, who tend to roam around and use their tools of locomotion. As a matter of fact, in the animal world the male is generally more mobile than the female (15); and in human beings, this is reflected in their hobbies and pastimes. Women tend to go to lectures, roundtables, club meetings, and luncheons. Men in contrast move and roam, and their pleasures are less of the listening variety such as concerts and lectures but more of the visual variety such as musical comedies or burlesque shows. Locomotion is associated with visual perception, while stationary behavior is more dependent upon sound.

Distance behavior has been variously identified with the upper class, indifference with the middle class and closeness with the lower class. The lower class has to put up with closeness because of crowded living conditions or closeness to nature. In the upper class, where more cubic feet of space are available for each individual, inside the residence and outside, distance behavior is more in order. Furthermore, upper class children are cared for by servants, who do not evoke the same feelings that a mother might. Here everything gets stylized early in the life of the child. Finally, in the middle class, indifference is the order of the day, inasmuch as commitment to any idea or action may endanger the future position of a person; the middle class has to protect itself against attacks from below and above.

Patients who have conflicts about intimacy or distance fall into several groups. First we have those who provoke intimacy although the situation does not require such closeness; then we find those who have to maintain distance even though the situation does not lend itself to that purpose; finally there are those who are unable to be either close or distant and who display a somewhat impersonal, pseudo-friendly attitude. The person who is artificially intimate usually has strong incorporating tendencies; he monopolizes, restricts, controls, or overidentifies with the other person. The person who maintains distance does not wish to penetrate another individual's private affairs and avoids inquiring into the other person's likes, dislikes, personal habits, ambitions, and goals. A distant person dislikes sharing facilities such as baths, swimming pools, toilets, buses, and other conveniences, and on the whole avoids gatherings in which large numbers of people congregate.

The patient who has a need for intimacy has to be gratified. The therapist has to allow the patient to incorporate, to imitate, to explore, and to hang on. This is the patient's first way of establishing contact. However, the therapist has to be prepared for later regurgitation when the patient discovers that he took on too much and that what he accepted was not in line with his own needs. He begins to be resentful and throws overboard what he previously adored. This gradual spitting out process can be mellowed by analyzing step by step the patient's unpalatable incorporations. If the patient discovers that he is given freedom to reject whatever he considers unsuitable, the feelings of resentment or guilt can be minimized. And from a relationship of forced intimacy, the patient then is taught to gradually assume a flexible position in which intimacy or distance can be assumed according to circumstances.

With the distant patient, therapy begins in the same way. At first, he is allowed to be distant and impersonal. Contact usually can be established if the patient is allowed to avoid statements about emotions, values, and personal problems. Instead the discussion may begin with social, cultural, or economic problems. Sooner or later, however, the patient will get fed up with his distant behavior and will break down. Such a crisis may develop when the patient feels hurt, when an emergency occurs, or when the patient cannot hide his desire for intimacy any longer. After the crisis, the patient usually feels ashamed and becomes more distant than ever. The therapist has to forestall this reaction by his own lack of embarrassment and his otherwise spontaneous behavior. After repeated incidents of this kind, the patient usually discovers that there is little danger in being close. After he has made sure that he will not be coerced or abused, he will eventually begin to discuss personal affairs without fear. Since for these patients the experience of intimacy is connected with anxiety, the therapist has to give the patient plenty of opportunity to test out situations in which intimacy may occur. But he has to beware of the demonstration of pseudo-intimacy. To a girl, he may have to point out that sexual intercourse is not synonymous with intimacy and that prostitutes have for millennia practiced one of the most impersonal occupations known to man. Intimacy is an experience and not a display of external symbols that people commonly associate with intimacy.

THE TOPOLOGICAL ORIENTATION:
BELONGING AND MARGINALITY

People of the core group · Marginal people · Therapy with core people · Therapy with marginal people · Remaining safe and reaching out

The assessment of similarities and differences with respect to others clarifies one's own position and tells where one belongs. The basic elements which later enter into the identity formation of the individual are acquired by children through imitation (4). Spontaneously the child will copy other human beings, and when the adult rewards this behavior, sameness acquires a pleasure value. Once a behavior pattern has been successfully established, deviation from it may arouse anxiety. Fear of exclusion from the group constantly reinforces the sameness aspects, implicitly containing directives as to what not to do. Children hear fathers and mothers comment on how their family's beliefs, attitudes, and practices contrast with those of other groups. The clearer these comments are, the more is the position of the child defined. Within the core group, differences are established in much the same way. If a mother likes one child better than another, she may reward the preferred child for imitative behavior while the other may be scolded if he dares to do the same thing. This child, then, may be able to secure the mother's attention by becoming the "black sheep" of the family. By imitating in reverse, he belongs as much to the group as his brother, who conforms to the required standards.

Marginal people derive from several sources: children who grew· up in core-group families where strife and conflict reigned may be confused as to where they belong and so become marginal. Others may be born into marginal families and acquire through indentification a marginal personality. Again other children may be displaced through war, disease, or economic circumstances and acquire so many different identities that they do not know which is to prevail. Marginal people—people who really do not belong—feel like fish out of water. Somewhat rejected but not completely, agreeing in some respects but not in others, they acquire a relatively mobile position within the group. While core members can simply take over the solutions devised by the group, marginal people have to examine each problem anew. They perpetually have to clarify their position and, depending upon whether they belong or not, accept or reject the proposed solution (6). Thus it is not accidental that the marginal group has intellectuals and artists who question the premises of their time and that the core group is mostly made up of technicians, business men, and administrators who perpetuate that which is in existence.

Members of the core group usually show psychological problems of unawareness and prejudice, and therapy therefore revolves around a broadening of their field of awareness. In order to adapt their individual needs to those of the group, they have to repress and conform; and whatever they do not know they do not care about. If, in spite of all psychological precautions, some conflict should penetrate awareness, prejudices will serve the purpose of keeping the individual uninvolved (1). Core people thus have to be helped to tolerate impurities and contradictions without getting anxious. This is achieved by inducing the core person to talk with foreigners, strangers, and members of minority groups; to travel; and to attempt to view himself through the eyes of others.

Therapy with marginal people revolves around narrowing their field of awareness. Since marginal people cannot rely upon cultural tradition or upon conformity to a group norm, they have to assess every step they make. This over-awareness of differences, conflicts, and injustices makes them unacceptable to the core group and often to themselves. The therapist endeavors to make marginal people accept the technical implementations of the core group—the practices dealing with traffic, communication, trade, finance, and social manners. That the deeper layer of conviction and belief cannot be touched goes without saying. But his acceptance that "how to do it" is a problem eventually incorporates the marginal person somewhat into the core culture. This is achieved by discussing daily life events and pointing out how a core person would do it. Furthermore, reading and occupational or casual social contacts with the core group will improve the situation.

The marginal person maintains his identity by being different, and the core person maintains his identity by being similar. In therapy, then, the complementary mechanisms have to be acquired. The core person must learn to tolerate differences and the marginal person to tolerate similarities. The core person's position in society is unquestioned, but the price for his conformity is tension disease or psychoneurosis. The position of the marginal person in society is fluid, and his symptoms are found in disturbed human relations. The marginal person does best living in marginal society—in bohemia, in the anonymity of the big urban center, among intellectuals and artists, or as a guest in a foreign land. Here the outsider can become an established outsider, and countless are the American and English expatriates who lived for generations abroad because they could not tolerate their own core culture. The core person, in contrast, has to stay with his own group, but he can move to the periphery of his circle. As a traveler, patron of the arts, or nature lover he learns to reach out while maintaining his safe position within the core group. He never questions the basic assumptions of his culture; he merely enjoys what others do that he cannot do himself.

THE GOAL ORIENTATION: SUCCESS AND FAILURE

Value judgments · Facts and evaluations · Nominal aspects of experience · Concern with the outcome · The language of success and failure · Converting failure into success

The person who feels inferior or superior, the person who views himself as a failure or as a success, the person who judges actions in terms of good and bad, the individual who appraises objects in terms of the expensive or the cheap tends to evaluate events on a uniform scale. After having pinned a value on action, person, or object, these people need not pursue the subject any further. Such people usually have difficulties in communicating, and classification into value categories usually hides serious emotional disturbance. While the healthy person uses value terms to compare otherwise uncomparable things and to reach a decision (10), the sick person labels events without ever reaching a conclusion. To use a metaphor, one might say that the "value spouter" runs around with price tags in his pockets, pinning these on the objects, people, and actions he encounters without bothering to buy or sell goods or services. Actually the naming of values in the emotionally disturbed person is an obsessional phenomenon. This ritual apparently had some significance in the family of origin. Mother might have used such comments as "a good boy does not wet his pants," whereby the subsequent interaction revolved not around the practical handling of bladder control but upon being good or bad. In the face of anxiety, then, the adult person copies mother's behavior and concentrates on evaluation.

The naming of values enables an individual to dispose of complex problems in a simplified way. Aware of this oversimplification, the therapist attempts gradually to reintroduce complexity. An interview might assume the following form: The doctor asks, "Are you married?" The patient replies, "I should be, but I haven't gotten around to it." Or when the doctor comments, "You are late," the patient might reply, "It's my damned right to be late; I pay for the hour." If the therapist understands that the patient is an extremely immature person or is anxious, depressed, or in a state of regression, he will tender kind support and avoid arguments. As time goes on, the therapist, little by little, can eliminate value terms. This he achieves not by challenging the value reply of the patient but by treating the patient as an individual whose range of understanding is narrow. So when the patient says, "I shouldn't have been frightened when I saw the ladder fall," the doctor emphasizes the fact that he was frightened and, in the circumstances, did the best he could. The patient is made to understand that consideration of what he should or should not have done is reserved for those situations in which he really has a choice and is functioning optimally.

The translation of a value statement into an operational statement can occur as follows: If the patient says, "New Yorkers are snooty," the doctor inquires, "Whom did you meet?" If it then comes out that the patient was ignored by a John Doe who came from New York, the doctor may say, "Suppose he lived in New Jersey; do you not think he would have cut you in the same way?

You obviously do not like this John Doe, and that is what you want to state." The patient thus learns that it isn't the emphasis on value but the experience that matters. Once this idea has been put across —that social intercourse consists of an exchange of experiences— the patient will become much more fascinated with exploring his own experiences and those of others than with pinning upon these events labels that preclude further understanding.

Statements about success and failure consider the nominal aspects of events only. To have or not to have achieved a set goal is more important to the individual than whether the goal is gratifying or appropriate. Concern with the outcome implies that the person chooses an arbitrary point on a continuous scale and labels this as the success point: to have won the election, to have signed the contract, to have discovered a new drug. Omitted from consideration are the periods before and after the critical date (11). This viewpoint represents a peculiar distortion of life, as if it consisted of this single critical event. Forgotten is the fact that years may elapse before and after such a point is reached. And if the state of success is to last, more and more such points must be maximized. More battles have to be won, more contracts obtained, more honors accepted—regardless of whether these make any sense. The person who indulges in failure does somewhat the same thing. A given point is maximized and considered representative of a whole life. A flunked exam may be viewed as the end of the world.

The language of a person who is concerned with success and failure has many metalinguistic implications. A person may state, "I am a failure," making the other person appear as a success because to maintain his own psychological household he needs to associate with people who are more successful than he is. In this instance, then, the professed statement "I am a failure" has to be translated into "I want you to be powerful and successful so that you can protect me." Conversely, the person who blows his own horn, drops names, and impresses others with his success may be a person who can relate only to people who are less successful. He requires their admiration and perhaps their hatred and envy, and he wishes to reassure himself that he can do things for others. His orientation with regard to success and failure (3) may structure his human relations to such an extent that no other considerations can develop. This preoccupation in both thought and word, of course, begs one question: Success or failure by whose standards? A hobo might be considered a failure by middle class standards, but in his own eyes he might be quite a success. These and other implications the therapist can appropriately introduce in order to shake the foundations upon which the patient's preoccupation is built.

Therapeutic communication with these cases can follow two distinct lines. If the therapist accepts the patient's orientation as unalterable, he merely sees to it that the patient builds a style of life which fits his orientation. If the patient is preoccupied with failure, his drive can be reconstructed towards success if he is given an opportunity to deal with people who have experienced failure—disaster victims, war casualties, or criminals. The patient may become a Franciscan monk, a martyr, a missionary; he may join the French Foreign Legion or become a social worker or a Red Cross worker. The drive to succeed in turn can be implemented by having the patient choose an occupation where target dates and promotions occur at regular intervals. The patient thus is directed towards occupations which deal with emergencies—fire, disease, police work—or with sales. If, however, the therapist wishes to be more fundamental, he has to work through all those memories of childhood conditions which induced the patient to become oriented towards success or failure. Through the uncovering of unconscious motivations the patient learns to reorient his implementations; and if the therapist succeeds in training the patient not to consider the ultimate outcome but to take each step as it occurs, then the patient may be able to obtain gratification from his daily actions.

References

1. Adorno, T. W., Frenkel-Brunswik, E., Levinson, D. J., and Sanford, R. N.: *The Authoritarian Personality*, 990 p. New York: Harper, 1950.
2. Alcoholic Foundation, Inc.: *Alcoholics Anonymous*. 400 p. New York: Works Publishing, Inc., 1939.

3. Brachfeld, O.: *Inferiority Feelings in the Individual and the Group.* 301 p. New York: Grune & Stratton, 1951.

4. Grinker, R. R.: On identification. Int. J. Psycho-Anal., 38, 1–12, 1957.

5. Hollingshead, A. B. and Redlich, F. C.: *Social Class and Mental Illness.* 442 p. New York: Wiley, 1958.

6. Mann, J. W.: Group relations and the marginal personality. Hum. Relat., 11, 77–92, 1958.

7. Ripley, H. S. and Jackson, J. K.: Therapeutic factors in Alcoholics Anonymous. Amer. J. Psychiat., 116, 44–50, 1959.

8. Ruesch, J.: Experiments in psychotherapy: II. Individual social techniques. J. soc. Psychol., 29, 3–28, 1949.

9. Ruesch, J.: Social factors in therapy. Pp. 59-93 in *Psychiatric Treatment* (ARNMD #31). Baltimore: Williams & Wilkins, 1953.

10. Ruesch, J.: Values and the process of communication. Pp. 27–40 in *Symposium on Preventive and Social Psychiatry, 15–17 April, 1957.* Washington: Walter Reed Army Institute of Research, 1958.

11. Ruesch, J. and Bateson, G.: *Communication: The Social Matrix of Psychiatry.* 314 p. New York: Norton, 1951.

12. Ruesch, J., Christiansen, C., Patterson, L. C., Dewees, S., and Jacobson, A.: Psychological invalidism in thyroidectomized patients. Psychosom. Med., 9, 77–91, 1947.

13. Ruesch, J., Harris, R. E., Christiansen, C., Loeb, M. B., Dewees, S., and Jacobson, A.: *Duodenal Ulcer.* 118 p. Berkeley and Los Angeles: University of California Press, 1948.

14. Ruesch, J., Harris, R. E., Loeb, M. B., Christiansen, C., Dewees, S., Heller, S. H., and Jacobson, A.: *Chronic Disease and Psychological Invalidism.* 191 p. New York: Amer. Soc. Res. Psychosom. Probl., 1946. 2nd printing, Berkeley and Los Angeles: University of California Press, 1951.

15. Scott, J. P.: *Animal Behavior.* 281 p. Chicago: University of Chicago Press, 1958.

Chapter Six

Disturbing Modes of Inner Experience

PREVIOUS experience, obviously, influences the content and mode of communication. On the one hand, this experience may be related to one's own organism; on the other it may be related to encounters with the environment. Experience thus includes all that happened before up to the moment of the ongoing event. It involves emotions, feelings, thoughts, memories, sensations, and whatever other functions occupy the human being. In talking about experience, we presume that all present functions of the organism and all traces of the past are active to some degree in shaping the events of the moment. That past experience shapes communication is obvious, in that perception is primed, evaluation slanted, and expression available only in those areas where learning has occurred. Granted that at some time in early childhood there must have been a first experience, this was in the nature of a reflex action. Only after part functions have sufficiently matured, some time in the course of the first year, can we truly speak of experience rather than of response. And as experience is superimposed upon experience and the functions of communication are practiced over and over again, a reciprocal relation develops. Inner experience shapes communication and communication shapes inner experience. Certain forms of inner experience are so significant that they loom like a thunderstorm over the individual, pervade his every activity, and are consciously felt with such intensity that they barely leave room for any other feeling. These overvalued experiences are often the driving forces which compel a patient to consult the psychiatrist.

LONELINESS

Cultural loneliness · *Situational loneliness* · *Loneliness as a character feature* · *Loneliness and growth*

The subjective experience of loneliness has many roots: it may be culturally determined or it may be brought about by physical circumstances; it may be imposed by others or individually sought. But regardless of its origin, loneliness seems to be a painful, frightening experience which people tend to avoid at all cost. Culturally determined loneliness together with a decline of personal face-to-face encounters is a phenomenon of the twentieth century. The mother's social activities outside the home, the father's business obligations, and the absence of grandparents in the same home deprive the youngsters of much needed contact. While intimate associations within the kinship group are on the decline, impersonal relationships are on the increase. The gigantic growth of the population and the rise of collectivism induce government employees, doctors, and lawyers to think in impersonal terms. Station-to-station communication has replaced person-to-person communication. Particularly in the higher echelons of competitive striving, where fear and mistrust accompany the man in his work and at play, the lack of good fellowship results in a feeling of unbearable loneliness (4).

Forced separation is another source of loneliness. The homesick young soldier, the nostalgic sailor, and the prisoner of war are well known examples. When forced separation occurs at a young age, as in the case when a mother has to go to the penitentiary, the baby may develop an anaclitic depression (16). Closely allied to forced separation is the mourning of the bereft, who counteracts pain by identifying with the deceased. Then there are cases in which separation is imposed by social or geographical conditions: isolated outposts, people lost in the wilderness, solitary confinement in prisons, or prisoner of war camps. Here sensory deprivation and separation from other human beings seem to produce intense feelings of loneliness.

But the loneliness the psychiatrist encounters in his patients is of a more permanent nature. The combination of the patient's narcissism, megalomania, and hostility is a character feature which is difficult to tolerate; people therefore respond in a hostile way, and the patient withdraws (19). Therapeutically, Fromm-Reichmann recommends that the therapist convey to the patient that he is available and that he has knowledge of the patient's feelings of loneliness (8). As Farber (7) puts it: "It is only when the therapist has exhausted every conceivable device for reaching his patient that he may, from the very heart of his despair, cry out with his entire being, as if to his Maker. Such a cry is as far from dialogue or confirmation as it is from love or sympathy; any response awakened by it will be a response to pain and loneliness." And when the patient perceives this deep felt experience of the therapist, he may for the first time forget his own loneliness.

For the feeling of being helpless and unconnected which is part of the experience of Western man (3), the therapist perhaps can do a little more. We are all born of a mother and go through a cycle, being inside of her first, later outside, and then in the group, until finally death detaches us from the living. The loneliness of dying seems to be something absolute: definitive for the dying person as well as for the survivor (18). In the terminal phases of life, the therapist can only have the attitude of standing by; he cannot encourage, educate, or promise. He can only respect the patient's struggle to come to grips with himself and what he has to face (6). But with the younger person who still has a full life ahead, the prospects are somewhat brighter. The basic principle is to guide the patient towards personalized relations and to induce him to abandon his striving for power. He must face the fact that after work he has to have personalized relations which include all age groups and both sexes, and involve a variety of activities. He must supplant the old kinship group by interest groups which convene because they have in common some assumptions about life and are devoid of competitive striving. Leisure time has to be reserved for experience and not for success, for pleasure and not for striving, for exchange and not for warfare. Unless the patient rebuilds his life in another way, he will experience futility, emptiness, and loneliness over and over again.

INSECURITY

The delusion of security · *Tradition as a defense against insecurity* · *Managing feelings of insecurity*

Once upon a time, man took it for granted that life was precarious and that at any moment violence, famine, or pestilence might threaten his existence. His physical insecurity was brought home to him in the course of his daily pursuits, and ancient man therefore turned to less materialistic interests. The life expectancy of the Roman citizen was twenty-seven years as compared to our seventy years of today. Indeed, longevity has, as Masserman puts it, contributed to our delusion of immortality (12). Modern social security in terms of old age pensions, unemployment and medical insurance, and all the other protective devices is likely to give the individual a feeling of immunity and induces him to take security for granted. But when man is confronted with the ugliness of war, the pain of disease, or the hopelessness of the deprived, he awakens from his dream and feels threatened. But when he gives up self-reliance and association with friends and relatives for support in time of need, he has nothing but the system to turn to; and if the system has no solution, when it cannot provide for further illusions, comfort, or anesthetics, the individual feels lost. Self-esteem is bound to self-reliance, and self-reliance is based upon well-functioning personal relations. The insecurity experienced by many of our patients is an awareness of the realities which contrast with the picture painted by the propagandists of our day. To have feelings of insecurity is a social stigma—a sign of deviation. It means not to share in the universal delusion, and this brings the individual to the psychiatrist.

In previous centuries, the insecurity of the moment was compensated for by idealism and a sense of historical perspective. If one was not to succeed, then one's son might reach the goal; and if one failed, one brought shame not only upon oneself but upon one's whole family. Modern mass man is a creature without a past but with a boundless future. The future, however, is fantasy; and fantasy vanishes at times of stress. Man's failure to be anchored in tradition and historical continuity creates a feeling of being adrift. Modern man cannot tolerate uncertainty; he has to know and he believes in control; and in his frenzy for certainty and control, he feels deeply insecure when nature and other suprapersonal forces raise havoc with the order he has created. To cover this insecurity, modern man has acquired a public face; externally he presents the picture of a calm, smiling, relaxed individual who is always in control, even if he is ready to explode.

The patients who reach the psychiatrist are either those who cannot successfully mask their insecurity or those who believe that insecurity is abnormal. The first group of patients can be helped by reinforcing their conformist tendencies. They are helped to believe in security and longevity, to deny the existence of death, and to ignore any realistic considerations. This procedure is not without danger. Sooner or later, the intelligent and alert patient is going to consider the doctor a fool and will cease to trust him. Therefore this method works only with a naive, not too intelligent person with great dependency strivings which can be satisfied through the usual conformance rewards: approval, togetherness, and inclusion. This procedure also is very suitable to tide the patient over acute emergencies until more favorable circumstances allow a more radical reappraisal of reality. The second group of patients—those who believe that insecurity is abnormal—can be helped to relinquish the idea of security altogether. The patient has to face squarely his own negligible power, his exposure to the elements from without, his instability within, the lability of life and all matters human. Once he has reached bottom and given up his ideas of immortality, omniscience, and power, he learns to enjoy life as it is without wishing that it were different. By relinquishing his anticipatory behavior concerned with security, a more acceptable adjustment is likely to develop.

INFERIORITY

Inferiority as a character feature · Institutionalized inferiority · Coping with inferiority

The combination of a certain genetic endowment with traumatic social experiences may in fact place a child in an inferior position. As a result of these experiences, the individual may develop an attitude of doubt about his abilities and capacities. He may believe himself to be of lesser intelligence, strength, beauty, status, or achievement than others and as a consequence he begins to defend himself against both the inner experience of inferiority and the outer situations which might expose his feelings. If an individual cannot successfully protect himself, he often resorts to the opposite method; he openly declares himself inferior in the hope of obtaining special consideration and support.

Whether the sense of inferiority in the human being and the problem of dominance and submission observed in the animal world are related is difficult to decide. Differences in pecking order (15) and similar phenomena certainly indicate that animals respect superiority. But animals do not possess the ability to institutionalize inferiority; whereas in our human world special schools for the mentally retarded, treatment for neurotics, social security in old age, and deferment from military service protect the old, the weak, the sick, and the orphans.

When the therapist has to cope with feelings of inferiority of his patients, he first has to diagnose whether he deals with an individual feature or with manifestations of a cultural institution (5). If he reaches the verdict that the individual's sense of inferiority is based on some social or group discrimination, he had better inquire into its usefulness first. To appear inferior in certain cross-class contacts has often been a successful way of handling people, as exemplified by the beggar who makes a good living by being inferior. However, if the doctor concludes that inferiority is an individual feature (2), he might be inclined to look to Adler's theories (1). Therapeutic communication then is directed at two distinct tasks: first, to strengthen the actual skills of the patient so that in terms of achievement and human relations he performs better than before; and second, to break into the neurotic process which perpetuates the inferiority complex, and through exposure and understanding to induce the patient to find more rewarding pursuits. The working through of inferiority feelings follows traditional lines: verbalization of the conflict; study of relevant examples; involvement of the therapist and other people in the patient's struggle to remain inferior; analysis of the present situation and gentle refusal of the therapist to play the power game; gradual reorientation of the patient, who searches for means of contact with the therapist outside of the power issue; and acceptance of the residual conflict by both patient and therapist.

UNINVOLVEMENT

Fading away · Conscious and unconscious observation · Experience of the Gestalt · Commitment and skill

"Nothing really makes sense to me" is a statement frequently uttered by patients. They do not love; they do not hate; they have no special interests. Working, eating, and sleeping run off according to schedule; but in the absence of danger to life, health, or economy, living becomes a bore. Nothing really matters. Concomitant with this uninvolvement on a larger scale there exists, on a smaller scale, an alienation from interaction (9). Many of these patients are unmarried or are married but have no children. In personal encounters, they may exhibit aloofness or show preoccupation with subject matter, with self, or with technicalities, all of which preclude a direct approach to the other person. The cues that betray an uninvolved person may be a movement that is not properly timed, a gaze that is not focused, or a voice that is not appropriately pitched. Even if an aloof person mimics involvement, the participants sense a certain disinterest which cannot be overcome by ordinary means. A committed individual, in contrast, gives the impression that all his expressions and actions are coordinated and that his behavior is well integrated.

Uninvolvement is another way of saying that people act as observers. If we distinguish among the outside observer (scientific observation), the self-observer (conscious self-observation), and the unobserved observer (unconscious observation) (14), we also will have to admit that as long as an individual is capable of observing his own actions he is not capable of full participation. Being able to make a distinction between his inner self, his visible actions, and other people prevents him from blending completely into the situation. But if he manages to forget himself, to trust unconscious observation, and therefore to fuse self with action, then subject and object become one. This process is best known to the masters of Zen (17), who train their pupils for years to achieve oneness (10).

But the psychotherapist is not a Zen master. He does not select his patients and therefore does not leave the unsuitable ones to rot in the cesspool of their own neuroses; on the contrary, he will attempt to aid the uninvolved ones to become more involved. Although the patient's ability to utilize his unconscious for better performance may be a far cry from the skill of a master archer who can split an arrow at fifty paces, the secret of therapy, I believe, is to work towards unconscious, automatic control of action. I have played with children and I have helped them to learn to swim, to sail, to ride, or to play ball. I have worked with adults, and I have helped them with their doctoral theses, their music, their woodwork; and the principle that I used was always the same. Beginning with the simplest movement and progressing towards the more complex, I avoided pouncing on details. Children are taught to swim by having them in and around the water and by equipping them with life preservers so that they can experiment to their hearts' delight. After action in water has been thoroughly experienced, the time has come to practice specialized movements such as jumping, plunging, diving, or kicking. Around horses, the children may pet, groom, lead, feed, and catch the animals in the pasture. After they have become thoroughly familiar with the gelding or the mare, riding becomes easy. At the piano, the patient is familiarized with a few chords. The neophyte begins to read chords rather than musical notes, tries to find the necessary chords to fit the tune, and learns to be free of anxiety when playing with others. A beginner can participate in playing together by taking over the bass and learning to play by ear the C, G, or F chords. After an individual has mastered the Gestalt of musical denotation and the nature of musical interaction, he can finally be started on technical exercises. The principle is to give children, and patients, a chance to familiarize themselves with the setting, the atmosphere, the layout, the meaning, or whatever other words are used to indicate the over-all pattern. Once the total Gestalt has been grasped, involvement usually follows.

Involvement derives from pleasure and mastery; it is geared to the present and minimizes anticipation and recollection. Any action forces an individual to coordinate and to integrate lest he be killed, mutilated, or ridiculed. But our technological civilization no longer exposes people to situations of immediacy and therefore people do not learn the essentials of commitment. Modern social conditions do not require many bodily skills—not even speech—making pidgin English quite satisfactory for getting along in this world. But the person without skill is uninvolved, and the ancient contempt for unskilled people was an expression of scorn for the individual's lack of commitment. The therapist has to counteract these trends. He has to induce the patient to become a master in some small area: the collection of stamps, embroidery, or the playing of a musical instrument will do the trick. There exists a carry-over of mastery from one field to the other, and so the patient's skill will help him in many ways. Through his skill, he will have occasion to meet other dedicated people, and eventually interest, commitment, skill, and human relations will become inseparable.

SENSITIVITY

The extrovert · The introvert · Traditional therapy is geared to the extrovert · Coping with the introvert

Our modern technological civilization favors the extroverted person, whose reasoning and judgment organize the untidy and coerce the accidental things of life into regular patterns and whose rational functions and conscious sensations are more skilled than his unconscious perception and intuition. The extrovert's sense for facts is highly developed. His life consists of an endless series of contacts with concrete objects. He makes little use of his own accumulated experience; and when he does utilize it, it serves as a guide for better sensation.

"Still waters run deep" . . . "Almost more even than the extraverted is the introverted type subject to misunderstanding: not so much because the extravert is a more merciless or critical adversary than he himself can easily be, but because the style of the epoch in which he himself participates is against him." These words of Jung (11) are as true today as they were a quarter of a century ago. The introverted person is often inaccessible to external judgment because of his inability to express himself. He is constantly undervalued by public opinion because his habitual communications express very little of that richness of his inner experience; and if he speaks out as a thinker, sage, visionary, or prophet, he finds that he is, at best, ignored and perhaps treated as subversive or eccentric. The inner-directed person (13), the individual who in a most sensitive way reacts to himself as well as to certain events in his surroundings, is indeed in a sad position in our culture.

Present day psychotherapy and psychoanalysis are geared to the extrovert, and they are dependent upon the therapist's skill. Writes Jung (11), "the judgment would entirely devolve upon the observer—a certain guarantee that its basis would be his own individual psychology, which would infallibly be imposed upon the observed. To my mind, this is the case in the psychologies both of Freud and of Adler. The individual is completely at the mercy of the arbitrary discretion of his observing critic . . ." Because some of these methods are unsuitable for introverts, a large number of sensitive persons who come to the psychiatrist are thrown into that basket called "borderline case" which labels such patients as unsuitable for ordinary treatment methods.

But what are the alternatives? The experiences that a borderline patient brings with him are not likely to be rational and tidy, and therefore the therapist cannot concentrate on his verbal productions. In the realm of the nonverbal and of the unconscious, logic is replaced by intuition. The therapist therefore has to gradually feel his way into the patient's mode of living and experiencing. If the therapist can understand the other person's inner experience, he begins to reduce the gap that separates him from the patient. By abstaining from the appraisal of phenomena which cannot be understood logically, the therapist gains the confidence of the patient. To the patient, logic appears as an absurdity, and he pities the man who wishes to measure "the length of sorrow" or "the depth of despair." Communication with the sensitive person consists of an exchange of personal experiences—a truly private phenomenon. While therapy with the introvert centers around understanding, therapy with the extrovert centers around agreement. But the therapist has to beware of agreeing to an experience of another individual lest he become an impostor. The introvert will immediately interpret this agreement as coercion—for how can another person know what happened to his psyche? Therefore the therapist confines himself to understanding and limits agreements to visible actions. And as the patient is made to feel that his inner experience is worth while, he becomes more adjusted and progressively complies more with the requirements of daily life.

References

1. Adler, A.: *The Practice and Theory of Individual Psychology*. (Tr. by P. Radin). 352 p. London: Kegan Paul, Trench, Trubner, 1945.

2. Ansbacher, H. L.: The significance of the socio-economic status of the patients of Freud and Adler. Amer. J. Psychother., 13, 376–382, 1959.

3. Boss, M.: *Indienfahrt eines Psychiaters*. 260 p. Pfullingen: Neske, 1959.

4. Bowman, C. C.: Loneliness and social change. Amer. J. Psychiat., 112, 194–198, 1955.

5. Brachfeld, O.: *Inferiority Feelings in the Individual and the Group*. 301 p. New York: Grune & Stratton, 1951.

6. Eissler, K. R.: *The Psychiatrist and the Dying Patient*. 338 p. New York: International Universities Press, 1955.

7. Farber, L. H.: The therapeutic despair. Psychiatry, 21, 7–20, 1958.

8. Fromm-Reichmann, F.: Loneliness. Psychiatry, 22, 1–16, 1959.

9. Goffman, E.: Alienation from interaction. Hum. Relat., 10, 47–60, 1957.

10. Herrigel, E.: *Zen in the Art of Archery*. 109 p. New York: Pantheon, 1953.

11. Jung, C. G.: *Psychological Types*. 654 p. London: Kegan Paul, Trench, Trubner, 1946.

12. Masserman, J. H.: Faith and delusion in psychotherapy. Amer. J. Psychiat., 110, 324–333, 1953.

13. Riesman, D.: *The Lonely Crowd*. 386 p. New Haven: Yale University Press, 1950.

14. Ruesch, J. and Bateson, G.: *Communication: The Social Matrix of Psychiatry*. 314 p. New York: Norton, 1951.

15. Scott, J. P.: *Animal Behavior*. 281 p. Chicago: University of Chicago Press, 1958.

16. Spitz, R. A. and Wolf, K. M.: Anaclitic depression: an inquiry into the genesis of psychotic conditions in early childhood. Pp. 313–342 in *The Psychoanalytic Study of the Child*. Vol. 2. New York: International Universities Press, 1946.

17. Suzuki, D. T.: *Zen Buddhism*. 294 p. Garden City: Doubleday Anchor Books, 1956.

18. von Witzleben, H. D.: On loneliness. Psychiatry, 21, 37–43, 1958.

19. Zilboorg, G.: Loneliness. Atlantic Monthly, January, 1938.

Part Three

The Doctor's Therapeutic Operations

The therapist's operations are essentially symbolic in nature. He either speaks, gestures, or listens. And if he engages in action, the communicative aspects of his activities are of perhaps even greater significance than their physical impact. As the therapist communicates or acts, he forces the patient to make inferences about his —the doctor's—values, attitudes, and goals. These inferences then can be discussed, and the patient's interpretations can be checked against the therapist's initial intentions. As the exchange progresses, the initially unexpressed assumptions of both doctor and patient gradually become an integral part of the therapeutic process.

The doctor's therapeutic operations therefore involve the following component parts: the physical and social setting of the encounter; the doctor's silent assumptions, perceptions, and evaluations; his verbalizations; his actions; and finally his observation of the effects he has achieved through his impact upon the other person.

Chapter Seven

Therapeutic Attitudes

THE HYPOTHETICAL construct called "attitude" is employed to refer to an individual's readiness to respond in certain predictable ways. The term does not imply that the individual has to behave consistently in all circumstances. It merely means that, over the long term, definite ways of behaving can be detected. Attitudes perhaps more than any other character features can be molded—even at a later age—in certain ways. Whereas in the therapeutic process doctors are not capable of predicting with certainty the specific turn of events, they have nonetheless a pretty good idea as to the kinds of attitudes which are needed to meet the problems of the patients (6). Discussion of attitudes not only indicates the long-term orientation assumed by therapists but also points to the effect these have upon patients. If the patients assume some of these attitudes themselves, they will become capable of better understanding, communication, and cooperation with their own surroundings.

DISCRIMINATE PERMISSIVENESS

Permissiveness is not indulgence · *Goal-directed permissiveness* · *Permissiveness and strictness*

The absence of signs of dominance, the friendly encouragement to proceed, the guarantee that no unforeseen punishment is going to surprise the patient, the respect for his individuality—all of these may be included in the term "permissiveness." In practice, of course, the conclusion that the doctor is permissive has to be tested out over a period of time. The patient has to find out when and where the permissive therapist asserts himself; what kind of restrictions he imposes, in what matters, and when; what sanctions he invokes if rules of conduct are violated, if behavior becomes destructive, or if failure in action becomes evident. Permissiveness thus is not to be confused with absence of limitations, masochistic exposure to frustration, and ignorance of goals. Permissiveness is not synonymous with chaos. On the contrary, it is an extremely goal-directed attitude whereby the long-term task is clearly defined and contradictory behavior is utilized for purposes of correction. The patient comes to understand that his symptoms are tolerated, that his own ways of gaining satisfaction—although pathological—are respected, and that the therapist stands by to help if necessary.

But permissiveness on the part of the therapist cannot be indiscriminate. As Redl and Wineman (4) point out, children—and this applies also to adults—want not only friendliness, tolerance, and affection but they also need protection. When people show fear of other people, are apprehensive about loss of control, and dread situations which trigger pathology, permissiveness becomes poison and has to be replaced by firmness and the setting of limitations. Permissiveness thus is an attitude which is bound to certain times and situations and is dedicated to a specific purpose. It is not to be confused with *"laisser faire, laisser aller."* A permissive attitude helps the patient to experiment with his neglected communicative functions and to learn by trial and error.

When the therapist is strict, he influences the patient to such an extent or in such a way that his choice of messages is markedly reduced. In excited, confused, anxious, or depressed patients, or in an emergency period, unlimited choices become a burden because the state of mind does not permit evaluation of alternatives. The therapist's strictness therefore consists of leaving open only one possibility, both in communication and in action. Strictness is conveyed by ruling out, through subtle or drastic means, all unacceptable ways of communication. In behaving as if there were only one choice, the therapist leaves the patient no alternatives but to take this one choice or violently oppose it. Strictness on the part of the therapist reinforces the repressive tendencies of the patient, enabling him to focus upon one piece of information at a time and to regain his balance. With compulsive and rigid persons, however, the reverse applies. When the therapist is permissive, the choice of messages and actions is left to the patient, giving him a chance to consider alternatives. Permissiveness is implemented by accepting whatever the patient says without a definite reply. Permissiveness allows the patient to experiment, to make his choices, and to correct errors. This procedure is tedious, time-consuming, but it promotes growth.

BRINGING UP THE UNMENTIONABLE

Explicit and implicit designation   ·   Everything can be talked about   ·   Specifying the meaning

In society there exist rules about things that can be talked about and those that are expressed in an implicit way. In the process of justifying, for example, most people mention clichés while they omit pointing to their feelings as determinants of their actions. In a business setting, it is "unprofessional" to bring up the problem of fears, apprehensions, or personal taste; instead, human relations are cloaked in statements which refer to roles or functions. At a social gathering, in contrast, personal preferences, likes and dislikes, are routinely discussed and allusions to functional relations are omitted.

In the therapeutic situation, the patient has to learn that all the rules that apply to ordinary life are suspended and that the distinction between personal and official function is not made. He has to learn that in therapy there are no tabooed subjects and that the unmentionable can be mentioned. Although the airing of an obscure topic may not clarify the subject, the mere fact that is has been talked about takes away the magic power from the unmentionable. The attitude that everything can be talked about must be conveyed to the patient by demonstration. The therapist may introduce the unmentionable by referring to the patient's posture: "You have assumed a defensive body position; what do you expect to happen?"

Or he may point to the patient's elaborate make-up: "You are dressed for a party; whom do you wish to beguile?" The patient thus learns to talk about his feelings, and soon he doesn't hesitate to make his body, his expectations, or the therapist the subject of discussion.

The instructions to express whatever comes to mind convey to the patient the idea that in therapeutic communication no one subject, idea, or word has higher status or takes precedence over another. There are no good and no bad words, and not even expressions involving the therapist's person are exempt from this rule. There are merely words and gestures that describe what is to be described, and these may be more or less appropriate. By accepting the whole vocabulary of the patient, including slang and four-letter words, and all gestures, whether idle, obscene, or elegant, the therapist makes it possible to make the unmentionable accessible. He raises the questions, "How does this work?" "What does this indicate to you?" "What is its effect?" The patient has to learn that we are not concerned with tradition, manner, and form but with the feelings, ideas, or things words stand for.

EXPECTANT READINESS

The patient initiates · *The therapist patiently waits*

The catatonic who does not speak, the suicidal patient who is about to kill himself, the criminal with his bitterness against the world, the apathetic person who passively drifts along—all these people need human contact but they may not be ready to tolerate it. All the therapist can do is to convey the fact that he is ready, alert, and game whenever the patient feels like taking advantage of it, even if his first steps are tentative, shy, and inappropriate. Instead of bombarding the patient with verbal statements, the therapist shows his interest and curiosity. The doctor's attitude of non-interference, of course, stops when the conservation of life, property, and the social order are at stake; but non-interference is strictly maintained with regard to intrusion into the privacy of the individual's inner world of experience. A hospitalized patient may be visited daily and the doctor may stay in silence; after weeks or months some communicative exchange may develop.

It takes a lot of patience to assume effectively the attitude of expectant readiness. Sometimes a patient has to be sent away and told to come back when he is ready—in a week, a month, a year, or even longer. He has to be informed that the doctor is ready whenever he is and that he should feel free to come any time if he wishes. Under no circumstances should retaliation, punitiveness, or disappointment govern the therapist's actions; otherwise his attitude dooms him to failure. By being expectant, he expresses the fact that he looks forward to something that can take place if the patient should be ready for it. As a matter of fact, the therapist indicates implicitly that he knows that the patient would love to be in communicative exchange but is not ready for this task. And he also lets it be known that time does not matter and that he, the therapist, will wait. After the many lean years in the patient's life that have gone by without his fully experiencing the pleasure of human communication, a few months more really do not matter.

CATHARTIC LISTENING

Secrets burden the mind · *Talking eases tension*

The word "catharsis," which was introduced by Freud into the terminology of psychiatry, comes from the Greek word for purification. One of the beneficial effects of catharsis is abreaction, and the knowledge that one has a patient listener is certainly reassuring. The expression "cathartic listening" refers to an attitude of the therapist that implies the doctor's readiness to listen to the patient's concerns, his emotional qualms, and other expressions in an attempt to understand without interrupting, guiding, advising, or refuting whatever the patient has to say. In daily life, many of the father and mother confessors to whom people turn to tell their troubles have mastered the art of cathartic listening. It is their non-interference and their non-evaluative attitude which inspires confidence and induces the patient to tell. Apparently there exists a learned or inborn need in human beings to share information. A person feels uncomfortable when he has to carry a secret alone.

In the course of psychotherapy, the patient meets situations which tax his tolerance limits. When external events trigger his neurotic conflicts, his irritability increases and sometimes his tension is ready to overflow. To relieve himself, he has to engage either in action or in talk, and in many instances talk is the less harmful procedure. Through continued contact with the therapist, the patient may learn to become a good listener himself—an ability which comes in handy when dealing with other family members. The therapist's attitude, therefore, teaches the patient that expression of innermost secrets is beneficial.

CONDITIONAL COMMITMENT

The therapist's commitment · *Reacting to the healthy part of the patient*

Much has been written about the doctor's devotion to his patients, the necessity of maintaining an uninvolved objectivity, or the undesirability of countertransference. Most of these recommendations do not fall on fertile ground because the therapist is a human being who behaves at a given moment the only way he can behave. He really has no choice of assuming this or that pose or of regulating his degree of involvement. All that can be done is to help the doctor in training to gradually acquire an attitude which has proven useful to other therapists. The doctor's attitude towards the patient may be described as "conditional commitment." This term can be defined as follows: When the therapist is with the patient, he should, with all his mental and physical resources, be present, responsive, and engulfed in the problems at hand. The commitment goes to the now, to the patient, and to the situation without doubts or mental reservations. This attitude of commitment on the part of the physician can occur under one condition—that the patient seek therapy and be willing to do his share. If, however, the patient is reluctant, then an attitude of expectant readiness replaces the attitude of conditional commitment.

Conditional commitment should not be confused with indiscriminate approbation of the patient's actions. Many patients have an attitude that indicates, "my pathology makes me do that; since you are a psychiatrist, it is up to you to tolerate my behavior. If you don't like it, do something that makes me well." At this moment, the therapist must use his leverage. He can react to that part of the patient that can grow and communicate, but not to those features which escape interpersonal control. Such features, he may say, might be tolerated at best but not cherished or cultivated. The therapist can make the patient aware that everybody has some leeway and that nobody is entirely the plaything of his emotions. If the patient tries hard, the therapist will try equally hard to help. The emphasis here is not on successful action but on the patient's attempt to struggle. If the patient tries, improvement eventually may be forthcoming. If the patient is passive and leaves it up to the therapist, the latter's attitude reverts back to expectant readiness. By being conditional, therefore, the doctor implicitly expresses the idea that the patient's attitude determines in part what is happening. The patient must be made to feel that he loses something worthwhile if he does not assume responsibility for his existence. The experience of closeness promoted through conditional commitment eventually provides the driving force which stimulates further cooperation.

CONSTRUCTIVE SELECTIVITY

Tactical decisions · Pointing out potentialities · Pathology diminishes by default

One of the misconceptions that young doctors have bears upon the therapist's non-directive attitude, in which unresponsiveness, aloofness, objectivity, and freedom from value judgments are considered desirable features. Soon such a beginner discovers that he accomplishes little if anything with such an attitude and that the only patients who are likely to stick it out with him are those who respond to the ritual of the therapeutic situation. The experienced therapist who studies the patient and then arrives at a conclusion has to pass judgment. For example, he might make the decision to first tackle the patient's authority problems. With gentleness and through repetition, he demonstrates to the patient the various ramifications of the conflict. He shows the patient that an authority also can be kind and helpful, and that part of the patient's trouble is that he did not experience the friendly and constructive aspects of such a relationship. Selection of a topic requires a determined attitude on the part of the therapist. The doctor has to convey that all is not lost, that the patient is capable of learning, that many of his shattering experiences in the past need not be destructive if experienced in conjunction with another benign person. But to convey such an idea, the doctor has to be assertive and directive.

With an attitude similar to that of a teacher who has to decide which features in his pupil need further work, the therapist has to commit himself when it comes to coping with pathology. If the patient explicitly or implicitly raises the question, "What is so lovable in me that I should make an effort?" the therapist's implicit, or sometimes explicit, answer may be, "I like your unrealized potentialities, and I see in you what you might become." The therapist becomes a shareholder, as it were, in a common venture; and the sooner he commits himself vis-à-vis the patient's pathology, the less the patient is likely to use his pathology to coerce the therapist or to be self-destructive. Some patients have expressed this selective attitude of the therapist in the following words: "You have liked the child in me"; "You have treated me as if I were capable of living"; "I never got you to like my tricks, and this was perhaps the most disappointing experience, but a healthy one"; "At first you treated me like a project, but then I began to recognize that you were human and that helped"; "You showed me that I had potentialities, and your attitude helped me."

One of the most effective ways of dealing with pathology is to leave it alone. When the patient begins to mature, he has less need to rely on his pathology; and as time and energy are freed, he has time to cater to other but neglected personality features. As these functions begin to grow, the patient acquires new ways of gratification and the vicious circle is interrupted.

UNAGGRESSIVE DIRECTNESS

Vague and circumstantial patients · *Directness produces reorientation*

Some patients have great difficulty in steering a conversation to the subject of their concern. Although consciously aware of the nature of their condition and the purpose of their visit, they spend a lot of time in small talk, they beat about the bush, or they talk about the weather or the pictures on the wall. When they enter the office their minds seem to go blank, although before they entered they had a long list of things to talk about. These patients cannot be brief or succinct; they cannot give information and ask for information, but always appear vague and uncertain and what they say is contradictory. The same intangible vagueness can be observed in psychotic patients who are unaware of the necessities of daily life. Blithely they ignore the fact that they need a job, that they have to rent an apartment, or that they have to be considerate of others in the group. Intellectually confused and emotionally tense, they don't know in what direction to move.

With this kind of patient, the therapist has to be direct. He has to disregard all the embellishments, the niceties, the rationalizations, and the resentment. Cutting through all non-essentials means to identify the situation, the prevailing emotion, or the conflict that produces it. In spite of insufficient information, the therapist should draw some conclusions and make some interpretations in order to force the patient to clarify some of the confusion. The therapist has to use words that properly impinge upon the patient's emotional state. This can be done successfully only if he appreciates intuitively whatever is going on in the patient. At first this procedure looks like an authoritarian intrusion, but soon the patient discovers great relief when, through the therapist's pinpointing, some of the fog begins to lift. The unaggressive directness of the therapist teaches the patient that he himself has to clarify contradictions in his existence. As soon as the doctor has made a statement, the patient can agree with it or oppose it. In either case, he clarifies an issue. The disagreeable feelings connected with the facing of emotional and social realities are overcome when the patient has to corroborate or oppose. Eventually the patient learns how to cope with the confusion within himself by tentatively formulating a plan of action.

RESPONSIBLE PERFORMANCE

The pleasure of responsibility · *Responsibility to self* · *Responsibility means mastery of decision-making*

Privilege engenders responsibility; responsibility means that a man is accountable to an authority or to other persons for the confidence bestowed upon him. To assume responsibility means to assume power; but a responsible performance is characterized by self-awareness, group consideration, and goal orientation. People who put in a responsible performance do so with diligence, wisdom, tolerance, and skill. The acceptance of responsibility is something that is connected with pleasure. The young rider's interest in his horse is not an obligation but rather a pleasure involving skill in managing and caring for his mount.

In order to assume responsibility, a person must be in good health. The therapist has to convey this to the patient, saying, in effect: "The first consideration of any human being is to put himself into good shape, physically as well as mentally, and to provide for those conditions which favor growth and maturity." "But how can one be so egotistical?" may be the reply of the patient; "I always used to put myself last." "And what was the price you exacted in return?" the doctor may interject; "Others had to admire your humbleness, your selflessness, your excessive self-control." Only when a person is well off physically and mentally is he capable of participating with others in the complex tasks required by group and society. The person who cannot look out for himself, who is altruistic, masochistic, subservient, or self-sacrificing eventually needs the support of others and therefore becomes a burden.

Attending to one's growth does not mean ruthlessness, but it does mean to satisfy those needs that are imperative for one's development—freeing oneself from human connections, interests, and activities that have no function in one's present life situation. Responsibility means decision regarding the sacrifices one wishes to make, the price one is willing to pay, and the gain one might obtain. In due time, this attitude of the therapist is conveyed to the patient, who in turn will realize that the therapist's existence is not based on masochistic pleasure in taking care of others but upon the exercise of a skill that earns him a position and a living.

TAKING THINGS IN HAND

Therapeutic intervention · *Emergencies* · *The therapist's power*

There are moments in therapy when the doctor has to take things into his own hands. Neither legally nor morally nor medically is he permitted to let things ride. When a patient has become self-destructive, for example, he has to interfere; and if he chooses to hospitalize the patient, this procedure is generally accepted as correct. But in therapy there are many minor occasions when hospitalization is not indicated and the therapist has to take other necessary steps (4). Let us assume that the patient is a homosexual who specializes in seducing minors. In his responsibility vis-à-vis society, the therapist cannot very well say, "You continue until you get caught," but he might diplomatically convey to a reliable relative the danger inherent in the actions of the patient. In a case involving a juvenile, the mother has to be informed so that she can arrange for the son to be busy; or perhaps she can manage to be at home most of the time so that opportunities for seduction are reduced. Such manipulations, of course, are undertaken with the patient's consent, and the doctor explains to him that this is done in his own interest. In other instances, the therapist might have to talk with the practitioner who treats the patient for some physical ailment and inform him of the patient's self-destructive or manipulative tendencies which the other doctor, who is unfamiliar with the patient, may not be aware of. And again, such a conference might involve the teacher in school or perhaps the employer.

If the patient calls the therapist at night and says "I just swallowed thirty nembutals; I am saying goodbye to you because I am going to die," the doctor obviously cannot afford to lose time. In this instance, he will call the police department, inform them of the patient's whereabouts, urge them to break in and to take the patient to the nearest hospital; and this by telephone, because precious time can be wasted if the doctor waits until he arrives on the scene. Perhaps an even more difficult situation arises when it comes to the evaluation of homicidal impulses. Some statements may be interpreted as bragging, some may be threats that never will be carried out, and others which appear as harmless at a given moment may be triggered into action later. If all people with murderous intentions were to be committed, a large part of the population would sit behind bars. The problem thus is to distinguish between the criminal who kills for business reasons and the patient who might kill for personal reasons. The former belongs in the hands of the police; the latter in the care of a psychiatrist. If the doctor has any doubts about the patient's intentions, he should get in contact with the prospective victim and find out all that he can. He has to protect both the patient and the victim from irrational, impulsive actions.

Taking things in hand has a distinct function in psychotherapy. Aside from protecting the patient, the doctor's actions convince the patient that not all is talk. The realization that the doctor has actual power gives the patient a feeling of security. With definite action, the therapist shows that he sets certain limitations; that he does not tolerate anti-social or destructive behavior but that he is willing to find alternate solutions to the patient's problems. If the patient is properly prepared before and after such intervention, he usually profits immeasurably from it.

UNDERSTANDING THE LANGUAGE OF THE PATIENT

The primitive language of the patient · *Active help* · *Words as camouflage*

Present therapeutic practices derive mostly from psychoanalytic procedures which were adapted to the treatment of the psychoneurotics—that is, patients who had achieved some maturity in the use of symbolization systems. But patients with acute psychotic episodes may regress temporarily to more primitive forms of expression. And other patients never may have progressed to a state in which they can appropriately use verbal language for the expression of their innermost thoughts and feelings. Therefore, in dealing with acting-out patients, psychopathic personalities, schizophrenic patients, or immature individuals, verbal exchanges may often remain insignificant. In such cases, the therapist has to demonstrate to the patient that he too can use body or action language, although he may not do it with the same pleasure or to the same extent as the patient does. In hospitals, of course, the physician has greater opportunity to use action language; he can play with the patient, go for a walk, participate in some of the patient's hobbies, or engage in sports. In ambulatory treatment, this is much more difficult because of the limitation of time; nor is the doctor's office equipped with the facilities for engaging in physical activities. Here the use of action language may take such forms as giving a patient a book to read, having him bring photographs or other documents which may illustrate his life, inspecting objects or things he has created, or listening to a patient's playing the piano. I, for my part, do not hesitate to show a patient a book, to play a record, to have a cup of coffee, or to offer a cigarette if verbal communication has to be interrupted. If the patient senses that the doctor is secure in his actions and conveys with his actions a message that is difficult to convey in words, he will immediately appreciate this non-coercive kind of communication. And strangely enough, after such an action exchange a patient frequently talks more freely and uses words in a more meaningful way.

Particularly during emergencies, the doctor is called upon to use action language. I remember an episode with an alcoholic and barbiturate addict that occurred late one evening. Apparently the patient had begun to rave, shout, and be acutely disturbed as if suffering from a pathological intoxication; she had thoroughly frightened her female friend, whom she had picked up in a bar some two hours earlier. Finding a card with my name in her purse, the friend, being herself in psychiatric treatment, simply dumped the patient at my doorstep. Upon talking with my patient, I discovered that she had gone into a homosexual panic, helped by the consumption of about four drinks. As I talked to her she calmed down within twenty to thirty minutes. I then loaded her into my car and drove her to local public transportation, bought her a ticket home, and instructed her to take a taxi at the other end. This the patient did. The next day she came back, talked about the whole event, and, after that, remarkable improvement set in. Excessive drinking and consumption of barbiturates stopped, and her pathology shifted to entanglements with other human beings, which difficulties were resolved in due time.

Whenever the doctor shows ample flexibility in applying emergency help, the patient rarely abuses the attitude of the therapist. On the contrary, something spontaneous emerges on the part of the patient, appreciating that the doctor went out of his way to help. Patients who are laid up with chronic diseases or fractures can be treated at home as well as or better than if they were to come to the doctor's office.

Sometimes the therapist encounters patients who use bizarre verbal language. Instead of deciphering this often unbreakable code, the therapist does much better to look at the accompanying actions and gestures. The main message may be carried by silent movement, and words may be used only to amplify or obscure it. It is, of course, incorrect to assume that verbal statements of patients refer under all circumstances to some object, thought, or feeling. Very often words represent a noise-making procedure which the patient engages in to reassure himself. There are animals who growl or bark, and there are people who sing or whistle in order to obtain an external auditory stimulus which, through feedback, reassures them of being alive (3). This phenomenon can be ob-served in children who, before they develop skills, engage in noisy action. But as the proprioceptive control increases, noise decreases. In such situations, the noise made orients the individual and steers his actions. Withdrawn or sensorily deprived patients yearn to hear the voices of others; and as the patient is addressed in a personal way, the random noises that he makes as well as his hallucinations tend to disappear.

UNCONDITIONAL RESPONSIVENESS

Response replaces affection

In the last few years, we have heard a lot about the remedial effects of tender loving care, particularly for children. But what is love? (1). Can love be dispensed on prescription? And does the attitude of the physician imply love of his patients? Varied are the academic answers to these questions, although in practice the problem is less complicated. The patient soon perceives that the doctor does not pretend to be affectionate but that he is attentive, that he is not personally but professionally interested, that he does not love but he does respond. The doctor's readiness to acknowledge the statements of the patient does not mean that he agrees or is ready to yield to the wishes of the patient. But the fact that an expression is taken seriously and acknowledged is often worth more to the patient than an actual fulfillment of his wishes. Little (2) calls this the analyst's total response to the patient's needs, and I myself have formulated it as follows: ". . . when an individual— be it doctor, nurse, relative, or friend—responds unequivocally to the intention of the patient and the patient is given the opportunity to respond in return, the foundations have been laid upon which recovery can take place" (5).

Unfavorable attitudes of the patient towards his illness can be changed gradually, through responsiveness, into attitudes which will favor improvement. A sample of such attitudes may read as follows:

Initial Attitudes of the Patient	*Attitudes of a Therapist*
This is an illness, for which I am not responsible	This is a way of adapting, but perhaps there are better ways
I want to please you	What pleases me most is your functioning well
You do not understand me	I listen, and I try to understand you
Tell me what to do	We will discuss each problem as it arises

Initial Attitudes of the Patient	*Attitudes of a Therapist*
I cannot say it	When you are ready, you will talk
I want things to go my way	It takes a great deal of skill and thought to control people. You have a lot of learning to do
I expect to improve	If you work hard at it, you will improve
You will cure me	If you work on your problems, you will understand yourself better
If I get into trouble, you are to blame	If you get into trouble, you will bear the consequences

References

1. Harlow, H. F.: The nature of love. Amer. Psychologist, 13, 673–685, 1958.

2. Little, M.: "R"—The analyst's total response to his patient's needs. Int. J. Psychoanal., 38, 240–254, 1957.

3. Ostwald, P. F.: When people whistle. Language and Speech, 2, 137–145, 1959.

4. Redl, F. and Wineman, D.: *Controls from Within*. 332 p. Glencoe: Free Press, 1952.

5. Ruesch, J.: The schizophrenic patient's ways of communication. Pp. 198–207 in *Congress Report (1957) Vol. 4*. Zurich: 2nd International Congress for Psychiatry, 1959.

6. Szurek, S. A.: An attitude towards (child) psychiatry. Quart. J. child Behavior, 1; 22–54, 178–213, 375–399, 401–423; 1949.

Chapter Eight

Authority and Leverage

LEVERAGE IMPLICIT IN PROCEDURE AND SITUATION

Therapy as an institution · *Rewards for undergoing therapy* · *Faith* · *Threat* · *Breaking into an established relationship* · *Altering feedback characteristics* · *Remaining outside established family relations* · *Assuming functions for the patient* · *Assistance* · *Support* · *Opposition*

When a patient comes in contact with a psychiatrist, a clinic, or a psychiatric hospital, he has been primed by the radio, TV, press, cartoons (16, 20, 23), and idle gossip to expect certain things from the field of mental health. Formerly a hush-hush discipline, psychiatry has now become fashionable; it can be talked about, and people even pride themselves on having a therapist or analyst. In America, psychiatry has become a discipline that takes care not only of the mentally sick but also of marginal people. Those who do not manage to adapt to our technological civilization—be they criminals, senile, juvenile delinquents, alcoholics, ulcer bearers, psychoneurotics, or ordinary persons with character disorders— are referred by the medical profession and by the authorities to the psychiatrist. He is the caretaker of the insane, the non-conformist, the displaced, and the rebellious. Being able to get along with people who are ordinarily excluded, the psychiatrist is allegedly endowed with certain magic powers.

The relationship between patient and doctor cannot be seen as a relationship between two private individuals only. The psychiatrist is a licensed physician: the medical school gave him an M.D. degree, the State a license, and professional associations his standing as a specialist. If so many people and institutions honor him, the patient cannot fail to be impressed. Regardless of whether the patient finds himself on the psychoanalyst's couch, on the ward of a state hospital, or in a small office in a clinic, the therapeutic situation carries a connotation of public approval. That the patient's relationship to the psychiatrist is in part institutional can be seen in the fact that some patients have become dependent upon a hospital or an institution rather than upon an individual (17). Some patients have difficulties with interpersonal relations and they prefer contact with a hospital or clinic in which the attending physician changes. Dependence upon an institution, a methodology, or a specific school of thought has become a well-known substitute for dependency upon an individual or a group. In some way, this has become socially more acceptable than dependence upon an individual.

But approval by the group is not enough to keep a patient in therapy. In most theories of learning (8) it is implied that no behavior is pursued without the presence of a reward. In any therapeutic procedure, therefore, the patient has to be offered rewards if the operation is to be crowned with success. The way in which this is done varies. In the analytic situation, the reaction and interpretation on the part of the therapist become the reward; in group discussions, the approval of the participants and of the moderator serve the same purpose; in psychotherapy, the liveliness of the response of the physician, and on the wards, the reaction of nurses and patients are factors which tend to act as rewards and to reduce tension momentarily. These rewards satisfy the individual's need for understanding, affection, approval, recognition, and inclusion. No therapy seems to be possible without gratification of these three principal needs: understanding and knowledge, inclusion by the group, and self-respect. The more rewards impinge regularly upon these three needs, the more effective the procedure will be. Most therapeutic sessions, group meetings, and occupational gatherings are scheduled to recur at intervals, giving the participants an opportunity to repeatedly obtain these rewards.

The rewards that the therapist can give to the patient and the rewards embedded in the therapeutic situation furnish the therapist with the necessary leverage to steer the patient in the desired direction. Once the patient has experienced the advantages of personal growth, the pleasure of improvement becomes a third factor which gives the doctor leverage. But let us be clear that without a priori endowment of the therapist with some healing powers by patient and society, the patient would never begin or even know about therapy (5). And without skillful management of interpersonal rewards during therapy, the patient would never accept the frustration imposed by the therapeutic process.

SEPARATING THE PATIENT FROM AN AGGRAVATING SITUATION

To separate one person from the other, to threaten departure, to take away objects, status, or money are powerful tools of reinforcement which are widely used in public life. Our legal system operates with fines and loss of freedom; accident prevention bureaus conjure images of invalidism; cancer campaigns silently imply the loss of life; husbands threaten to leave the family and patients to separate from their psychiatrists; psychiatrists warn their patients that if they do not abide by the rules of therapy they might not continue to see them. Threats of separation, nonsupport, suicide, and loss of property thus are methods that bank on the fact that the other person might yield rather than take the loss.

But the physician usually does not deal in threats and eventu alities. If necessary, he actually and physically removes the patient from his customary surroundings and hospitalizes him. In this case, he not only breaks into a well-established social situation but he separates the patient bodily from his habitual surroundings. In the old days, doctors used to prescribe a voyage at sea or a spell at "taking the waters" in order to remove the patient from his habitual surroundings. The change of scenery was sufficient to force a re-adaptation—perhaps only a temporary one. In recent years, sanatoria and hospitals have replaced the spas, and psychiatrists view the mental hospital as a milieu (14) in which the patient can learn to function in new surroundings. Some of the patients may spend only the night in a hospital; others the day (1, 3). In this process, they meet doctors, nurses, attendants, teachers, and other patients and profit from an atmosphere which they do not possess at home. Sometimes only a partial removal from the aggravating situation is necessary. A patient may be advised to rest two hours at noon time, to play tennis every morning, to take a certain extension course, to hire somebody to take her place in the home; all of these suggestions, if properly implemented, reduce the number of hours spent in a given communication network. With fewer hours at home, the patient may be better equipped to cope with frustration than in his previous state of chronic fatigue.

THE ADDITION OF THE THERAPIST TO AN ESTABLISHED NETWORK

Several are the processes which enable the therapist to build leverage into the therapeutic situation. By introducing himself to an established communication system between two or more people, the therapist can change the existing relationship. People who berate each other may switch to a different form of interaction if the messages also reach a third person—the therapist. If, with the permission of all concerned, the therapist familiarizes each of the two persons with all the secrets of the other, the situation changes radically. Without being a "tattle tale," the doctor can simply indicate that such and such problems exist and the patient should discuss matters with his partner. Topics which heretofore were never brought out into the open now have to be considered. The psychiatrist may break into established feedback circuits between mother and child, alter a stalemate, and help her to fulfill her role in a more satisfactory manner. A therapist may interject himself into the sadistic-masochistic interaction patterns between husband and wife and therefore dilute the intensity of the assault.

By interjecting himself into the communication network of a family, the therapist disturbs the established order and changes the nature of the feedback circuits. The equilibrium of forces becomes asymmetrical, the system of checks and balances has to be reorganized, networks have to be rearranged, new ideas circulate in the system, and during this phase of turbulence the therapist can steer some of the changes in the desired direction. It is well to remember that the therapist breaks into established feedback circuits even if he sees only the patient. The mere fact that mothers, fathers, or mates know that the therapist has information about them changes their way of behaving. The therapist's participation in a given communication system becomes particularly evident after he has become a permanent member. Therefore every therapist has to see as many members of the family as is feasible in order to rectify whatever fantasies they may have about him.

THE THERAPIST'S ACCEPTANCE AND REFUSAL OF ROLE ASSIGNMENTS

There are families that excel in assigning roles to outsiders, and with this skill the family unit maintains its pathology. For example, there are parents who fix every situation in which their children might get involved. They pull rank, pay the wages at the teen-ager's place of employment, or buy a business for their children. They hire tennis trainers, horsemanship instructors, and tutors, and as long as strangers are bought, they do not have to face the child in person. Therefore it is not surprising that the child views everything that comes from the parents as a tentacle and an extension of their authority. If the doctor can demonstrate that he will not be a part of such a diabolical scheme and is not a hireling of the parents, he may gain personal leverage with the patient. The parents, in turn, are flabbergasted to find that there are professionals who cannot be bought, and they become intrigued. By refusing to accept the assigned role of employee, the therapist may get the parents to express their feelings and to interact directly with one another.

This does not mean that the therapist should avoid interviewing the other members of the family, but, as in the case of paranoid patients, such talking is best done in the presence of the patient so that he knows what has occurred. The therapeutic efficacy of the therapist here is tied to the patient's knowledge that he has one relationship that is free from the remote control that he was subjected to all his life and which he blames as the source of all his difficulties. Gradually, as the patient improves and gains sufficient confidence to know that the therapist is incorruptible, the doctor may include some of the other members of the family in the therapeutic scheme. However, if this inclusion occurs too early, the patient's improvement will be retarded indefinitely.

In many instances, the doctor will not be content with understanding the patient's problems but will have to act in his behalf. For example, he may assume the role of an expert and consult with another doctor who has examined the patient; at other times, he may have to become protective and get in contact with an agency. He may act as an intermediary between husband and wife or between the patient and officers of the law. Although a doctor may assume some of the deficient functions of the patient, he is careful not to make a rule of it. He has to convey to the patient that he is willing to help in an emergency and to guide him in mastering a situation, always with the goal in mind that the patient eventually will have to attend to his own functions. Although he gives the patient a feeling of security, he tries not to institutionalize the therapeutic symbiosis. The fact that the therapist is willing to stand by and help provides him with much needed leverage.

When the infant is small, the adult perceives, evaluates, and acts for him. In the course of his development, the child takes over some of these functions until by the time he reaches social maturity he has become an independent person. But if, for whatever reason, something prevents psychological growth or induces psychological or social pathology, the individual cannot take over some of these functions. If the psychiatrist takes over perception, evaluation, and, to a certain extent, expression, he either displaces another person who did this for the patient before him or he provides the patient with a first experience. In both instances, he acquires leverage to steer the patient's future development.

SUPPORT OF OR INTERFERENCE WITH ABNORMAL BEHAVIOR

In many cases, established abnormal-behavior patterns have to be supported before a change can occur. An addict is not confronted with a sudden withdrawal of his drug but is given a substitute drug. An excessive smoker may be offered chewing gum, and a restless patient may be given the opportunity to exercise. Here the therapist acknowledges the underlying craving but changes the menu, as it were. In other instances—for example, with compulsives—the therapist has to strengthen their pathology if he wishes his patients to function at all. Wisely handled, support of pathology may give the therapist much needed leverage which he can use later on to change the very same pathology.

The psychiatrist also may interfere with pathology. On a closed ward, for example, he can prevent the patient from being violent; he can restrain, sedate, or isolate him. The doctor does not undertake such interference in his own name but on behalf of the hospital and for the purpose of achieving health. Interference with pathology is accepted by the patient as situational, and much of the ward administration in terms of curtailment of privileges, weekends, and suicide precautions falls into this category. But it is the therapist's job to work through whatever interference he imposes. When the job is divided, decisions are more difficult to make.

LEVERAGE THROUGH RESPONSE

Initial power of the therapist · Gratification in acknowledgment · Group support · Impinging upon the other person's need · The patient's hostility · Negative feedback · Selective emphasis · Tangential response as therapeutic device · Infectious enthusiasm · Future reward · Prestige in groups · Deflation and reconstruction · Fear of insupport · Debunking apparent security · Technical advice · Visible and invisible suggestion · Prestige of the persuader · Technique of emphasizing · Mandatory reporting · Reversible and irreversible events · Acceptance of person; rejection of behavior · Freedom from threat · Investiture of authority · Verdict as integrative force

Under the term "leverage" are included all those forces which permit the therapist to manage minor details in therapy, eliminate external interference, promote communication within the therapeutic situation, and overcome internal resistances of the patient which prevent progress. The leverage of the therapist is exercised in action when an immediate response is required; his knowledge and wisdom, in contrast, come into play in strategic considerations which necessitate awareness of long-term goals and study of behavior in the light of larger time segments. If leverage of the therapist is generally attributed to the patient's assignment of power to the therapist due to transference distortion, we have to add to this definition the leverage that develops because of the gratification or frustration experienced in realistic communicative exchange. Leverage through response, therefore, can be achieved before any transference neurosis has developed. Such leverage is needed in the management of acute conditions, in the first interviews with a new patient, and in dealing with relatives, friends, and professional groups. Also, we shall here assume that for whatever reason the patient makes a move, the therapist must be prepared to reply—including the kind of reply which is represented by silence. We shall further assume that the patient's moves are essentially expressed through symbolic behavior rather than through gross physical action or bodily disease.

ACKNOWLEDGING

Inasmuch as the therapist's manner of acknowledgment steers the patient's future actions, it represents one of the principal tools of therapy. Acknowledgment proper may consist of a nod of the head, a simple "I understand," a question, or a comment. Out of a multitude of impressions received, the doctor has to sift out the relevant signals in order to appreciate the core of the patient's message, which may be contained in a wink or may be hidden in verbiage which covers one or more interviews. If the doctor, even after attentive listening, is unable to decipher the patient's message, he has to acknowledge this difficulty. Failure of the patient to communicate or of the doctor to understand has to be tactfully mentioned in a form such as "I don't get it," or "This does not make sense to me as yet." Sometimes the therapist can verbalize that part of the patient's message that is clear. Thus, acknowledgment, with progressive delineation of the part that has been understood, acts as an incentive towards further clarification. As time goes on and successful communication has been established, the messages tend to become briefer. Thus, in well established systems, any failure to communicate is explicitly acknowledged while successful communication is taken for granted.

The most potent force one can exert is to acknowledge the intent of the other person. Rarely is such intent explicitly formulated, and the doctor has to rely upon implicit cues. Acknowledgment of the full intent behind a communicative act provides deep gratification; tangential response or even complete disregard of the intent of the patient results in frustration (18). The psychiatrist's task is directed at gratifying the patient in terms of understanding and acknowledgment so that he will attempt to perfect the skills of communication. And as the patient seeks this gratification, the therapist has gained leverage. However, the psychiatrist has to beware of replies that are geared to assumptions rather than to specifically established facts. If a psychiatrist behaves like an actor, a salesman, or a TV announcer, he engages in parapsychological relations (10) and can be turned off as easily as a TV set. The patient, perhaps with the exception of hysterical characters and depressives, senses the phony attitude and loses confidence in the doctor.

ACTION RESPONSE

Whenever a goal can be reached only through the combined efforts of several people, each individual holds power over the others. Refusal to cooperate may sabotage the outcome, while "playing ball" or doing more than one's share brings about recognition by the group. In emergencies, the patient is dependent upon health agencies and medical teams. The physician's immediate therapeutic intervention consists of taking things in hand, making decisions, providing for hospitalization, and alleviating the anxiety of the patient. The leverage obtained by the medical person and his helpers is due to the fact that he belongs to a group that can help or destroy the patient.

The prestige of the medical team is implemented through action which, if appropriate, alleviates suffering. In the animal world as well as in human society, action not only implements practical needs but it also fulfills a symbolic function. Action well done or action matched to another person's action establishes rapport between people. Action thus becomes a language which the physician has to master. Unbearable pain, dislocation of joints, bleeding, anxiety, and confusion can be alleviated by medical intervention; and once the patient feels better and has faith, the doctor has gained leverage.

APPEALING

Appeal is directed at some built-in need or trait of the other person, be it his sense of duty, his eagerness for material gain, his desire for revenge, or his readiness to be destructive. Appeal whets the appetite and implies future reward. But to be effective, the appeal also must provide for immediate and direct stimulation; a seductive voice, the smell of a good dish, an appealing color combination, or a small sample of that which is to come convinces the other person more effectively than empty promises. Appeal works both ways. The patient appeals to the doctor (9, 22) and the doctor appeals to the patient. And the management of mutual appeals makes up part of the skill of the therapist. He appeals to the pride of the patient and to his sense of autonomy and independence; or he may appeal to him as an intelligent or rational creature, as a sexual being, or as a member of a group. Such appeal is designed to make the patient aware of what he has or is, so that he may use himself in a more successful way.

Appeal may be directed at some function of the other person. When the patient states that he is inferior, he appeals to the doctor's alleged superiority. And so he can state: "I am weak" (you are strong), "I am adaptable" (you control), "I am devoted" (you need some faithful followers), "I am crazy" (you had better take care of me). These appeals to complementary needs may at times be an expression of real needs which seek fulfillment. But more often than not they are manipulative devices to tie down the other person for some other purpose. The proverbial helpless female that catches her man by making him look strong is a well known example.

DISARMING

When a person accuses, insults, belittles, or assaults, the therapist has three alternatives. He can remain silent; he can take up the fight; or he can disarm. Depending on the occasion, the last method seems at times to be the most satisfactory. A popular way of disarming consists of not taking up the challenge. Implicitly the patient is told that study has replaced warfare. By turning the attack into something that can be laughed about, the patient is drained of his accumulated hostility. He is given an opportunity to use humor as a means of discharging tension (7).

But there are other ways. One therapist with his understanding kindness seems to melt away the attack; another may say, "You scare me when you come out charging like a bull," reminding the patient that the attack has an effect; again another therapist may say "Whom are you trying to destroy?" or perhaps, "Let's look at what makes you so furious." Most people get alarmed when attacked, and this positive feedback increases the tension of the patient. The absence of defensiveness or retribution on the part of the therapist makes the patient's charge obsolete and his tension diminishes. Negative feedback here is the effective operation. Once the patient has experienced the therapist's disarming ways, he endows the doctor with almost saintly properties.

IGNORING

There are many ways of ignoring. In conversation, certain topics, actions, or meanings can be minimized while others are responded to. For quite a while the therapist will use this selective method when he wishes to postpone the discussion of certain topics until a better relationship has been established. At times he may feel that certain topics should be avoided altogether. But the mere act of ignoring or avoiding gives the therapist leverage because the patient will attribute power to him who manages to elegantly postpone, avoid, or delay a response. This, of course, cannot be stretched too far, and sooner or later a definite stand has to be made in reply to a repetitive message of the patient.

Ignoring is also helpful in many other ways. When a stutterer comes for therapy, his speech defect can be ignored; when a society beauty plays on her appearance, it can be ignored. But this is effective only if the therapist at the same time points out that he is interested in another aspect of the message: what the stutterer has to say rather than how he says it; in what matters rather than how the patient asserts himself. Ignoring, therefore, has to be accompanied by an alternate reply. By responding to peripheral aspects of the patient's message and by ignoring the central intention, the therapist engages in what I have described as "tangential response" (19).

INSPIRING

On many occasions the patient announces in a somewhat hesitant way that he would like to pursue a certain skill or acquire a specific knowledge. If the therapist feels that the patient is ready and well motivated, he can further the patient's cause. An individual in his early thirties who has saved some money but never finished college, for example, can express the desire for more education. This plan may or may not make sense, depending upon a host of circumstances. But even if it is sound, the plan still may be indefinitely postponed if the patient has no suitable model to imitate. In one case, the therapist can point to his own and other people's achievements, to their knowledge, or to their ways of learning. Such exemplification may fall upon fertile ground when the attitude of the therapist betrays enthusiasm and conviction. Of course, the doctor should not be carried away and sway the patient to undertake something for which he is not ready. But enthusiastic support of or opposition to an educational or ethical principle helps the patient to clarify his own commitment. Inspiration thus is a procedure which grows out of the readiness of the patient, the knowledge and skill of the instructor, and the suitability of the situation. When the hunger of the patient is great and the therapist as a person has something to offer, then the cues fall upon fertile ground. Inspiration should not be confused with persuasion or permissiveness. Inspiration means merely to strengthen the anticipatory behavior of the patient in a direction in which his motivation is strong, and to furnish him with suitable ideas for practical implementation.

PROMISING

Any promise entails a future reward. If a promise is made by an eloquent person, it may exert an effect that is comparable to an actual reward. A fast talker can telescope time, present air-castles as real, and exhibit an attitude which makes others believe that fantasy is fact. Depending upon the past record of the one who promises, his ability to obtain leverage varies. If he is unknown, his promises will hardly be better than the word of a stranger. If he is known, his past record will influence his audience; if he paid off in the past, his promise is taken seriously. But there are many people who love to gamble, knowing that the odds are against them. And they believe empty promises because they think that they can beat the law of probability.

The therapist rarely pins himself down with overt promises because by so doing he limits his own course of action. But he does something which might be called "covert promising." He exhibits an attitude which indicates, "I have experience, and I know that you might grow and develop; there is hope for you in the future, so work hard and things will get better. I shall help you to achieve this goal." And this silent promise which reaffirms the belief of the patient gives the doctor some leverage.

SUGGESTING OR DEFLATING PRESTIGE

When a prominent patient complains about not having been asked to attend a meeting to which his competitors have been invited and he appears to feel low and left out, the psychiatrist may seize the opportunity to comment on his competence. "Don't you know of certain horsemen or skiers who have been barred from competition simply because they took all the first prizes and never gave anybody else a chance to win? This was bad for group morale; and sometimes people are left out just because they have too much prestige, not because they have none. The fact is that you have a good job, that you are well paid, that you function well; and this in itself should tell you of your own standing."

Prestige suggestion thus means a reinterpretation of the facts by applying a somewhat more sophisticated scheme of evaluation. It teaches the patient two things—first, that prestige is a many-sided thing; and second, that he lacks self-confidence and relies upon primitive and infantile means of assessing his prestige. Nobody can be included everywhere all the time, and the adult has to learn to be selective on the one hand and to react to averages rather than to single incidents. In some cases, the patient's prestige may not lie in his occupational field. He may excel in a hobby or an avocation, and his skill may be known to a limited circle only. Almost every person somewhere is respected by others. It is a question of working out when, by whom, and in what matter.

When a patient relates how others do not appreciate him, slight him, or suggest that he might leave the job, the time has come to study the patient's way of self-appreciation. The patient has to be shown that his high opinion of himself is not shared by others and that the discrepancy is due to an overvaluation on his part of his good intentions and an undervaluation of the effects he produces upon others. At first the patient will resist, but as the psychiatrist patiently presents fact after fact and demonstrates to him his actual failures, he says in effect, "If you revise your views about your usefulness, efficiency, and importance, other people will not be tempted to undermine you; you will become less vulnerable and will function better." At times the psychiatrist may be able to show the patient some self-destructive tendencies; perhaps the patient unconsciously plans to fail and merely uses his declarations of good intentions to hide his real purpose.

REGULATING SECURITY

The fear of insupport—economic, emotional, and physical—is a phenomenon about which many patients complain. Threatened loss of position, employment, status, love, health, or life and exclusion from the group are perennial problems. A patient's fear of insupport may arise because he measures his security in terms which are not applicable to his particular situation. A concert violinist who has lived in many countries and who contracts to play here and there may have fear of insupport because he does not belong to an ensemble. In this case, the psychiatrist has to point out to him that his personal security lies in the fact that he can join, for one evening, almost any orchestra in the world, that his security is not based on group membership but on his being a lone wolf with talent and skill, and that his talent should become the source of his security. To counteract the need for security based on a prescription which is advertised on the radio or taught in schools, the psychiatrist has to search for consistent behavior patterns which already exist in the individual's life and can provide him with future security.

The patient who basks in false security likewise needs the help of the psychiatrist. A civil service job may become unbearable, success in a TV show may not be permanent, and changes in age, economics, or fashion trends may bring reversals. Here the psychiatrist has to work on the presumption that the only secure thing is what the patient has mastered and holds within himself. A little debunking of phony security based on popularity or paper contracts does a lot to reorient the patient. Life is a precarious thing; and since one cannot predict all possible reverses, security must be found in personal skill, adaptability, and resourcefulness. If the psychiatrist emphasizes skill and aptitude and minimizes the external influences, he strengthens the patient and his belief in his competence. Freeing the patient from dependence upon external conditions increases his confidence and provides the therapist with leverage for future operations.

TRAIL BREAKING

Trail breaking is a strenuous pursuit. The first in the column of men hacking their way through the jungle or stamping in freshly fallen snow has the hardest job. But can the patient be expected to break a trail if he is not very strong? Sometimes the psychiatrist can be of some help. On one occasion it may be a suggestion, a catalogue, a book, or an address which breaks the trail. On another occasion, the suggestion that he make an appointment with a professor or a lawyer helps the patient to overcome his own timidity. Then again, it may be an innovation in procedure with a handicapped patient that does the trick. To lead is foremost in all educational procedures, particularly when the patient is stuck. In contrast to some widely held belief that gratification of the patient's dependent needs may lead to more dependency, there is evidence for believing that the patient will alter his behavior once he has had all the support he can take. The former view results in a weaning procedure; the latter in a saturation procedure. Perhaps a combination of both works out best. To let the patient take the initiative and to wait is fine for him who can; but for those who are immobilized, the doctor has to lead. And through imitation, the patient eventually will learn.

CUTTING THROUGH

Getting to the crux of the matter involves the discarding of irrelevant details. The patient has to learn to weed out the unessential from the essential. A young woman, for example, who was talking about daily events, looked pale and her voice sounded more serious than usual. When I said, "You look concerned; what is the matter?" the patient replied, "I'm pregnant." In this case, the patient did not announce her pregnancy but hid this important event in the midst of irrelevant details. In other instances, it is the anger which impresses the psychiatrist; and on still other occasions it may be avoidance. Thus in the general communicative behavior of the patient there appear indications that one or another emotion is dominating the scene. In cutting through the verbiage, the rituals, and the unnecessary actions, the doctor responds to and comments about the patient's visible emotions so that the patient is almost forced to elaborate the experiences that are connected with them. This is most commonly observed in mild depressions where the patient begins to accuse himself of all sorts of misdeeds and shortcomings. At such moments the doctor cuts through and says, "You are angry—angry at yourself and angry at me—but you really can't say it." In reply to this frontal assault, the patient has to pull himself together and to crystallize his feelings; and as a result he may feel much better. If the internal conflict can be externalized and anger in self converted into an activity directed against the other, then the whole procedure exerts an integrating influence. The skill and knowledge with which such an operation is undertaken gives the therapist leverage for future occasions.

ADVISING

In many instances, the psychiatrist holds specialized knowledge which qualifies him to advise the patient—for example, in the choice of a physician or a hospital for a medical or surgical ailment, in matters of choosing a proper institution of learning, or in finding another therapist for a relative. Advice is given not to make up the mind of the patient but to supply technical information which the patient would have difficulty in getting elsewhere. Some psychiatrists have ample knowledge in other fields—medicine, biology, semantics—or they may be expert hobbyists or sportsmen. If they see that the patient is stumbling along and does not know from whom to learn, where to go, and how to inform himself, advice as to how to improve his skill and knowledge is quite in place. Often such technical information is appreciated by the patient to such an extent that it changes his image of the psychiatrist from that of an impersonal doctor to that of a warm human being. Unhesitatingly the psychiatrist should make available his knowledge about areas in which the patient is uninformed. At times the patient will consider such information unessential, but some of it may stick, nonetheless. The patient has to be trained not merely to accept or reject information but to utilize those aspects that are useful to him. The skilled therapist indicates that he cares more whether the patient utilizes some aspects of the exchange than whether he accepts or rejects information on emotional grounds, and this attitude eventually rubs off on the patient.

SUGGESTING AND PERSUADING

Suggestion is a procedure in which one person presents an idea to another person by sneaking in through the back door. As Freud (6) says: ". . . what distinguishes a suggestion from other kinds of mental influence, such as a command or the giving of a piece of information or instruction, is that in the case of a suggestion an idea is aroused in another person's brain which is not examined in regard to its origin but is accepted just as though it had arisen spontaneously in that brain." In persuasion, in contrast, the author of an idea remains identified. All he does is to induce another person to believe by means of statistical argument, demonstration of advantages, or allusion to status gain (2, 11). In psychiatry, Dubois (4) used persuasion as a method of treatment; he tried to explain to the patient the over-evaluation of his illness and attempted to correct his faulty attitudes.

Suggestion and persuasion can only be carried out if the words of the speaker—in this case, the doctor—carry weight with the patient. This leverage is obtained through rewards embedded in the group situation. The positive, self-assertive behavior of one person is used to have the junior or weaker member of the group submit to the idea, which virtually insures the leadership of the assertive individual (13). While in persuasion the acceptance of an idea is based on a relationship of dominance-submission, in suggestion it is founded upon some personal, usually nonverbal, appeal. In order to be effective, a suggestion must fall upon a receptive attitude; the other person must have a need which either the idea, or the person who presents it, fills. Suggestion thus implies wish-fulfillment, and the person who is capable of providing gratification obviously has leverage in the eyes of the patient. The speaker sells himself; he presents himself and the others who share his opinions as lovable creatures; he points to the advantage of accepting his views. He says, in effect, "If you take my word, you shall be rewarded." Respect, admiration, affection, inclusion, and sometimes material advantages thus are offered on the condition that certain views be accepted. While on the one hand results achieved through persuasion may be short-lived, they also have definite advantages when followed by action. Suggestion or persuasion to dive into a swimming pool is quite successful when the subsequent swim turns out to be gratifying. In this case, the persuader does not rely upon the weight of his words alone but upon the experience of the subject in action. Skilled therapists use persuasion only when they are sure that action will bear out their words so that the subsequent events can be used as evidence. The sequential order of word and action therefore seems to determine success or failure of suggestion and persuasion (12).

DRIVING HOME

Blind spots in patients can be overcome by forcefully driving home a given point. I remember a patient who used to come drunk to the interview. She staggered, giggled, laughed, and fell down the stairs. I put her in a taxi and the next time she appeared I drove home the point that I did not wish to see her in a state of intoxication. This driving home, or "rubbing in," as Redl calls it (15), is achieved by nonverbal cues that indicate to the patient that this matter is serious, that the therapist means business, and that he is not going to put up with it. Apparently the patient is given to understand that the usual tolerance for experimentation does not apply, that the therapist will take steps to reinforce what he says with all the power at his disposal, and that he is not going to give in. These personal cues, apparently, together with the urgency of the voice and the seriousness expressed through attitude, indicate to the patient that something important is going on that he has not grasped sufficiently. Through the insistence of the therapist, the patient usually takes another look at the reality situation and may be able to fill in his blind spots. The driving home technique is the more effective the less often it is used.

PROHIBITING AND PROTECTING

Unlike a parent who can physically enforce a verbal command, the doctor is not in a position to utter more than sound. If he chooses to prohibit an activity, he is likely to get on slippery ground. Because if the patient wishes to defy him he can do so with impunity; and if he doesn't, the psychiatrist would not have needed the prohibition in the first place. To prohibit means to say, "I do not like to see you go to bed late, regardless of the reason. If you wish to undergo therapy, you have to work; and in order to work, you need rest. If you cannot keep in shape, my work with you is futile." In other words, certain prohibitions can be presented to the patient if the doctor is ready to enforce them with termination of therapy. This should not be a threat but a statement of consequences and a condition of treatment. The same applies to a patient who is in treatment and can afford to meet his financial obligations but leaves the doctor's bills unpaid. A forceful reminder usually suffices to convince the patient that he is the one who has problems and that he foots the bill, either in terms of money or in terms of frustration.

Some patients need protection from others, some from themselves. Prohibitions may serve the purpose of protection. An epileptic, for example, may be taken into treatment on the condition that he renounce illicit driving—a measure of protection for himself and for others. Children need to be protected from their own daring and old people from their lethargy and inertia. Although at first the patient may oppose such measures, he eventually recognizes the wisdom of such procedures and respects the therapist for his actions. Protective custody, protective separation, and protective exposure are other versions in which the manipulation of the physical situation regulates social contact. Also, the noxious influence of one family member upon the others may be attenuated when interaction is openly discussed.

CONTROLLING

Control literally means that the therapist reinforces that which he thinks the patient should practice. In the therapeutic hour, it means control of expression and awareness of the task. It may involve a step-by-step recitation of what the patient did yesterday or how far he got in his work. Perhaps the therapist wants to know how many drinks the patient has taken, and the necessity of reporting will induce the patient either to go on the wagon or to lie. Under supervision, the patient might not do many of the things he possibly might have undertaken without supervision. The therapist thus assumes the function of a parent who does homework with the child. The awareness that he will have to report often induces the patient to abstain from an action in which he otherwise would have participated.

Sometimes it is the absence of supervision which achieves an effect. Not to ask what happened, not to demand a report, but to accept the patient as a self-respecting individual who will report when he deems it necessary may help him to face his own behavior. Once the practice of reporting has been established, the patient will be accustomed not to hide conflicts. A depressive patient, for example, can be made to report in person or by telephone twice a day. The concrete task, the availability of the therapist, and the obligation to announce his whereabouts may prevent him from committing suicide.

ACCUSING AND REPROACHING

On occasions, the psychiatrist can force the patient to come to the point by means of an accusation. In one case, the psychiatrist said, "You did not tell me that you experienced premenstrual swelling in your right breast for the last three months. This is something that has to be looked into immediately." This accusation induced the patient to seek an immediate consultation with a surgeon, followed by a radical mastectomy. Accusation means "You did not do what I expected you to do or what we had agreed you would do," and it usually pertains not so much to the form of communication as to information which was omitted or belatedly brought up. If a patient walks in and says to the doctor, "I got married yesterday," he has to be made to understand that any anticipated action which might change his patterns of living has to be discussed in advance; and if he does not do this, then there is something the matter with the therapeutic relationship. And because the therapist is not in the habit of accusing, this accusation, when presented, becomes the more effective. It serves to signal the presence of irreversible events so that the patient learns not only to carefully weigh important happenings but to discuss them with others. It is the reversible event which an individual can take lightly; but the irreversible event places responsibility upon his shoulders which cannot be dismissed in an off-hand manner. The doctor's expressed wish that the patient take the significant and irreversible events in life seriously endows him with leverage for future operations.

REJECTING

Denying somebody something he wants, not asking him to express himself if such was his desire, or not acknowledging his messages may be included under the term "rejection." Rejection means not only frustration but a specific insult to the other person's pride. The issue is not merely of the order of "You can't have this," followed by a reasonable explanation; in rejection the implication is "You can't have this because of your personality," and this, of course, hurts. On occasions, the psychiatrist has to reject overtly—for example, when he does not accept a patient for therapy because he has no time or the patient is unsuitable for his kind of method. In a much subtler way, the psychiatrist is at times forced to reject certain of the patient's pathological behavior patterns. Paraphrased, it would sound as follows: "I do not like the implications of what you do; and although I put up with it at the moment, I do not accept it as a permanent feature. If it should be part of your behavior forever, I would have to reject you; but since it is probably only a temporary feature, I am with you and ready to help in the correction of your pathological behavior." To avoid a possible later rejection, the patient abides by the terms of the therapist and with an open mind may gradually strive for what heretofore had been unacceptable to him. Unconditional acceptance of the positive features and conditional acceptance of the pathological features gives the therapist a great deal of leverage; however, much of what is transacted as acceptance or rejection occurs on a preconscious or unconscious level (21).

THREATENING

Threats to life and limb, to security, to material possessions, and to beloved ones are effective methods of exerting leverage. Such methods are successfully employed by companies to sell health or life insurance policies and by drug firms to induce customers to consume a certain remedy. Threat usually includes the anticipation of an irreversible change in order to force a desired course of action. For millennia, threat has been a tool of the power policies of both gangsters and politicians. Threat gains time for the one who uses it because a person who is threatened may yield; but eventually the tables are turned. Once the victim gets mad, the one who threatens gets scared because he sees the end of his power. Therefore the therapist rarely uses direct threat because if the patient is not impressed the therapist either loses face or has to prove that he was right. In either instance, he loses his freedom to initiate the most appropriate procedure. But what the therapist is inclined to do is to expose the threats that burden the patient's mind. When these are brought into the open, they usually disappear. In the minds of some patients, the doctor is viewed as a threatening person, capable of hurting, omniscient, and the bearer of great skills. As therapy progresses, the patient recognizes that the doctor does not possess much magic. The discovery that the threats come from the patient's own conscience and not from the doctor actually gives greater leverage to the physician than the experience that he also, under certain circumstances, can hurt.

JUDGING

Verdicts are passed not only by judges, police officers, and other officials in the community but by any person who holds a position of authority. The passing of a verdict can have an intensely gratifying or a frustrating effect. When a patient consults a doctor, the result of the doctor's examination and his verdict may spell the difference between life and death, invalidism and health. Thus a doctor is vested with the potential power to pass a verdict, and if this verdict is favorable the patient experiences an emotional reaction and the doctor has obtained some leverage. Of course, this leverage is dependent upon the patient's knowledge that the doctor is capable of passing such a verdict; because were the physician to operate incognito, the other person would not vest him with the powers of healing. It is perhaps for these reasons that doctors often display their diplomas and other signs of accomplishment in a prominent place and that they wear white coats, so that the patient is primed as to their status in the office and hospital environment.

The verdict itself is a climax which clinches a whole set of expectations; it verifies, alters, or disappoints. At a trial, the verdict represents an end point; it makes public the thoughts that were private; it implements the reaction of others; it places the individual within the group. In a medical verdict, secret thoughts are made explicit and the patient's future is predicted. This very function of connecting—regardless of whether the verdict is favorable or unfavorable—exerts a therapeutic effect. The physician who passes a verdict increases his status and at the same time draws emotions upon himself. Psychiatrists often are leary of passing judgments, in order to avoid an authoritarian position. But at times such a role is the only thing that will temporarily help the patient over his acute discomfort.

References

1. Bierer, J.: *The Day Hospital.* 56 p. London: Lewis, 1951.
2. Brembeck, W. L. and Howell, W. S.: *Persuasion; A Means of Social Control.* 488 p. New York: Prentice-Hall, 1952.
3. Craft, M.: Psychiatric day hospitals. Amer. J. Psychiat., 116, 251–254, 1959.
4. Dubois, P.: *The Psychic Treatment of Nervous Disorders.* 466 p. New York: Funk & Wagnalls, 1906.
5. Frank, J. D.: The dynamics of the psychotherapeutic relationship: determinants and effects of the therapist's influence. Psychiatry, 22, 17–40, 1959.
6. Freud, S.: Hypnotism and suggestion. Pp. 11–23 in *Collected Papers,* Vol. 5. London: Hogarth Press, 1950.
7. Grotjahn, M.: *Beyond Laughter.* 285 p. New York: McGraw-Hill, 1956.
8. Hilgard, E. R.: *Theories of Learning.* (2nd. ed.) 563 p. New York: Appleton-Century-Crofts, 1956.
9. Hill, L. B.: Anticipation of arousing specific neurotic feelings in the psychoanalyst. Psychiatry, 14, 1–8, 1951.
10. Horton, D. and Wohl, R. R.: Mass communication and para-social interaction. Psychiatry, 19, 215–229, 1956.
11. Hovland, C. I., Janis, I. L., and Kelley, H. H.: *Communication and Persuasion.* 315 p. New Haven: Yale University Press, 1953.
12. Hovland, C. I. and others: *The Order of Presentation in Persuasion.* 192 p. New Haven: Yale University Press, 1957.
13. Minnick, W. C.: *The Art of Persuasion.* 295 p. Boston: Houghton Mifflin, 1957.
14. Redl, F.: The meaning of "therapeutic milieu." Pp. 503–515 in *Symposium on Preventive and Social Psychiatry, 15–17 April, 1957.* Washington: Walter Reed Army Institute of Research, 1958.
15. Redl, F. and Wineman, D.: *Controls from Within.* 332 p. Glencoe: Free Press, 1952.
16. Redlich, F. C. and Bingham, J.: *The Inside Story.* 280 p. New York: Knopf, 1953.
17. Reider, N.: A type of transference to institutions. Bull. Menninger Clin., 17, 58–63, 1953.

18. Ruesch, J.: *Disturbed Communication*. 337 p. New York: Norton, 1957.

19. Ruesch, J.: The tangential response. Pp. 37–48 in *Psychopathology of Communication* (P. H. Hoch and J. Zubin, editors). New York: Grune & Stratton, 1958.

20. Steig, W.: *The Rejected Lovers*. 152 p. New York: Knopf, 1951.

21. Tagiuri, R. and Petrullo, L. (Editors): *Person Perception and Interpersonal Behavior*. 390 p. Stanford: Stanford University Press, 1958.

22. Taylor, F. K.: Awareness of one's social appeal. Hum. Relat., 9, 47–56, 1956.

23. Vertes, M.: *It's All Mental*. [85 p.] New York: Tudor, 1948.

Chapter Nine

Attributed Power and Frozen Communication

Two PEOPLE who spend hours, days, or weeks together begin to react to each other. Sometimes they want to get rid of the partner or want to run away; sometimes they wish to make love; and again they might want to control and advise the other person. But whatever the reaction, the other person becomes an important consideration which takes up time and energy. Whatever effort is spent in coping with this other person is of course an investment from which an individual expects returns. These returns are not necessarily received immediately, and they may not even be personal. A teacher, for example, who has spent hours in coaching and instructing his pupil in playing the guitar may not expect gratitude but may be quite content to see the student play and perform in a satisfactory manner. It is unnecessary to state that any personal investment is mutual and that the pupil likewise has an investment in his teacher. The term "investment," borrowed from banking, literally means that something is given to someone else so that he may operate with it in order to earn, among other things, a return for the investor.

Therefore one might say that anyone who communicates with another person for any length of time eventually develops certain expectations. These may be realistic or unrealistic, but in any case they constitute the driving force which makes therapy possible.

DISTORTION OF THE THERAPEUTIC REALITY

The caricature of a psychiatrist · The denial of identifying features · Exaggeration of the psychiatrist's influence · The psychiatrist as technician · The psychiatrist as omniscient expert · Rules and rituals · A plan for living · Rigidity of principle and flexibility of implementation

The psychiatrist is a real person with a body and a soul, and his personality permeates all transactions with his patient. Through the influence of movies, newspapers, and cartoons, the patient has been primed to compare the therapist to a variety of clichés (8). These assumptions are particularly convenient if the patient wishes to obliterate the fact that the therapist is a human being with a name, an address, a family, and all the other features which characterize people.

The psychiatrist is either male or female and is either young, middle aged, or old. If a young and attractive patient denies the fact that her slightly older doctor is a healthy male, unmarried, and available, she introduces a gross distortion of facts. To deny that which exists not only produces a distortion but vests the patient with imaginary power. Just as the assignment of roles in the transference situation invests the therapist with leverage, so does the denial of actual characteristics give the patient license to treat the therapist like a rubber ball. If the therapist is caught in this trap, he really supports the magic thinking of the patient. The therapist, therefore, has to stand his ground and if necessary open the subject for discussion, so that he stops being a mythical figure for the patient. In the eyes of the patient, he has to become an individual with a name, age, sex, address, and certain character features which include sensitivities and deficiencies of various kinds.

The psychiatrist not only has a personality but he is in effect also a significant person for the patient. But he is significant only in the therapeutic situation and not necessarily in the home life of the patient. Frequently the patient, who is seen for one or two hours a week, pretends that all other hours of the week also are determined by the therapeutic situation. Thus the therapist becomes all important and permeates all actions of the patient. In another kind of distortion, the therapist is treated like a dentist—the patient comes, sits down, goes away, and pays, and that is about all there is to it. The withholding of proper and realistic acknowledgment of the role of the psychiatrist on the part of the patient and of the function of therapy is a symptom of the patient's struggle with human relations.

The difference between a transference distortion and a distortion of therapeutic reality is contained in the management of roles. In a transference neurosis, it is the emotional gratification of having established a specific kind of relationship which stabilizes the situation. To treat the doctor as a father substitute is an unconscious attribution of role (13). With a father—a good one—career, marriage, or hobbies may be discussed or chess may be played, always with the assumption that he will look out for the son's well-being. But in distortions of the therapeutic reality, the unconscious attribution of role is secondary. The other is not viewed as a person; therapy is not viewed as a relationship. The therapist is merely a tool and therapy is merely a technique. These distortions occur regularly before the transference neurosis begins to develop and when the patient has to find a realistic means of coping with the doctor. At this stage, preoccupation with the technique, the couch or the chair, means of payment, hours of appointment, the field of psychiatry, or theory is rather prominent. And the patient's exaggeration of the therapist's virtues is merely intended to sugar-coat the bitter pill.

When transference and transference neurosis do not develop, the psychiatrist becomes the subject of fiction—a man who is supposed to have a lot of power, who is supposed to delve into the sex lives of patients, to know all about people, to threaten the existence of the clergy, to dabble in religion, and to change existing values. Frequently the psychiatrist is called upon by the patient, and by organizations, to pass judgment and to utter his opinions on matters far removed from his daily activities. He is supposed to say something about the mental health of the nation, or to utter opinions about the atom bomb, or pass on pending legislation. These atitudes are evidence that the person in question has no relationship to the psychiatrist, that he vests him with imaginary skills and tempts him to go into fields which the psychiatrist has not mastered. This temptation is commonly used by lawyers who wish to nullify the effect of an expert witness's testimony. They draw out the psychiatrist to talk about things he does not know and then they prove to the jury that he is either an idiot or a charlatan. All of these exaggerated attributes are culturally determined and vary from group to group (14). Therefore, the sooner the patient's exaggerations and distortions are corrected, the sooner therapeutic progress is likely to fall into more productive lines.

The most powerful antidote against distortions of the therapeutic reality are the rules of therapy. Investments are usually protected by law; emotional investments are safeguarded by certain behavioral practices. Therapists have established rules which force the patient to consider the realistic aspects of therapy: waiting lists, regularity of appointments scheduled at specific intervals, cancellation of appointment well in advance, payment for missed appointments, loss of the monetary investment if therapy is abandoned too early. Traditions and rituals of therapy were established in order to avoid unpleasant experiences. By establishing a therapeutic routine, mutual investments are protected.

But the rules of therapy are not confined to behavior in the doctor's office. The patient must learn to safeguard his investment by exposing himself to life experiences which will further his development and avoid situations that might threaten his growth. The therapeutic situation is analogous to the home situation in childhood; the parents control, to a certain extent, the extrafamilial experiences to insure optimal development. Similarly the therapist lets his guiding hand be felt on many occasions; he induces the patient to work and to play, and he helps him to introduce sex into his life in an acceptable manner. This does not mean the dispensing of recipes but the working out of detailed plans for living. And what is good for one patient may not be good for the next one. While one patient has to abstain from overwork, the next one has to renounce loafing.

The therapist does well to adhere rigidly to abstract principles and to be flexible in his practical implementation. For example, continuity there must be, but how, when, and with whom, are individual questions. Diversity of experience with different people and groups is a must, but how this is equated with necessary solitude is again an individual question. The code of the mature person is to be consistent and true to himself in matters of abstract principle but flexible and tolerant with the many little things that interfere. This attitude, which in due course of time is conveyed to the patient, is eventually incorporated in the latter's thinking.

TRANSFERENCE AND COUNTERTRANSFERENCE RECONSIDERED

Historical Development · Transference as a social phenomenon · Phenomenology · Transference in ordinary circumstances · Abnormal transference · Arrested growth · Transference in the nonverbal mode · Stimulation of proximity receivers · Transference and anxiety · Counter-transference defined · Unconscious acknowledgment of transference · Mutual investment

The concept of transference has undergone many transformations since Freud's first allusion to it in 1895 (1). Having considered it at first as synonymous with suggestion (7), Freud later viewed transference as a displacement of affect, then linked it to the phenomena of resistance and fixation (5), and finally recognized it as a repetition compulsion (2). These concepts became the cornerstones of psychoanalytic theory. But psychoanalytic ideas did not remain confined to the field of psychoanalysis proper, and when the notion of transference was examined in the light of different behavioral theories, a number of puzzling questions arose. Even to this day the issue of whether transference and countertransference are pathological phenomena has not been settled to everyone's satisfaction. Some hold that transference includes only neurotic and irrational manifestations on the part of the patient in therapy (12); others believe that it embraces the whole doctor-patient relationship; finally, there are those who feel that the concept should be extended to include irrational elements in all non-therapeutic, spontaneous relations of daily life.

When Freud first described the phenomena which he grouped under the name of transference, he was clarifying something which had been used unwittingly by physicians in their treatment of the sick throughout the ages (16). As a matter of fact, he described some fundamental characteristics of communication, although at that time he believed that the events subsumed under the term of transference were limited to therapeutic activities. But they can all be found in daily life. Crushes of adolescents upon older members of the same or the opposite sex, emotionally involved teacher-pupil relationships, the reliance of dependent employees upon authoritative employers, or the relation of certain spinsters to their household pets are of the same order.

Freud (4) described the transference phenomenon as a process in which the patient sees in his analyst the return—the reincarnation —of some important figure out of his childhood or past, and consequently transfers onto him feelings and reactions that do not pertain to the present situation. In psychoanalysis, the tendency to transfer is unusually intensified; it shapes the whole analytic situation and sidetracks the patient's rational aim of becoming well and free from his troubles. Instead, there emerges the aim of pleasing the analyst, of winning his applause and his love. This becomes the driving force for the patient's collaboration, and under its influence the patient achieves things that would otherwise be beyond his power; his symptoms disappear and he seems to have improved.

Although the manifestations of transference and countertransference appear to be manifold, they actually can be reduced to a few relevant facts. Transference invariably involves two persons, one of whom is usually status superior in terms of age, experience, skill, beauty, material possessions, or the ability to provide protection and support. In the affective sphere, one of the participants tends to display outspoken signs of like, dislike, or pronounced indifference which are not matched by similar responses on the part of the other person. The same disparity can be observed in the cognitive-intellectual sphere; one person usually makes assumptions, displays attitudes, and develops fantasies which do not correspond to the thoughts of the other person. Finally, in the realm of action, the activities of the first person are tolerated by the second person without effort at specific negation or outspoken cooperation. On the whole, either one or both participants are aware of the existing discrepancies of status, affect, thought, and action and sometimes may perceive that the emotional flavor of the relationship does not fit the actual social circumstances. With advancing age, the participants often spontaneously come to recognize that once they dissolve such a relationship they tend to embark upon another similar one. The absence of complementary behavior on the part of the two participants, the repetitiveness of the patterns, and the questionable fit of the affective responses into the actual social setting thus become the identifying characteristics of what in the therapeutic situation have been labeled transference and countertransference relationships.

Daily life communication is unthinkable without transference. The child, the adolescent, or the adult necessarily must draw upon previous models of human relations when encountering strangers and meeting new social situations. These assumptions derive from past experiences and consist of attributing character features to self and to the other person. Although these initial assumptions rarely correspond to the reality situation, they do not as yet constitute a disturbance of communication. Only if in the course of events the initial assumptions are not validated and corrected (15) may we be permitted to talk about pathological transference and disturbances of communication. If two persons' mutual adaptation fits like a key to a keyhole and the behavior blends into the larger social framework like a doorlock into the style of the door, behavior is by definition adaptive, rational, and normal. Nobody would think of calling a young mother's tender love for her baby transference, although on the mother's side a great many feelings, thoughts, and actions constitute a transfer from earlier experiences.

The correction of initially false assumptions is facilitated by a variety of circumstances. If the other person is seen in widely differing situations involving a number of other people, distortions tend to be minimized. If, however, the situation is a rigid one, as in therapy, teaching, or employment, a favorable ground for fantasy elaboration and distortion is created. The same holds true for people who live in relative isolation—persons in hospitals, boats, prisons, or desolate outposts. In other words, when the possibilities of varied human contact are reduced, when the exchange of messages becomes redundant, or when communication is handicapped by stringent rules, feedback phenomena cannot be relied upon to correct distorted assumptions.

When the child at the time of the oedipal period fails to progress beyond simple two-person exchanges and cannot master communication in the primary group composed of self, mother, father, and any existing siblings, later role distortions are the result. Successful identification with the parent of the same sex—or the resolution of the oedipal conflict—indicates that the child learned the meaning of multiple roles vis-à-vis father, mother, and siblings, that he mastered complex and varying rules with different people, that he acquired some knowledge of discursive language, and that he became capable of dealing with the intricacies of human relations and group communication. Those less fortunate ones who did not master the oedipal conflict had to be content either with ineffective communication or with an exchange limited to two-person situations with prevalence of nonverbal language, use of proximity receivers in perception, and use of nonverbal action in expression. Fixation at the oedipal or pre-oedipal level implies a lack of flexibility in human relations, the inability to grow by interpersonal experience, and the necessity to cope with human relations in terms of transference.

This inability to correct is intimately related to the characteristics of verbal and nonverbal language. When people confer with each other, they use spoken or written verbal signals to elicit in the other person images and fantasies which by their very nature are analogic. But no two persons' sensations and interpretations are completely identical, and this analogic imagery is suitable for understanding only. In order to carry out a discourse, verbal language is indispensable, inasmuch as it enables people to isolate certain aspects of events and to delineate the areas in which they wish to reach an agreement. It follows that people whose mastery of verbal communication is shaky have great difficulties in stating agreements or disagreements, and therefore they have trouble in utilizing interpersonal communication for the correction of assumptions and beliefs. Consequently, people whose language is prevailingly nonverbal tend to distort and transfer more than those whose communication is based upon an integration of verbal and nonverbal language.

But since in Western civilization the concepts of education and maturity are intimately linked to the use of the distance receivers and verbal expression, the skillful integration of verbal and nonverbal methods of communication is rarely achieved. While structured group situations, with the exception of sports, necessitate the use of verbal-discursive language, the two-person relationship favors the use of the less rigid, nonverbal language which includes perception through smell, taste, touch, vibration, temperature, and perhaps pain, and which in turn provokes actions that are designed to appeal to these very same modalities. Therefore, when in a two-person situation the participants seize the opportunity to free themselves from the artificiality of verbal logic and desire to emphasize the free, analogic, nonverbal methods of exchange, they discover that they are poorly prepared for such an eventuality. Since in adolescence and adulthood the individual was scarcely allowed to elaborate and refine his nonverbal means of communication, he has to fall back upon the nonverbal methods he used in his childhood. The cultural taboo on touch and expression through action, and the fact that man's earliest social experiences occurred in a two-person situation in the nonverbal mode, explain the fact that interpersonal communication in adolescence and adulthood so frequently is associated with what has been called transference.

Freedom from distortion is achieved when three conditions in the development of the individual have been met: first, people must have had such a variety of experiences that any single event or relationship becomes submerged in comparison to the composite; secondly, there must exist opportunities for interpersonal communicative elaboration; thirdly, the first and early experiences should not have been too intense. However, when experiences are extreme relative to the tolerance limits of the individual, and when there is no opportunity for communicative elaboration of events, and when in the formative years there is no variety of interpersonal contacts, distortions are likely to occur. Memories which never have been symbolized in digital or verbal terms are buried in the mind in terms of analogic imagery, feeling, or sensation. In later interpersonal situations, these memories are then acted out with scant or no awareness on the part of the individual. Thus we have to add to the concept of transference as an interpersonal event the fact that it occurs in a nonverbal, analogic mode (9).

The development of transference in therapeutic situations is bound to the same conditions that apply to ordinary life situations. The anxiety aroused by the contact with the therapist is overcome by means of transference—that is, by relying upon assumptions that have proven to be useful in the past. If these assumptions operate successfully and the anxiety diminishes, the transference neurosis is established. In ordinary, short-lasting doctor-patient relationships, the doctor can either avoid or act in accordance with the distortions of the patient. If he wishes to minimize transference, he will meet with the patient in diversified situations, avoid two-person contact or space it far apart, beware of stimulating closeness receivers, and refrain from transmitting messages in terms of nonverbal expression. If he acts in accordance with the developing transference situation, he will silently fit into the role which the patient assigns to him with all of its nonverbal concomitants. The satisfaction and freedom from anxiety on the part of the patient at having established a relationship in the nonverbal mode that is familiar to him has to be used by the therapist for purposes of suggestion or guidance before the patient becomes aware of his distortion. Those forms of therapy that rely upon working through of the transference neurosis actually proceed to translate the idiosyncratic fantasies, sensations, and feelings into language symbols, thus providing the patient with the tools of self-correction and consensual validation. The wishes to eliminate, touch, bite, caress, or make love or, conversely, the wishes to be hurt, rejected, or destroyed which occur during the height of the transference are subjected to mutual inspection and verbalization. As the patient learns to coordinate nonverbal with verbal language, he acquires the means of operating in a group. There he learns that many of his physical desires can be sublimated and satisfied by social means —a fact which makes him less dependent upon two-person situations and obviates the necessity for transference.

Countertransference is transference in reverse. The therapist's unresolved conflicts force him to invest the patient with certain properties which bear upon his own past experiences rather than to constitute reactions to the patient's actual behavior. All that was said about transference, therefore, also applies to countertransference, with the addition that it is the transference of the patient which triggers into existence the countertransference of the therapist.

If in the process of communication the patient treats the doctor as a malicious father figure, the therapist will, if he is sensitive, at times comply with the wishes of the patient. He will, in effect, assume the complementary role because if he were not sensitive enough to react he would be unable to experience the demands of the patient. To fit into the complementary role and to experience a corresponding emotional attitude is a diagnostic tool of the therapist. This procedure does not fill any particular desires of his, nor does it express a conflict, nor is it the result of a projection upon the patient. On the contrary, it is an extremely realistic attitude which allows the therapist to take the patient's communicative behavior at face value and allows him to experience its impact. But such exposure cannot be entirely passive. No competent horseman will draw his conclusions only from seeing a horse. Invariably he will want to ride, and only in action does he experience the qualities of the animal in the proper way. The therapist is in a position similar to that of the horseman. He has to experience communication through his own response and not only through passive observation.

But now comes the danger. Some inexperienced therapists may be caught in this exploratory phase and the trial period becomes permanent. If the patient seduces the therapist to play the complementary role and if this should satisfy in every respect the sense of fit, balance, and symmetry of the therapist, he may get caught in this path of least resistance. It takes either obtuseness and incompetence or extreme skill to be able to reply to a person in ways which are not complementary.

Not to be confused with countertransference are experiences which the therapist has in common with the patient. After several hundred hours of therapy, a body of experience is shared with the patient, and this exerts a bond which can by no means be labeled counter-transference. It is a realistic experience of learning in which the meaning of signals and signs is understood and a two-person language is created. With the instructional, explanatory, and interpretative schemes shared in common, a complexity and efficiency of communication is reached which cannot be duplicated without a great deal of effort. The therapist has an investment in the patient because he has put many hours of work into the task of understanding his communications; and the patient, in turn, does not wish to abandon what he has gained. Investment and counter-investment of effort thus represent the driving force which keeps therapy going. Neither participant wishes to lose the work he put into it, and this eventually forms the basis for further progress.

FROZEN COMMUNICATION

REPETITIVE BEHAVIOR AND RESISTANCE

The experience of repetitive behavior · Resistance in psychoanalysis · Resistance in psychotherapy · The four basic replies

Any experienced therapist is familiar with communicative exchanges which have become stereotyped, redundant, and repetitious. In such a situation, both the therapist and the patient have assumed entrenched positions which differ little from interview to interview. This type of frustrating experience is an absolute must for the patient if he is to face his neurotic conflict. After the patient has blamed the deadlock variously on the incapability of the therapist, the method of therapy, his relatives, or some other reason, he eventually comes face to face with the repetitiveness of his own difficulties and his inability to correct them.

Frozen communication can be perceived and experienced by alert lay people and by therapists as well. It is a ubiquitous phenomenon which occurs in many social situations. In the psychoanalytic situation, it is referred to as "resistance." When, in the course of psychoanalysis, the patient's associations stop short or wander far away from the subject under consideration and he experiences painful feelings at the discussion of the crucial theme (3), then the psychoanalyst knows that he deals with resistance. Conceptually, resistance is conceived of as a force which becomes manifest when the patient, with the help of his analyst, attempts to become conscious of his unconscious. If reluctance to give up symptom formation is one source of resistance, unconscious guilt represents a second, and repressed impulses a third (6). When these roots of resistance are uncovered and worked through, the forces which oppose the improvement of the patient gradually weaken.

For purposes of therapeutic communication, we may now reformulate the problem of resistance in a somewhat different way. Frozen communication is detected in the patient's expressions which are inappropriate to the situation, repetitious, and not amenable to correction. The patient's statements are not adapted to the statements of the therapist; instead, the patient is satisfied to maintain this unsatisfactory exchange and to structure the relationship with the therapist according to a preconceived, though unconscious, plan. This may involve maintenance of a role, seeking of an emotion, avoidance of an experience, control over painful memories, or evasion of the struggle with certain values. The management of this sterile state of affairs is directed at making the patient experience the consequences of his own behavior. If management is successful, the patient is at first puzzled; but as his communications become more adaptive, things seem to fall into place and at the end of therapy communication once more has assumed the function of flexible social implementation.

The tactics used in managing resistances—that is, redundant behavior which escapes ordinary correction—are tied to the nature of the therapist's reply. If he does not deal with diversified topics but emphasizes the periodicity and repetitiveness of the performance of the patient, the stereotyped roles and attitudes become crystallized. For this purpose the therapist uses four types of reply:

–The immediate reply is a response which is matched in every way to the characteristics of the patient's initial statement.

–The delayed response is a reply to a statement which ocurred earlier in the session or at another date altogether; the response is matched to the patient's initial statement.

–The longitudinal evaluation is a response to which the therapist has given some forethought; it is less spontaneous, more abstract, and considers the patient's statement in the light of many facts that have been established over a period of time.

–The interpersonal evaluation does not emphasize the face value of any of the patient's statements but interprets them as messages to the therapist.

And now for the details.

CHANGE OF UNIVERSE OF DISCOURSE

The art of switching topics · New symbols · Switching and clarity of view

When behavior is repetitive and the verbal exchange is stereotyped and the psychiatrist wishes to reinstate a flexible exchange, he may do so by switching the universe of discourse. Instead of accepting the verbal behavior of the patient at face value and therefore reinforcing whatever goes on, he can:

–Emphasize the history of this segment of behavior, try to understand the circumstances under which it was learned, and trace its development.

–Or he can project present behavior into the future and therefore shift the focus of attention from what is happening now to what might happen in the future.

–Or he can take one segment of behavior and focus the patient's attention on the implications and effects it has upon other people at the present time.

–Or he can look at the patient's behavior and discuss the effects he experiences himself.

–Or he can point out similarities and differences between what is happening in therapy and what is happening in daily life.

The switches that the therapist can make, therefore, are manifold. He can change from overt to covert content, from present to past and future, from one coexisting situation to another, and from content to interpersonal relationship. Theoretically, the efficacy of switching the universe of discourse is easy to explain. Memories and ideas are codified in certain symbolic systems. A switch introduces another time element, another position of the observer, another symbolization system. By trial and error, the therapist attempts to explore to which symbolic element the resistance is linked and then attempts to express the same idea in terms of a different system. As soon as the patient can operate with the new symbols, the resistance may begin to wane.

A switch in the universe of discourse is very similar to the inspection of a statue in a museum. There one can look at Venus from different angles—from the back, from the front, from the side, from below, from above. One can emphasize the material it is made of, the artist who made it, or the model who posed for it. Each time we take up another viewpoint, the image of the statue becomes clearer in our mind. Since we operate in therapeutic communication with the thesis that missing information is the link that prevents the patient from accepting certain unconscious facts and integrating them with his conscious information, any of these switches may help in two ways: first, to make the patient aware that something is missing; and second, to detect what it is that is missing. In other words, if a patient is not capable of tolerating contradictions between his emotions and his intellect, his ideas and his desires, his conscience and his activities, he develops resistance. This is expressed in a monotonous, stereotyped exchange which is designed to stabilize the situation and prevent painful adaptation. The switch of universe, by necessity, adds new aspects and new information. In one instance it may be the repressed memory of certain events that is missing; and when this is brought forward, the individual may be able to handle the conflict.

SWITCH OF LANGUAGE

Appropriate language · Home visits · Experience is language bound · Awareness is bound to contrast

Words do not exhaust the description of behavior, and certain experiences can never be verbalized. But sometimes expression can be improved by using a different kind of language. Body language, action language, and verbal language (10) all have different realms of application. If the patient narrates an anecdote in verbal terms it may fall flat because what he needs is action language to make it alive. Sometimes it is a demonstration, close inspection, or "the thing itself" that is needed to supply proper expression. The therapist who is skilled in all three forms of language is sometimes in the position of switching the patient onto the right track. When a more appropriate language is used, missing information may be unearthed and resistances overcome.

In once case it may be an intercurrent disease which offers an opportunity to use action or body language. I remember a patient who broke his leg, and I continued the therapeutic sessions in the hospital. The action of moving myself to the patient instead of waiting for him to come to me sufficed to establish a rapport which had not existed up to then. Another device is to visit patients in their own surroundings. Office visits are suitable only for those patients who have mastered symbolic behavior; but for those who have not, a home visit is very profitable. I arrange for the home interview as if it were the home visit of a general practitioner. I make an appointment, stay for an hour, and come back another time if necessary. The patient then shows me his home, his children, his hobbies, personal documents of interest, and so on. Only when one has seen people talk to their dogs and horses, seen them interact with their children, studied the kind of style they abide by (11), and seen them in action on their boats and in their gardens does one obtain the "feel" of the situation. And many times this procedure offers the only opportunity to utilize "action" or "somatic" language with the patient (10).

But the principle of switching codification can be applied within the verbal universe also. I have spoken to foreign born patients in the English language, and then one day I spoke in their native tongue—Italian, German, or French—and all of a sudden the whole relationship changed. This peculiar phenomenon is due to the fact that memories are codified in part in terms of the language in which the experiences occurred. If a child spoke Italian until he was eight and then came to America, many of the memories before the age of eight are accessible in Italian only. A change of language in the patient's youth usually means also a change of friends and people. The patient himself may be unaware of such a break in continuity, and only when the therapist unites these two phases by speaking both languages can the material that was isolated, suppressed, or otherwise inaccessible become integrated. The unity of language and experience is re-established because the transition from one memory to another is experienced with one and the same person.

Those who have studied Latin or Greek know that the process of translation forces people to decide what a term signifies. Corresponding words in two different languages rarely cover the same ground, and as we become aware of the differences and overlaps we discover the gaps in our knowledge and experience. In dealing with resistances, we become aware that blind spots can be bypassed and emotionally charged topics avoided by translating the subject in question into terms that the patient is capable of managing. This principle applies particularly to the integration of nonverbal with verbal memories. At the age of two or three years, action is the principal experience. To reactivate these memories, it would be most desirable to put our patients in sand boxes or on swings, or let them glide down the big slides. But since we cannot do so for physical reasons, we have to be content to have patients observe action in their own children. Such observations trigger memories which the patient has been heretofore unable to bring forth, and resistances may disappear.

INFORMING PATIENT AND PARTNER OF THEIR MUTUAL PATHOLOGY

In many instances another family member is blamed for stereotyped or broken down communication. One patient may name her husband's infidelity as the cause of her perpetual complaining; another may point to his drinking as the reason for marital failure. One of the ways to break into such a stereotyped accusation is to study the relationship of the two partners. For example, a successful businesswoman spent very little time at home with her two children, allegedly because her husband regularly belittled and ridiculed her in every possible way. At home, this woman behaved in a helpless and incompetent manner, although she was able to run her own elaborate business quite successfully. The interaction between husband and wife thus was characterized by a role distribution in which she played the incompetent wife and he the superior husband. Without entering into a discussion of the circumstances that induced each of these two partners to establish such a behavior pattern, it was sufficient to point out the existence of the pattern and to demonstrate that the wife seduced the husband into being critical. The husband apparently could only operate when she assumed an inferior role. Discussion of behavior inhibited the action in progress, and the re-establishment of communication at home also changed the stereotyped behavior of the patient in therapy.

DEBUNKING THE OUTCOME

Inner freedom and ability to learn · Preoccupation limits scanning · The fiction of the end state

Frozen communication frequently is associated with the patient's inability to face consequences realistically. For example, a woman who was extremely unhappy with her husband once stated, "Separation or divorce is out of the question." By eliminating this solution, the patient prevented herself from considering all possible solutions and she felt trapped. After therapy, when she allowed herself to admit that divorce was a possibility, the patient regained her inner freedom and she who dreaded divorce before therapy now accepted it as one of the possible solutions. Having gained freedom to conduct her own existence in the way she saw fit, she became less resentful of her husband, and therefore, paradoxically, had no desire to leave him. Not being limited by her self-imposed straitjacket, she chose to live with him.

Again, there are people who cannot talk about certain subjects such as sex or money because of anticipated consequences. In these cases, the patient has to learn to scan all the possibilities instead of being preoccupied with one or two of them. If a person can regain his freedom to scan and to make choices, he once again can learn and make mistakes. If a child is not pushed to be first in his class but merely is encouraged to be a good pupil, he will function far better than if his parents expect him to be Number One at all times. If a boy does not feel compelled to emulate his famous father and a daughter her socially prominent mother, they can develop their own lives in a more original way. Those who must reach a particular goal at all costs may not do justice to their intelligence, ability, skill, or interest.

A patient may be freed from these internal obligations by a method which may be called "debunking the outcome." These patients have demonstrated that their preoccupation with goals led to failure; concern with the outcome interferes with thinking, scanning, and adaptation. To bring the patient back to realistic considerations, the therapist has to raise such questions as "What can you not express? What are you anticipating? What are you afraid of?" Thus the therapist patiently points out the emotional factors that limit the patient's decision-making ability. He is brought back to the currently prevailing circumstances, and eventually the craze to achieve an anticipated end state is recognized as fiction. Life is an ongoing process, and end states exist only in man's imagination.

CHANGE OF PRACTICAL ARRANGEMENTS

Transference neurosis is situation bound · Verbal communication may be unsuitable · Mode of expression and context have to be varied

If communication between doctor and patient has been frozen for some time, a change in practical arrangements occasionally alters the steady state. Change in the frequency of interviews, vacations from therapy, talking to other members of the family, introducing an activity into the therapeutic sessions rather than talking—all can be tried. I remember one patient whose fantasy was very restricted and who could hardly talk at all. She was working on her master's thesis in education, and I decided that I would spend the next sessions in carefully studying the manuscript with her. After that, corrective feedback became established, talking became easy, and the patient made rapid progress. Another patient, who had suffered from anorexia and who refused to talk, I encouraged to play the piano. As I listened to her playing, an interchange about musical literature developed; and eventually this was expanded to include other aspects of her existence.

Frozen communication may arise because the patient lacks the tools of communication. Sometimes the patient is not used to self-expression; in some cases, it is the verbal language that is the obstacle; in others, it may be the two-person situation which is frightening. The shortcomings inherent in communicative behavior cannot be improved through interpretation. If symbolic expression is underdeveloped and if the patient's favorite way of relating is through direct action, any interview situation will break down because the patient lacks the basic skills of communication. The patient is unsuited for the verbal method. Freud considered persons with narcissistic neuroses as incapable of developing a transference neurosis and therefore beyond reach (4). Today we have to add that transference neurosis develops in all cases to varying degrees. But the infantile feelings may be expressed not in attitude or word but in action. In the narrower sense of the word, transference neurosis presupposes a certain maturity in the patient, experience with symbolic systems, and ability to express feelings. But if the patient's significant experience occurs in the nonverbal mode, the transference neurosis cannot be talked about. It can only be experienced, and by engaging in action the therapist will discover its full impact.

The physical arrangements, therefore, play an important part; and if they are altered in order to facilitate nonverbal action, the results are frequently astonishing. With nonverbal persons, the therapist has to become a child psychiatrist. Play, recreational, work, and physical therapy have to replace the verbal exchange. Once the contact with the therapist is organized around action, the patient usually is willing to correct his behavior.

SWITCH OF ROLES AND CHANGE OF RULES

When the therapist focuses the limelight on himself · When the therapist focuses upon the patient · Flexible rules

Like the change of physical arrangements, a switch of roles and rules in the therapeutic situation may have a significant impact. If the therapist, heretofore silent and rather unobtrusive, becomes involved in a state of frozen communication, he may begin to talk about himself or about a given subject, perhaps for several interviews. In proceeding actively, the therapist demonstrates how he thinks and feels. This may give the patient an idea of how to approach the therapist. If the patient is unable to explore people with his own devices, the therapist illustrates how a well-functioning person operates. Removing the focus of attention from the patient may induce him to struggle with the problems he previously ignored. Particularly those patients who have been exposed to a great deal of attention from adults but who have never met adults who included them in their own problems may react favorably.

The reverse procedure is indicated in patients who constantly wish to involve the therapist or who desire to argue, oppose, or rebel. By assuming a completely passive role, the therapist forces the patient to be concerned with his own affairs and to remove the focus of attention from the therapist. But the change of roles and rules is not limited to the therapeutic situation. After some experience in therapy, some patients can be induced, for example, to assume the role of expectant observer with other members of their families. Those who tend to participate too much then experience relief, and for the first time they obtain from others something that they never received before—spontaneous expression. A woman, for example, who ruled her husband's life, was amazed to discover that when she assumed an expectant attitude much of her husband's behavior changed. Instead of being seclusive and dutiful, he became interested and participating.

To formulate this idea in more abstract terms, one might say that the consistency of the therapeutic situation is embedded in the therapist's attitude of firmly but supportively promoting the emotional growth of the patient. Whatever supports this goal is acceptable as a method. Therefore it does not seem feasible to freeze rules of conduct and procedure except for the formulation of some over-all principles. The therapist has to remain flexible in his implementations; he has to adapt the rules of therapy to fit the case rather than to fit the patient into a straitjacket of rules: and, above all, he has to change some aspects that govern social organization and human relations in order to promote the growth of his patients.

Skirting pathology · First doing, then talking

The state of frozen communication, regardless of its origin, is, in the long run, not conducive to the growth of the patient. When the patient has found a status quo which is bearable—a state that is relatively free from anxiety but not necessarily conducive to growth —he has to be helped to abandon this equilibrium and to be prepared for more anxiety and insecurity in order to resume his growth. When the patient becomes opportunistic and forgets his long-term goals, when he does not handle his conflicts but appeases them, it is the task of the therapist to help him break through. As a rule, the patient has to experience several months of such frozen communication to understand its sterile character and to comprehend the security operations which underlie it before he will undertake steps to correct it.

An experienced therapist will probably use a combination of ways to help the patient resume a state of growth, and it does not matter whether we label this "working through" of the transference neurosis, "reconditioning," or "education." The issue at stake is the lack of progress of the patient in working towards self-realization. Understanding of the causes of frozen communication alone will not help the patient unless approaches are found to get him out of the stalemate. First, the therapist will attempt to strengthen those functions of the patient that operate reasonably well. In one case, this means to help the patient to practice ways of communication which are new; in another, it may involve improvement of skills, familiarization with wider social problems, or emphasis upon solitude and meditation. A patient who is well coordinated and loves dancing may take ballet lessons. A teacher who has her credentials but never taught can be encouraged to take a job. A doctor who is interested in human behavior but has no background in social science can be encouraged to take courses, to read, or even to take a psychiatric internship. Once healthy functions have been strengthened, communication about these activities opens up. And once the patient begins to talk, the management of the transference neurosis through interpretation becomes easier.

References

1. Breuer, J. and Freud, S.: *Studies in Hysteria.* 241 p. New York: Nervous and Mental Disease Publishing Co., 1936.

2. Freud, S.: *Beyond the Pleasure Principle.* 90 p. New York: Boni and Liveright, 1922.

3. Freud, S.: *New Introductory Lectures on Psycho-Analysis.* 257 p. New York: Norton, 1933.

4. Freud, S.: *A General Introduction to Psycho-Analysis* (Tr. of rev. ed. by J. Riviere.) 412 p. Garden City: Garden City Publishing Co., 1943.

5. Freud, S.: The dynamics of the transference. Pp. 312–322 in *Collected Papers,* Vol. 2. London: Hogarth Press, 1946.

6. Freud, S.: *The Question of Lay Analysis.* 125 p. New York: Norton, 1950.

7. Macalpine, I.: The development of the transference. Psychoanal. Quart., 19, 501–539, 1950.

8. Redlich, F. C.: The psychiatrist in caricature: an analysis of unconscious attitudes towards psychiatry. Amer. J. Orthopsychiat., 20, 560–571, 1950.

9. Ruesch, J.: Transference reformulated. Acta Psychotherapeutica, Psychosomatica et Orthopaedagogica, Suppl. Vol. 3, 596–605, 1955.

10. Ruesch, J.: *Disturbed Communication.* 337 p. New York: Norton, 1957.

11. Ruesch, J. and Kees, W.: *Nonverbal Communication.* 205 p. Berkeley and Los Angeles: University of California Press, 1956.

12. Silverberg, W. V.: The concept of the transference. Psychoanal. Quart., 17, 303–321, 1948.

13. Spiegel, J. P.: The resolution of role conflict within the family. Psychiatry, 20, 1–16, 1957.

14. Spiegel, J. P.: The family of the psychiatric patient. Pp. 114–149 in *American Handbook of Psychiatry* (S. Arieti, editor). New York: Basic Books, 1959.

15. Sullivan, H. S.: *The Interpersonal Theory of Psychiatry.* 393 p. New York: Norton, 1953.

16. Thompson, C.: Transference as a therapeutic instrument. Psychiatry, 8, 273–278, 1945.

Chapter Ten

Therapeutic Dialectics

IF PLANS of treatment and objectives of psychotherapy correspond to the strategy of warfare, the events in the therapeutic hour more accurately resemble military tactics (6). But unlike the soldier's primarily physical task, the therapist's work deals mostly with symbols and verbal exchange. This activity can be conveniently referred to as dialectics, which Webster defines as the art of disputation, and particularly of discrimination between truth and error in matters of opinion. Although the therapist's method may be distinguishable from that of the lawyer or the philosopher, the use of verbal communication and the prominent place of dialectics nonetheless makes all of these procedures first cousins. The psychiatrist's endeavors, of course, are not geared to competitive argument but to teaching and understanding. By means of the tactics of the psychiatrist, the patient learns ways of communication which in turn enable him to understand and later improve his behavior. But the road may not be an easy one and the psychiatrist does well to familiarize himself with the various dialectic maneuvers of the patient if he wishes to be effective (3).

PINPOINTING

When a patient has accepted the fact that he has a problem but does not fully comprehend the situation, the psychiatrist helps him to pinpoint certain aspects of the picture. Such pinpointing may be directed either at some small but relevant detail or at a view of the over-all picture. Usually the patient labors under the influence of some generalization or abstration which interferes with working out a solution on a practical level. If, for example, the patient blames his marital difficulties upon differences in religious denomination, the psychiatrist can point out some of the difficulties that he had before he married; if he believes that his problems developed because he left his native country, the psychiatrist can call his attention to the difficulties he had before he emigrated. To ask the right kind of question, to view the problem from various standpoints, to discuss possible solutions and implementations is the function of pinpointing. By adding a crucial piece of information at the right level of abstraction at the right moment, the therapist may be able to mobilize information which the patient possessed all along but could not use in its original form. Sometimes the information is too scattered and has to be condensed; or it is too concentrated and has to be diluted. Sometimes the translation of an abstraction into operational terms fulfills the same function. As long as a patient sees only the desired end goal of a development he is not able usually to take the first step. But working through a problem by discussing it step by step often enables the patient to tackle his problem. Whatever the difficulty may be, the therapist has to point his finger at the spot where more intensive work will help to solve the problem.

DOCUMENTATION

When a doctor listens to a patient, he uses the information brought forth in two different ways. First, he takes the words of the patient which purport to refer to certain events and proceeds to reconstruct the situation until he knows what the patient is talking about. Second, he watches the process of communication for evidence of distortion which might influence this reconstruction. Therefore he is constantly on the lookout for evidence to support or correct the picture that the patient presents. He may interrupt the patient by inquiring, "How did you arrive at this . . . ?" or, "What made you conclude that . . . ?" always pointing to the need for evidence. With such comments, the psychiatrist transmits to the patient the idea that words stand for real events and that these can be examined if appropriate and accurate symbols are used to represent them.

The events that occur in the therapist's office can be used as a further means of documentation. If the doctor points to what transpires in the therapeutic session and connects it with similar events in the past, the picture of what is talked about becomes more accurate. The psychiatrist may remark: "Twice before you were late"; or "Do you remember the session that upset you so much that you walked out? Today's session reminds me of that day." On other occasions, the therapist may remember a verbal comment of the patient's and fit it into the ongoing discussion. Progressively then the patient learns to bring more and more evidence in support of his conclusions; and he also will learn that none of these conclusions will stand for long because new evidence perpetually alters the picture.

TRANSLATION

Translation from English into French, from lowbrow into highbrow, from scientific into ordinary language forces the participants to define accurately that which they have in mind. In fitting an idea into various language patterns, the individual discovers that allegedly corresponding terms are based upon different assumptions. The German word "*Erlebnis*" and the English word "experience," for example, are by no means the same. In translating, the individual is forced to define to himself what he really means. What happens in the process of translation is that the idea to which a word refers becomes separated from the verbal codification and that the individual gets a feeling for the technical problems of language. In therapeutic communication, the doctor can make good use of this process. He may, for example, remark to the patient: "I do not quite understand. Please say it in another way"; or he may proceed to reformulate what the patient said and check whether the new version makes more sense to the patient.

A special form of translation is embodied in the analogy. Since study of behavior per se is not part of the daily pursuit of people, patterns often are more easily understood if they are illustrated by means of analogies. Berne (1), for example, advocates the use of the terms "parent," "adult," and "child" to designate superego, ego, and id components in the personality scheme. Others have advocated machine analogies (2), and still others have resorted to aphorisms. The nature of the metaphor does not matter so much as the fact that the juxtaposition of two analogies indicates features which direct expression is incapable of achieving.

REFORMULATION

While translation stays at the same level of abstraction, reformulation involves a greater symbolic change. In summarizing a long-winded account, in pulling together what was said over many interviews the doctor may be capable of giving the patient a somewhat different view. When evaluative statements are reformulated in operational terms, when feelings are tied to what is experienced in the body, and when logical statements are analyzed in terms of the words used, things begin to make sense to the patient. Thus when experiences are formulated in operational, localizable, accessible terms, the magic is taken out of them. For example, to experience anger is one thing; to explain that we feel guilty over anger is another thing. Also, the idea that we have feelings about feelings may be new to the patient and may act as a relief. Alan Gregg wrote: "The hallmarks of a good exposition are that it translates or formulates *the less familiar into terms that are more familiar;* it translates *the obscure into the clear, the variant into the constant, the complex into the simple, the vague into the precise, forms into functions,* and *states into forces.*" (5).

AMPLIFICATION

Almost anybody's view on a subject changes if information becomes more complete. This can be achieved in two ways: by mobilizing heretofore inaccessible experiences inside the patient, by adding new information derived from other people, or by direct observation. As the therapist listens to his patient, he may interject some probing questions which may induce the patient to volunteer information that he never knew he possessed. As the patient talks about her mother, the therapist may say, "I don't yet understand; I have to listen to you some more." In another instance he may respond to what the patient says and add some well established facts—"Are you aware that the majority of people masturbate at some period of their life?" Or he may, for example, give the address of a plastic surgeon after the patient mentions that he has to consult a specialist for a little tumor on his face. Also, the doctor may point to areas where information is missing and urge the patient to inquire, for example, into the conditions for enlisting in the Coast Guard. Pointing to the incompleteness of information, adding information, or inducing the patient to correct false information sets the patient on a path which may continue many years after therapy has been terminated.

CONCRETION AND ABSTRACTION

Rambling, long-winded reports need to be condensed, not only in words but in the mind of the patient. The first step in simplification consists of weeding out the unessential by defining the purpose of the message. The second step requires that separate events be telescoped into one. The third step involves the process of abstraction, which consists in choosing some common aspect out of the multitude of features that are being considered. But abstraction is a one way street; from the concrete, descriptive, and denotative to the abstract, the road is easy; from the abstract back to the concrete, the road is difficult and distortions may occur.

Contradictions can be solved by switching levels of abstraction (7). A contradiction which appears difficult to resolve at one level of abstraction may not appear at another. Although the tiger impresses people by its fury and the cow by its docility, the contradiction in the behavior of mammalian animals can be resolved by saying that both animals show ingestive-destructive qualities—one vis-à-vis other animals and protein, and the other vis-à-vis plants and cellulose. But deduction from the general to the particular and induction from the particular to the general are processes that have to be taught inasmuch as the intellectual processes of the emotionally disturbed usually do not operate satisfactorily. Either emotions cloud clear thinking or logical reasoning rides rough-shod over the organism. With the therapist's help, the patient learns that concretion and abstraction, and the process of switching levels of abstraction, are prime methods of coping with anxiety.

COMPARISON

Comparison is a process that leads to the establishment of similarities and differences. To compare events that occur in several places or at separate times, juxtaposition of statements with slight distortion of place and time characteristics is necessary. In therapy, comparison of the present with the past, of self with others, of one situation with another allows the therapist to state differences or changes that have occurred over time. Comparisons help in establishing the uniqueness of the patient's behavior patterns and the generalities he shares with others. But the therapist has to beware of patients who constantly engage in comparisons to reassure themselves of their strength. In using comparisons the therapist leads the patient to tolerate both similarities and differences without experiencing too much anxiety; he sharpens the patient's ability to observe and to get to the gist of a problem.

CONTRADICTION

Contradiction serves the purpose of challenging the patient's opinions and conclusions. "I have never seen a person die of constipation" was an answer given to a patient who stated that unless regular enemas were given to her baby he was going to get seriously sick. Or a patient who puts great stress on her personal tragedy of twenty years ago can be simply and effectively contradicted by saying, "You know I certainly believe what you have said about the terrible experiences to which you have been exposed; but today, two decades later, you are dwelling on it because you do not want to face recent difficulties. You are anxious about something that happened not very long ago." The therapist has to be very careful to be precise in what he says and avoid any generalizations. The contradiction does not serve the purpose of proving the therapist right; however, it forces the patient to think of alternatives which heretofore he had not considered. The anger that is generated in the process of opposing the other person rallies the patient. He gains more of a sense of identity and has a chance to clarify his ideas.

CONFRONTATION

In this procedure, the therapist does not oppose the patient's opinion with his own but he confronts him with facts. Confrontation is a method frequently used in courts of law where the accused is brought face to face with evidence that seriously challenges his testimony. Confrontation contains an element of aggressiveness and is designed to produce shock. Once the patient has perceived the discrepancy between his report and certain facts, the therapist can go about helping him solve the riddle. For example, if a married woman is confronted by the therapist with the fact that her motherly attitude in public is viewed by her husband as belittling and insulting, the patient has to reconcile these contradictory views. Eventually she may come to recognize that she uses her motherly behavior—although it is perhaps solicited by her husband in privacy—to set him down a notch or two in other people's eyes. Confrontation thus usefully demonstrates discrepancies between intent and effect, between word and action, between stated rules and actual practices. One of the most effective ways of confronting is to gather information from an outside source and to present the patient with the other person's testimony. If the two people are husband and wife, confrontation often helps in mending broken down communication and the two partners may begin to talk (4).

ARGUMENTATION

The process of argumentation consists of formulating reasons, making inductions, drawing conclusions, and applying them to the case in discussion. In the course of an ordinary conversation, then, reasons and proofs are offered to convince the other person of the correctness of the speaker's conclusions. Frequently this will take the form of a debate in which the other person offers counter-arguments in order to demonstrate that the conclusions were incorrect. Although in therapy debate is infrequent, the presentation of an argument—facts and inferences—is a daily occurrence. When the therapist makes a statement, the patient may find flaws in it; paradoxically, for many patients, this is the only way in which they can accept the statement made by the therapist. Eventually some of the therapist's reasoning will rub off on the patient, and instead of debating the issue he may learn to utilize some of the therapist's comments for his own benefit. But the argument of the therapist, like that of the lawyer, has to be airtight. Facts must be lined up with facts; but in contradistinction to the lawyer, the conclusion is left to the patient. At no time should the therapist's superior position and authority supplant missing data. The patient will accept an argument only when the therapist is able to back up the inevitable conclusion with ample and convincing material.

ACCEPTANCE AND NEGATION

Among other things, the patient has to learn to separate fact from fantasy. But often he is incapable of determining what facts and circumstances exist and what is wishful thinking. In many instances, therefore, it is necessary that the psychiatrist accept as a fact that which the patient rejects and, conversely, declare a figment of imagination that which the patient considers reality. If a thirty-five-year-old man, for example, complains of his recently acquired impotence, he says in effect that he cannot accept his present condition. The therapist must convey to him that by accepting the state of affairs as it exists today he does not imply that it will last forever. But unless the patient accepts the existing realities he cannot initiate any remedial measures. If he spends his waking hours dreaming about how it would be if he were potent again, there is really no need for him to do anything about his condition. Acceptance is a state of mind in which a person views the status quo as unalterable, avoiding mental subterfuges, excuses, reasons, or modifications which would explain away the existing conditions. That which exists now is the only thing that a person can cope with. This clear-cut attitude of the psychiatrist focuses the patient's attention upon the facts in his life and conveys to him the idea of coping with the tangible. The doctor demonstrates his acceptance of the patient's reality by reviewing the events of the preceding day or week and by planning for the immediate future. This does not imply an inventory of pathology but a preparation for getting to work tomorrow morning or for paying the tax bill that is due.

There are aspects of his existence which the patient is likely to negate. Negation is a kind of convenient neglect; it does not have the connotation of denial or repression; it is simply non-consideration. A woman may, for example, overlook the fact that because of the demands made upon her by her young children she may have curtailed her social activities, neglected her meetings with friends, and thereby may have lost the recognition she used to receive. Here she negated her need for male recognition which in turn had contributed to her self-esteem and attractiveness; and once those facts are established, the picture becomes more understandable. Negation on the part of the therapist is useful when he wishes to neglect certain aspects of the patient's existence. It may be therapeutic to simply forget for a while that the patient has hay fever or hives. If the therapeutic situation provides for enough understanding and gratification, the patient will tacitly fall in line with the therapist's procedure. And the negation of the symptoms teaches the patient to talk about his problems in living rather than about his bodily health.

INTERJECTION

To be interrupted while speaking becomes more tolerable if the intruder adds something worth while. While in many instances the patient will resent intrusion, he may at other times welcome it; it breaks a performance which he himself may have considered to be undesirable. Interjection thus is a technique which is widely used in psychiatry to interrupt a rambling account, to sidetrack a streak of mockery, or to expose submissive arrogance. Even silence can be terminated by skillful dialectics on the part of the doctor. Interruption tends to provoke acute anxiety—particularly in compulsive persons whose main aim is to finish a statement or an action which is on the way. Here the interruption has to be very gentle until, in the course of therapy, the patient learns to interrupt his own compulsive activities without undue panic.

Interjection serves the purpose of steering the communicative exchange in a different direction. A new topic which is introduced obviously must have some connection with the ongoing subject; otherwise such a move might be interpreted as a hostile act. Frequently the therapist picks up the patient's words to give another slant to the discussion: "My father has a cattle ranch . . ." whereupon the therapist asks, "Do you like to live out in the country?" In this case, the doctor wants to explore the patient's experience in a rural environment rather than to ascertain what his family is doing. Interjection also may serve to focus upon a subject that the patient glosses over lightly. If he says "In 1953 I had three operations," the doctor may interrupt to nail down the details.

DELAY

Perhaps the best known of all dialectic devices is to wait for the patient to proceed. The therapist thus conveys the idea that one can wait without anxiety, and that silence is a perfectly acceptable way of behaving. Waiting is particularly appropriate with the hyperactive person. This attitude sooner or later forces the patient into a discovery of his zest by contrast with the therapist's underactive behavior. To give the patient plenty of scope is a procedure that is borrowed from public relations. Eventually the events speak for themselves.

On occasions it is necessary to postpone some declaration of the patient because he himself is not yet ready to make such a statement. In other instances, action has to be delayed, particularly if the patient tends to manage his frustration by engaging in premature activity. Providing a satisfactory incubation period to delay statement or action is one of the most important procedures of the therapist. He achieves this end in one of several ways. First, he can identify the need of the patient by overtly acknowledging the impending activity. This in itself may obviate the future action altogether. Or the therapist can state that a certain statement or action is needed but that the patient is not ready. "Eventually you will have to leave home, but I believe that the best time will be next spring . . ."

INTERPRETATION

Upon receipt of the patient's message, the therapist has four alternatives. He can remain silent, he can acknowledge the message, he can respond to the nominal or face value of the statement, or he can talk about the message and analyze it. The latter procedure we shall call "interpretation." Absence of response usually is a signal to proceed; acknowledgment indicates that the intent of the speaker has been perceived; response is a sign that the psychiatrist is willing to enter the situation as a participant; interpretation means that the doctor has chosen a particular kind of response which is characteristic of psychoanalysts and dynamic psychotherapists.

Whenever the psychiatrist chooses to be a participant he reacts like an ordinary human being, accepting the presuppositions of the patient's message and avoiding evaluation and interpretation. If, for example, the patient says "May I smoke?" and the doctor replies "By all means, do," the response is explicit and unambiguous. No interpretation is made, and neither participant knows quite what the other is thinking. However, if the therapist chooses to interpret, the patient's message becomes the subject of study. Interpretation therefore consists of connecting the statement of the patient with other information, thus enabling the patient to consider his own actions in a broader perspective. Explicit interpretation restricts the patient's thinking; it coerces action, appeals to the rational functions of the other, and is analytical in nature. A direct response without interpretation increases the adaptive behavior of the other person, is nonanalytical, and appeals to the emotions. The leverage that the psychiatrist gains through interpretation is due to the increase in understanding that it affords, although it rarely has an immediate therapeutic effect.

Interpretation means to connect the past with the present, the inside experience with the outside effect, the self with the group. Such connections produce a feeling of relief in the patient, things begin to make sense, growth is experienced, and the patient endows the therapist with leverage because he made such an experience possible. If an interpretation is directed towards a discussion of content or meaning, the signifying properties of symbols are taken at face value and an attempt is made to reconstruct the original situation. In this case, therefore, the therapist tacitly admits that he was not present when the original events took place and that he has to rely upon somebody else's report. If an interpretation is directed at a discussion of the processes of communication, the therapist emphasizes the speaker's and the receiver's ways of handling symbols rather than the symbols themselves. In discussing the patient's relationship to the symbols he uses, the therapist can rely upon first hand observations collected in the therapeutic hour.

When a therapist shifts the discussion from the overt content of a statement to the motivation of the speaker, he increases anxiety and thereby changes the speed of mental functions. Conversely, by acknowledging the content or the "what" of a message he produces a feeling of gratification in the patient and slows him down. Any time the therapist wishes to put the seal of the unalterable upon a statement, he has merely to take it at face value; if he wishes to render the situation more dynamic, he shifts the emphasis to whatever lies behind a statement. This emphasis speeds up the patient because he has to be in readiness for anything new the discussion may bring. The content becomes relative and the past ceases to be burdensome because the patient discovers that the way of remembering or telling alters considerably the purportedly unalterable facts of the past. This discovery acts as relief. For example, when the patient relates with deep emotion the death of his father, the therapist may comment, "Should there be a connection between the memory of the loss of your father and my going on a long vacation?" This comment pulls the patient out from the past, puts him right into the present, and the painfulness of the past loss is reduced and the present frustration increased. But the present can be handled while the past remains unalterable.

ANALYSIS AND SYNTHESIS

Analysis leads from larger to smaller units, from more complex to simpler levels of organization, from larger time segments to smaller ones. Analysis may mean to break down an event into its smallest constituent parts or to trace it to its source of origin. The process of synthesis proceeds in the reverse way and gives a macroscopic picture of the constituent parts and a chronological account of various phases of development. Analysis helps the patient to clarify foggy notions; synthesis, in turn, is gratifying because it puts things together that did not fit into a pattern before. There are people who talk in big terms, who tend to see the larger connections, who neglect somewhat the detail; here, analysis rather than synthesis is in place. Compulsion neurotics, in contrast, who are unable to focus upon larger patterns and configurations, have to be steered towards the understanding of relationships and larger Gestalten; here synthesis is needed.

In therapy, analysis comes first and synthesis follows later. Only after the patient has understood many of his dreams, has recalled many details of his biography, or has understood the present as it evolved from the past is he ready to synthesize disjointed pieces of information. Preparation for integration is analogous to the learning of skills; detailed movements have to be practiced separately until they can be made up into a more complex pattern. In football practice, for example, tackling, running, and blocking are practiced separately; but during a game these maneuvers follow one another fluidly. And everybody is familiar with Sherlock Holmes sitting in his study and putting little pieces of apparently unrelated material together. The result of such synthesis is a sensation of making things fit, which in turn produces pleasure and relaxation.

Synthesis thus is not synonymous with interpretation. In interpretation it is the psychiatrist who puts one piece together with another piece. In synthesis it is the patient who coordinates, and all the psychiatrist does is to occasionally point to an element that the patient has collected before but may have overlooked adding to the present puzzle. Or when the patient is groping for an answer, all the psychiatrist has to do is to point out that his information is incomplete and that he has to search for more information. If the patient learns to give himself time, he has gained immensely. Because as life progresses he will join more and more pieces together.

References

1. Berne, E.: Ego states in psychotherapy. Amer. J. Psychother., 11, 293–309, 1957.

2. Colby, K. M.: *Energy and Structure in Psychoanalysis.* 154 p. New York: Ronald Press, 1955.

3. Feldman, S. S.: *Mannerisms of Speech and Gestures in Everyday Life.* 301 p. New York: International Universities Press, 1959.

4. Garner, H. H.: A confrontation technique used in psychotherapy. Amer. J. Psychother., 13, 18–34, 1959.

5. Gregg, A.: On the reading of medical literature. U. S. Armed Forces med. J., 7, 1596–1604, 1956.

6. Masserman, J. H.: *Principles of Dynamic Psychiatry.* 322 p. Philadelphia: Saunders, 1946.

7. Ruesch, J.: *Disturbed Communication.* 337 p. New York: Norton, 1957.

Chapter Eleven

The Various Stages of Therapy

THE BEGINNING

THE "HOW" OF COMMUNICATION COMES FIRST;
THE "WHAT" COMES LATER

THE INITIAL PHASE of therapy is devoted to the process of getting acquainted. This involves exploration of the patient's ways of communication, elimination of emergencies so that work can go on smoothly, and waiting for the transference neurosis to develop.

The initial form and content of therapeutic communication is dictated by the patient. The first contact has to be made through whatever media and channels will reach the patient—conversation, play, or work. The patient chooses the language and the psychiatrist attempts to reply in the same mode. Frequently it is necessary to abandon conventional ways of communication because the chance to establish corrective feedback may be greater with another approach. For example, helping the catatonic patient when he dresses and assisting him with his socks may be more therapeutic than fifty interviews. Therefore the therapist's mode of response has to be varied and flexible, and no formula can be established which is valid for all cases. But once the therapist has discovered a type of interaction which will induce the patient to reply, the foundations for future exchange have been laid. Eventually the patient will get used to the pleasure of being responded to and will actively seek people in the hope of obtaining satisfaction from more diversified sources.

If therapy begins with restricted and selective communication and the procedure is successful, it ends with unrestricted, gratifying communication which covers a variety of topics. The selectivity begins with the diagnosis of the patient's communicative difficulties and the organization of remedial exercises. The patient who is fuzzy in his thinking needs pinpointing and sharpening; the individual who is too concrete has to be oriented towards more general considerations. The patient who does not respond must be given the opposite treatment; his presence and his messages have to be acknowledged over and over again. Where overconcern with people prevents the patient from recognizing what goes on inside of him, reinforcement of the internal experience is in place; if the patient is concerned exclusively with himself, the effects of his actions upon others have to be documented and focused upon. The doctor's corrective actions may be initiated by a concrete statement; but eventually it is the repetitiousness of his performance and his insistence which exert a therapeutic effect.

Correction of faulty ways of communication in the initial phase often produces the impression that therapeutic communication neglects content. The patient may resent the fact that the exchange between him and the doctor does not follow any logical pattern. This, of course, is intentional. Content can only be discussed meaningfully if perception, evaluation, and expression function properly and feedback is not distorted. For example, there is no sense in discussing with a highly self-centered individual the merits of his solipsistic view of the world; but he can be confronted with the effect he produces on others. Thus the communication therapist steers away from consideration of content, in the early phases of therapy, and utilizes the patient's productions to include him in a flexible exchange.

But when the therapist does consider content, he focuses upon concrete problems of living. The fact that the patient needs to have funds to pay for therapy, that he has to adjust to whomever he lives with, that he has to pursue an occupation that interests him— all that has to be discussed early. The patient is trained to take up in each interview that which happened yesterday and to focus on the problems of today. Discussion of yesterday's events makes the patient aware that alcoholism centers around the first swallow, that debts are a problem of the first dollar spent, and that acquiring a mate is a problem of the first smile. Over and over again, the patient is brought back to these concrete tasks, and only when he is capable of observing, reporting, and evaluating his daily behavior is he allowed to turn his sights to events of the remote past.

THE EAGER AND THE SHY

Most patients are overwhelmed by their own problems and spill them out readily when talking to the therapist. They present their complaints, ideas, and theories about their illness, and they may blame others for their distress. In these initial phases, the doctor listens—occasionally pinpointing one problem or another—until he gets a clearer idea of the central problem of the patient. In the process of collecting material, the therapist has to beware of too fast a pace, lest the patient become frightened. Sometimes, therefore, the task is one of slowing down the patient by entering into a discussion of overt problems and thereby directing attention away from unconscious or covert problems. Before a good relationship has been established, it is bad therapy to have unconscious problems emerge too soon. People have a hierarchical order in which they discuss problems, moving from the general to the more specific and personal. But many patients, unaccustomed to human relations in a twosome situation, try to become intimate too fast, disregarding their own apprehensions and getting themselves into a situation in which they feel uncomfortable. On occasions, the opposite is true. The patient may have nothing to say, and in these cases the therapist may have to cut through the obvious to get to the more covert problems of the patient. This is achieved by talking about motives, intentions, wishes, and all the things that commonly are not talked about.

In the early phases of therapy, the therapist has to beware of maintaining too great a distance. With some warmth, abreaction may be facilitated and the ice broken, whereupon the patient gains confidence. The patient is shown that everybody has conflicts and that ambivalence—even about therapy—is a conflict that has to be coped with. Catharsis and abreaction serve the purpose of clearing the atmosphere and setting up the conditions which are necessary for later more systematic working through.

Some patients overwhelm the doctor with inquiries. Here are some samples:

"What do you want me to say?"

"I read that others lie on a couch."

"Don't you want to hear about my dreams?"

"I have a diary that I want to show you."

"I have kept careful notes about my sex life."

"Would you like to call up Dr. X? He examined me a year ago and said that there was something wrong with my hip."

"Should I talk with my wife about these things? She is very eager to know what happens here."

"How long do you think it will take us to get anywhere?"

"Which school of therapy do you belong to?"

"Can you hypnotize me to get the secrets out of me?"

"What shall I read? What is my homework?"

"I hear that Mrs. X is being seen four times a week. If you see me twice, does that mean that you use another method?"

The therapist does well to take each of the questions at face value and answer it to the best of his ability. There is no sense in explaining at the beginning of therapy that some of these questions are manipulative in character and that they merely serve the purpose of structuring the situation in the desired way. There is no sense in explaining that therapy is based on growth, learning, and a change of attitude, because initially the patient cannot comprehend what is taking place. Most patients are eager to familiarize themselves with the method they have heard so much about, and the best way to do this is to take their inquiries seriously. But the therapist should beware of discussing the philosophy of therapy, of explaining the differences between schools of thought, and of speculating on how therapy works. To cope with the next day's and the next week's problems is the task of the moment, and explanations should be confined to the immediate task ahead.

MANIPULATORS AND TALKERS

Not necessarily during the initial interview but perhaps later, the interviewer may be faced with patients who adhere to particular modes of communication. Although these may not deserve the label of disturbances, they nevertheless may not fit with the interviewer's ideas of free exchange, or they may affect the therapist in that his training or natural qualifications have not prepared him to cope with such approaches.

The patient who continuously asks questions is relatively easy to deal with. His questions are reflected. If the patient asks, "Do you advise me to quit my job?" the reply is "What do you think about it?" If a question such as "Why are you always wearing the same necktie?" bears upon the psychiatrist's dress and is not relevant to the patient's problem, the reply may be "Does it bother you?"

The patient who makes announcements and resolutions has to be coped with in another way. His statements *ad eternitatem* have to be reduced to something that bears upon the present. The patient's statement that "My wife and I resolved never to fight again" may be countered with "And when did the next fight come?" Similar are the promises of the alcoholic who says "I shall never take a drink again" and shortly thereafter lifts the bottle to his lips. In its timelessness, such a resolution bears upon the intent of the speaker and not upon his actions. By using words which refer to the future, he avoids coping with the present. Also, the declarations of intention often serve to alleviate the guilt feelings which have been engendered through drinking or enjoying some other forbidden fruit. By reciting the correct principle, by promising and asserting his good will, the patient purges himself and is free to pursue his old vice anew.

The patient who threatens the psychiatrist is more difficult to deal with. Threats can be crude and blunt or they can be subtle and complex. In the first case they are designed to frighten; in the second, to stimulate unresolved conflicts of the therapist. To be the object of bribe, temptation, and blackmail is for the psychiatrist part of his day's work. One of the most frequent threats is a challenge of the doctor's skills, whereby the patient says, "I have been coming to you now for six months and I do not see much change; perhaps your method is not suitable for me, or maybe I should go to somebody else." At this point, there are several ways of steering communication into a different channel. One is to say, "Are you threatening me?" or "Do you expect me to justify myself?" Another way of responding is to carry out a little calculation: "You are now thirty years old; you have lived about eleven thousand days, or 264,000 hours. If we subtract one third of that for sleeping, we still arrive at something like 176,000 waking hours. You can hardly expect patterns that took that long to be established to be undone in fifty or one hundred hours."

Some patients are particularly apt to point out to the therapist that he is caught between the devil and the deep blue sea. Suicidal patients, for example, may say, "If you hopitalize me it means that you don't trust me, but then again I might commit suicide if you don't." This "double-bind," as Bateson calls it (1), is something that the psychiatrist has to learn to cope with, inasmuch as the patient may wish to stimulate the doctor's ambivalence and to reduce his decision-making ability. The therapist has to try to stay free of these influences by responding not to the manipulative tendencies of the patient but to the underlying feeling of loneliness or depression.

Patients who jump from subject to subject and expand on irrelevant details have to be educated to stick to the topic. To teach a patient to focalize his thoughts is beneficial for the scatterbrain. It is achieved by always coming back to the main topic, patiently and without disrespect. The patient can be confronted with the fact that it is hard for the therapist to follow him in his flight of ideas and if he would make an effort it would be a little easier. Also, the tolerance of therapists varies. Some can tolerate people who "run off at the mouth" and consider irrelevant problems, while others are less tolerant. Under no circumstances, however, should scattering be mistaken for free association. The latter method was designed to help the rigid and logical thinker, who even at best can hardly be detracted from his central theme, to loosen up.

There are patients who say that they have nothing to report. By not having anything to say, the patient usually tries to force the psychiatrist to "do something." In these situations, the therapist's answer may be, "Finally there are no more emergencies and no more pressing questions which need an answer so that from now on we can study your daily behavior patterns." At this point, the psychiatrist may comment on the patient's anxiety about not having any ideas, thoughts, or feelings. The patient is informed that to have no feelings is as relevant as to have feelings; and as soon as the patient sees that every person always thinks or feels something, he is likely no longer to blackmail the psychiatrist into activity.

There are patients who use abstract language—particularly compulsive talkers, intellectualizers, and theoreticians (7). Scientists in particular are likely to have over-all systems with which they attempt to find answers to all their problems. Connotative words and abstract statements do not contribute to an understanding of the actual events that the patient is talking about, and he has to be educated to use denotative terms. If the patient says, "I feel rejected," the psychiatrist may counter with, "Tell me when this feeling arose—on what occasion, in whose presence." If the patient says, "I do not like my mother," the psychiatrist has to explore not only the external circumstances but the internal feelings of the patient as well. In the end, it may turn out that he is very attached to his mother and resents his loss of freedom. The opposite situation arises in patients who are so specific that they are incapable of perceiving larger Gestalten. The therapist approaches this difficulty by summarizing all the ramifications of a problem, by condensing content, and by expressing the issue in connotative terms. Eventually the patient will follow suit.

There are patients who make excessive use of value judgments. One person may say, "I am no good at this job," or "My wife is a terrible cook." Here the task is to translate the value judgment into operational terms. So the psychiatrist inquires, "At what time does your wife enter the kitchen? When does she shop? Is she economical in her purchases? Does she select dishes that you like? Is the dinner ready in time?" With such replies, the patient is made aware that a formulation of the technical aspects of a problem may contain the seeds of its solution.

There are patients who omit certain aspects in their reports. A patient may talk about a party he attended and about the people who were there but omits to mention his own activity, feeling, or thought. Conversely there are other patients who concern themselves entirely with their thoughts, feelings, sensitivities, and misgivings, and one hardly learns about the situation, the other people, or the conversation that took place. In such cases, the patient has to be trained to include both self and others in his report. The patient harbors enough information which can be ferreted out to complete the picture. Consciously, he then can go about to include in future considerations the aspects he tends to omit.

EXPERIENCE MATTERS MORE THAN FACT-FINDING

At the beginning of therapy, the patient may list his symptoms, mention his difficulties with other people, describe some fears or concerns, and perhaps demonstrate his anxiety. Gradually he has to be educated towards reporting his total experience at any one moment. If the patient begins by talking about the political situation of today, the doctor may call his attention to the fact that he has made some accessory movements with his foot. The purpose of this exercise is to give the patient to understand that an appreciation of the political situation and its impact upon the patient can be achieved only if he also considers his bodily reaction. The doctor has to convey to the patient that anger, for example, changes the appraisal of the political situation and that all people have to learn about the impact of emotions upon their thinking.

When a patient says, "I have nothing new to report but I can tell you about yesterday's baseball game," while being near tears with a slight tremor, the doctor might reply, "At the moment you are very anxious and you try to hide it. Perhaps you and I can sit here for a while and find out what this anxiety is all about." The earlier we admit that in many instances we cannot run away from anxiety, the easier it becomes to tolerate it. The history of many patients reveals that anxiety may disappear when the person is busy, meets a lot of people, and talks about irrelevant things. If, during the interview, the patient says, "I almost feel like bursting; I've got to do something," the doctor might reply, "Have you ever talked to anyone about these feelings?" and the answer usually is "No." At the end of the hour, the patient may have gained composure because of his experience that anxiety becomes more bearable if faced and talked about.

If the term "experience" refers to the insider's view of events, the word "reality" denotes the consensus of a number of people who attribute to it a concrete counterpart in the outer world. The therapeutic emphasis upon experience rather than speculation about a hypothetical reality does not mean that the patient should not familiarize himself with the opinions of his contemporaries. People with whom he lives such as mate, parents, and children reach certain conclusions which have an impact upon him. The patient has to be able to see himself as others see him; he has to explore the conventions that govern his human relations and the traditions and values that shape his and other people's behavior. This is the social reality.

Experience is the total state of the organism felt at a given moment. Experience cannot be dissected into words, although some aspects can be discussed. The patient thus has to be trained to understand that the psychiatrist is not interested in the description of an event as somebody else might have seen it—the exact details of an accident, for example—but rather in the patient's experiences at that moment. However, the psychological reality—or what goes on in the patient—has to be correlated with the physical and social reality—or what goes on around the patient. We thus have two kinds of things to work with: first we have the inner experience as related through words; and then we have the consensus about these events, which we call reality. A complicated relationship arises when experience is aligned with experience and thence compared to reality.

It is surprising to see how often people, particularly patients, ignore social reality. Some are oblivious to the fact that they do not blend into the landscape, as it were; others ignore conventions, shirk responsibilities, or take on duties which are not theirs. The therapist, familiar with the locality and the people among whom the patient lives, has to steer the discussion in such a way that the patient becomes aware of these social forces. It is not the doctor's task to confront the patient and to act as the representative of society. Without spoiling the therapeutic relationship, the therapist can call attention to some areas which need clarification. I remember a mother of two children, the wife of a professional man, who slept until after noon and left her young children to answer the telephone. This they did by announcing that mother was asleep and could not be disturbed. It had not occurred to the members of this family that such behavior struck others as peculiar, since among middle-class Anglo-Saxon housewives this was hardly the custom. As the therapist, I suggested that the patient should talk with other women, particularly about when they got up and who answered the phone. These discussions made the patient aware of the impact she had upon others and called attention to the damage she inflicted upon her husband and her children.

SEPARATING THE WHEAT FROM THE CHAFF

As the therapist begins to work with the patient, the information that he receives and the observations he makes will eventually crystallize and fall into distinct patterns.

First he will be concerned with the evironmental situation that the patient has to adapt to. If the patient has chosen a naval career or if he is an archeologist or an anthropologist, he will lead the life of a nomad. He will travel to different places without being able to take his family with him. At other times he will take them along and then his children will deplore the fact that every so often they have to relinquish their friends, give up what became dear to them, and start all over again. Then there are those who have chosen unusual environmental surroundings to live in—the desert, the high mountains, or an island. We also find persons whose time schedules differ from those of others—the entertainer, the night watchman. And then again we have the people whose life experiences are seasonal—the fisherman or the resort operator. In all of these examples, the external life situation is relatively unalterable and the patient has to adapt to it if he wishes to continue to live as he has. In order to determine the patient's adaptability, the doctor has to familiarize himself with two aspects: the rigidity and duration of the patient's behavior patterns and the changes that occur naturally in the external situation.

The autonomous psychic processes that make up the inner life of the patient are the next concern of the doctor. He will explore the nature of the patient's ideals; the rigidity of his conscience; the awarenesses of his blind spots; the hopes, wishes, and unfulfilled ambitions; and all those features which are relatively independent of the surroundings. These processes are not conceived of as a static, compartmentalized structure but as ongoing developments which have been predetermined in part by previous experiences. The autonomous behavior is predictable, relatively independent of outside situations, and not always adaptive. If the patient is feeble-minded or exceedingly intelligent, submissive or dominant, over-powered by his conscience or irresponsible, his behavior patterns will continue to exist irrespective of the situation.

If adaptive processes are responses to the external reality situation and autonomous processes are responses to the internal environment, there exists a third type of process which is aimed at a change of the existing reality. These processes, subsumed under the heading of control, imply the exertion of effort and the intent to influence self and others. If the patient owns a big and powerful dog who attacks the mailman and the delivery boy, he will have to control the dog, train him, or get rid of him. If he wishes to successfully race a sail boat he will have to keep the boat in tip-top condition.

If he wishes to raise flowers or crops, he will have to control soil, pests, irrigation, and other features. And if the patient does not control the features that are controllable, he obviously gets himself into trouble.

After the doctor has obtained a clearer idea about the patient's intrapsychic autonomic functioning, the things he has to adapt to, and the features which he has to control, he will attempt to illustrate these three ways of functioning. This, then, brings the doctor to the point where he will meet certain features in the patient which he has to accept as unalterable. These, of course, appear to the therapist as limitations of his own effectiveness. He thus makes an inventory of the features which can be changed and of those that cannot. In one case, this may mean an increase in the patient's adaptability; in another, it may consist of strengthening his autonomous character features; and in a third it will result in a control of the environment.

THE FIRST STALEMATE

After the patient has gone through the phase of getting acquainted and after the doctor has explored the past history of the patient, there comes a period in which everything seems to proceed smoothly, only to give way soon to what might be called the first stalemate. The patient has given out much conscious information, the relationship to the therapist is consolidated, attitudinal organization of feelings has begun, and repetitiousness of ways of communication has set in. The first resistance, which signals the beginning of the transference neurosis, is usually accompanied by the patient's wish to change something in the standing arrangement.

At this point, the art of therapy consists of retaining the patient in treatment. It is too early to discuss the relationship to the therapist, and it is too late to discontinue therapy. The patient intuitively shies away from the involvements of the transference neurosis (5) and goes through the motions of proving that he can get along without therapy. He may view the first stalemate as boredom; he may declare that he is well, that the therapist has nothing to offer, that therapy is not for him. Or he may proposition the therapist— "Why do we talk about all this nonsense when we could have a much more pleasant time together?" Or he may ask, "When am I going to have the revelations I read about in books?" Regardless of the specific version, the patient experiences a feeling of stagnation and the therapist does well to call his attention to the repetitiousness of his experience, reassuring him that this occurs in most cases when therapy progresses properly. The therapist has to convey to the patient that his behavior and his experience of a stalemate is not an artifact or an undesirable by-product but a kind of experience which forms the very essence of what occurs in therapy. The doctor can go on to explain that in daily life a person is likely to force, at this point, a change in the social relationship to others. He may seek better company, he may withdraw, or he may change the degree of intimacy. The physician has to explain that inasmuch as the patient is in therapy, he now has an opportunity to look at those inner events which urge him to manipulate relationships. Once the patient has accepted this phenomenon as part of the program, he usually ceases to be apprehensive about the consequences of this peculiar relationship to the therapist.

As the transference neurosis develops, the therapist does well to consider all the silent partners in the therapeutic situation. The patient's mate, his children, parents, siblings, boy-friends, mistresses, and sometimes his employers are to be considered here. And neither should the doctor's family be neglected. As the patient becomes fortified in his position vis-à-vis the therapist, he may try to win the therapist as an ally against one of his relatives or to make the relative an ally against the therapist. It is well to remember that when a significant experience is worked through in therapy there are usually more than just two persons involved. In the original family situation, for example, a girl may ally herself with her younger sister against her older brother in order to oppose mother, while at the same time she may vie for father's attention and compete with her younger sister. In whichever role the therapist is cast, he will have to cope with the silent partners that the patient unconsciously includes in the situation.

Early the patient's attention can be called to the fact that his feelings towards his relatives are likely to change. He is instructed that during the beginning of therapy no major decisions about changes in family status, occupation, or residence should be undertaken unless an emergency occurs. Where to live and with whom, and what to do are problems which can be solved in due course of time but not at the moment when the transference neurosis develops. The patient thus is familiarized with the idea that although he and the therapist may sit alone in the room, there are many others who await with eagerness the outcome of the encounter. Sometimes the doctor has to talk to the patient's relatives. They can be warned that some rough times may be ahead but that the patient's experiences in therapy do not necessarily reflect his permanent attitude vis-à-vis others. On some occasions, the doctor's relatives may be involved. Jealousy concerning the therapist's wife, husband, children, dogs, cats, or flowers may not only occupy the fantasy of the patient but also become the concern of the patient's relatives. Interviews with the patient's silent partners will enable the therapist to prevent wholesale distortions.

UNDER WAY

Connecting the past with the present · Painstaking work · The real and the imagined · Internalization of therapeutic experience · Acceptance of pathology leads to its elimination · Need for concomitant life experiences · Lacunae in life experience · Optimum relation of experience and therapy · The therapist's delusions of omnipotence · Acting out · Commitment to a style of living

WORKING AT, THROUGH, AND BEYOND

The middle phase of therapy is concerned with the exploration of the unconscious, the acceptance of existing conflicts, the understanding of resistances, and the struggling with the transference neurosis—in brief, with working through. If one translates these analytic concepts into operational terms, one finds that in the middle phase of therapy communication revolves around very specific topics in which past events are equated with present happenings and unresolved experiences are relived in the therapeutic situation.

By this time, the patient usually has accepted the therapeutic procedure without questioning it. He has become aware that learning is slow, and he has had glimpses of what progress means so that he will work for more of the same. Symptoms and initial complaints usually have disappeared or have given way to new ones. The relationship to the therapist has become stabilized and therapy has become part of the patient's existence. In terms of hours, the middle phase may be reached after twenty or thirty hours in one case or after one or two hundred hours in another case. The initial phase will last longer if the patient is infantile or psychotic.

The "working through" phase is characterized by detailed work. Broad generalizations, speculations about the future, and anecdotal reconstructions of the past are avoided in favor of painstaking work. Daily events, dreams, or episodes of the past are brought to light, scrutinized, and, as it were, collected in order to be integrated with other experiences that have not been discussed as yet. The patient may yearn to put the various pieces of information together, but he must have patience and accept the uncertainty inherent in incomplete knowledge. The middle phase is a period of education, and that which was traumatic and repetitive has to be undone. That which was not learned at home has to be acquired now. And since unlearning and learning cannot be accomplished by rote but by experience only, therapy takes time. Just as a baby takes a year to learn to walk and several years to learn to speak, so does the patient take time to get over such things as rejection and lack of self respect. But the doctor also will meet insuperable difficulties. There will be problems the patient works at indefinitely without getting through, and then again there will be problems that can be solved and the patient can move on. The principle has to be kept in mind that the doctor does well to develop first those areas that are underdeveloped. As the patient gains more satisfaction and confidence through growth, the conflicts can be handled with more success.

When two people meet, they perceive each other not only in terms of their momentary impressions but also in terms of their own expectations which are set by past experiences. As time goes on, the influence of past experiences recedes in favor of more recent impressions. In the therapeutic situation, the therapist relies upon this phenomenon in that he knows that the patient's experiences gained in therapy are superimposed on the traces of earlier experiences. Eventually the experiences shared by doctor and patient establish a common bond and the patient begins to see in the therapist a friend, a helper, a person who sets limitations and abides by rules, a person who is permissive on the one hand and firm on the other, a man or a woman who is living and has a family, friends, and outside interests. It is this realistic contact with a functioning human being which gradually replaces the patient's attributions, projection, and assumptions which previously distorted his view of the personality of the psychiatrist.

As therapy progresses, the resolution of the transference neurosis creates a new bond between doctor and patient. Since whatever happened in therapy was real and took place between two living beings, neither doctor nor patient can whisk away these events by simply saying, "It was just therapy." Both patient and doctor have to accept the fact that their cumulative body of experience was modified by what they experienced in common. A sort of attachment, positive or negative, therefore will remain until such time as the doctor's experience of the patient wanes because new and more recent cases occupy his attention and the patient's experience of the therapist dims because he has formed new attachments in life. The patient's memory of the therapist's existence has to recede before the patient can function well. The therapist, as it were, supplies the corrective experiences. These experiences of course can never remain the mainstay of a person's existence. As long as they do, the patient is not well.

In the initial phase of therapy, current events cannot be related to the past experiences of the patient because the doctor is unfamiliar with the case and the patient himself may have difficulties in recalling certain pertinent events. This set of circumstances changes in the middle phase. Without consulting his written notes, the therapist can mobilize the mental notes he made during many sessions with the patient. He may remember that on two or three occasions the patient was late or canceled an appointment and that the cancellation was always preceded by a dispute in his family. If events happen repeatedly, the therapist can safely assume that similar events occurred a long time before therapy began. After his discovery of situations which are similar in terms of context, motivation, and effect, the psychiatrist can superimpose one episode upon another. This condensation enables the patient to recognize all the ramifications of his actions and he obtains a richer insight into what is going on, particularly if these behavior patterns occur again. When repetitive events are telescoped into a construct, they are assigned a permanent place in the memory of the patient. This procedure enables the patient to come face to face with his own neurotic behavior.

If the patient experiences behavior as automatic and beyond voluntary control, he may realize his inability to correct it. The acceptance of the repetitive behavior and recognition of its unalterable character lead the patient to concentrate on behavior patterns that are non-repetitive. This results in growth which in turn may obviate the previously so necessary repetition of behavior patterns.

THE PRIVATE LIFE OF THE PATIENT

In the middle phase of therapy, one important prerequisite for improvement is the true life experience. Unless the patient can experiment and test reality in the areas of his difficulties, no amount of insight, discussion, and reconstruction is capable of altering repetitive behavior patterns. If a man tends to quarrel with his sweetheart or wife, isolation from women will not teach him how to get along with girls; and if somebody has difficulties at work, staying home will certainly not resolve the occupational dilemma. Here we meet one of the realistic limitations of therapy in that its success is dependent upon concomitant life experiences. If a young man who never held a job before is faced with the prospect of earning a living, the therapist can be instrumental in discussing this task. If the job prospects are commensurate with the age of the patient and his past record, he probably will pass with flying colors. But the therapist has to help the patient not only to expose himself to those experiences which are commensurate with his age, sex, and social role, but to catch up the best he can with those experiences he has never had.

But the problem is not always that simple. If a child was sick during his grade-school years, perhaps paralyzed by polio, he obviously missed the play that served to acquire coordination, and he probably will never be able to completely compensate for this missing experience. Or the teen-aged boy who is ill at the time when boys meet girls may have to begin at the age of twenty-eight to meet members of the opposite sex. A woman of forty-five who has never been married is likely to approach members of the opposite sex as she did her high-school sweethearts. When her romantic notions are not reciprocated, she is likely to be disappointed and to withdraw, remaining unaware of the fact that romantic love is an experience of youth. This patient, for example, may believe that she can find an unmarried man in his middle forties. But people who have lived for nearly half a century have commitments, attachments, and past experiences, and furthermore a man of forty-five is not likely to marry an old maid. Thus the therapist can sometimes, although very poorly, compensate for the missing life experience by focusing upon the problem, commenting and explaining, suggesting reading, and favoring discussion with others who may have similar problems. But the lacunae in life experience remain.

There is reason to believe that the so-called "successes" in therapy are cases in which the concomitant life experiences were favorable and therefore helped the working through of the problems discussed in the doctor's office. When either the nature of the pathology or external circumstances prevent experience in action, therapy remains a symbolic exercise. Words, not having a counterpart in experience, leave the patient untouched. When the patient cannot coordinate therapeutic communication with life experiences, he may misuse the relation to the therapist. Therapy itself can become a substitute for outside experience, and the patient then clings to the doctor year in and year out, incapable of intense experience except for the few moments when he is together with his doctor. We must recognize, of course, that such defects in the ability to experience exist and that some patients may have to see a psychiatrist for a good part of their lives.

In order to encourage concomitant life experiences, the doctor must cultivate a special attitude. If he views everything that the patient experiences as being causally related to what happens in therapy, he becomes the victim of a delusion of omnipotence. It is absolutely absurd to assume that because a patient spends two hours a week with a doctor the remaining 166 hours should be entirely steered by what happened in these two hours. Though one cannot deny that this may be the case, it is highly improbable. If the patient is exposed to such a delusion of omnipotence of the therapist (8, 10), he may react in either of two ways. He may be fascinated by it, submit to it, and participate in a *folie a deux;* or he may rebel, which behavior is frequently labeled "acting out." In this case, the patient goes to great lengths to demonstrate that the therapist does not and cannot control his—the patient's—extracurricular activities. Such acting out may be interpreted as a message to the therapist, and the only appropriate response is for the therapist to give up his omnipotent ideas. As soon as he acknowledges the independence of the patient and the limitation of his own power, the troublesome acting out usually stops.

Acting out can be minimized if the therapist responds in terms of both content and manner to the other person's needs and refrains from superimposing upon the patient ways of communication that are alien and ideas that do not correspond to reality. Almost all patients go through some form of acting out during therapy. If action behavior is not related to omnipotent ideas of the therapist, it may be the result of the doctor's inability to cope with action language. But once he has handled acting out successfully, the patient usually begins to cooperate with the plan of therapy.

As the patient pursues independent life experiences, he begins to commit himself to certain viewpoints, roles, and courses of action. Just as ability is mostly the result of repetition and elbow grease, so is the value of existence tied to what a person has done with himself. Most patients, however, do not know the economies inherent in commitment. They do not know that once a girl has decided to become a doctor certain avenues are open to her and others are closed; and once she has taken this choice, she does not need to make other decisions. In the middle phase of therapy, then, the therapist works with the patient on the latter's style of living. This task may range from a consideration of dress to a choice of reading material and from dancing lessons to a discussion of the budget. To be committed to a kind of life means to have made some choices which in turn will prejudice future choices. A woman of forty has to reconcile herself to the fact that if she has not married up to now, the chances are that she will continue on her maiden path. In accepting these facts and committing herself to a course of action in which she will have to rely on her own earning ability as well as her capacity to live alone, she will have undertaken the first step towards more gratifying living. To make a commitment does not mean that a person has to stick to it forever. Commitment means that under the prevailing circumstances the path chosen is the one that suits the individual best, for just as long as it makes sense.

TOWARDS THE END

Self-correction begins to work · Experience replaces value judgments · Substituting another person for the therapist · Successive therapists · Multiple therapists · Therapeutic consultation · Diminishing returns · Gradual rather than sudden termination · The patient makes the decision · "Let's be friends"

The later phases of therapy are characterized by the fact that some conflicts have been worked through so that various aspects of the patient's existence appear to be more consistent. Correction by the other person is accepted and self-correction begins to work. Since both patient and doctor can look back upon many hours of hard work, a common bond has been formed. The patient's view of the therapist is no longer self-determined but is arrived at by consensual validation. Events of daily life are taken up and discussed with the assumption that in anybody's life there exist difficulties which have to be solved. The patient feels free to plot his own course, not in secrecy but in consultation with the therapist.

By now the patient has learned that he may oppose and contradict without asking the permission of the therapist. Therefore oppositional behavior diminishes and transference attachments usually give way to some realistic bonds which are based upon the gratification obtained from the ongoing exchange. And just as children outgrow their parents, so does the patient grow beyond the help of the therapist.

The date of termination of therapy is usually set by arbitrary means. Vacations, beginning of a new year, moving away, shortage of funds, and similar reasons instigate a separation from the therapist. But leaving the therapist does not terminate the work. If by now the patient has reached a state of functioning in which correction and self-correction operate satisfactorily, he still has to make up for the many years of his life in which correction did not operate successfully. As he gains life experiences in areas where he was avoidant, observes things he did not see before, and carries out actions that he previously left uncompleted, the patient becomes capable of acquiring a system of evaluation which will enable him to replace the value scales provided by his elders with standards which derive from his own personal experiences. It may well take two or three years before this process is completed and the effect of therapy comes into full force.

INTERMITTENT THERAPY

Some of my patients have, after an absence of many years, returned for a short review. They address me less in the capacity of therapist and more as a person who knows them well and who has had an understanding of their long-term development. And without feeling relegated to the role of the patient who struggles with transference and transference neurosis, they discuss current developments. Often in two or three sessions the problems and conflicts that have been worked through earlier and have been put to test in a life situation can be clarified. The new experience fills a certain gap in understanding, and all the patient needs is some help in putting the pieces together.

However, there are some patients who are stuck with their transference neurosis and who cannot accept correction from others or proceed with self-correction. When a patient has reached a plateau in which nothing significant happens, and therapy as well as ordinary life appears as humdrum routine, it may be expedient to interrupt therapy. Theoretically it is safe to assume that in the long run every patient creates a social milieu for himself in which he can function. If the therapist has been included in a neurotic stabilization of human relations, the only chance for change is contained in an alteration of the existing social balance. This the therapist achieves by withdrawing from the situation. A vacation of six months or even longer may alter the situation altogether. The resistance surrounding a certain conflict may be lived out with another person, and after that the therapist is again in a position to exert leverage. By necessity the patient will rearrange his relations so that the gap left by the withdrawal of the therapist is filled by another person. This theoretical explanation is backed up by the fact that many patients improve only after therapy has been interrupted. What apparently happens is that the interpersonal ties are so precarious that the patient cannot risk any goal changing behavior. The void that the departure from the therapist leaves, however, acts simultaneously as relief and as frustration. This becomes enough of an emotional impetus to seek attachments elsewhere. Sometimes it may be a new therapist—more often another partner or another group. After a year or so, the new situation is stabilized again in a new equilibrium. At this point, the therapist has to decide whether to remain an outsider or to re-enter the social network of the patient. If he sees the patient only a few times, he remains an outsider and indicates to the patient to continue as he is. If he resumes therapy, he interferes with the new set-up, forces a re-adaptation, and re-activates the transference neurosis with the exception that the pattern will be slightly different.

CONTINUATION OF THERAPY WITH ANOTHER THERAPIST

The usefulness of a therapist is exhausted after two or three years because the mutual adaptation of physician and patient leads to a steady state in which the awareness of the problems diminishes. At this point, the patient has to be referred to another therapist. However, I have always found it expedient to insert an interval of three to six months before the patient continues with the new psychiatrist. The new therapist has to be carefully selected. Let us assume, for example, that the old therapist was nationally, socially, culturally, and religiously of the same origin as the patient. The interaction was that of an insider who helps another insider; also, he may have exerted unconsciously the kind of control that members of the same group exert upon each other. The new therapist, in contrast, who should have culturally, socially, nationally, and religiously different characteristics, might enable the patient to understand himself as an outsider might see him; with such a therapist the problems of opposition, rejection, and cooperation become more prominent.

A similar situation arises when doctor and patient suffer from similar character difficulties. A phobic patient who works with a doctor who is basically a somewhat phobic character may at first make rapid progress, only to bog down completely later on. This particular difficulty can be overcome by simultaneous treatment by two therapists. In this case, the patient is not actually referred to another psychiatrist but arrangements are made with a colleague —preferably one of the opposite sex—to see the patient once a week while the first therapist continues as usual. Although this procedure may at first look unusual, it is rather practical. And after a few interviews the second therapist may cease to see the patient and confine his work to consultation with the first therapist (2, 3, 4).

Unfortunately, problems of status, the therapist's feelings of omnipotence, the need to make a living, and the inability to confess to limitations in therapy are largely responsible for little use of the suggested procedure. Every therapist is secretly afraid that the other one will find flaws in his procedure, and although he is willing to show these to someone who is considerably older and status superior, as is customary in supervision, he is not willing to do this with a contemporary. Not too long ago, medicine operated on the same principle. A doctor took care of all ailments of his patient, and specialists were unknown. Today, specialists consult with practitioners; and perhaps the time will come in psychiatry when the principal therapist will feel free to call in consulting therapists who might work out subordinated problems for the benefit of the patient (6, 9).

DISCHARGE

No absolute criterion for discharge from therapy exists. Usually both patient and doctor agree that after hundreds of hours of work the point of diminishing returns has arrived. This is particularly true of patients who have little money and live on a tight budget. They will weigh the merit of the fee against the pleasure obtainable from trips, vacations, cars, or houses, and eventually they decide that the expenditure is no longer warranted. With well-to-do patients, of course, this need does not exist, and often the wealthy patient hangs on to his doctor for decades. Here the doctor has to take a firm hand, and unless he deals with an absolutely defective character who needs constant supervision, he will have to tell his patient that therapy must terminate. What I do in such a case is to tell the patient that I do not wish to see him for a whole year and that he should abstain from telephone calls, letters, and personal appearances. After one year, I will see the patient briefly two or three times to determine the progress he has made. Then a decision can be made whether to continue therapy, terminate, or refer the patient to another therapist. In coping with people whose monetary resources are so abundant that fees do not play a role, this procedure proves highly successful.

Another version of termination occurs as follows: When the therapist has the feeling that the time for discharge has come, he puts the patient on a call basis. If the patient has not very stringent reasons for consulting the doctor, the effort and expense involved in making an appointment and in going to the psychiatrist prove enough of a barrier to prevent his frequent reappearance. Without appointments that set aside a certain hour of the day or week for the interview, the patient eventually loses the habit of going to the psychiatrist. On a call basis, he will decide whether he has to have more interviews, whether he can manage alone, or whether he needs to return occasionally. If he does not call at all, he evidently has decided not to come back.

The term "discharge" gives a false picture of what is really going on. It isn't the doctor who decrees, "You are well and hence need not see me." On the contrary, it is the patient who decides whether he needs further therapy and who verifies this tentative conclusion with his doctor. And whether a termination of therapy becomes a final discharge can only be seen in retrospect. Before terminating, I explain to the patient that he may come back if he deems it necessary; but I put the responsibility for calling, writing, or asking for an appointment squarely upon his shoulders. In this way, the patient obtains a feeling of self-determination and responsibility for his own well-being. It is he who decides whether he can manage alone or whether he needs help.

As time goes on and therapy has become a matter of diminishing returns, a patient may have formed a realistic attachment to the therapist and can't let go. Such patients have found in him a person with whom they can sensibly discuss problems; and if they are lonely, the therapist fulfills the function of a friend. Sometimes it is a young girl who wishes to retain the therapist as a father substitute, or it is an older patient who has nobody to turn to who seeks in the therapist a friend. Before terminating therapy, these patients may suggest, "Let's be friends." There is nothing to be said against it if a patient wishes to become a friend of the psychiatrist. But usually there exist some natural obstacles which prevent such a development. The therapist, having developed an attitude of watchful protectiveness, can only with difficulty relinquish this role. Soon the patient discovers that he has little to offer to the therapist—except for being a patient—and that the relation was based upon the patient's need for help and the doctor's need to make a living. When money-making is eliminated as an incentive, many of the proposals of "Let's be friends" die a natural death. Of course there are exceptions. The patient may offer the doctor social advantages, and if he is a social climber he will take social opportunities in lieu of money. If the patient has unusual skills, which may vary from skiing to boating or from composing to playing an instrument, the mutual interest may convert the doctor-patient relationship into an interest relationship. But on the whole it takes so much to re-organize well established relationships that it may be easier to interrupt than to reconstruct. Actually the task of the therapist is to keep his time and energy free to tackle new patients and new work and to keep a perhaps curious and friendly contact with his old patients in order to check on his own work. An adult with a full life usually has to drop a relationship so he can find time and energy for a new one. Therefore, self-regulation superbly takes care of the problem, "Let's be friends."

References

1. Bateson, G., Jackson, D. D., Haley, J., and Weakland, J.: Toward a theory of schizophrenia. Behavioral Sci., 1, 251–264, 1956.

2. Bock, J. C., Lewis, D. J., and Tuck, J.: Role-divided three-cornered therapy. Psychiatry, 17, 277–282, 1954.

3. Dreikurs, R.: Techniques and dynamics of multiple psychotherapy. Psychiat. Quart., 24, 788–799, 1950.

4. Dyrud, J. E. and Rioch, M. J.: Multiple therapy in the treatment program of a mental hospital. Psychiatry, 16, 21–26, 1953.

5. Fenichel, O.: *The Psychoanalytic Theory of Neurosis.* 703 p. New York: Norton, 1945.

6. Gans, R. W.: The use of group co-therapists in the teaching of psychotherapy. Amer. J. Psychother., 11, 618–625, 1957.

7. Gitelson, M.: Intellectuality in the defense transference. Psychiatry, 7, 73–86, 1944.

8. Marmor, J.: The feeling of superiority: an occupational hazard in the practice of psychotherapy. Amer. J. Psychiat., 110, 370–376, 1953.

9. Spitz, H. H. and Kopp, S. B.: Multiple psychotherapy. Psychiat. Quart. Suppl., 31, 295–311, 1957.

10. Wheelis, A.: The vocational hazards of psycho-analysis. Int. J. Psycho-Anal., 37, 171–184, 1956.

Part Four

Long-Term Therapeutic Goals

Chapter Twelve

Education and Growth

WHEN therapy extends over many months or years it becomes an educational experience. But no examiner can verify the content of this alleged course of instruction. Learning in therapy does not, as in school, involve memory, arithmetical reasoning, or any kind of performance which is amenable to measurement. Its objective is to fill the gap in a person's emotional growth. Hence terms such as emotional maturity, reality awareness, and sense of responsibility have been used in the past to denote this very feature. Today we might say that if the patient succeeds in establishing within himself a model of self and of the world which resembles more closely than before that which other people perceive, then he has truly benefitted from therapy. At first sight, such a definition implies a greater degree of conformity. But if conformity is restricted to those assumptions which enable us to communicate with others, it does not impinge upon thought or feeling; on the contrary, it facilitates the realization of uniquely individual features. Well-functioning communication enables the patient to perceive relevant cues, to express himself appropriately, to make the necessary decisions, and to test reality. Once so equipped, the patient is able to accept guidance from his emotions instead of being misguided, to initiate or learn the procedures necessary for daily living, and to get along with his fellow men.

GUIDING PATIENTS TOWARDS APPROPRIATE
SOCIAL EXPERIENCES

*One-sided experience · Remedial experiences · Tolerance for change ·
Change of goals · Therapy and learning theory*

Because of the selective nature of experience, all people possess
more knowledge about one subject than about another. This incompleteness of information does not refer to technical information only
but includes skills as well. Uneven development is usually the result
of overspecialization in human relations during the formative years.
A youngster, for example, may have had scant exposure to other
children or may have missed the experience of close contact with
mother. A particular family situation may have forced him into the
role of silent listener, preventing decision-making and restricting
verbal expression; and the special assumptions and symbolization
systems used inside the family circle may not have been readily
understood by outsiders. Perhaps the child was not taught the proper
use of abstraction, or he may have been induced to disregard his feelings. Perhaps the subtleties of roles and rules never were conveyed
to him, or social change may have destroyed his sense of belonging.

Be that as it may, the therapist can suggest a program in the course
of which the patient will be exposed to situations and people that
he has not met before. Therapy has to be conducted in such a way
that the patient realizes the need to seek life experiences which will
compensate for his earlier deficiencies. The therapist cannot leave it
entirely to the patient to select his own social situations because he
unfailingly will seek those situations that are known to him. By gently
urging the patient, the therapist must make a conscious effort to
steer the patient towards a life that will fill these lacunae in his body
of experience.

But there are people who cannot tolerate change. Though these
persons assume certain social roles, they cannot switch these roles;
although they can follow rules, they cannot tolerate a change of rules.
Conversely, there are people who cannot hold a role for any length
of time or cannot observe a rule without attempting to change it.

The psychiatrist thus is faced with the task of conducting therapy in such a way that the patient learns to tolerate rates of change that are strange to him. The unstable personality—for example, the psychopath or the schizophrenic—tolerates a fast rate of change and has to be taught to slow down, while the compulsive or depressive patient has a slow rate of change and has to be speeded up (14). But the adaptation to change and lack of change is only the first step. The second step implies the consistent pursuit of goals (3). The patient must learn to achieve goals, to see an action through, to complete that which he has initiated, and to stick to his task. After he has mastered this second step, he then can tackle the third step—that of changing goals that have proven unsatisfactory.

When patients begin in therapy they frequently are overconcerned with change. Having set their sights, they use the thought of change as a defense to maintain their status quo. They dislike themselves, abhor what they are doing, but abstain from correcting their behavior because they believe that things—as if through magic—are going to change; therefore they have no responsibility for their own growth. The therapist thus has to maneuver the situation in such a way that they will go through step one—acceptance of the existing; thereafter step two—correction—follows easily; this leads to step three—change of goals. Fortunately the therapist is not always forced to wait for these steps to be completed. Often the filling in of a gap will help the patient to integrate older memories which previously remained inaccessible. For example, if an individual includes feelings as a type of information used in the evaluation of others, he may begin to understand people and be able to accurately predict his behavior in certain social situations. In this example, the experience of utilizing feelings and correlating observations about self with observations about others is an entirely new experience. The result of this combination of data may signal the beginning of goal-changing behavior.

Since details of the therapeutic process as seen from the standpoint of learning theory have been excellently reviewed by Dollard and Miller (4) and by Mowrer (8), it suffices to state that at the end of successful therapy the patient does not remember too distinctly what he has learned. But in a general sort of way he now is capable of learning, of tolerating change, and of inducing change himself. And this state is brought about not only by the experiences gained in the therapeutic sessions but to a major extent by experiences gained in a milieu in which such processes are permitted to take place. In a conventional milieu, the emphasis is upon maintenance of the status quo. The individual who wishes to experiment with strange ideas and methods has no other alternative but to leave and seek new surroundings. In a milieu where change is tolerated, the individual may be encouraged to experiment on his own. It is the task of the therapist to steer the patient into a milieu that will be beneficial to him.

SOCIAL SITUATIONS CONDUCIVE TO LEARNING

Copying and imitation · Teaching models

Learning through copying, imitation, and finally identification requires, for the child, the continuous presence of another person. The feeling of belonging, of being a part of, of being rooted, or of acquiring mastery over a skill, develops only if the persons who teach have such a relationship to the youngster that he can accept and utilize the cues that are presented and the rewards that are given. Each patient is like a child who has to learn anew. Some can perceive social cues if they are exaggerated, others if they are repeated. Some learn from their peers, others from slightly older teachers. Lovemaking is a subject that can only be learned in a two-person context; other activities may be learned in group situations. The way a teacher molds his pupil is perhaps mostly a problem of personal preference. However, even if he is free to shape the situation to his heart's content, he still must fall back, as Thelen (16) points out, upon a number of basic models:

–In the Socratic discussion, the teacher invites the pupil to present his argument and then proceeds to point up the inconsistencies in the latter's logic.

–At the town meeting, the teacher is a moderator rather than an expert, and the course of action is decided upon by the majority vote. Here the pupil learns to subordinate his own wishes to those of others and is faced with the task of convincingly expressing his thoughts before and at the meeting.

–In an apprenticeship situation, the pupil learns his skills first in a low status role. He usually goes through the ranks and as his activities change so do his status and his relationship to the teacher. The latter is varyingly boss, supervisor, colleague, fatherly adviser, and friend.

–The employment situation is characterized by a boss who gives the orders and the employee who carries them out. The pupil learns to perform tasks at a clearly defined level and not to trespass on other people's territory.

–In the business situation, the plan calls for an exchange of services or goods and the pupil learns to fulfill his obligations at the same time as he sees to it that others stick to their obligations. Learning to bargain and to market depends largely upon how good the partners are.

–Teamwork teaches immediate short-term reaction rather than consideration of long-range effects. If the individual learns how to play along, it eventually shows in the team's performance, and the gratitude of the other team members constitutes the reward.

–The guided tour, the bird's eye view, or the orientation course is a way of guiding the neophyte through new territory. Its purpose is to give an over-all idea of an operation so that when the individual works on details he knows where they fit into the master plan.

For therapeutic purposes, these teaching models are relevant because they give the therapist an idea as to what kind of situations a patient should be exposed to. Patients often avoid some of these learning situations altogether. One person seems to be unable to participate in teamwork; another cannot start at the bottom and work his way up. Still another cannot tolerate being an employee. Whatever the reasons for such voids in experience may be, they handicap the patient in many ways. Because of limitations inherent in the therapeutic situation the therapist cannot fill all of these roles himself, and the patient will have to gather these experiences outside of therapy. Age, of course, is another limiting factor in that a man of forty often has a hard time to become once again an apprentice or a student. But with the helping hand of the therapist the patient may expose himself to situations he would not have dared to face without such help.

DEVELOPING UNDERDEVELOPED FUNCTIONS

Inhibition and ignorance   ·   Objective evidence   ·   Focusing upon non-neurotic functions

A distinction has to be made between neurotic inhibition and lack of experience. A person who until the age of thirty had been an excellent swimmer and then developed a fear of the water has a different kind of problem than the individual who actually never learned to swim, had no outdoor experience, and is fearful to go into the ocean. It is this latter type that has to be educated. In the same category fall people who have never worked, never had sexual relations, never earned money, barely learned to speak or read, lived with uncorrected vision, or, if deaf, never mastered lipreading. Guidance, encouragement, actual help in terms of making appointments and gathering information, and support in the decision to take on a learning situation are necessary to strengthen underdeveloped functions.

Let us take the example of a woman who never had to work, either at home or in the office. The therapist not only conveys the idea that work is a skill that people have to learn but he helps the patient in the process of learning to work. The therapist inspects the daily schedule of the patient, comments on various inefficient ways of handling things, and points out that there exist more appropriate methods. If the patient works in an office, for example, he may suggest that she go to business school at night to perfect shorthand and typing. But there is a more tangible task. This is the apportionment of time. The patient should put on paper the time it takes to go to the office, to shop, to prepare dinner, and then compare the expected duration with the actually elapsed time. If the time durations do not match, analysis of the failure reveals what features contribute to the wrong estimate. The therapist has to step outside the attitude of benevolent amiability, which merely helps to cover up the patient's inability to cope with things. Instead he has to acquire detailed information on the activities of the patient; he has to inspect reports of others, documents, samples of things produced, pictures of the relatives, or newspaper reports. This attitude in turn transmits to the patient the idea that he can check on his own performance.

A somewhat different problem presents itself when the therapist deals with patients in their thirties who never developed a sense of direction. While it is acceptable that a young man of twenty can hold any kind of a job, a man of thirty-five should have a job and an occupation through which he can cumulatively profit from earlier experiences and utilize these in gainful employment. And while a young girl of twenty is doing all right in dating young men, a woman of thirty-five should have found more permanent relationships. The help that the therapist can give concerns the long-term outlook. The patient has to renounce one kind of gratification to obtain another. And by sticking to a pursuit for a sufficient length of time, he may reap the fruits of skill and seniority. What the therapist does in effect is to shift the patient's attention from his neurotic conflicts to areas he has not been concerned with. If the patient is capable of investing time and energy in these underdeveloped functions, he will taste the pleasure of success.

ESTABLISHING INTEREST

Talent · Interest through repetition · Invisible interests · Interest exploration

Interest is usually conceived of as an a priori feature, and the learning of a skill or the acquisition of knowledge, then, is considered the result of such interest. But what we call interest is to a large extent a learned feature which was transmitted to the youngster by people and was acquired by repetition. Without denying that there are innate differences in ability, it is nonetheless the environment, the culture, the group, or the parent that provides for the opportunities to develop innate abilities. Since psychotherapists rarely deal with normal persons who possess an endowment that has been properly developed, we can forget about this group of people. That leaves us with those who were born with lesser capacities, or those who were introduced to skill and knowledge in a deviant way, or who have had insufficient practice so that they appear as if they had no interests.

It is well to remember that interest is also the result of vested effort. If somebody has spent hundreds of hours building a barn, he has a vested interest in his building. The countless patients who claim to have no interests can be given an interest by sheer repetition of their existing activities. At first, the learning of an activity and the attempts at participation may be halting and hesitant; to all concerned it may look like a mere attempt to satisfy the wishes of the psychiatrist. But repetition leads to a broadening of experience and eventually to establishment of a real trend. The patient cannot let go of his investment. Interest and competence are ninety per cent elbow grease, sweat, and tears. I remember a physician who, after having obtained his Ph.D. in chemistry and his M.D. in medicine, complained that neither of the two fields really interested him and that none of the subspecialites in medicine were to his liking. Upon careful examination, it was revealed that all his life he had played with flasks and tubes or with the improvement of apparatus, only to lose interest when the machine worked. His interest, therefore, was in scientific instruments, experimental set-ups, and the creation of gadgets not heretofore existing. He was, as it were, an inventor at heart, playing, with his hands and his brain, to improve the mechanical gadgets of the profession. Once aware of his interest, he found a position appropriate to his talent.

Many patients do not have interests which fall into an established category, and it depends upon the skill of the therapist to detect the consistencies in the patient's behavior patterns. If the patient's interests are not in law, medicine, architecture, real estate, farming, or any other such occupation (17), the psychiatrist has to search further. The patient may use, primarily, a mode of perception such as looking, hearing, touching, or tasting, or a mode of expression such as shaping with the hands or moving through space. These modes may involve concern with the hands or feet, with surfaces or inside things, or may deal with words or rhythms. If the patient is sensation-, action-, organ-, or situation-bound, his affinity is towards a subject that can be labeled not with a noun but only with a verb or adverb. This so-called "predicate orientation" (10) can be formulated and the patient's attention can be called to the fact that he has been specializing for a long time. He may like to smell things that come fresh from the fields, or he may prefer to touch highly polished surfaces. But regardless of which bodily system or activity is involved (5), the patient will be gratified as long as he can engage in this, to him, significant pursuit. Therapy in this case consists of strengthening the patient's belief in himself; once he grasps his skill he usually becomes more inclined to follow his talents.

With a patient who professes to have no outspoken interests, the psychiatrist has to explore systematically whether parents, relatives, or outsiders have ever made any attempts at teaching an area of knowledge or skill. The second thing the psychiatrist has to ascertain is whether the individual has been schooled in any area of endeavor, even though he may not have liked it, perhaps during his military service, in prison, or in high school. If these explorations yield negative results, he then can examine a third feature: what has this patient done in the years before he came to see the psychiatrist? Perhaps he worked with wood; or he might have been selling things. Obviously the title of his occupation or the superficial description of his leisure time activities does not do justice to the minute actions that an individual carries out. One man who says that he loves gardening may actually shovel earth for his wife and build seed beds; another one may prune shrubs and fell trees; and a third may cultivate roses. Once the psychiatrist has established the actual physical movements and the context of the activity, he can go about furthering these existing tendencies. The man who likes to build seed beds can learn more about soil, fertilizers, plowing and disking; and the man who likes to prune shrubs or to fell trees may learn more by working with a tree surgeon. The more proficient and professional the patient becomes, the more likely he is to harvest the fringe benefits that go with his activities.

ENCOURAGING EXPERIMENTATION

Two types of learning · Learning by trial and error · Intrapsychic obstacles · Tolerance of uncertainty

There are, fundamentally, two types of learning. In trial and error learning, the individual himself proceeds to isolate certain cues which might help in solving the problem. The source of the reward is mastery of the action itself. In social learning, the cues and the reward are handed to the individual by other people. In the case of copying, the cues derive from one source and the rewards from a different one. For example, the child who receives lessons from a tennis trainer may be praised and acknowledged by his mother; while in imitation the person who is a model and the person who rewards are one and the same, and the impact is more powerful. In identification, finally, the processes of copying, imitation, and learning by trial and error can no longer be separated. The delineation of the identity of the individual (4) is based on thousands of little experiences which indicate where a person belongs, what his power and property are, what the differences and similarities vis-à-vis others are, and what he thinks about himself.

The therapist who wishes to encourage problem-solving activities on the part of the patient may run into resistance. On the whole, patients do not seek situations they have not experienced before. They avoid contexts with which they are unfamiliar unless confronted with an emergency. The doctor thus has only an indirect influence upon the patient's problem-solving pursuits; he can encourage and reward the testing of new situations and activities, and above all he can help the patient to tolerate the failures when his experiments do not succeed. In order to grow, a person must be permitted to fail, be able to correct the action that led to failure, and then improve the performance. People who are not permitted to fail do not learn to correct their performance. Many patients never were permitted to experiment; they were told how to proceed, and any deviation from the prescribed scheme was reprimanded. The psychiatrist has several ways in which he can help the patient to learn from people. One of these ways is to establish satisfactory human relations. If the patient is capable of communicating, he will be able to associate with those who have something to teach and who are wise enough to tolerate temporary failure.

Intrapsychic conflicts which manifest themselves as guilt or fear over an anticipated action inhibit or prevent learning. High-pitched ideals and rigidly set standards make any performance look poor. The patient therefore conceives of himself as a failure. This the patient may avoid by carefully skirting any action in which he might fall below his high standards. The result is passive behavior. The psychiatrist can tackle high-pitched ideals by slowly reconstructing the events that led to this character formation. Actions of father and mother can be reconstructed; and once the bridge to past events exists, the patient begins to understand that he has largely identified with the ideals of his parents. But these may now be outdated.

Excessive need for control of events to come or omniscience is another source of inhibition. This disease affects many compulsive characters who feel that they have to know in advance what they are letting themselves into. Uncertainty creates anxiety and they are unable to tolerate it; the result is passive inaction. Therapeutically this inactivity may be handled by provocation or confrontation. An impasse can be set up in which doing—as opposed to not doing—is the lesser evil. If the therapist informs his patient that unless he accepts employment therapy cannot be continued, the patient, in order not to discontinue, might go and find a job. Provocation, of course, appeals to the innate desires of the patient to engage in action, and when the immediate pressure is great enough the anticipatory reaction to the new situation can be temporarily minimized. This shotgun method has to be followed up by working through with the patient the almost certain failure which is to follow. In order to appease his desire for omniscience and to avoid facing uncertainty and limitations, he is inclined to return to his previous state of passivity.

INCREASING FRUSTRATION TOLERANCE

Time-stretching function of fantasy   ·   Delay of gratification   ·   Psycho-pathic personality   ·   Psychosomatic patients   ·   Exercising and restricting fantasy · Situational stress

Fantasy is a buffer system which adapts sensory input to motor output, compensating for missing gratifications and elaborating on the frustrations of daily life. For example, when external stimulation fails, fantasy provides for internal stimulation (6). When external stimulation is too powerful or threatening, fantasy alters perception in such a way that the perceived becomes tolerable for the individual. Recollection of past and anticipation of future events therefore are closely linked to action. Fantasy enables the individual to delay gratification and to tolerate frustration. By setting a long-term goal, a person is able to accept delays of many years; and during this time the anticipated reward substitutes for actual gratification. Fantasy thus is a time-binding and time-stretching device which helps us to extend minutes into years and to condense months into seconds.

Disturbances of behavior can arise if fantasy is systematically misused. The psychoneurotic patient may, for example, delay gratification indefinitely, thus depriving himself forever of what he needs. He tends to live in his fantasy, content to plan things without ever carrying them out. Therapy therefore has the task of reducing fantasy elaboration and the concomitant frustration brought about by the disregard for actual events. Patients with excessive fantasy should not be allowed either to free-associate or to indulge in fantasy elaboration. Instead, a continuous clarification of what is, of what goes on, of what people do, and of what they are may help the patient to gain some insight into reality.

Conversely, the psychopath who has to gratify his wishes immediately cheats himself out of skills and knowledge and all the things that can be acquired only if long-term goals are kept in mind. Here, action substitutes for fantasy elaboration. Without forethought, he may indulge in impulsive action, seeking to gratify his wishes without delay. This rashness of procedure gets the patient into trouble.

By means of dream analysis, play techniques, and other measures directed at the unconscious, the therapist attempts to reawaken the fantasy that the patient possessed in his childhood. Gradually the therapist will observe that the period between anticipation and re-alization of action becomes longer and fantasy begins to fulfill its intended purpose.

Similar observations can be made in psychosomatic conditions, where the paucity of fantasy and imagination is demonstrable by projective techniques (11, 12, 13) and dream analysis. In the pres-ence of stress, psychosomatic patients cannot tolerate frustration be-cause they do not possess a buffer system in the form of a well-de-veloped fantasy. Instead, they start reacting to the overstimulation —not, as in the case of the psychopath, in terms of action, but in terms of systemic contraction of smooth muscles and secretion of glands. The action thus involves only selected muscle groups and the whole process can be likened to a spilling-over of tension (1). Development of fantasy in psychosomatic patients is undertaken by training the patient to become aware of his dreams and by promoting daydreams and preparations for future action. Once fantasy develops, it is usually accompanied by disappearance of symptoms.

Too much fantasy and the subsequent frustration of real needs is countered by repeated confrontations with reality. The patient is at first not aware that reality blurs into fantasy; the line has to be drawn for him. And the therapeutic communications should not cen-ter around his fantasy productions but around his daily actions. Once he begins to understand that much of what he talks about is "hot air," he also will become aware of his pitifully ineffective actions. The converse procedure is indicated with patients with too little fantasy. The psychopath who cannot tolerate frustration can be helped with the most powerful tool of the therapist—interpersonal elaboration. Neither the psychopath nor the psychosomatic patient is, on the whole, used to talking with another person about frustrating events. For such patients, the act of interchange is a first experience, and as time passes his frustration tolerance will increase. Apparently the interpersonal elaboration is internalized and eventually the patient learns to elaborate events within himself. At the same time, it acts as a permission to bring secrets out into the open. This method is second to none to ease tension and to help in the integration of diversified experiences. It is the basis on which healthy fantasy—that which is publicly accessible and not hidden by proprietary feelings —develops.

A totally different method of coping with frustration can be employed when the patient's difficulties deal with real events. The distribution of frustration over time helps in coping with difficult situations. When a person is faced with financial reverses, he should not make decisions about marriage. And if a man is told that he has cancer, he should not burden himself with the chore of moving to a new city. The stress of living has to be distributed over time; and when stressful events demand the full attention of the individual, no additional burdens should be taken on. Unfortunately, most patients manage to get exposed simultaneously to various stresses without knowing the secret of apportioning these over time. Under such circumstances, the therapist takes over and decides for the patient; the principle of "first things first" is thereby imparted to the patient.

BOUNDARIES AND STEP FUNCTIONS

Setting of limitations · The next step · Exceptions · Calling a halt · Standards and norms · Conventions

To pursue a task means to accept limitations. The task determines what comes first and what comes second, and it induces the individual to mobilize his resources. Poorly educated children conceive of limitations as things that are forbidden, whereas a successfully educated child conceives of limitations as something that helps in the pursuit of a goal. One cannot become an expert at playing the saxaphone if one watches television all the time, nor can one become a quiz kid if one does not read and study. The setting of limitations therefore, helps in organizing a program which minimizes all those features that interfere with the attainment of a goal. In childhood, tasks are set to correspond to the youngster's resources. With patients, the same principle is used and limitations are set in order not to scatter the patient's efforts.

Concern with the next step in a series of actions means to divide an action into various parts. It is easier to predict the events in the near future than those that lie in the remote future. That which is going to happen in the next minute, the next hour, the next day, or the next month has to be attended to immediately; things that might happen five years from now can be attended to later on. Most patients with a developed fantasy engage in gigantic flights in which the next fifty or one hundred steps are taken for granted; but it is always the next step that determines the ultimate outcome. Concern with the immediate future deals with such specific items as allocating time for work and pleasure, budgeting money, organizing human relations, and balancing family with outside contacts or choosing between solitude and social gatherings. This budgeting, planning, and preparing for the thing that comes next is a task which is concretely learned by children when they engage in camping, fishing, mountain climbing, riding, sailing, canoeing, hiking, or bicycling. That the success of an expedition largely depends upon its preparation (15) is a notion that the patient may not have accepted. The therapist therefore discusses from interview to interview whatever the patient's next step will be.

The patient has to learn that there are exceptions to routines just as there are exceptions to traffic rules or to court procedures. It is difficult for the inexperienced to recognize when such an unusual condition exists. While many patients are inclined to constantly invoke emergencies so that the exception becomes the rule, there are others who are so engulfed in routine that they cannot make exceptions. But the recognition of exceptions can be taught. The irreversible event takes precedence over the reversible event. When somebody is sick, when an issue of life and death arises, when a decision involves a whole career or a marriage, exceptions can well be taken. The patient has to be taught to assign priorities to the various problems at hand and he has also to learn to inform others that such priorities exist. And if he takes the trouble to communicate, others will usually acquiesce.

Assuming that every living being expands and trespasses on the territory of others unless called to a halt, we must teach our patients to defend their boundaries and to respect the boundaries of others. One can borrow a hatchet from a neighbor in an emergency, but one cannot—without prior special arrangements—borrow another tool every day. People love to have week-end guests or vacation visitors; but if they overstay their welcome, they have to be helped to leave. One can contribute in money and time to a community effort, but one's own personal affairs should not be disrupted. One can have children play and roam in and out of the house, but this needn't interfere with the activities of others. Although most patients see the need for establishing boundaries, they are afraid to publicly state where these boundaries are. The psychiatrist has to teach the patient that it is far better to call a halt to any procedure that trespasses on somebody's inalienable rights—particularly within the family—than to tolerate infractions. Those persons who remind each other not to trespass are those who function successfully. They do not suffer from resentment, and they rely upon each other to keep in line.

While the setting of limitations and the establishment of boundaries have to be arrived at by mutual agreement, there also exist in society norms which the individual has not been asked about. They were established a long time before he was born. The incest taboo, for example, is one which since ancient times has been rigorously enforced—except in the case of gods. How much of the body can be exposed and which of the bodily activities must be carried out in private and at what age are prescribed in all civilizations. Fire regulations, building codes, and traffic rules all serve to make life easier. The patient as well as the child therefore has to accept the idea that there are some things which cannot be managed according to the whims of the individual but have to be handled according to tradition. The culturally imposed norms may range from appropriacy of dress, language, and eating habits to respect for private property or the safety of others.

Isolated or withdrawn patients and those who pride themselves on nonconformity often have not learned the conventions which govern social intercourse. The patient has to learn the obvious truth that by obeying conventions he buys his freedom and by violating conventions he invites antagonism. Although psychiatrists cannot instruct the patient in the usage of many of the conventions, they certainly can comment on the conventions that govern a particular kind of social situation. In middle or old age, it is difficult if not impossible to learn new conventions, and particularly immigrants who come to this country at an advanced age may never fully adapt. But for those who were raised in the same culture there exists a solution. The psychiatrist is equipped to mobilize the latent knowledge of standards inherent in the patient. He can be helped to review those past experiences which will teach him to draw the necessary conclusions himself. Many of the patient's experiences have not been analyzed properly and elaborated upon with another person, nor have the conclusions been put to a test.

ACCEPTANCE OF INTERNAL AND EXTERNAL CONTROLS

Ego alien controls · Control by people · Control of conscience · Control through physical laws

By avoiding or rebelling and sometimes by passively submitting, some patients express their opposition to the control of other people. Some individuals cannot accept the dictates of their own consciences; they have to get drunk or become self-destructive to express their rebellion against themselves. The factor that makes a person accept or reject controls is found in the personality of the authority. The way in which control is taught, by whom, at what age, and under what circumstances determine its acceptance or rejection. As long as controls are imposed upon the individual, they are rarely accepted; but if they are viewed as devices which improve the performance and insure more gratification, they are eagerly sought. Reasonable control is not intended to inhibit; it is designed to facilitate better timing and quantification of action and more appropriate decision-making.

Control results in the skillful execution of an action; and if this action involves other people, we talk of social control. The police, firemen, the military, the courts, the tax assessor, and the employer all exert social control. Group action is possible only if social controls are accepted by people. The acceptance of social controls depends upon a person's good relations to one or two other people. The patient with a working relation to wife and children is more likely to accept social controls than the lonely person, and this is the goal towards which the psychiatrist works.

The control exerted by the conscience over impulse or action is the result of introjection of earlier interpersonal controls. In helping people overcome their self-imposed restrictions, psychoanalytic techniques are at their best. Reconstruction of the original events and recollection of the external controls that were imposed connect these depersonalized values with concrete situations. When conscience and ideals, which in the mind of the patient stand as depersonalized monuments, become connected with people and activities, the awesome quality of the superego forces begins to diminish.

So far we have mentioned external social control and internal self control. But there exists a third form of control which is built into the situation and is determined by physical laws. In skiing, for example, control over the skis is impossible if balance and weight distribution are ignored; and although the control in this case is with the skier, it is determined by physical laws. There are patients who cannot accept nature and its laws. They do not learn that it takes time to go from one place to another; they do not know that accomplishment requires exercise. They ignore the fact that certain bodily needs have to be gratified. In this age of control over nature, the individual is trained to disregard physical limitations and he abuses his organism until it breaks down. Therapy is directed at making the patient accept the controls of nature. The patient has to realize that while controls from conscience and from other people may be modified, the laws of nature never can be changed. No man has defied death or aging for long, and no man has changed the law of gravity. Reality testing therefore becomes the exercise that informs the patient about the effects of nature.

GUIDING, CORRECTING, AND REWARDING

Acquiring an attitude · Guiding through attitude · Correcting · Sharpening cues · Gratification of others

An attitude is conveyed through repetition. For example, were the therapist to tell his patient, "Try to be more permissive with your daughter," the patient probably would confuse permissiveness with inconsistency. Through demonstration of when, where, and in what subject-matter permissiveness is indicated, the therapist conveys his attitude. And frequently an attitude emerges only when the patient has been exposed to contradictory experiences. For example, the patient may have to learn that, because of the experience gained, an apparent failure may contribute to later success while easily won victory may deprive him of acquiring much needed experience. The therapist thus conveys that there are consistencies of human conduct at a higher level of abstraction which the patient can gain after having been exposed to a basic variety of experiences.

The attitudes that the patient has to acquire do not revolve around specific subject-matters. Therapy is not here to develop attitudes towards pets or bicycles, towards cousins or employees. No, it is a question of mastering conflicts within the self and with others. The first thing that the patient learns, therefore, is that conflict is part of life; it has to be treated as a daily event without the concomitant resurgence of anger, shame, or guilt. The attitude of the psychiatrist that daily life is characterized by difficulties is gradually transmitted to the patient. Understanding, patience, fairness, control, and a host of other features help in solving problems, one after the other, as they arise. To disregard temporary annoyances, to be able to lay aside the pressures of work during leisure time, to become unresponsive to certain interfering suggestions, to be selective, and to establish hierarchies in the importance of events—all this is learned implicitly. Through example and general bearing, the psychiatrist thus educates the patient. Learning through copying, imitation, and identification and the learning of learning (2) itself are the primary processes of therapy.

The patient looks upon the therapist as the teacher who shows him how to do it, as the arbiter of success and failure, and as the judge who awards the rewards or punishments. This attitude, which derives from analogies borrowed from social life, has to be converted into a more operational one: Whatever contributes to correction is desirable; whatever does not becomes ballast. Of course the therapist does reward, judge, and teach, but these are not his major functions.

Correction is the core of the matter, and it is willingly accepted by the patient if it is done according to the formula— "This way, not that way; here, not there; now, not later; or later, not now." But if instead of correction the therapist delivers a value statement: "You are wrong; it is too late; nothing can be done," such a statement is usually resented, and the way is closed to future communications.

One of the foundations of correction of performance often is related to the clarity of cues. If the patient does not perceive certain aspects of social behavior, it may be due to the fact that they have never been spelled out clearly for him. In correcting, then, the therapist aims at clarifying clues for his patient. Just as a tennis trainer teaches the pupil how to hold a racket and the skiing instructor shows him how to distribute his weight, the therapist teaches the perception of social cues. For example, when the patient gives a long intellectual account of what happened in a conversation with a friend, the therapist interrupts and says, "Was your friend depressed?" The cue which specifies the mood of the other person may solve the whole problem. Or when the patient tells of a premature decision of his, a simple remark such as "Were you tired?" may give a lot of answers. The principle employed is simple. If the patient overemphasizes cues bearing on feeling, the therapist focuses upon thinking and logic. If the patient emphasizes thinking, the doctor has to give attention to feeling. If the patient concentrates only on what happens within himself, the outside situation and the reactions of other people have to be emphasized. Through such compensatory comments the patient may gain a balanced picture of the total situation.

If support and criticism are ways of rewarding and frustrating the patient in the therapeutic situation, the patient in turn has to learn to do the same with others. He has to learn to talk the language of the people, to play their games, and to acknowledge their needs. He has to try to encourage others; and a friendly "You can do it" or "Why don't you find out for yourself" will get him remarkable results. The patient thus has to learn that by gratifying others he gratifies himself; and unless he looks out for the gratification of others he will not achieve proper human relations.

SEEING A TASK THROUGH

*Checking details · Hurdle help · Task adapted to emotional maturity ·
Satisfaction from integrated tasks*

There are parents who are content to see their child started on
an enterprise without paying any attention to its execution. A
mother may give a child a tennis racket and balls without seeing
to it that there are opportunities to play and to practice; and another
mother may be quite content to see that the child sits at a table
apparently doing his homework without checking on whether the
work is actually done. Helping another person to see a task through
consists of attending to minute details. In the case of a child, it
is, "Let me check the math problem you are working on just now."
With a graduate student, a conversation about the book he is just
reading is helpful; and with the patient, a careful inquiry into his
handling of his daily affairs may convey the idea that concern with
details is the secret of seeing a task through: "Did you consult your
dentist?" "What is your budget?" "Did you pay all your bills?"
"How much time do you allow to go to work?" People have to be
taught to look after little troubles and not wait until the difficulties
have grown to such proportions that they can hardly handle them.

Every child and every patient has to learn to seek help when he
is lost in some phase of his work. While supervision and concern
with detail convey to the patient how he can operate, he must be
trained to seek help when he feels that he cannot manage alone.
Once the patient can ask for help, the need for constant supervision
is eliminated. The patient who is trusted to judge for himself when
he needs help feels greatly strengthened. This, however, implies
that the therapist is available, or that other people are available,
in case of need. At first, of course, it will be left to the teacher or
therapist to give help at critical moments so that the patient understands when he needs assistance. This kind of assistance has been
aptly termed "hurdle help" by Redl and Wineman in describing
therapy with aggressive children (9). Help appropriately given can
thus prevent outbursts, abandonment of the task, and lowering of

self respect.

As the task progresses, it is important that both the child and the patient be accompanied through the various stages of development by one and the same person. In the elementary school, the youngsters have at first one teacher for all subjects, and only later in the advanced grades do they have different teachers—one for each subject. When a patient has little self-confidence and when he is unfamiliar with the task, he cannot be burdened with adapting to a variety of instructors. He must be familiar with his mentor and must be able to anticipate his reactions to such a degree that he can concentrate on the task at hand. The tutor, in turn, is capable of rewarding the achievements of the patient in individual terms. He sounds him out as to whether or not he has given his best; and if he has, he will reward him for his performance. Only much later, when the patient's performance can be measured by generally accepted standards, is an objective appraisal in place. The same principle applies to youngsters, whose performance adults gauge to the level of development of the child. Thus a sentence written by an eight-year-old is gauged differently than a sentence written by a sixteen-year-old. When somebody is beginning to learn a skill he can only be judged within his own league, and it would be a great mistake to apply absolute standards to the tentative attempts of patient or student. Just as we talk about intelligence quotients and mental ages, so do we have to consider emotional levels of maturity.

To see a task through thus means to accompany the patient from the beginning to the end of his venture, becoming familiar with every detail of the enterprise, introducing outside help if indicated, rewarding when necessary, and correcting on other occasions. In the case of a youngster, this means to initiate, to construct, and finally to use the thing that has been constructed in play or work. A task that has been seen through does not come to an end until it has been integrated into a meaningful place in the life of the patient. If somebody has gone through the struggle of learning a musical instrument, the ultimate crowning success is not the winning of a prize but the ability to play with others and to make music a regular part of life.

MAINTAINING IRRATIONAL ASSUMPTIONS

Rationality and probability · *The institutionalization of irrational assumptions* · *Hope and faith as survival mechanisms* · *The utopia of rational man*

Whenever an individual acts in conformance with established facts or whenever his evaluation of events is in agreement with that made by other people, we speak of this individual as a rational person. Also, when an individual attempts to predict events to come and his expectations correspond to statistically established probabilities, he can again be spoken of as a rational person. However, the border between rational and irrational behavior becomes blurred when we try to predict events the probabilities of which are unknown. Whether an action is worth the risk depends upon what is at stake. If it is a matter of life and death, even a ten per cent chance to succeed may look inviting, while under different circumstances a 75 per cent chance of succeeding may deter an individual from embarking on a given enterprise.

If growing up implies that the individual has to become more and more rational, a point may be reached at which he is unable to answer his own questions. This is the case when human understanding ceases and questions such as what is beyond our universe and what comes after death cannot be answered by rational means. When things stop making sense, people begin to make irrational assumptions. As Masserman points out, nobody would be able to survive without making highly improbable assumptions (7). Among these are the delusions of invulnerability and immortality, the delusion of omnipotence, and the delusion of man's kindness to man. The rational scientist, for example, who in his work makes nothing but rational statements, goes to church and there obtains reinforcement for his irrational assumptions. The business man who knows how to estimate risks and probabilities tries his luck in gambling, knowing that the chances are against him. It seems as if, in every individual and in every organization, the rational and the irrational assumptions are bound into one system. Every culture possesses its own institutions to accommodate these highly improbable assumptions made by human beings. In Western civilization, the irrational aspects of life have in the past been institutionalized by the church, thus enabling people to be informally rational in their daily lives. But today the situation has changed. The power of the church is waning; science has institutionalized rationality; and irrationality is left to the individual to cope with. Perhaps we owe to these conditions the upsurge of movements which cater to the wishful, irrational thinking of people—the interest in extrasensory perception, the concern with affluence, and the popularity of dictatorial forms of government—as if any of these activities would solve basic human problems.

Mental health seems to depend upon the relationship of a man's rational and irrational assumptions regarding himself and the world. When an individual makes irrational assumptions which do not affect his social life, he is considered mentally healthy; thus he may paint utopia, he may model eternity, or he may compose whatever he likes; but if he goes out and assumes he can walk on water or drive on the left hand side of the street, he gets into trouble. Conversely, if an individual is so rational that he is constantly aware of the precariousness of living, he will be unable to spend a quiet minute and eventually he will succumb. The soldier who goes into battle has to believe that he will survive; otherwise he is unlikely to protect himself. Therapy can be called successful when the patient has learned to distinguish fact from fantasy, when he has learned to predict accurately, and finally when he has learned to tolerate the uncertainties inherent in ignorance. Wishful thinking and irrational assumptions have to be called upon to aid in tolerating uncertainty of living and certainty of death. In ordinary language, these are called hope and faith, and without them life, progress, and therapy are unthinkable.

Therefore the communication therapist, being aware of the irrational needs of human beings, will not go about to propose—as so many other therapists did in the past—that rational man is the goal of therapy. He will only go so far as to state that man ought to be rational in those matters which affect his social functioning; beyond that his irrationality should be left unchallenged, and on occasions it should be promoted. We can hope to be rational in our communication, and we look forward to basing our exchange of messages on probable assumptions. But in the sphere of action an element of unpredictability will remain; this we have to accept. The person who bridges uncertainty with wishful thinking and completes an action is more successful and healthier than the one who surrenders to the uncertainties and does not act at all. Because he who believes in complete rationality is himself a utopian and a most dangerously irrational member of society.

References

1. Alexander, F.: *Psychosomatic Medicine—Its Principles and Applications.* 300 p. New York: Norton, 1950.

2. Bateson, G.: Social planning and the concept of "deutero-learning." Pp. 81–97 in *Science, Philosophy and Religion,* 2nd Symposium. Edited by L. Bryson and L. Finkelstein. New York: Conference on Science, Philosophy and Religion, 1942.

3. Deutsch, K. W.: Communication theory and social science. Amer. J. Orthopsychiat., 22, 469–483, 1952.

4. Dollard, J. and Miller, N. E.: *Personality and Psychotherapy.* 488 p. New York: McGraw-Hill, 1950.

5 Erikson, E. H.: *Childhood and Society.* 397 p. New York: Norton, 1950.

6. Lilly, J. C.: Mental effects of reduction of ordinary levels of physical stimuli on intact, healthy persons. Pp. 1–9 in *Research Techniques in Schizophrenia.* Psychiatric Research Reports #5. Washington: American Psychiatric Association, 1956.

7. Masserman, J. H.: Faith and delusion in psychotherapy. Amer. J. Psychiat., 110, 324–333, 1953.

8. Mowrer, O. H.: *Learning Theory and Personality Dynamics.* 776 p. New York: Ronald Press, 1950.

9. Redl, F. and Wineman, D.: *Controls from Within.* 332 p. Glencoe: Free Press, 1952.

10. Ruesch, J.: *Disturbed Communication.* 337 p. New York: Norton, 1957.

11. Ruesch, J., Harris, R. E., Loeb, M. B., Christiansen, C., Dewees, S., Heller, S. H., and Jacobson, A.: *Chronic Disease and Psychological Invalidism.* 191 p. New York: Amer. Soc. Res. Psychosom. Probl., 1946. 2nd printing, Berkeley and Los Angeles: University of California Press, 1951.

12. Ruesch, J., Christiansen, C., Patterson, L. C., Dewees, S., and Jacobson, A.: Psychological invalidism in thyroidectomized patients. Psychosom. Med., 9, 77–91, 1947.

13. Ruesch, J., Harris, R. E., Christiansen, C., Loeb, M. B., Dewees, S., and Jacobson, A.: *Duodenal Ulcer.* 118 p. Berkeley and Los Angeles: University of California Press, 1948.

14. Ruesch, J. and Prestwood, A. R.: Interaction processes and personal codification. J. Personality, 18, 391–430, 1950.

15. Tenzing, N. and Ullman, J. R.: *Tiger of the Snows.* 294 p. New York: Putnam, 1955.

16. Thelen, H. A.: *Dynamics of Groups at Work.* 379 p. Chicago: University of Chicago Press, 1954.

17. U. S. Government Printing Office: *Occupations, Professions, and Job Descriptions.* Price List 33A. Washington: Superintendent of Documents, April, 1958.

Chapter Thirteen

Timing, Correlation, and Patterning
of Experiences

GUILT ABOUT COMMUNICATION AND PARTICIPATION

Thought and action confused · Communication as intimacy · Removing guilt about communication · Freedom of thought; restriction of action

PERHAPS THE MOST significant factor which interferes with group participation and communication is the shame or guilt experienced by the individual when he exposes himself. Direct and successful communication may throw the patient into a state of panic. If relating to others is experienced as a procedure that has to be avoided, the patient usually is unaware of his guilt. These patients consider the symbolic preparation for action—be it silent thinking, sentiment, attitude, or feeling—as well as its verbal expression as synonymous with physical action. When such a person has hostile fantasies, he magically attributes destructive power to his feeling. Such attitudes develop, of course, during the formative years when the parents do not talk about aggression, inhibit the expression of anger and resentment, and ignore the existence of sex. By excluding certain persons, feelings, or thoughts from social intercourse, the parents convey to the child the idea that there are things that are much too powerful to talk about. A statement such as "You should like your aunt" or "You have a dirty mind" conveys to the child that it is wrong to harbor certain thoughts and feelings. Communication is a great threat to such patients because the process of exchange stimulates thoughts and feelings which may be forbidden. This reaction may induce some patients to abandon therapy prematurely.

A variant of this guilt about communication is found in patients who treat their relations with others as a unique secret. This attitude seems to constitute a perseveration of the affectionate relationship and the communal experience with the mother in the first few years of life. These early experiences involve washing, bathing, rocking, cuddling, touching, and other affectionate components which some mothers continue well into adolescence. When such a patient talks to the psychiatrist, his divulging any information may be conceived as a disloyal act because any kind of communication or soundmaking is equated not with the management of ideas but with bodily or spiritual intimacies. Communication therefore can only be achieved at the price of guilt.

In such cases, the therapist is faced, from the beginning of therapy, with the task of coping with the guilt about communication. This he can do in either of two ways. If he confines the discussion to a superficial level, he may focus upon occupation, job, or career. After a month or two, the patient may mention that therapy should embrace more than vocational counselling, and this comment may signal his readiness to talk about the difficulties he experiences when he touches upon the subject of his personal relations—particularly his mother. If the therapist tries to tackle the guilt in the early interviews, he has to resort to somewhat premature interpretations. He may point out the patient's feeling of shame when talking about intimate subjects and how he is content with generalities instead of giving examples; how he emphasizes the impersonal family roles and abstains from mentioning any feelings; and how such topics as desires, wishes, and sexual fantasies are avoided altogether. The therapist thus concentrates on citing the things that have not been mentioned, making the patient indirectly aware of the presence of a selective mechanism. Eventually the patient will come clean and confess that his feelings are not intended for the ears of strangers. In so doing, the patient discovers that nothing special occurs when he talks about himself and that the secrets and intimacies that he reserved for mother, and later for the introjected mother, are in no way unique. Eventually the patient relinquishes this particular attitude.

The patient's tendency to maintain a most impersonal relationship from which private and personal information is omitted may stem from the confusion of thought with action. To counter this tendency, the patient has to be trained to distinguish between action on the one hand and the verbal and nonverbal preparations for action on the other. He must be made to realize that undue selectivity in thinking and feeling handicaps action. He must be familiarized with the fact that thought control by others is impossible and that people control each other by control of action. Once the patient has understood that fantasy and thought have no magic effect unless implemented, he usually feels a great relief. He now can have bad thoughts and bad feelings; he is free to fantasize; and he is now more than ever willing, because of the freedom experienced, to control and censor his actions.

CONTENT AND FORM OF COMMUNIQUÉ

The "what" and the "how" of a message elicit separate responses ·
Disjointed expressions · Content is subordinated to emotions

The content of a message is intimately linked to the means of expression. Popular opinion has it that we choose our expressions to fit the content of a message; however, child development seems to belie this assumption. As the child matures, his channels and modes of communication develop in a predetermined order. In his early years, the range of expression is subordinated to the development of speech. Only later, when maturity and learning have reached a certain level, does he possess a limited freedom to choose language and mediums of expression. In interpersonal situations, the content of a message is coordinated with the nonverbal forms of communication. Commonly, "I like you" is expressed with a different pitch and inflection of the voice and a different facial expression than is "I hate you." From experience, the listener knows that certain forms of communication are associated with certain contents; misunderstandings may arise if a person's voice, for example, elicits a hostile kind of response while the content consists of an innocuous question.

One of the therapeutic efforts is devoted to matching ways of expression with content of the message. The patient is taught this art by demonstration. The doctor discusses how he listens to the "music" of the patient's statements and how he decides whether form is matched to content. He further explains that if this is the case the listener can react to the statement, but when it is disjointed more clarification is needed. A Janus-faced statement, for example, forces the listener to explore the nonverbal modifiers; he has to ascertain whether the other person is angry, anxious, fearful, guilty, or depressed and he has to inquire into the other person's intent—whether the other is looking for a victim, an authority, a love partner, or a trading opportunity. The nonverbal modifiers of a statement inform us about the human user's relationship to the signs he employs, and only after we have explored this relationship can we concern ourselves with the events the signs purport to refer to.

Most patients show a serious schism between form and content, and the therapist begins by making an a priori assumption: the nonverbal modifiers are closer to the unconscious than the verbal content. As a result of this assumption, the doctor attempts to adapt the content to fit the emotion. Once the patient has learned that feeling and movement represent him more truly than his verbal expressions, he will try to choose his words more carefully. In later stages of therapy, when the patient has learned to express himself, the procedure may be reversed. Then the nonverbal components of expression may be adapted to a given topic. But if this is done too early, play-acting may be the result.

SEPARATING WHAT DOES NOT BELONG TOGETHER

Task orientation and rivalry · *Goals and implementations* · *Displacement* · *Separating fused elements* · *Original event and secondary elaboration*

Separation of elements of behavior which in the course of events have become linked but which do not belong together is an essential therapeutic task. For example, there are people who start out to do a job and invariably get involved in fighting with others. Instead of completing their task, they become dedicated enemies. Opposition and enmity replace the original goal of action, and the individual cheats himself out of the fruits of his labor.

A fusion of implementation and goal of an action occurs when an implementation which originally was secondary gradually displaces the goal and becomes an end in itself (4, 14). The acquisition of social status is such an example. Prestige is secondary to personal achievement or birthright; but there are people who strive outright for status, notwithstanding their lack of skill, achievement, or position. These social climbers therefore are greatly surprised to discover that after having improved their status they still feel dissatisfied.

A similar fusion of elements is encountered in displacement (9). In psychoanalytic theory, modes of action characteristic of the sex organs can be displaced onto other parts of the body—for example, the mouth. Erikson (5) has devised a scheme to understand such displacements in a more systematic manner by separating the erotogenic zones of the body from their modes of action. Any displacement of functions to other objects, body parts, or persons usually requires the attention of the therapist.

In practice, the therapist delineates the behavior of the patient by matching instinct, implementation, and goal. An effective process for reinstating the vanished goals of action, for example, consists in calling the patient's attention to the fact that an adult is not loved because he eats up the food on his plate. This behavior pattern constitutes a fusion of the implementation of eating with mother's approval, which in turn replaces reliance upon satiation. Whatever elements get fused together—rewards from one universe of endeavor with implementations from another or qualifications of one set of circumstances with actions pertaining to another—have to be carefully traced to their roots. Once the patient has cognitively separated the various elements, he must try to gain a gratification which is inherent in the action itself. Until he can do this successfully, the therapist's support makes up for the missing gratification.

In the process of tracing fused elements, the memories of past experiences have to be separated from memories of secondary elaborations. It isn't merely the memory of the big dog which ran over little Johnny, but in addition it is little Johnny's reaction to the dog, his anxiety, and the anxiety of his parents, and the subsequent communicative exchange which is imprinted upon his memory. As psychiatrists, we cannot alter the terrifying experiences which our patients were subjected to in the past; but what we can achieve is separation of the primary event from its secondary elaborations. In many instances, the process that prevents the integration of a traumatic experience with all the other experiences is a discrepancy between content and secondary elaboration. Apparently partial and unsuccessful communication shortly after an alarming experience is responsible for the special treatment which the memory of this experience receives in the mind of the patient. This breakdown may be a result of the patient's inability to express himself or it may be due to the absence of an understanding listener or to an oversolicitous or anxious listener. In contrast, the most terrifying conditions can be tolerated (7) if elaboration of these events becomes possible. In therapy, then, the doctor attempts to provide for a belated opportunity to ventilate traumatic experiences in order to enable the patient to integrate the incident.

FOCUSING

Selective suppression

Knowledge of when and how to say something and when to remain silent marks the therapist with experience. In therapeutic communication, the timing of a reply has to be adapted to the readiness of the patient. French (6) has called attention to the fact that in most therapeutic situations the thoughts and feelings of the patient tend to polarize around certain topics. The experienced therapist learns from little hints or omissions of the patient that his thoughts and concerns are crystallizing. When a patient is working on a theme and his actions, feelings, and statements tend to revolve around one topic, the task of the therapist is to permit polarization and to avoid competing themes. And when one subject is exhausted, the patient will bring up the next one. Thus out of the wealth of memories of the patient, a few are illuminated at a time, lifted into consciousness, and, after they have been in focus, allowed to be forgotten. They are available upon request but do not bother the patient at other times. Much of the confusion of the patient is due to the fact that circumstances did not enable him to sift out the essential from the unessential and to arrange things in a proper order in his own mind. In therapy, then, the opportunity is offered to settle one problem at a time, to elaborate details, to look at it in slow motion, and to experience step by step the progress made.

THE EXPERIENCE OF INSIGHT OR FIT

The nature of insight · The analysis of non-fit · Learning to appreciate fit

Empirically speaking, the experience of fit—the "aha" phenomenon or "I get it"—is accompanied by a sensation of relief or exhilaration. But the objective description of the experience of insight is not so easy. Expressed in terms of learning theory, one might say that insight occurs when an implementation is combined with the proper cues to insure the reward. In psychoanalytic theory, it would mean that an unconscious association has become conscious (8). In communication theory, it would be defined as a recombination of pieces of information to form a larger Gestalt. Whenever one piece of information is fitted to another piece, either by means of verbal exchange with others, by solitary experimentation, or by some psychic process of combination, release of tension is experienced. The conditions that make for such an experience are manifold, but the element of timing seems to be foremost (20). When an external social situation fits with an internal preoccupation, when a missing link in the chain of information is presented when needed most, when through experimentation a solution is found to a burning problem, then insight occurs.

The psychiatrist helps the patient to obtain the experience of fit by dissecting action in terms of its constituent components—let us say needs, implementations, cues, and rewards. Then he can readily see when a gratification does not match an implementation or when cues do not solve the problem. The patient who is fascinated by a woman and then discovers his impotence obviously is not taking into account some basic conflict. The girl who works in a clinic and who arrives all dressed up, wearing elaborate jewelry, is confused about the situation. The man who cannot accept compensation for work done, although he needs it, obviously has a conflict regarding rewards.

Without a sense of fit, the individual will not experience insight. An awareness of extraneous elements that enter and distort experience and an appreciation of timing are needed. Just as a fashion designer may decide that a certain color does not match with another in the design of an evening dress, or an interior decorator may remove a piece of furniture that disturbs the formal style of the room, so has the patient to sharpen his perception of non-matched elements in his behavior. This presupposes an appreciation of style in the wider sense of the word. When feeling, thought, and action progress in unison, when behavior is fitting for the occasion, when responses of one person match the responses of another person, and when all this produces satisfaction, then the base has been established from which integration can proceed. Literally, the patient must become dependent upon an internal sensation of satisfaction whenever the experience of insight and the cognizance of fit occur, so that he will seek more of the same.

THE EXPERIENCE OF SEQUENCE

Step functions · Sequence as learning principle

Polarization and fit are two types of experience which lead to clarification. However, there is a third one to be added: the sequential order of events. When problem after problem is discussed in therapy, the participants should be aware that every single session eventually contributes to a cumulative experience and that the order in which this happens will determine the ultimate result. The shift of focus from interview to interview is engraved in the memory of the patient like a kinetic impression. If he masters each step function, he automatically becomes ready for the next and more complex development. A successful therapist is a person who can gauge length of exposure and rate of change to the capacity of the patient. There is perhaps no better description of such an experience than in Herrigel's *Zen in the Art of Archery* (11). The author wanted to become an archer, but in his third year of training he had not as yet seen a target. In his fifth year, however, he was capable of splitting an arrow, and thereupon he became a master archer.

The therapist of course cannot undo the kinetic impressions gained before the patient came to therapy. If a girl had to mother younger siblings at the age of ten, or if a boy became a father at the age of seventeen, these premature experiences cannot be undone. Furthermore, the remembered experience is in all probability but an example of a whole series of improperly timed experiences to which the children of that family were exposed. Sometimes, therefore, the therapist has to introduce the patient for the first time to a series of experiences which, when lived through, will imprint the patient with a kinetic impression of sequence and growth. The criteria employed by the therapist are simple: he remains at each station until that particular problem has been understood and acted upon. When the patient reaches a feeling of satiation and the therapist a feeling of boredom, the focus shifts to another problem.

INCREMENTS AND DECREMENTS

Shock · Regulating the load · Quantifying the next step

Our sensory organs are built to perceive differences. If the increment or decrement of a stimulus is too small, no change is perceived. If the change is too great, shock may result. The process of repetition stabilizes new patterns of behavior; shock tends to break down established patterns. In psychiatry as well as in ordinary living, shock has been widely used to shake people in their very foundations. In therapeutic communication, however, exposure to stimuli has to be timed and quantified in such a way that shock is avoided and growth is promoted.

To a certain extent people control the amount of stimulation and the increments or decrements to which they expose themselves. In athletic training, progressively more difficult tasks are introduced as the individual grows. After reaching a certain age, the man in his advancing years has to decrease the amount of exercise and stimulation. But people with psychological problems—among them, ulcer patients, for example—are notorious for taking on responsibilities which tax their physical and psychological resources, and some immature personalities may be so ambitious as to take on tasks which are well beyond their means (18). To fit the task to the resources of the patient, to adapt the stimuli to his receptive capacity, and to adjust his output to his strength and skill are among the major tasks of the psychiatrist. The occupation has to be matched to the educational background, hobbies to the interests of the patient, spending to the pocketbook, and sex to the morality of the individual. The patient thus has to learn to make decisions which are geared to what he is or to what he could be under optimal circumstances, and he has to learn to renounce his pipe dreams which are not commensurate with his intellectual, emotional, social, physical, and economic resources.

To teach a patient proper control of stimulation, the psychiatrist has to analyze action sequences in detail. Whenever the patient reports events of the previous day or the previous week, the psychiatrist carefully scans what he has heard for elements which appear to be out of proportion. He gently reminds the patient to consider the next step, not the ultimate goal. "How did you plan the party for tomorrow night? How many people are coming? Does your husband know what to do? What about food and drinks? Can you afford the expense? Have you got enough help?" After the party, the psychiatrist then inquires how things went, and failures are carefully analyzed. When, over a period of years, the affairs of daily life are carefully planned and the results analyzed, the patient learns to properly set for himself the increments and decrements he can tolerate. Perhaps a girl has to learn to give a party for two or three people first, and then increase the number of people; or perhaps she should obtain the help of a friend who shows her how to do these things. Glossing over dozens of steps and thinking about the outcome rather that the intermediate operations can lead but to failure.

In planning for the next step, we are concerned not only with the logic of the next move but with its intensity. What is the additional load if a man becomes a member of another committee? And when he retires, what kind of pursuits will replace his previous work load? We have to avoid shock on the one hand and deprivation and underload on the other. And if a change in load is indicated, it must be undertaken over time so that the organism has an opportunity to adapt.

SPEEDING UP OR SLOWING DOWN

Stress and change · Personality and rate of change · Childhood patterns Control of mental speed through response

War, epidemics, and catastrophes force a quick adaptation of practical procedures to the demands of naked reality. In times of peace and routine, values remain rather stationary and practices are changed slowly. The speed with which ideas, values, and attitudes can be changed seems to depend upon whether or not the individual is subjected to stress. In general, we can say that skill and knowledge reduce individual stress and slow down the rate of change while lack of skill, ignorance, confusion, and absence of emotional attachments seem to promote stress, randomness, and quick change. These truisms about behavior under stress (10, 12) apply of course also to human communication. When two people converse with each other and one of them is a fast person with a quick grasp of words, moving speedily from one idea to the next while the other one is a slow person, doggedly sticking to the same topic, both participants feel frustrated. But this frustration forces a mutual adaptation; the fast one will become slower and the slow one faster, if they wish to reach an agreement.

Magnitude and rate of change are vitally important concepts in psychiatry. Psychopathological diagnostic categories seem to be based principally upon criteria that refer to excessive rates of change. References to the impulsiveness of a psychopath, the mood swings of a manic-depressive, the sudden withdrawal of a schizophrenic, or the repetitious performance of a compulsion neurotic all imply minimal or excessive change. Schizophrenics, for example, frequently subject the physician to such a speedy assessment that it usually escapes the observation of the average person. The naive observer may be tempted to say that the schizophrenic is an unapproachable and extremely static person in whom no change occurs at all. More careful observation, however, will reveal that the intrapsychic and interpersonal changes are so fast that the average individual does not keep up with them. The initial warming up period and subsequent stabilization of patterns are missing; instead, the patient retains his freedom of choice and forces the other person to adapt. These features give the schizophrenic a swift and fleeting quality, as well as the ability to consider the fantastic, the theoretical, and the new. The neurotic, in contrast, with his slow rate of change, assumes a role only gradually but perpetuates the same position for an undue length of time even in the face of changing conditions. Thus the compulsion-neurotic is sometimes referred to as the most stable, most regular, and most reliable individual— a view which ignores his lack of adaptation and inability to make choices.

The childhood patterns that produce people with flexible rates of change are rather striking. Emotional deprivation, absence of skin stimulation, and absence of complementarity of action tend to produce people with fast rates of change. Overprotection, pedantry, and lack of diversified social contact lead to an overstabilization of patterns. Because of these peculiarities in velocity and rate of change, both the schizophrenic and the neurotic patients are out of step with the world and with reality (15, 19). By relying upon rates of change which differ from those of their surroundings, they create more conflict than is really necessary.

In almost all therapeutic situations, the therapist is faced with the necessity to speed up or retard mental processes. Response to the face value of a statement and concern with its conscious components tend to slow down the mental process. In accepting a statement at face value, the therapist does not question premises, and the attention of the participants is focused upon the issue. Mental speed remains relatively stable because the idea that is being discussed does not change. An example might illustrate the case:

Patient: "I have headaches."

Doctor: "Describe them to me."

Through the simple comment, the patient is pinned to the subject; he has to analyze his statement, and his idea is not challenged. However, if the therapist chooses not to respond, the patient will tend to make other statements in the hope that these additional utterances will evoke an acknowledgment from the therapist. In so doing, the patient will speed up slightly. If the therapist consistently responds by focusing upon the premises that underlie the statement, upon the ways of expression, or upon previous and related statements, the patient will speed up considerably. For example:

Patient: "I have headaches."

Doctor: "Do you notice that you clench your fists, that you grit your teeth, and that your armpits are wet?"

This comment shifts the cognitive concern with headaches to an interactional response and the mental speed increases. It is the task of the therapist to gauge the tempo of the patient. With patients who are in a state of excitement and who have a fast rate of change, the therapist ought to abstain from questioning the underpinnings of the patient's existence but should accept his statements at face value. But in situations where the therapist feels that the patient is caught in a state of inertia in his thinking, feeling, or personal relations, he does well to speed up the patient by responding to the implicit meaning. In so doing, the therapist imitates what most schizophrenic patients do spontaneously. By jumping ahead and skipping some intermediate steps, he omits consideration of the next step. By rushing to the next highlight or by replying to a tangential aspect of the message, the physician forces adaptation upon the patient and thereby introduces change.

EFFUSION AND SUPPRESSION

Decontamination and expression · Action and inhibition · Listening as nonverbal action

The old idea that substances or thoughts contained within the organism were foreign bodies which should be released led to the belief that purges would get rid of whatever evil befell the mind or the body. The medical and religious procedures of purging led to the ritual of decontamination, which in its more spiritual form developed into the practice of confession (2). Breuer and Freud's work (1) on the psychic mechanisms of hysterical phenomena in 1893 inaugurated a new era, and the method of lifting into consciousness some unconscious material has been the objective of psychoanalytic technique ever since. The older concepts of decontamination and confession have been combined with the newer notion of repression in such procedures as catharsis and abreaction in modern theories of therapy. At present, to listen, to help the patient to express himself, and to let him abreact are all part of the therapist's daily procedure.

The psychic processes of the schizophrenic patient contrast sharply with those of the hysterical person. The schizophrenic is aware of his own and other people's unconscious, and he lacks the repressions necessary for healthy functioning in a human society; so far, no effective methods have been developed to prevent the patient from spilling unconscious thoughts and feelings and from being overwhelmed by them. The only device known to the psychiatrist is to initiate action. If the therapist talks or acts, the patient is compelled to adapt, which in turn exerts a suppressing effect. When a man balances himself on a tightrope, all other considerations are temporarily suppressed until he reaches solid ground. When a schizophrenic patient contracts pneumonia or breaks a leg, his hallucinations and delusional experiences tend to recede until he is well again. To a lesser degree, this is also true of the many small events of daily life. The therapist who works in a hospital is quite familiar with action therapy. To drink a cup of coffee, to have a little snack, to go for a walk, to play a record, to talk about something that happened conveys support, not in word but in attitude. Many schizophrenics on the verge of a breakdown can be helped in this manner. By doing, the therapist nonverbally points out that the little things of daily life really are worth while. As long as the patient can do something with the doctor, he will postpone some of his preoccupations to another time. The stronger the proximity stimulation and the more absorbing the action, the more will other preoccupations of the patient recede.

Suppression, of course, goes hand in hand with expression. Sometimes it is necessary to listen to a patient all night, and if the patient is at home the relatives can take turns. Such acute phases usually last but a few days, and the doctor's task is to support the relatives so that they in turn can listen to the patient. The only thing that should not be done is to enter into a discussion of the patient's preoccupations. Inasmuch as the verbal feedback circuits do not function, only the more compelling nonverbal actions are registered. This observation is similar to that of mothers who report that babies quiet down when somebody is nearby. In the presence of others, therefore, selective suppression and expression are more operative than when an individual is alone.

ALIGNING THE TWO BASIC CODIFICATION SYSTEMS

Analogic and digital codification · *Transposition* · *Forcing recodification*

In human communication, psychic images or actual pictures of objects and people are examples of analogic codification; they are replicas of what goes on in life and are self-explanatory. Words and numbers, in contrast, are artificially created, discrete entities, and a legend or a person has to be consulted in order to find out what each symbol stands for. Thus when we deal with the word "horse," we have to go to the dictionary to find out that it refers to a certain large, four-legged, solid-hoofed, herbivorous mammal, domesticated by man. But if we have the image of a horse in our head or a photograph in our hand, we have no difficulty in recognizing such an animal when we encounter it in a pasture.

Analogic codification—an image in our head or a photograph on the table—expresses a multitude of things at once, whereas digital codifications—numbers in our head or words in a book—have to be serially aligned and one thing expressed after the other. The difficulty of synchronizing the two denotation devices is due to the different treatment of time: analogic codification encompasses many features all at once; digital codification takes one aspect at a time. Infantile characters and artists think in analogic terms; compulsive patients, scientists, and logicians think in logical-verbal terms. For each of these people it is difficult to learn the other method of codification. While the predominantly analogic type has difficulty to master extrapolation and interpolation and to study part functions one at a time, the digital type often cannot see the whole and does not understand patterns. A digitally oriented person at times may appear to be self-destructive because no amount of logic will tell him when he is tired or sick. In psychoanalysis, the process of translating fantasy and dreams into words and ordinary words into metaphors such as oral, anal, or genital is one of the therapeutically effective exercises. Once the patient is capable of transposing one codification system into the other, he is able to view himself and the world in a more complex manner. Not only can he understand things as they are at the moment—analogic codification—but he can also learn to project them into the past or into the future—digital codification.

In practice, the coordination of the analogic and the digital is accomplished by letting the patient verbalize his daydreams and fantasies; by the therapist's verbalization of the patient's actions, gestures, and movements; by relating the patient's general and abstract statements to concrete events in the hope that these will evoke a specific imagery in the patient's mind; and by responding to the patient in words which will evoke action or in terms of action which will provoke a verbal response. What recodification achieves is obvious. Because spatial and temporal aspects of events, part and whole functions, continuities and discontinuities, vision and sound are treated so differently in each of the codification systems, any transposition reveals new aspects.

SWITCHING FRAMES OF REFERENCE

*Keys to interpretation · Social context · Cultural background · Aware-
ness of differences · Sharpening discrimination · Adaptation to changing
frames of reference*

The notion of "frame of reference" is convenient when discussing
differences of views due to varying positions, pursuits, and biases
of the discussants. A visitor who spends one day in a clinic obviously obtains a different view than the nurse who has been working there for ten years. The pilot of an observation plane flying at
one thousand feet has a different view of the terrain than the man
who is standing on the ground. Most disagreements between people
can be traced to differences in the frames of reference used, and
experts in communication are careful to state their own as well as
to pinpoint the other person's frame of reference.

Among the determinants of the frame of reference we find, first
and foremost, the social context; it governs the manner of speech,
the style of writing, and the nature of the content. When a patient
reports a dream in which his wife is accidentally killed and the
subsequent discussion revolves around his death wishes, it goes
without saying that his statements are to be interpreted within the
framework of therapy. Such death wishes are of quite a different
order from the "intent to kill" in the legal sense, where the motive
of an accused is explored in court. Therefore a person who is a
skilled communicator includes in his diagnosis of the frame of reference a statement about the social context and the date at which a
statement is made.

Awareness of a person's prevailing cultural orientation helps in
the interpretation of messages. The assumptions about life and
the worthwhileness of preserving life, for example, differ from
country to country. In a locality where the birth rate is low, where
the principles of equality and liberty flourish, and where high
standards of living prevail, life may be cherished. In another place,
where the birth rate is high and where a low standard of living is
combined with an authoritarian class and caste system, life may

be cheap. Depending upon such basic outlooks, the character of medicine, therapy, and the values placed upon helping another individual may vary.

Awareness of differences can be stimulated through travel. In foreign lands, the patient gains certain experiences that he has not had at home. Traveling widens his horizons because it makes him aware of different frames of reference. Awareness of differences also can be stimulated through therapy. This is concretely accomplished by explicit remarks on the part of the therapist as to the assumptions other people might have made when in contact with the patient. What does the patient's wife think about money, science, and retirement? What are her a priori assumptions about women and sex? In painstaking work, it is demonstrated to the patient that ethnic, social, occupational, and religious factors influence the frame of reference and that if he wishes to understand people he had better study the other person's values.

Patients frequently are unaware of their own frames of reference, and the thought is relatively new to them that other people, by necessity, have different views. Apparently they have not acknowledged the fact that people's experiences are not alike and that age changes the outlook on life. Young people, for example, going to a dance have different experiences from those of a mother trying to match her daughter with a wealthy widower. The task of therapy, therefore, is to help the patient to separate actions and statements into two parts: the frame of reference and the content. To implement this task, the therapist calls the patient's attention to the cues that label various contexts. He then trains the patient to identify interviews, conferences, celebrations, briefing sessions, and informal bull sessions. Once the patient is capable of understanding the purpose of a gathering, he most likely is able to understand others and the statements they make.

The work that the therapist does with regard to frames of reference can be boiled down to the following: The individual's interpretation of a given subject matter will vary with his frame of reference, which is determined by a multitude of factors. But frames of reference and roles of the participants are frequently changed during a conversation; within one and the same sentence, a man may talk as a scientist, private citizen, taxpayer, and government employee. At one instant the content of a conversation may be concerned with the disbursement of funds from the standpoint of an agency; in the next instant the issue may be inflation, and it then may move on to taxation. Although all three deal with the topic of money, they may also be considered from the standpoint of the government, the public at large, and the private citizen.

FUNCTIONING IN UNISON

Fantasy and action · Words and action · Synchronization · Preparation for synthesis

The ability to anticipate distinguishes man from animal; it has made human civilization possible and contributed also to mental malfunctioning. Without anticipation there would be no neurosis, no worry, and perhaps no hallucinations or delusions. In the experience of man, memory and fantasy have a time-stretching or time-condensing function. Unfortunately, fantasy may be abused. Instead of being related to ongoing action, it may fulfill a compensatory, antagonistic, or supplementary function. In some cases, the fantasy may substitute for action; in other instances, the patient may suddenly experience a delayed emotional reaction. The anger that should have been expressed on the spot comes out at home, when the patient berates his wife.

Fantasy is not the only factor that may interfere with appropriate action. Verbal activity represents perhaps an even greater danger. Some persons are willing to take words or symbols as representative of inner events; others feel that words are representative of the conscious aspects of behavior only. Be that as it may, the word may supplement, disguise, forecast, or even replace practical implementations. Therefore the psychiatrist has the task of ascertaining in each case how the individual uses words and what relation, if any, these have to action. Only when feeling, thought, and action occur in unison can the individual be expected to function optimally.

In therapy, then, the doctor strives to coordinate the patient's feelings with his thoughts and actions. When a mother says to her child, "I love you," and then pinches him until he is black and blue, there exists a discrepancy between word and action. When a person reassures another of his cooperation but shows signs of anger and resentment, then speech does not correspond to feeling. The job of synchronization can only be undertaken when the therapist himself is an astute observer so that he can perceive the slightest desynchronization. Inappropriacy may be detected in one sphere through the patient's erroneous judgment; in another through faulty logic; and in a third, through displaced feelings. Only life experience and maturity can teach the young psychiatrist to detect asynchronous performances of patients.

Once the therapist has detected an asynchronous expression, he has to focus upon the underlying conflict. Each of the aspects of the conflict has to be discussed separately, and in each session, one or more hurdles are worked upon. The trail of the therapist thus resembles an obstacle course, whereby he travels one path until he meets the next hurdle. After the groundwork has been laid, the patient may suddenly put things together; feeling is matched to cognition, and fantasy prepares for action. As time goes on, the patient will simply experience and respond, and the observer will perceive fewer and fewer asynchronous and inappropriate reactions.

SYNTHESIS AND INTEGRATION

Old and new experiences · Emotions as index files · Task awareness · Switch of levels of abstraction · Adaptive responding · Integration of complaints · Competitive communization · Integrating individual with culture

The integration of a new experience into the treasury of past experiences can proceed efficiently only when the memory of part items is accompanied by a memory of the whole structure (16). But when part of an experience is considered in isolation from other parts, a loss of information is the result. The process labeled integration deals with the time-binding capacity of the organism to combine past and recent experience into a new whole. For this purpose, experiences have to be properly recorded and classified, as it were, so that they are readily available when needed. Without becoming technical, such a process can be conceptualized as follows (3):

Incoming signals stimulate the organism;

Some of the signals are dissociated from the rest and impinge upon what is called "memory";

Memories and new impressions are recombined into new patterns;

The new pattern is connected with other patterns, and its origin becomes obliterated.

If we follow this little scheme in our work with patients, the therapeutic task is easy to recognize. When the patient recalls memories which are contradictory and confusing, the therapist separates each item and discusses it in detail. By concentrating on one thing at a time, the patient relegates other contradictory pieces of information into the background. Since the emotional concomitants of a thought enable the person to properly classify an experience, the therapist pays particular attention to the affective concomitants of expression. Experiences, in turn, are closely tied to perception. Perceived and mediated through different sensory modalities, an impression may have gustatory and osmic components in addition to tactile, visual, and auditory ones. The coding remains bound to the modalities in which the impression occurred, and the recall of the experience as a whole is dependent upon the synthesis of the various sensations. Although an osmic stimulus, for example, may reawaken visual or auditory memories, recall will be clearer and distortion less marked if the stimulus is similar to the earlier one. If the outside stimulation, which might initiate perfect recall or recognition, is missing, talking about the experience can help in the correction of some of the distorted aspects of the memory process.

Information about action can be comprehended much better if the individual is aware of the points of departure and destination of an action (17). In physical action, these two points are clearly defined as, for example, in the case of travel. In social action, the state before and after the action replaces the points of departure and arrival. Granted that such slicing may be arbitrary, it none-theless is practical if an action is to be talked about. In almost any description of action, the point of departure is more difficult to fixate than the point of arrival, for the individual who is engaged in action is usually aware of the goal he is striving for. Task-oriented groups are notoriously more efficient and have a higher morale than groups that have lost their sense of direction. In therapy, the crystallization of the state of affairs prevailing at the present and a statement of future goals helps the patient to clarify and define his actions; it forces him into selective focusing and suppression of irrelevant details.

Integration of experiences is by necessity associated with a certain amount of distortion. A certain violence has to be done to fit various experiences into specific classifications or molds. In therapy, the patient learns to observe analogies and homologies, and under the guidance of the physician he learns about the nature of his distor-tions. The therapist thus helps the patient to fit his ordinary experi-ences into an over-all organization by abstracting the features which these experiences have in common. In thought and speech, the change of levels of abstraction is a necessary device for the promotion of integration. The healthy person continuously switches from the abstract—that is, the over-all pattern—to the concrete—that is, the detail—and vice versa. In speaking, this switch makes for clarity of expression; in terms of integration of experiences, it brings order. But the main purpose of switching to a different level of abstraction is to eliminate contradictions in information. When the therapist helps the patient to flexibly switch levels of abstraction, both in interpreting perceived events and in expressing himself, he provides a base upon which integration can take place.

After the therapist has worked on the intrapsychic processes of de-lineation, abstraction, concretion, translation, and interpretation, the time has come to train the patient in the interpersonal processes of human communication. First, the patient has to be able to perceive and adapt to any change in the communicative behavior of the therapist; a change in the position or role of the therapist has to be accompanied by a corresponding change in the patient. In reciprocal communication, a statement of the therapist requires a complementary response on the part of the patient; if the doctor makes a joke, the patient cannot reply in a serious vein without transition. If the other person is speaking in terms of the present, the reply cannot be in terms of the past. Although the art of replying cannot be imparted directly, the changes of pace can be demonstrated and rehearsed. Finally, when the patient is able to carry out such maneuvers, he usually discovers that he has gained some inner flexibility. This means that the patient can assume a number of differing positions, roles, and rules in adaptation to another person and that through this device he has gained in scope.

The integrative efforts of the therapist may be opposed by certain specific forms of pathology. Some patients complain that nobody cares for them, that they feel excluded and lonely, and that life holds no meaning for them. "What is the use of doing anything?" is their complaint. At this point, the therapist has to interfere. By separating the more meaningful from the less meaningful material, the doctor expresses through his efforts that there is something worth discerning in the patient. A complaint means that the doctor has to proceed with an operational analysis of the problem. By demonstrating this receptive attitude, the therapist gradually conveys to the patient the idea of being a participating member, and the resulting feeling of inclusion makes the task of communication appear worth while and reduces the patient's sensation of loneliness and exclusion.

Competitiveness is frequently the result of defective communication, whereby the feeling of isolation induces the patient to do what others do. Lonely people frequently seek group activities and sameness in action in order to avoid communication. Competitive patients—the "me too" people—have great difficulty with integration. Their competitiveness forces them to take on tasks which other persons have set for themselves, even though these tasks may not fit into their plan for living. This type of activity, which substitutes for true communication, has been called "communization" (13). Only when the patient is seriously sick and hospitalized does the therapist communize with him; otherwise the communizing experiences are reduced to a minimum and the communicative behavior is maximized.

Many patients are social deviants and, as such, are in a minor or major state of opposition against the group or culture of their origin. To them, relatives and other significant figures become police officers who implement and reinforce silly rules and obsolete traditions. It is the task of the therapist to gradually familiarize the patient with the fact that the value system of his culture constitutes a cumulative body of knowledge which has been acquired through the centuries. Through trial and error and the impact of various events, generations of the past have accumulated information about how best to cope with people and surroundings. To know about culture means to possess knowledge about social relations which fits the circumstances, the people, and the climate of a given region; it also means to be acquainted with the devices used to reconcile conflicts. Each culture prescribes the desirable behavior to be displayed when people are under stress. This may consist of explanation, assumption of roles, or the pursuit of certain activities. Therefore when the patient has ventilated his hostilities against parents or in-group and when his self-destructive tendencies have been exposed, the time has come for him to look again at the ways his own people handle the problem. Perhaps he has to visit the place he came from and talk with representatives of his group. An Irishman might have to go back to Ireland; a Catholic might talk with his priest; a New Englander living in the West might have to visit back East; a girl born on a farm might have to inspect the playgrounds of her childhood and the people who lived there. Out of such confrontation arises upheaval and sadness. Fantasies have to be buried; concessions have to be made; and as a result, the identity of the patient becomes clarified.

References

1. Breuer, J. and Freud, S.: *Studies in Hysteria.* 241 p. New York: Nervous and Mental Disease Publishing Co., 1936.
2. Bromberg, W.: *Man Above Humanity: A History of Psychotherapy.*

342 p. Philadelphia: Lippincott, 1954.

3. Deutsch, K. W.: Communication theory and social science. Amer. J. Orthopsychiat., 22, 469–483, 1952.

4. Dollard, J. and Miller, N. E.: *Personality and Psychotherapy*. 488 p. New York: McGraw-Hill, 1950.

5. Erikson, E. H.: *Childhood and Society*, 397 p. New York: Norton, 1950.

6. French, T. M.: *The Integration of Behavior*. 3 v. Chicago: University of Chicago Press, 1952, 1954, 1958.

7. Freud, A. and Burlingham, D.: *Infants without Families*. 128 p. New York: International Universities Press, 1944.

8. Freud, S.: *A General Introduction to Psycho-Analysis*. (Tr. of rev. ed. by J. Riviere.) 412 p. Garden City: Garden City Publishing Co., 1943.

9. Glover, E.: *Psycho-Analysis* (2nd ed.). 367 p. London: Staples, 1949.

10. Grinker, R. R. and Spiegel, J. P.: *Men Under Stress*. 484 p. Philadelphia: Blakiston, 1945.

11. Herrigel, E.: *Zen in the Art of Archery*. 109 p. New York: Pantheon, 1953.

12. Marshall, S. L. A.: *Men Against Fire*. 215 p. New York: Morrow, 1947.

13. Morris, C. W.: *Signs, Language, and Behavior*. 365 p. New York: Prentice-Hall, 1946.

14. Mowrer, O. H.: *Learning Theory and Personality Dynamics*. 776 p. New York: Ronald Press, 1950.

15. Rank, O.: *Will Therapy and Truth and Reality*. 305 p. New York Knopf, 1945.

16. Ruesch, J.: Part and whole. Dialectica, 5, 99–125, 1951.

17. Ruesch, J. and Kees, W.: *Nonverbal Communication*. 205 p. Berkeley and Los Angeles: University of California Press, 1956.

18. Ruesch, J., Harris, R. E., Christiansen, C., Loeb, M. B., Dewees, S., and Jacobson, A.: *Duodenal Ulcer*. 118 p. Berkeley and Los Angeles: University of California Press, 1948.

19. Ruesch, J. and Prestwood, A. R.: Interaction processes and personal codification. J. Personality, 18, 391–430, 1950.

20. Symonds, P. M.: *Dynamics of Psychotherapy*. 3 v. New York: Grune & Stratton, 1956–1958.

Chapter Fourteen

Identity and Self-Realization

AT ONE point in therapy, many patients raise the question, "What am I doing? What is this all about? What is my future? Is life worth living?" The patients who raise these questions consider themselves superfluous members of society. Perhaps they are unattached people without husbands, wives, children, or parents; or if they live with others, they might not know how to fulfill their function satisfactorily. The purpose of living, the goal of their strivings, the meaning they have for others does not seem to have been defined by their own experiences. Here the therapist's task is clear. He has to free the patient from measuring life; he has to teach the patient that the external yardsticks suitable for measuring achievement and possessions cannot be employed for this purpose. The individual has to learn to weigh his existence within his own personal framework. Unless a person experiences pleasure in living, in creating, and in constructively being with others, his life will make little sense (5). Unless his talents are mobilized and he is able to pursue that for which he is talented and prepared, he will consider himself a failure. To help the patient to experience gratifyingly is the goal of therapeutic communication.

ACQUIRING A SENSE OF IDENTITY

Identity defined · Identity as experience of self · Conditions favoring the sense of identity · Acquiring an identity through therapy

In the popular sense of the word, identity refers to the answer given to the question, "Who are you?" In psychiatric terms, identity refers to a person's awareness of what he is, a feeling of being a self-contained unit regardless of situation, group, or activity. To have an identity means to possess an absolute core that defines what is good for self. Identity cannot be acquired without attachment to people or without human experience in a variety of situations. To have an identity implies commitment to long-term goals, enabling the individual to minimize activities undertaken for reasons of expediency or boredom. Identity also means responsibility, above all, towards self, compelling an individual to look after his own welfare and growth and to avoid all those things that are detrimental to body and soul. By keeping in good shape, the individual actually contributes to society and culture.

The sense of identity is the result of a long, slow, and complex development (10). When children know where they belong, whom they can trust, who likes them, what they have to learn, what their limitations are, what they can expect, and who will help them when they meet some difficulties, they have in effect acquired a sense of identity (2, 3). What goes into the sense of identity is codified within the organism in the analogic mode. It cannot be appraised logically and has no quantitative or numerical value; it cannot be tested; it can only be experienced. The sum total of the experience of oneself in a variety of situations leaves a feeling of familiarity—something that serves as a guidepost for future reference. Evidence of this transformation is manifold; some people call it unselfconsciousness, some refer to it as pride, and others call it spontaneity. All of these terms encompass the fact that to function well an individual must have self-respect and must have knowledge in action and be able to apply it in whatever situation and with whatever person.

The sense of identity is acquired by long-term contact with one and the same person so that the diversity of external conditions can be elaborated with this person and fused into a whole. But personal contact is not enough; to develop a sense of identity an individual must have continued contact with the same landscape, the same situations, and the same groups. An unidentified person, in contrast, is one whose life experiences were too diversified, who changed place of residence, culture, language, and people, and who lacked continuous contact with one and the same person. To give such an individual a sense of identity it is necessary that, through many action sequences, an image of self is created which embodies the more time enduring aspects of the personality. Working through historical material and all those past experiences which were disjointed, isolated, or repressed and connecting them with present-day events gives the patient a sense of continuity. Thus he learns to be proud of things he has done or felt and acquires the habit of discriminating between that which is characteristically his, that which is generally human, and that which is typically somebody else's. The end result is a heightened awareness of self and a sense of confidence and well-being.

Although the primary and secondary processes of identification (4) influence the sense of identity throughout a lifetime, the sense of identity at any one moment is almost synonymous with the sense of integrity, independence, and usefulness that an individual possesses. Through his explorations, the therapist conveys that he is searching for the patient's identity, his role as a man or as a woman, his sense of self-respect, his interests, and his pleasure in living. This subtle, tender, and consistent attitude indicates to the patient that there is something worthwhile in him to develop. And as the therapist searches, he is careful not to intrude and not to destroy. This something of value that has to be studied, protected, and developed, this part of the patient that is alive and trustworthy, is the substance out of which the patient's sense of identity develops. At the beginning of therapy, the patient will tend to please the doctor and imitate the things that he does or says. Over and over again, the therapist will point out to the patient that whatever he takes over from others must be sifted and screened; what he can use, he keeps; and what he cannot use, he forgets.

YOUNG PEOPLE WITH A FUTURE

Encouraging new experiences · Support in the face of failure · Growth curve and expectations · Expectation and reality

Young people who stand at the beginning of their life cycle harbor in themselves unrealized potentialities which the psychiatrist helps them to attain. At this age, past experiences have not yet established precedents which are completely unalterable and commitment to various plans of living may not have occurred. The young enjoy the moment and await the future for those things that have not happened as yet—the apprehension of the expectant mother, the excitement of the bride-to-be, the doubts of the young man who has his first command position. The belief in the future is one of those powerful ideas (6) which keep people going, seeking, and searching. To have a future means to have hope and faith. To have a future gives meaning to life.

Therapy with the young, therefore, consists of encouragement to pursue activities and situations that have not been tested as yet and to reject that which is unsuitable. The therapist stands by as the patient makes his choices; he acts as a benevolent parent, but without the apprehension and personal involvement of the natural parent, and therefore with less obligation and guilt on the part of the patient. To have a kind of mentor is for many people a first experience for which they have waited all their lives. When a young person's belief in the future collapses in the face of the first reverses—loss of a beloved person or failure of achievement—the therapist reinforces the idea that a single reverse is but an interlude and that the loss of one battle does not mean the loss of the war.

Young people extrapolate from their own rapid growth and assume that their future development will follow a similar pattern. But the growth curve flattens out and eventually reverses itself in the early twenties. Unfortunately, many people do not take account of this change. They continue to assume that next year they are going to be stronger, bigger, and better in spite of the fact that their strength and speed may wane. Or, to put it into different words, a man's expectations have to be adapted to his growth curve (9). A healthy individual has to learn to tailor his expectations to actually established probabilities. These are determined by the situation and the individual. By confronting the patient with the statistical probabilities that apply to person and circumstances, the therapist may gently teach the patient to base his extrapolations on recent rather than remote experiences.

A young person's identity is tied to his belief in a future. Correction of unsound expectations does not imply destruction of this elementary force; on the contrary, it means that the outlook should be based on average probabilities for a person of this age and type. That individuals may deviate from such probabilities, that they might disregard safety or scoff at established rules, is the privilege of youth. The therapist's guidance at this point consists of spotting talent, or diagnosing missing experience, and of steering patients towards the acquisition of skills. This procedure is a mixture of vocational and character guidance. Expectations taken over from parents may not fit the patient's endowments and have to be altered. A slowpoke may not fit into emergency work, nor an artist into bureaucratic procedures. The short-legged butterball is not fit to become a ballerina, and the near-sighted boy cannot become a ball player. The therapist thus stakes the territory in broad terms. He points to a style of life and patterns of human relations that fit age, sex, talent, body build, and past experience of the young person. He helps, in other words, to match the individual's expectations to existing biological, social, and economic conditions. Once the expected is somewhat proportionate to the real, less tension is generated from the discrepancies between anticipation and fulfillment.

OLD PEOPLE WITH A PAST

People remain the same · Transitional phases · Mastery of symbolization systems · Upward, collateral, and downward identification · Providing a source of identification and belonging

People who have lived for some time have established commitments and allegiances; they have assumed responsibilities and are shareholders in various human enterprises. If such people get into trouble later in life, they cannot be changed radically but can be helped towards a continuation, elaboration, or slight modification of whatever they stood for and did in the past. If they were total failures, it is almost impossible to help them acquire a new identity or to provide them with a new plan for living. Fortunately, most people have something worth salvaging, and it remains for the therapist to decide what elements in the patient's personality can be used for future development. To make a liability an asset, after all, is part of the art of therapeutic communication.

People with a significant past often believe that life comes to an end when they have completed one of its phases. When a person is through with college and has to establish himself, when an executive in a company is moved up to the board of directors, when a line officer is promoted to a staff position, when a woman feels that she has lost the charm of her youth or when she is afraid that she might not catch a husband, and when children leave home— these are the moments when the psychiatrist may be called upon to help.

The termination of a significant phase in a person's life means that the individual has to reorganize his human relations, acquire new roles, live by new rules, and adapt his implementations to new circumstances. As long as the individual believes in his future, temporary difficulties can easily be overcome. However, older persons who possess an insufficient mastery of the systems of symbolization may get into trouble. In the older age groups, influence is not exerted by direct action but by remote control. The age at which people begin to rely upon symbol manipulation usually coincides with the age—between forty and fifty—at which complete mastery of communication is attained. But if such mastery is delayed or postponed, the psychiatrist's first task is to develop the communication system of the patient. To cope with symbols and words, to experience at the sight of symbols when reading, observing, and listening, to be able to create with symbols or to influence people is the art that has to be taught. Once this is under way, the person can resume his development.

Another difficulty that is found in older people is related to the inability to identify with authority figures. Early in life children identify with their parents and other heroes; middle aged people identify with their peers and with groups; older people identify with their children and with the generation of the future. Thus the object of identification is always the person who is in the prime of life. The individual thus goes through a cycle: he begins with upward identification, continues with collateral identification, and finishes with downward identification. Personality difficulties may not always show up in youth. Some people, when young, look up to others, submit, rebel, and serve. As they get older, they are the ones that get into the position of control, but their need for upward identification may interfere with efficient operation. As long as they could identify—even ambivalently—everything was all right; to become the object of identification, however, may be unbearable.

To help unidentified people is relatively easy as long as they are young because the therapist himself can become a source of identification. But with older patients who do not look up to others or to a future, who sometimes are lonely and without children or grandchildren, the task is more difficult. Almost every person believes in his own immortality, and each religion makes detailed provisions for life after death. An assumption of some kind of immortality is necessary for healthy living, and if people cannot look towards a future they become self-destructive. The therapist thus has to see to it that older people can maintain their belief in their own immortality. This can be achieved by having old and unidentified people participate in a movement with a clearly defined goal. The human authority they so much seek is embodied in the officers of the organization; the belief in the future is rekindled by the goal of the organization, which may stand for social progress, peace, education, or art; and immortality is achieved by identification with an idea, regardless of whether it is philosophical, ethical, or religious. The idea must be embodied in a symbol that is more powerful than the individual. The psychiatrist can discuss these ideas with the patient and help him to find a movement with which to identify.

COMMITMENT, EXPERIENCE, AND EXISTENCE

Commitment · The brain as a calculating machine · Man as a responsive animal · Self-selection and opportunity · Self-realization

The pleasure of living is dependent upon a person's ability to experience and to be involved at the moment. Commitment in this sense means that a person can mobilize all his resources for what he is doing at the moment. But when the adult individual is not capable of committing himself to the present and dreams of either the past or the future, problems are likely to arise. The life history of successful people indicates that full participation and involvement with what was going on at the moment and little concern about what would come in the future are outstanding features. Current existential philosophy and associated therapeutic schools (7) maintain the position that the analytic schemes of the past detract from the individual's being in this world and his feeling of oneness within himself and the surroundings (1).

The logical, analytical, deductive approach does not encompass all of man's psychic phenomena and does not do justice to the instantaneous experiences of the moment which exist largely in the analogic mode. Images, sensations, and feelings are continuous events which are not split into subject and predicate, and under no circumstances can they be expressed in terms of numbers. Digital or verbal codification relies upon symbols that refer to one aspect of the event after another, and the impression of the whole is achieved by serial alignment of symbols. Extrapolation and interpolation are essentially digital-verbal functions upon which the processes of prediction and analysis are built.

But let us not forget that man is half calculating machine and half animal; and the animal side, with its analogic imagery and its responsiveness to stimuli, is the one that usually gives trouble. American Indians, tribes of the South Pacific, or other primitive people have excellently developed analogic systems of communication. They are integrated people, skilled, and relatively content; but because of their undeveloped digital system they are technologically inferior and their numerical systems, their ability to calculate, and their scientific knowledge are poor. Our patients, in contrast, who have been trained for twenty or more years in the use of numbers, words, and logic, are familiar with analytic techniques; but they are immature in the analogic sense. They lack the ability to comprehend the obvious; they are poorly integrated; and they are constantly dealing with part aspects of events. They lack the ability to meditate and to give a meaning to their lives, which can be achieved only by a mixture of solitude, contact with nature, and the empathic understanding of man. And while natives such as the North and South American Indians were killed by the technical superiority of the colonizers, the white man is likely to be exterminated by his lack of intuitive understanding of his own organism and its limitations. Therapy with the white man is largely devoted to a strengthening of the analogic way of experiencing and of the adaptive way of responding.

In some of the non-technical native civilizations, the prevalence of analogic modes of codification, responsiveness to stimuli, and skills induce people to do what they are fitted for. In our civilization, where the lure of varied opportunities and their selection by so-called experts prevails, people often get themselves into careers or situations for which they are ill suited. When we need scientists, youngsters are pushed in one direction; when we need salesmen, they are pushed in another; and when a state of war exists, they all become soldiers. Under such conditions, the individual cannot make maximum use of his cultural endowment, his physical constitution, and his personal talents. In places where the digital-verbal modes of codification prevail, control is preferred to adaptation; and with this dwindles the chance for self-realization.

Self-realization can be encouraged if the therapist has a profound knowledge not of therapeutic theories and formulations but of people and their personal experiences (8). Above all, he must keep in mind the ways in which nature sets limitations. He knows that women in their late forties seldom bear children, that a pianist needs some five to ten thousand hours of practice spread over a period of many years to become really proficient. Knowledge of ranges, maxima and minima, helps the therapist to confront the patient with the cold facts of life. Mental patients are helped to ignore obvious facts through the arbitrariness of the digital-verbal codification system. The therapist's emphasis thus is directed towards the analogic, which maintains a closer relationship to actual events; a photograph speaks louder than a verbal description of a scene. Experience rather than exposure, inner satisfaction rather than external success, talent rather than opportunity, and the present rather than the future are the points of emphasis. Through the "now," fully committed to the problems at hand, and rich in inner experience is the road to self-realization. The therapist's methods are simple; by commenting at crucial moments, he sways decisions and reminds the patient to be true to himself, to bank on his talents, knowledge, and skill, and to favor long-term development. Only a well developed person who has realized his own potentialities will become a useful member of society.

References

1. Berg, J. H. van den: *The Phenomenological Approach to Psychiatry.* 105 p. Springfield: Thomas, 1955.

2. Erikson, E. H.: *Childhood and Society.* 397 p. New York: Norton, 1950.

3. Erikson, E. H.: The problem of ego identity. J. Amer. Psychoanal. Assoc., 4, 56–121, 1956.

4. Fenichel, O.: *The Psychoanalytic Theory of Neurosis.* 703 p. New York: Norton, 1945.

5. Kyle, W. M.: *Mind and Experience.* 162 p. Brisbane: University of Queensland Press, 1956.

6. Masserman, J. H.: Faith and delusion in psychotherapy. Amer. J. Psychiat., 110, 324–333, 1953.

7. May, R., Angel, E., and Ellenberger, H. F. (Editors): *Existence: A New Dimension in Psychiatry and Psychology.* 445 p. New York: Basic Books, 1958.

8. Sechehaye, M. A.: *Symbolic Realization.* 184 p. New York: International Universities Press, 1951.

9. Welford, A. T.: *Ageing and Human Skill.* 300 p. London: Oxford, 1958.

10. Wheelis, A.: *The Quest for Identity.* 250 p. New York: Norton, 1958.

Part Five

Therapy with the Disturbed Individual

Part Five

Therapy with the Disturbed Individual

Conscience. But over half a century of psychiatric experience, belief

Chapter Fifteen

Personalities and the Course of Therapy

THE DICHOTOMOUS way of thinking prevalent in Western civilization has not left psychiatry unscathed. Diseases have been grouped in pairs such as psychoses and neuroses, organic and functional disorders, or psychoneuroses and personality disorders. For therapeutic purposes, these classifications are meaningless. They originated in the nineteenth century, and psychiatrists then believed that diagnostic categories might have etiological and prognostic significance. But over half a century of psychiatric experience belies this assumption. The criteria for classifications are vague and cannot even be used for cross-cultural comparisons. What is called schizophrenia in one hospital or one country may be labeled manic-depressive in another. However, there is some justification for classifications in the state hospital. A diagnosis can be used as an index of the severity of a condition and the kind of nursing care that is required. And when the commissioners of mental hygiene submit their budgets to the legislators, they at least have words to indicate that different kinds of patients have been hospitalized (26).

But if the psychotherapist cannot use psychiatric diagnoses as an aid in his therapeutic work and if he disgustedly abandons classifications that do not help him, what does he accept in their place? Unfortunately there is at the present time no scheme available which would do justice to the various degrees of difficulty with which the psychiatrist has to cope. In one instance, an acute schizophrenic may be helped in a matter of one month while a person with a character disorder might require ten years. In the next instance, a person with a simple personality disorder may be helped to cope with some difficulties in a few sessions while the borderline schizophrenic may never learn to cope with his difficulties at all. Short of an actual exploration of the patient, there is no way of predicting what is going to happen. However, within the first eight or ten hours of therapy the psychiatrist comes up with a pretty good estimate of the patient's difficulties if he focuses upon personality instead of upon pathology and if instead of dwelling upon the unusual he concentrates on the usual. The communication patterns of some of the types (19) that are regularly met in clinical practice are described on the next few pages.

THE INFANTILE PERSONALITY

Self-insufficiency · Five phases of development

The infantile person (17, 19) usually seeks the aid of the psychiatrist during a period of acute stress in which either physical symptoms or anxiety become disturbing. The infantile person displays a cross section of almost all disturbances of communication: poor observation of other people, difficulties in decision-making, and inability to express self. Therefore, when life makes increased demands, the patient is unable to cope with people and situations. The factors which contribute towards retarded emotional development are difficult to specify. In some instances, the patient has grown up in social surroundings in which symbolic systems and communication were neglected. The family interaction may have been kept at an immature level, and growing up could have been achieved only at the cost of alienating self from the family. In other cases, immaturity is the result of traumatic events; and again in others it is due to insufficient and discontinuous contacts with adults. But all of these circumstances have in common that the patient developed only a rudimentary sense of identity.

The over-all therapeutic program is geared to helping the patient to mature, and the infantile person should continue therapy over many years. In the first phase, when the patient demonstrates bodily functions, displays somatic symptoms, and has an urge for contact and "hypodermic affection," physical therapy, dietary measures, or drugs may provide the much needed sensations of physical stimulation. The second phase begins when the patient starts to engage in action. This kind of action is not designed to implement personal needs but is supposed to convey a message. Not having mastered communication through action, the patient now has to catch up on what he missed earlier; and therefore this kind of acting out behavior has to be tolerated. In the third phase, the patient, being impatient with what he has not learned as yet, may revert back to his physical symptoms or go through a mild depression. But with the steady support of the therapist he may master this stage and begin to learn to express himself through word or gesture. Phase four, then, is characterized by symbolic behavior which is connected with bodily sensations. Now the patient no longer needs physical contact but can have physical experiences upon perception of verbal or gestural signals. In the fifth phase, the patient learns to minimize the extent of bodily sensations connected with symbolic behavior and attempts to become more task oriented. In this phase, group participation is indicated; but in contrast to the person of action, whose goal is power and control, the infantile person makes it his purpose to be liked, to identify, and to gratify bodily desires. If therapeutic communication results in improved skills, the patient can function on a higher level of complexity. If therapy is supportive, the therapist merely constitutes a refuge to which the patient returns when he has been bruised by life.

PEOPLE OF ACTION

Action as message · *Putting action into its proper place*

The psychopath, the acting out kind of person, the adventurer, the explorer, the athlete, the soldier, and the pioneer are all people who use action as their principal form of expression (19). Therapy with persons of action is among the most difficult and exhausting tasks the doctor can encounter. Patients manipulate, they force action replies, they expect split-second timing, they get easily angered when action is not perfectly fitting, and they disregard most of the overt content of messages. Verbal communication to them is decor—a ritual, as it were, which one has to play with until one can get to the real thing.

Persons of action can be helped in two ways. First, they can be induced to master action beyond the stage of showmanship; competition with real experts may help them to achieve this goal. The patients know that their mastery of skills leaves much to be desired because, in using action for communication, they emphasize those aspects that are visible to others. Expert performance, in contrast, is geared to results rather than to noisy activity. The second way to help is to encourage participation with others around a common task. The natural tendency of the psychopath is to carry out a task on his own; subordination is hard for him to learn. A step-by-step description of such a procedure therefore would read about as follows: In the first phase, the patient gives lip service to cooperation with the therapist. As his frustration mounts because the therapist does not reply in terms of action, the patient begins to act out, usually away from the doctor's office but occasionally involving the therapeutic hour. After a period of acting out, most psychopaths quit therapy. However, if the patient should stick it out, a mild depressive reaction usually follows. This is based upon the insight that action cannot be used as self-expression, and the patient's world seems to crumble. As the patient emerges from his depression, reconstruction occurs in the fourth phase. He then applies his talents in action to the pursuit of an occupational or recreational skill. If, with the continued support of the therapist, the patient begins to act like a professional rather than an amateur, his acting out and expression through action are replaced by more complex symbolic exchange. In the fifth and last phase, finally, consolidation takes place. After the patient has been established in the group, he can share in cooperative activities, use symbolic means to communicate in group or two-person situations, and use action for personal satisfaction.

THE DEMONSTRATIVE INDIVIDUAL

Audience control · *The deflationary period* · *The reconstruction period*

The demonstrative or exhibitionistic person (19) who does everything in order to obtain approval and applause is of a type that has found great acclaim in our culture, not only on television, in the movies, and on the stage but also on automobile row and in the advertising world. All his efforts, all decisions, and all opinions are shaped by just one desire—to make an impression. He is dependent upon his audience and willing to shape himself to the demands of the audience (22).

Therapy with the demonstrative person begins with a deflationary period in which the patient's exaggerated opinion of himself has to be tackled. But the balloon must be punctured with care and the air should leak out at a slow rate; otherwise collapse of the patient or interruption of therapy might be the result. By confronting him with his phoniness, the therapist shows the patient that whatever he does and says is a step towards achieving either applause or disapproval. Many of the things he does or says have no particular significance for him except that they provoke a reaction in the other person. The patient has to understand that these provocations may be quite well received, particularly by masochistic characters. The second phase of therapy has begun when the patient begins to understand his reactive attitude, his lack of ego strength, and the absence of long-term plans. At this point, the patient may begin to drink, use drugs, or go to doctors for imaginary or real ailments; he may become promiscuous with members of the opposite sex, enter a homosexual phase, or go through a moderate depression. At this point he needs support from the therapist because some of the sources of external applause have fallen away.

In the third phase, an attempt is made to pick up the trends that were abandoned in early childhood—interest in other people, technical skills, or creative talents. In developing the patient, the doctor perpetually confronts him with the question: Do you get some real satisfaction from what you are doing? As he gradually relinquishes his phony beliefs in popularity, fast money, quick success, or tragic involvement, the patient usually begins to be more independent of applause, competition, or disapproval. He may become more interested in his existing family, his mate, and his children; or if he is single, he might consider the benefits of marriage. In the fourth phase, a study is made of how to use the patient's knowledge of people and situations in a productive way. The patient is superbly suited to occupations such as salesman, manager, politician, or public relations expert where he is in a middle-man position. But the show-off tendencies do not mingle well with top executive positions, and the patient usually has to resign himself to the fact that he will not give the orders. His dependency upon the audience usually prevents him from making really far-reaching decisions.

THE LOGICAL PERSON

Behavior is not logical · *Debunking* · *Understanding life*

The logician, the philosopher, the intellectualizer, and the fast talking administrator are all people who believe in the supremacy of words and numbers. They neglect nonverbal symbols, intuitive understanding, and appreciation of complex patterns (19). The therapeutic course with these patients is a tough one. The psychiatrist does well to keep his mouth shut, because whatever he says the patient might use against him; the patient might, for example, point out that a statement is illogical, contradictory, and nonsensical, not realizing that logic is a game of words that man invented himself. The patient cannot understand that some people, such as the therapist, are not interested in the "truth" game of the lawyer or the logician but are more concerned with the effects that man produces in others and the way he experiences the world around him.

It is almost impossible for such a patient to grasp the fact that man and nature are not logical (10). In the first phase, the only comments that the therapist makes are directed at calling the patient's attention to his emotional state. In reply, the patient usually begins to rationalize why he is anxious, depressed, or angry. Soon, therefore, the therapist has to introduce a rule: logical matters are not discussed in therapy; instead, the focus of attention is upon feelings and overt behavior in an attempt to correlate inside events with the effects that the patient produces in others. Soon the second phase is reached when the patient's complete inability to deal with human, emotional, and intuitive matters becomes obvious. Once the patient realizes that a whole set of considerations has been omitted in his life, he may begin to learn, becoming aware of his unbalanced —sometimes violent and sometimes primitive—emotional states which he has controlled successfully through his rationalizations. He begins to pay more attention to the nonverbal, non-rational aspects of living. At this stage, the therapist has to stand by and support the patient until he can find somebody in real life to share pleasure and sorrow with.

As the patient begins to equilibrate and synchronize the emotional with the rational aspects of living and begins to make decisions which include such aspects as gratification, pleasure, and displeasure, the third phase has begun. Now he understands that what he considered logical, rational, and intellectual approaches were nothing but rationalizations which justified his own behavior. This phase may be long drawn out until he reaches the fourth level, where he may emerge as a "reformed" intellectual. No longer is he a drawing-room "lawyer," "philosopher," or "social scientist." Instead, he begins to be a human being who understands children and animals, who may appreciate movement, color, and form, and who, above all, realizes the limitations of the verbal-intellectual approach. This shift is frequently accompanied by a change in his occupational orientation in which he gets bored with what he did before and now seeks emotionally more gratifying fields. Occasionally the therapist can muster some outside help to speed up this process. Readings in Zen Buddhism (27, 30) and particularly the study of the Koans puncture the balloons of the intellectual completely. Personal contact with people familiar with Zen Buddhism is of immense help in getting the patient out of his logical bind.

THE WITHDRAWN PERSON

The introvert · Fantasy as a block · Learning social conventions · The introvert in an extrovert culture · Schizophrenics

Withdrawn, shy, and introverted persons may be either highly sensitive and creative or sullen and peculiar. At times, the withdrawn person is diagnosed as suffering from a character neurosis; at other times he is considered to have a schizophrenic or a manic-depressive reaction. A withdrawn person doesn't care for people who interfere with his inner life; he tolerates others with a bemused look on his face, sometimes being polite and sometimes very rude. Being uninvolved in the petty strivings of human beings, he often is more of a realist than his contemporaries; but his Achilles heel is his sensitivity to coercion and interference. Having taken refuge in a world of his own, he may feel dissatisfied unless he can find a creative outlet for his fantasy. Outwardly the introvert's development reveals fewer traumatic incidents than that of the extrovert; but his suffering may be equal if not greater, and he carries his difficulties in silence and often with dignity.

The therapeutic task with the withdrawn person is to free him from living in a dream world and to bring him back to the enjoyment of his body, of sensuous pleasures, and of other people. First the patient has to be made aware of his magic thinking, of his belief in the omnipotence of thought and the gratification provided through fantasy. The inventory of his way of living has to include a statement of the paucity of his practical implementations, his lack of experience with people, and perhaps his intolerance for others. The fact that his exchanges are confined to self and his immediate surroundings—perhaps including music or books, but not social interaction—has to be illustrated.

Phase two begins when the patient has realized his shortcomings and makes an effort to overcompensate for his antisocial attitude. At this point, the therapist has to make it quite clear that love of people is not required but tolerance for people is. To live and let live is the motto the patient has to adopt. The patient will have to experiment with practical implementations, perhaps rearranging his occupational life so that he will participate to a minimal degree in all those activities that are necessary in the pursuit of a career. He might learn to attend parties, to talk shop with colleagues, to go to a town meeting, or to drop in on neighbors. The withdrawn person is in no way capable of keeping up a sustained "social effort." Unlike the organization man (31), he cannot keep up year in and year out with entertainment, occupational meetings, drinking bouts, and the like. If he drinks, he often drinks alone. But showing him good will is often enough to get him out of his isolation and to permit other people to approach him. In America, most withdrawn characters are in positions which are well below their capabilities. By socializing, they may achieve, to a certain extent, more satisfactory job conditions. An introverted person sometimes is able to find a mate or a friend who will tolerate his whims and sensitivities, his intolerances and projections, and who will take on some of his social obligations. This is a division of labor which often works very satisfactorily.

The last phase, which is rarely achieved even after many years of work, is devoted to finding a place in the sun in which the patient's introvert qualities can be appreciated. This is more likely to occur in Western Europe, where the introvert has a respected position and people who deal with ideas are valued. In the American civilization, which is geared to the extrovert, many of these patients are likely to remain misfits. But in accepting their character and their inferior social position, they frequently can develop a satisfactory existence. They are the eggheads, the intellectuals, the teachers, and the artists. In peacetime, the successful businessman looks down upon them, but at times of emergency they are called upon to rise from obscurity and provide others with solutions which the extrovert is incapable of thinking of. With the advent of the atomic age, it appears possible that the introvert might find a more respectable position in American society.

Therapeutic communication with schizophrenic patients who are outright psychotic presents a challenging problem (20). Although some therapists maintain that it is perfectly possible to

analyze certain schizophrenic patients in the same way as psychoneurotic patients (2, 16, 25), most therapists have abandoned
the classical technique (4, 5, 9). To them it seems unnecessary and
undesirable for the patient to lie on a couch and free-associate.
Treatment of chronic schizophrenic patients in the earlier stages
is essentially nonverbal (7) and the therapist has to be more alert
to cues such as tone, rhythm, volume of voice, and body movements,
noting the timing and context of verbal productions rather than attempting to decipher their obscure content (11). A schizophrenic
patient may talk straight either when he is physically sick or when
he respects the therapist, whereas his "schizy talk" has to be considered a way of testing out the doctor (3).

To understand the patient's behavior and his needs, the therapist
must be aware of interpersonal impacts and situational conditions.
Catatonic patients require a greater degree of physical handling;
the hebephrenic patient demands intuitive appraisal of his verbal
productions; the paranoid patient expects encouragement and
nurturance. The crucial point in the rehabilitation of schizophrenics
seems to be that any person with whom the patient has consistent
and prolonged contact be given an opportunity to form durable
relationships with him. Only in such a way can this person learn
the special forms of communication that the patient engages in
(21). Intimate contact with one and the same person over long
periods of time allows the patient to relive, both in action and in
fantasy, his anxiety-laden wishes (15, 24).

ANXIOUS AND FEARFUL PEOPLE

*Anger, fear, and anxiety · Communication during alarm · Management
of the alarm reaction · Diagnosis of alarm-producing situations · Overcoming fear*

Reaction to danger is described in terms of anger, fear, or
anxiety. The initial reaction to an alarming signal and the subsequent instigation of psychological and physical preparedness for
action is known as the alarm reaction, which readies the organism
for fight or flight. In anger, impending danger and interference

have been perceived as a threat which can be managed, fought, and conquered. In fear, integrated action is initiated to avoid the interference. If, for internal psychological or external environmental reasons, flight or fight is impossible, the fear or the anger changes into anxiety (18, 23). A state of anxiety develops when the massive impact upon the organism of stimuli—self-generated or deriving from the outside—becomes so overwhelming that the individual feels paralyzed. As a result, the preparedness for action cannot be consummated and the vascular, muscular, respiratory, and endocrine phenomena persist for undue lengths of time. The same thing may occur when the individual has perceived subtle signals that indicate the presence of danger which he cannot cope with. This condition is felt by the individual as anxiety.

The rehabilitation of the anxious and phobic person has been amply described in the psychotherapeutic and psychoanalytic literature (6, 8). What is of interest is that neither anxiety nor fear interrupts communication unless the patient is in an acute state of panic. Feedback is operative, except for those topics that are threatening to the individual. Like a horse or a deer that pricks his ears in the direction of noise, the human being concentrates in the direction of the expected danger. His anticipations, therefore, influence that which he is going to perceive and make him somewhat obtuse for stimuli which derive from persons, objects, animals, and situations that fall outside the realm of the anticipated. Communication with alarmed people taxes the resources of others. The angry, anxious, and fearful persons demand and expect a reply to their preoccupations. The angry person longs for a soothing hand or a fight; the anxious person expects that the other one will become anxious too and thereby justify his own anxiety; the fearful person, finally, wants protection against the fear-inspiring stimulus.

To the psychiatrist who has to deal with a disturbed patient, it does not matter whether anxiety is brought on by situational stress, by an intolerable internal conflict, or by a combination of these (29). The therapy of all anxious people, regardless of the type of pathology, is much the same. The voice of the therapist should not be threatening; it should be firm. The sentences should be short and uninvolved, and they should refer to simple things—"Sit down," "Have a cup of coffee," "Let's walk." The comprehension of the patient is rarely beyond these short, command-like sentences. The fact that somebody else makes decisions and takes over serves as a relief, even if the command imposes restraint. If the therapist can manage to remain relatively unperturbed himself, he will, through negative feedback, convey to the patient that the apparent object of anger, fear, or anxiety is not so important as the patient thought it was. By not being angry, anxious, or fearful himself, he exerts the greatest therapeutic effect (23). In order to comfort the patient without increasing his anxiety, touch works exceedingly well. A gentle patting of the hair, holding the hand, or putting an arm around an excited person works miracles. Touch and togetherness apparently reinforce the inbred notion that within a herd there is safety (28). Stimulation of the proximity receivers seems to bind the person more to the present situation and drag him away from anticipatory behavior which aggravates anxiety. Once the immediate excitement is under control, the therapist can see to it that the patient is temporarily separated from the anxiety provoking situation and tranquilizers may be used to quiet him. When the patient is more relaxed, a review of the precipitating factors or the personality features which induced him to react with anxiety is in place. Listening, understanding, and acknowledging have an effect which rather rapidly will help the anxious person. Serious decisions are postponed until a later date, and everything is geared to re-establishing the status quo ante.

When the patient has regained his equanimity, the therapist takes a second look not only at the circumstances but also at the personality structure which permits such temporary breakdowns. He may discover that previous traumatic experiences or idiosyncrasies make the patient vulnerable to certain kinds of situations. The inability to engage in action, difficulties in expression, threatened dependency, isolation, authority problems, and a host of other factors may be the precipitating cause; and if exhaustion, boredom, or malnutrition is added, a breakdown may result. Once the specific personality feature and the environmental stress have been identified, the patient can learn to avoid this for him dangerous situation.

In the next phase, the patient will tentatively test out the limits of his tolerance for the traumatic situation. It goes without saying that the patient is more inclined to be avoidant than to expose himself, but with the encouragement of the therapist he may attempt to approach the danger from a somewhat different direction. Understanding of his shortcomings may enable him to prepare himself in a way which was not possible before. As he meets the dangerous situation anew, the patient experiences another phenomenon: he will learn to abandon his crutches—particularly the association with people who act as protectors in fear-arousing situations and as sharers of anxiety in post-mortem bull sessions. He will learn to experience, not with tubular vision but with a wider field of awareness. Instead of clinging to one protector, he will learn to rely more upon himself and upon information.

THE DEPRESSED PATIENT

Feeling low · Redirection of anger · Lowering of ideals · Inner-directedness

Depression is a symptom which may be observed in a patient with a manic-depressive temperament, in a person who suffers from a situational reaction, in a middle-aged person who goes through the involutional phase, in an alcoholic who has ceased drinking, or in a patient with a duodenal ulcer that has healed. The person who is depressed has restricted his network and cut himself off from communication with others. Reacting slowly and with anger towards himself, he is redundant in his thoughts and preoccupied with self-accusation; he feels unworthy and is incapable of achieving the goals he has set for himself. Loss of a beloved person or abandonment of a cherished idea often signals the onset of the depression.

The therapeutic course varies somewhat, depending upon the severity of the depression (1, 12, 13). In mild cases it is often possible to convert the anger against self into anger towards another

person, and therefore a somewhat aggressive therapist often manages
to get a release of anger with a subsequent lifting of the depression.
In the more severe cases, however, it is impossible to change the
direction of the anger. The severely depressed patient needs continued support and steady company for twenty-four hours a day.
The patient becomes very demanding in these phases—so demanding that he is afraid of his own appetite and possessiveness. He has
to be reassured and permitted to be demanding; and when he discovers that the other person is not afraid, he improves. Therefore
continued support and company, avoidance of all decisions, protection from overstimulation and coercion, and postponement of
resumption of duties may help the patient to find himself. Whether
or not hospitalization is necessary and shock or drug therapy indicated has to be decided in each individual case.

No depression lasts forever, and in the second phase of therapy
the patient may attempt to recapture what he has lost. Spontaneously or after a variety of treatments, the patient begins to substitute some other person for the one that he lost, and he may again
pursue the old ideal or a close substitute with new vigor. That
these strivings may be on the somewhat unrealistic side does not
matter as long as the patient resumes functioning. When the patient is out of his depression, an appraisal of realistic goals has to
be made. His perfectionistic tendencies and high level of aspiration
are of course deeply embedded in his personality, but the patient's
ideals and standards must be reduced to something which is compatible with his skills and the external situation. Only by re-anchor-
ing the patient's self-respect to other aspects of his existence and
freeing him from his dependency upon that one person or that
single idea will the doctor be able to avert future depressions. The
lowering of standards is achieved by working through the original
situations that imposed such a need. When the patient is able to
recognize that high standards are in part compensatory mechanisms
to cover failure in action and in part a reflection of his parents'
ideals, he gradually may be able to accept his own experiences as
guideposts for behavior.

The last phase of therapy is characterized by recurring depressions, but they are milder than the previous ones. In this phase, the patient learns to work himself out of his depressed mood without external assistance. He becomes aware of the fact that his anticipatory behavior outraces his actual skills and that his extrapolations do not take account of his resources. After intensive work with the therapist, the patient's outrageous appetite for love and respect may diminish and be replaced by communicative exchange demonstrated by the therapist. When the patient has learned rational approaches, elation and depression can be muted and he may learn to put on the brakes consciously. The outer-directedness (14) of the patient, which previously led to elation or depression, is gradually replaced by a more stable inner-directedness. Instead of relying upon exhilarating incorporation, the patient learns to rely upon practical implementations and productive activity.

THE SADISTIC-MASOCHISTIC CHARACTER

The sadistic-masochistic game · Weaning the partners · Dilution of intensity · One or two therapists

There is no sadist without a masochist. Communicative exchange between these two types is characterized by the absence of specific replies, with all the concomitant frustration. In order to force acknowledgment, the sadistic partner resorts to cruelty while the masochistic partner prides himself in not giving satisfaction. Both sadist and masochist learned their approaches in childhood. The patients' specific messages were not acknowledged and the verbal statements which emanated from the parents often did not match their attitudes and actions (19). The child then had either to resort to tricks to force a response or submit to the arbitrary expressions of the parent. These patients learned that verbal communication can be used to frustrate the other person by withholding acknowledgment. A step-by-step analysis of the sadistic-masochistic game would read as follows: When the masochistic person makes a statement, he knows that the other must interpret and reply. As soon as the other actually replies, the masochistic person changes his frame of reference and indicates that he has not quite caught on. When the other good-naturedly tries again, the masochistic person uses the same trick. Finally the other person feels cheated. He then decides to force a reply and resorts to cruelty. Then the masochist may yield and acknowledge; but by this time the sadist has had enough, and frequently the roles are reversed.

Team pathology is characterized by the fact that the partners are deeply involved in each other's neurosis. Normal communicative exchange with other people means little or nothing to them. In these cases, the therapist does well to take on both partners and work with them simultaneously, not in order to break up the relationship—time will take care of that—but in order to make both aware that they are sick people who are addicted to their pathology. Premature separation has to be avoided in that it would merely result in the patients' teaming up with others, and the therapist would deal with two pathological teams instead of one. In weaning the patients from their addiction and from each other, the therapist is helped by the patient's disgust with his own dependence. He would like to free himself from perpetual and frustrating arguments; but when he is on the verge of establishing a new relationship with a human being who does not play this involved game, he finds that life becomes meaningless. The therapeutic task therefore is to make the patient tolerate boredom, play down dramatic scenes, convert life from an obstacle course over emergencies to a routine performance, and care for the practical aspects of existence. When the therapist talks with both partners at different hours of the week or when he sees them together, he discusses scene after scene and event after event and points to the feelings of deep significance and equally deep frustration that both partners provide for each other. The relationship of the patients to the therapist can be characterized by dependence, rebellion, or aloofness. Under no circumstances does the therapist accept a role in which he becomes the significant person with whom this sadistic-masochistic game is played. Although such an attitude robs the therapist of some leverage, it nonetheless gives him a chance to set an example of a well-functioning communication system without undesirable side effects.

By working with both partners, the therapist applies the principle of dilution: the more diversified human relations these patients have, the less intense each relation becomes. Inasmuch as it is lack of intensity which the patients have to learn to tolerate, conscious participation in social groups is recommended and intimate face-to-face relations are to be avoided. Once this is accomplished, mutually interdependent partners may become less involved, which is the preparatory step for the dissolution of the relationship.

The therapeutically effective agent apparently is embodied in the fact that a third person has moved into a well-established equilibrium and disturbed the balance. Once the secret purposes of the partners have been verbalized and their procedures exposed, the patients no longer feel as free to engage in their pathology as before. At this point, the question can be raised as to whether one of the partners should seek another therapist. The decision depends upon the mutual roles of the partners, the financial circumstances, and the theoretical beliefs of the psychiatrist. If husband and wife are to stay married, they should be seen by the same therapist. If the daughter is going to leave home anyway, she might be sent to another therapist. And if a man wishes to separate from his mistress, the therapist might do well to refer her to a colleague.

References

1. Abraham, K.: *Selected Papers*. 527 p. London: Hogarth Press, 1942.
2. Bion, W. R.: Notes on the theory of schizophrenia. Int. J. Psycho-Anal., 35, 113–118, 1954.
3. Burnham, D. L.: Some problems in communication with schizophrenic patients. J. Amer. Psychoanal. Assoc., 3, 67–81, 1955.
4. Bychowski, G.: *Psychotherapy of Psychosis*. 328 p. New York: Grune & Stratton, 1952.
5. Federn, P.: *Ego Psychology and the Psychoses*. 375 p. New York: Basic Books, 1952.
6. Fenichel, O.: *The Psychoanalytic Theory of Neurosis*. 703 p. New York: Norton, 1945.
7. Freeman, T., Cameron, J. L., and McGhie, A.: *Chronic Schizophrenia*. 158 p. London: Tavistock, 1958.
8. Freud, S.: *Collected Papers, Vol. I.* (1924). 359 p. London: Hogarth Press and The Institute of Psycho-Analysis, 1948.

9. Fromm-Reichmann, F.: Notes on the development of treatment of schizophrenics by psychoanalytic psychotherapy. Psychiatry, 11, 263–273, 1948.

10. Gitelson, M.: Intellectuality in the defense transference. Psychiatry, 7, 73–86, 1944.

11. Hill, L. B.: *Psychotherapeutic Intervention in Schizophrenia*. 216 p. Chicago: University of Chicago Press, 1955.

12. Kraines, S. H.: *Mental Depressions and Their Treatment*. 555 p. New York: Macmillan, 1957.

13. Lewin, B.: *The Psychoanalysis of Elation*. 200 p. New York: Norton, 1950.

14. Riesman, D.: *The Lonely Crowd*. 386 p. New Haven: Yale University Press, 1950.

15. Rosen, J. N.: *Direct Analysis*. 184 p. New York: Grune & Stratton, 1953.

16. Rosenfeld, H.: Considerations regarding the psycho-analytic approach to acute and chronic schizophrenia. Int. J. Psycho-Anal., 35, 135–140, 1954.

17. Ruesch, J.: The infantile personality: the core problem of psychosomatic medicine. Psychosom. Med., 10, 134–144, 1948.

18. Ruesch, J.: The interpersonal communication of anxiety. Pp. 154–164 in *Symposium on Stress (16–18 March, 1953)*. Washington: Army Medical Service Graduate School, 1953.

19. Ruesch, J.: *Disturbed Communication*. 337 p. New York: Norton, 1957.

20. Ruesch, J.: Psychotherapy with schizophrenics. Pp. 199–216 in *Schizophrenia* (Edited by A. Auerback). New York: Ronald Press, 1959.

21. Ruesch, J.: The schizophrenic patient's ways of communication. Pp. 198–207 in *Congress Report (1957) Vol. 4*. Zurich: IInd International Congress for Psychiatry, 1959.

22. Ruesch, J.: Mass communication and mass motivation. Amer. J. Psychother., 14, 250–258, 1960.

23. Ruesch, J. and Prestwood, A. R.: Anxiety, its initiation, communication, and interpersonal management. AMA Arch. Neurol. Psychiat., 62, 527–550, 1949.

24. Sechehaye, M. A.: *A New Psychotherapy for Schizophrenia*. 199 p. New York: Grune & Stratton, 1956.

25. Segal, H.: Some aspects of the analysis of a schizophrenic. Int. J. Psycho-Anal., 31, 268–278, 1950.

26. Stanton, A. H.: Psychiatric theory and institutional context. Psychiatry, 17, 19–26, 1954.

27. Suzuki, D. T.: *Zen Buddhism*. 294 p. Garden City: Doubleday Anchor

Books, 1956.

28. Trotter, W.: *Instincts of the Herd in Peace and War.* 264 p. London: T. Fisher Unwin, 1921.

29. Wallin, J. E. W.: *Minor Mental Maladjustments in Normal People.* 298 p. Durham: Duke University Press, 1939.

30. Watts, A.: *Way of Zen.* 236 p. New York: Pantheon, 1957.

31. Whyte, W. H., Jr.: *The Organization Man.* 429 p. New York: Simon & Schuster, 1956.

Chapter Sixteen

Disturbed Functions of Communication

EVERY organism is characterized by the ability to perceive, to evaluate, and to transmit messages—and transmission also includes action which was not intended for communication but was incidentally perceived by others. Whenever one of the three fundamental functions is disturbed, repercussions can be observed in other parts of the network. A disturbance of perception distorts evaluation and expression; when judgment is faulty, perception is selective and action inappropriate; if expression is deranged, it exerts, through feedback, a distorting influence upon evaluation and perception. For therapeutic purposes, it is useful to isolate features which seem to be primarily or at least more grossly related to one rather than to another aspect of communication. Without implying any causal or etiological connections, the pinpointing of the principal pathology is the first step towards correction.

DISTURBANCES IN PERCEPTION

Shared and individualized distortions · Widening awareness · Erroneous interpretation · Misunderstandings between introvert and extrovert · Intolerance of difference in values · Over-specialization · Sharpening perception · Sensory distortions have a useful function · Coping with hallucinations · Shifting delusions · Sensory deprivation · The anxiety of the blind · The deaf

SELECTIVE INATTENTION

In recent years some fascinating experiments have shed light on the selectivity of perception (6). If, for example, photographs of two different people are mounted in a stereoscope and presented to an observer, he will describe neither of the two faces but a combination of both (10). What a person sees is what is significant to him, and "significant" is defined as whatever leaves an emotional impact. In other experiments (18), a subject is shown a distorted frame—a window or a room—in which he sees another person; he has the choice of perceiving either space or person as distorted, depending upon the relationship. Once the distortions have been chosen, constancies are assigned to these in order to obtain a consistent picture of self and of the world (2).

People do not bother about things that don't matter or about things that will go all right anyway. But pathology develops when they ignore events that do matter. People are inclined to ignore significant details that are anxiety producing. The absence of focal awareness, which Sullivan has termed "selective inattention" (35), insures the avoidance of unpleasant emotions. A person who pursues such a security operation may assume a role which does not fit the actual situation; for example, a person may behave as if he were on intimate terms with another, although he actually is not. A similar distortion occurs when a patient deliberately assumes that the context of a situation is different from what it really is, by negating physical disease, ignoring debts, or assuming responsibilities which are not his.

In former times, fugue states, sleepwalking, hysterical anesthesia, concentric restriction of the visual field, and similar distortions of perception were cured by producing shock. Slapping a patient's face was not an uncommon practice, and people with hysterical blindness have been restored to full vision upon such angry treatment by a physician (1). Therapeutically speaking, the directness of the approach that hits at the center of the selective inattention forces the individual to respond. At some level, of course, the individual knows what he consciously denies and a frontal assault produces anger which reorganizes his behavior.

In modern times, such shock methods are frowned upon unless the doctor is faced with an emergency, such as might occur in the high mountains, in an airplane, or in a boat. But under ordinary circumstances he will prefer to tackle the conflict that underlies the distortion of perception, although suggestion or hypnosis may at times be helpful. In long-term therapy, the doctor will help the patient to sharpen his perception, particularly in the social sphere. This he achieves by verbalizing the nonverbal aspects of the patient's behavior, by emphasizing the latent content, and by making him suspicious of whatever he ignores. Thus the patient can be trained to react to his own avoidances.

SOCIAL IMPERCEPTIVENESS

For the psychiatrist, social perception is an empirical problem that has to be handled on the spot. If people do not recognize the cues that characterize roles, do not inquire into the prevailing rules, fail to ascertain contexts, do not identify the signs of pleasure or frustration in others and in themselves, or cannot perceive the minute shadings which a raised eyebrow may give to a verbal statement, they are obviously at a loss to understand or interpret messages properly. But even if perception functions, a message has to be properly interpreted if misunderstandings are to be avoided. If, for example, an individual improperly assesses a cue and considers an isolated aspect of behavior as if it were representative of the other's personality all of the time, he may be misled. Or if he decides that a person's casualness, which he observed under ordinary circumstances, will continue under stress, he may be in for a surprise. There are many stereotyped interpretations which people use when they have identified a trigger cue; as a result, the other person becomes identified as a type or a case and group characteristics are substituted for individual features. Then there are those distortions in perception-evaluation which are brought on by our own behavior. We force the other person to adapt in some measure to our expectations, and sometimes, of course, the other will not adapt and then we are displeased. This displeasure, in turn, may cloud our own perceptions.

People who have different modes of experience are inclined to misinterpret each other's behavior, and the introvert usually looks askance at the activities of the extrovert, and vice versa. As

Ichheiser (17) puts it: "The introverted-contemplative person, therefore, will look frequently upon the extroverted-activistic as upon a busybody who conceals from himself his inner emptiness by releasing his restlessness in various meaningless pseudo-activities . . . To the activistic extrovert, on the other hand, the contemplative introvert looks like an irresponsible dreamer who conceals from himself his inability for responsible action by indulging in an attitude which 'does not lead anywhere.' The contemplative introvert wishes to understand why people feel and think and behave as they do; the extroverted-activistic person wishes 'to do something about it.'"

Another kind of social imperceptiveness is based on intolerance of differing assumptions about life, death, and the social order. In social situations, one has to understand the nature of the other person's values as well as the hierarchy which these values have in the person's life. If a person upholds the value of equality, he will obviously have to sacrifice liberty; if he observes the value of superiority, he will have to disregard equality. The merits of an isolated value can be neither understood nor reasonably discussed; but this is exactly what happens in many of the conversations that lead to heated, unsatisfactory discussions.

Some people are unaware of the social context of a situation. By ignoring furniture arrangement, composition of the group, state of health of the participants, or time of day, they can actively distort the communicative exchange. What somebody says in a late evening hour under the influence of liquor at a gay gathering may not stand up to scrutiny the next morning; nor does the observation of a person's leisure time activities give insight into his professional conduct.

Individuals who by nature and training have devoted most of their time to the perception of special situations may overlook or misinterpret cues if they fall into another field. There are those who focus upon "how to do it" and neglect the "what"; therefore they have difficulty in getting along with those who are idea oriented. The formalist, in turn, who perceives manners, grammar, and etiquette has great difficulties in perceiving a person's intentions.

Correction of social imperceptiveness is a long drawn out affair. The doctor has to spend a great deal of time with the patient in reconstructing events and pointing out omissions and distortions. He can say, "From what you have told me, it would appear to me that . . ." and thus familiarize the patient with the doctor's impressions; and through continuous back and forth exchange, a clarification usually can be achieved. The therapist also can rely upon events that occur in the therapeutic hour. He can point out that the lighting of a cigarette at a certain moment indicates the patient's need for intake and that this occurred when the doctor raised his voice. What, then, happened inside the patient at this moment?

EXTEROCEPTIVE OR INTEROCEPTIVE PREFERENCES

Informative stimuli may arise inside or outside the organism. Well integrated individuals can combine the information derived from different sources of stimuli, but patients tend to emphasize one set more than the other. The interoceptively handicapped person disregards warning signals such as hunger, thirst, fatigue, pain, desire for affection or sex, and makes life dependent upon the clock, the calendar, the opinion of others, or the rules set up by state and church; on the whole, he surrounds himself with logical or mechanical devices to compensate for his rudimentary intuition and his disregard for animal instinct. He is unaware of what goes on in himself and therefore he is likely to deprive himself of necessary gratifications to the extent of abusing his body beyond its limits of tolerance. Such a person usually is obtuse to the changes that age brings about and has difficulty in adapting his way of living to the needs of his advancing years.

The exteroceptively handicapped person does not heed external warning signals—traffic signs, printed rules, or precautionary measures. He disregards storm warnings and consequently often runs into a tempest. Associated with this disregard of external cues may be an inability to take instructions from others or to gauge the effects of self upon others.

Therapeutic communication with such people is obviously directed at strengthening the perception of the stimuli that they are ignoring. At any one time, the sensations arising within the organism have to be combined with those arising on the outside; only then can the individual decide what is good for him. In therapy, this is achieved by pointing to the missing information in the patient's experience. When a husband tells of his wife's sickness and reports medical details at great length, there comes a moment when the therapist interjects, "And how did it affect you? What did you feel?" If another patient wallows in a sea of feelings, reactions, and sensitivities as a result of a disagreement, the therapist interrupts and says, "Now give me a blow-by-blow description so that I can get a clearer picture of what happened. Who was there? What did you discuss? Have you had previous arguments of this kind?"

SENSORY DISTORTIONS

Illusions and hallucinations are very real to the person who experiences them. If voices call the patient by his name, he experiences being wanted by somebody else. If the voices accuse him of wrongdoing, he believes that another person is after him. And if a thirsty trooper lost in the desert perceives a mirage of a refreshing oasis close at hand, he obviously gains new strength to continue his march. To understand sensory distortions, we have to ask ourselves the question, "What function does this experience have in the psychological household of the patient?" Correction of sensory distortions occurs not through arguing or confrontation but through concrete experience.

A therapist who is interested in his patient and responsive to his unconscious intentions will observe that the voices calling the patient by name disappear after the relationship to the therapist improves. These voices are clearly a substitute for human relations. Accusatory voices, or the projected reproaches of the conscience, are more difficult to deal with. When the patient feels that he deserves punishment, he imposes punishment upon himself. If he cannot tolerate the ensuing frustration, he projects the origin of the punishment upon an imaginary outside source. Under such circumstances, the firmness of the therapist can teach the patient that he is in contact with an authority capable of punishing and rewarding. As soon as this has occurred, the patient maneuvers the situation in such a way that the therapist is tempted to assume an accusatory attitude. If he does assume this role, he has taken over the function of the accusatory voices which herewith become superfluous.

Although delusions are not sensory distortions in the strict sense of the word, they nonetheless influence perception. False beliefs help people to disregard whatever does not fit into their system. To correct such a system is almost impossible unless the delusions are shifted to another area of interest. If a patient's interest can be shifted from reading the minds of his neighbors to having a spiritual seance with his deceased ancestors, therapeutic success has been achieved. Now the belief is not accessible to ordinary testing, and whatever may be false about it does not show; it enables the patient nontheless to function satisfactorily in other areas of living. To accomplish such shifts, the therapist has but one tool at his disposal: the interpersonal relationship. If the relationship becomes gratifying, the patient will incorporate all significant transactions and confine himself on the outside to impersonal matters or to transactions that deal with his immediate entourage. And this is exactly what the normal person does.

SENSORY DEFECTS

There are people who suffer from congenital blindness or deafness; others have acquired organic diseases of the central nervous system and may suffer from an impaired sense of vision, hearing, touch, taste, smell, equilibrium, pain, or temperature. If the defect is temporary, the problem is not severe. If the defect is permanent, a complete readaptation has to occur if the patient is to survive.

Sensory deprivation through experimental reduction of stimulation (20), through natural loss of contact with the environment (24), or because of damage to the sensory pathways results in an intense desire for extensive sensory stimuli and bodily motion, increased suggestibility, impairment of organized thinking, oppression and depression, and in extreme cases in hallucinations, delusions, and confusion (34). In this case, the missing external input is replaced by an internal input so that the total sensory input remains constant (22). Similar reactions have been observed in people who are temporarily or permanently blinded. Operations on the visual apparatus, particularly when the individual is older, tend to be accompanied by symptoms of sensory deprivation such as hallucinations or confusion (16, 21, 25).

The rehabilitation of people who suffer from blindness does not fall into the province of the psychiatrist (37). There exist excellent schools and institutions which have specialized in the training and rehabilitation of the blind and are highly effective (3, 19). However, there are aspects of blindness that fall into the realm of the psychotherapist. Aside from hysterical blindness—a psychiatric disorder in the proper sense—the therapist might treat people who are apprehensive about future or anticipated loss of sight. A careless remark made by a physician or comments by oversolicitous but hostile relatives may instill in a patient the idea that vision will gradually diminish. A near-sighted child may be threatened that unless he wears his glasses faithfully he might go blind. In all of these situations the blindness is not really so threatening as is the person who expresses the threat. The anxiety that arises is the consequence of the hostile impact of a human being upon the patient. The patient is unable to cope with this hostility because it is phrased in terms of an act of God and not in terms of purposeful hostile action of the other person. Therapy here is geared to untie the prospective visual defect from interpersonal embroilment.

The psychiatrist rarely sees a person who has been blinded recently. More often he comes in contact with people who have been suffering from visual defects for some time. It has been pointed out by Cholden (7) that an individual can express feelings with any degree of comfort only if he is aware of the manner in which his expressions are received. The cues derived from the other person's facial expression, posture, or movements are not available to the blind person; instead he has to rely upon other cues such as the rate of breathing, coughing, or the noise of movements. The inability to gauge the listener's reaction is in part responsible for the relative blandness of the communications of the blind. Some of these difficulties can be discussed in group situations which help the patient to realize that his problems are not unique. Such meetings bring home the idea that deficient visual feedback can be compensated for by increased emphasis in other sensory modalities. Furthermore, the group therapeutic situation lends itself for discussion of the attitudes of the public towards blindness and for instruction of relatives and other well-meaning people in how to deal with handicapped people.

The deaf and the hard of hearing present perhaps an even more serious problem than the blind (3). People who have defective vision usually are aware of their disability, but the hard of hearing often are unaware, especially if the condition is progressive; and there are some who, for vanity's sake, deny the fact that they do not hear well. Because impaired hearing interferes with auditory feedback, misunderstandings occur more frequently and the patient becomes more isolated. In consequence, deaf people are frequently classified as rude, egocentric, or arrogant. Such social withdrawal results in substitution of intrapsychic for interpersonal feedback circuits (33).

If deafness afflicts children, they usually show severe disturbances in speech development because the auditory control of sound formation is missing. These children then have to be taught to speak. For the communication therapist, the rehabilitation of the deaf is out of the question. But he can help in different ways. First, the patient has to accept the existence of his disability as unalterable so that all possible steps known today for the remedy of deafness can be initiated. These involve the examination of the ear and the hearing functions, the application of hearing aids, and remedial training (36). The second task of the psychiatrist is to cope with the feelings of isolation and inferiority of the patient which result from his being handicapped. If the psychiatrist himself cannot contact the patient by means of the spoken word, he should resort to written communication. How this can be done has been shown by Farber (11), who himself has had the misfortune of becoming deaf. Apparently therapy through writing can be successful.

Disturbances of temperature and pain sensation as well as disturbances in equilibrium and the vibratory and tactile senses may occur in a variety of organic diseases of the central nervous system (14). The psychiatrist rarely if ever deals with such patients, and if he does he is usually more concerned with the personality problems involved than with the disturbances of sensation. All he can do is leave the treatment to other specialists, help the patient to accept his disability, and reduce the impact of the relatives' well-meant but often misdirected elaborations.

DISTURBANCES IN EVALUATION

Thinking, association, and codification · *Compensating for one-sided codification* · *Prediction* · *Mood* · *Empathy and sympathy* · *Ambivalence* · *One thing at a time* · *Scanning* · *Commitment and risk* · *Declining intellectual functions* · *Abiding by tradition* · *Experience to replace conscience* · *Flexible standards* · *Repression* · *Amnesia* · *Memory disturbance and brain disease* · *Inability to utilize past experience*

The disturbances of evaluation can be subdivided into disturbances of thinking, of feeling, of decision-making, and of memory. Although evaluation is an integrated process involving all of these functions, it is easier to discuss these processes one by one.

DISTURBANCES OF THINKING

In the era of association psychology, disturbances of thinking preoccupied the psychiatrists (28). This period was followed by the psychoanalytic era, which utilized the method of free association for therapeutic purposes. Today we have moved on and are preoccupied with methods of codification and decision-making. An observer has access to the thinking of another person through the interpretation of verbal behavior. Words thus are taken as an index of what is going on in the head of the patient; but it is well to remember that what we call thinking or association and its verbalization reflect but one mode of codification of an intra-psychic event. What really takes place is that inner events may be expressed through movements other than speech. Only the interpretation of combined verbal and nonverbal denotation gives us a representative picture of what is going on. For practical purposes, therefore, it is convenient to associate logical thinking with digital-verbal denotation and imagery with analogic-non-verbal denotation (32).

Logic is an exercise in the skillful use of words and numbers according to specific man-made rules (26). Among patients, there are those who try to make decisions in accordance with the laws of logic. Here the therapist has to demonstrate to the patient that the choice of what to eat or the position in a chair is not based on logic but on the reaction of the individual to what is most comfortable, what he likes best, and what gives him the greatest amount of satisfaction. Some patients have difficulty in admitting that they are governed by emotions and steered by gratification; they cannot admit that they are not rational at all. These patients have to be taught that their logic serves frequently to camouflage some instinctive desires. They have to learn to distinguish when logic is in order—for example, in solving a mathematical problem— and when it is out of place—for example, in reacting to small children.

In therapy, we frequently encounter the compulsive thinker who tries to analyze other people in terms of logic, the unintelligent individual who has difficulties in coping with abstractions, and the hypomanic who floods others with words. The counterpart of these digital-verbal types is the dreamer, to whom thinking is anathema because it destroys the Gestalt of his impressions. He prefers to express himself through media other than language. In coping with these two types, the therapist does not treat disorders of thinking or daydreaming per se. Instead he seeks to achieve an integration of the two modes of codification. To the logician, he replies not by argument but by pointing out the lacunae in his report: "How did you feel when your wife left you?" or "I see tension in your face and your fists are clenched." To the dreamer he points out that certain factual information is missing; he analyzes his behavior and points out the need to be rational. On the whole, the disturbances of behavior which look like disturbances of thinking come about because the patient leaves out analogically coded information which informs others of the pragmatic relationship between his statement and other dimensions of his personality. Only when all the components—analogically and digitally coded information—are available to the patient and to the observer can understanding be gained.

Prediction is dependent upon the individual's ability to assess probabilities. From his own and other people's experience, he knows about frequencies of occurrence, and these he is supposed to apply to predict future events. Difficulties in prediction arise when people confuse wish fulfillment with probability, when they do not believe in the regularity of occurrences, as in the case of the gambler, or when they have forgotten what happened before. To learn to use probabilities is part of the patient's education; to deal with the patient's inability to cope with probabilities is a task for the therapist. This he does by recounting to the patient those incidents that are similar to the one under discussion. For example, a therapist may remind the patient about his being late four times, or having been late to his own wedding, or having been late in applying for college. By pulling all these things together, the therapist points out that the patient does not act on the established probability of his being late and therefore does not compensate for his deficiency. Many people who have difficulties with probabilities believe in luck, which runs counter to statistical probability. It is a sort of belief in magic, to be able to beat the laws of nature. Once this omnipotent attitude is broken, the patient usually learns to predict with greater accuracy.

DISTURBANCES OF FEELING

The mood of a person is the sum-total evaluation of the state of the organism which affects his thinking, his feeling, and his attitudes towards other people. Mood is controlled by factors which are mostly unknown; this, however, does not prevent people from connecting many internal or external conditions with the existence of a given mood. Mood sets the tone for interaction. If somebody is elated, he is ready for enterprise; if somebody is irritable, he is ready for quarrel; and when somebody is depressed, he is ready for hibernation or suicide. The task of the therapist is to make the patient aware of his own mood at a given moment and to induce him to minimize its effect. The patient can learn that if anger is felt he should not drive, nor drink, nor make decisions. Although this does not affect the mood in question, it prevents some of the catastrophic impacts the mood may have.

In contrast to mood, feeling is something that refers to a part function of the individual. People may be suspicious towards certain individuals and trusting towards others, or they may be desirous of salted food and avoid a bland diet. Feelings, therefore, can be considered as a kind of information that indicates what action the organism has to engage in to satisfy specific needs. Discussion of feelings gives the therapist an opportunity to pinpoint emotional sources of information. Feelings, as it were, always give an answer to the pragmatic question: "How does this event affect me?" If a child gets a *D* in arithmetic he feels badly, and this feeling may induce him to work harder or to give up altogether.

In therapy, the processes of empathy and sympathy acquire a special significance. The Greek term *sympatheia* means "suffering with" the other, while *empatheia* literally means "suffering in" the other. In sympathy, therefore, the observer adapts his mood to that of the other person and becomes, as it were, a brother in joy or tears. In empathy, on the contrary, the observer-therapist disregards his own feelings and puts himself into the other person's place to understand what is going on. While most people are capable of sympathy, empathy has to be learned. The most flagrant absence of empathy is met in mothers who, although able to sympathize with their children when they hurt themselves, are incapable of putting themselves in the child's place to find out how a child may react and feel under a given circumstance.

Some people are not capable of sympathy, or the spontaneous feeling for another person. There are those who scorn others or who keep to themselves, and because of excessive control seldom show any emotion. In therapeutic communication, an attempt is made to share some emotions with the patients. This is achieved by positively pointing out when such sharing has occurred—for example, when a supersonic boom rattles the house, both doctor and patient may be sympathetic with each other's experience.

The skill of empathy has to be imparted to young psychiatrists, who have to learn to feel their way with other people. One of the ways to teach this skill is to obtain a tape recording of an interview of the young doctor with his patient. From the tape, it is possible to reconstruct what took place. Words seldom do justice to this process, and it is from the nonverbal sound cues that the supervisor gets the idea of the extent of his trainee's understanding. Vis-à-vis the patient, every therapist has to constantly check whether his empathic understanding is agreed to by the patient or whether the latter wishes to make some corrections. The patient's modification of the doctor's empathic understanding is one of the most crucial therapeutic procedures.

Ambivalence is a feeling which any normal person may experience, but after a brief period of hesitation the ordinary person arrives at a decision; this consists either of a clear-cut choice or of a compromise. But the abnormal person cannot maximize, minimize, or compromise. Both sides of the story exist side by side, and none of the affects involved gain the upper hand (5). Ambivalent feelings prevent a person from reaching a conclusion. When, at times, one feeling predominates and at times another, the individual cannot commit himself to any plan of action.

In therapy, ambivalence is clarified first by documenting its existence. In a second step, the therapist points out to the patient that he erroneously considers commitment as if it were to last for eternity. He calls attention to the fact that when too large a time segment is considered, no commitment can ever be made by anybody because opposing forces have to be considered. Therefore the third step of therapy consists of reducing the time duration of the patient's conscious commitment to a matter of minutes or seconds. For example, a smile can be responded to by another smile, but this does not imply that in the next second the same person would not be free to frown. And because the patient orders a hamburger now, it does not mean that he will like it tomorrow; as the next day arrives, he can eat something else, in another place, if he so pleases. The principle of "one thing at a time" is applied here by considering, in word and action, a time segment which is small enough not to include any opposing forces. In practice, this is achieved by pointing out to the patient that right now—this second —he might state in all fairness that he deeply resents his wife. This does not mean that a little while later he may not state that he adores his wife. After all, the double bind (4), in which all solutions to a problem prove equally painful, was probably set up by parents who telescoped in time certain action sequences which should have been properly separated. A typical example of a telescoped statement is the tangential response (30), whereby verbal statements and actions are connected that should have been set off from each other. Because the concomitant affective responses to each statement or action are likely to be different, they cannot be blended into a whole. By separating ideas, thoughts, feelings, and actions in time, the therapist makes a reintegration possible.

DISTURBANCES OF DECISION-MAKING

Decision-making is a complex process in which a sensory input is scanned against a background of memories. If, in the course of this scanning process, a signal impinges upon traces of earlier impressions, the resulting product becomes a sign that has informative value. This sign, in turn, has to be scanned against a background of possible choices. The action of another person, for example, must be evaluated against a background of what this person might have done under different circumstances (31). The various alternatives raised by both old and new information are carefully considered and eventually a reaction to the input occurs which substantially changes the present situation. Or to put it into scientific terms: when an input is followed by an output that changes the parameters of the system, the result can be called a decision. However, there are a number of things that can go wrong in this process.

Some patients cannot scan and some engage in erroneous scanning. The paranoid, for example, invariably sees only one facet of an idea; he may take the nominal aspect of a sentence and ignore its affective concomitant, or he may see only those things that are directed against him and not those that favor him. Other people have difficulties in arranging their experiences in an orderly way so that they are ready for future reference. These people, it appears, have not indexed their past experiences in a proper manner. Then there is the host of neurotic patients who are incapable of recollecting their own past experiences because they have amnesia for certain periods of their lives. Others deny the existence of certain desires—particularly those related to sex and anger. To scan well, people have to be in a state of awareness which can be likened not to heightened tension but to the relaxed, almost sleepy, alertness of a dog who is ready to pick up any signal from whatever side it may arrive. Preoccupation with self or with a particular problem in the surroundings distinctly reduces the possibilities of accurate pick-up and reduces the outlook for appropriate scanning. Therapeutically speaking, the patient can be taught to scan. This is done by sharpening perception and by bringing into awareness those aspects that the patient has repressed, partially ignores, or selectively distorts. The mobilization of repressed memories occurs in the usual way; and as the field of awareness increases and the patient experiences a greater accessibility to his unconscious, his ability to scan rapidly improves.

Decisions are dependent upon a person's ability to confine himself to the choice made and to renounce the possibilities which are inherent in the other alternatives. The ability to commit oneself is based on the mobilization of all resources for a given task. Difficulties of commitment occur when the patient wishes to have his cake and eat it too, and therefore does not mobilize his resources. Anyone who attempts to take a shower and eat a piece of cake simultaneously is likely to discover that he gets neither clean nor fed. Or if a person could eat without considering his waistline, or if he could be prominent without the danger of being envied or resented, he would not shy away from commitment. Therapeutic work teaches the patient to run the risks inherent in commitment. The therapist, far from making decisions for the patient, merely helps him to bear the consequences of his actions. This involves a redirection of attention away from the things that might have been to the things that are and away from the non-chosen to the chosen. Gently, the therapist confronts the patient with the realities that require his undivided attention; and once he has given his undivided attention to a subject for a period of time, he is committed.

When people get older, their ability to absorb new information, to adapt to changing situations, and to meet strangers becomes limited. They live, as it were, on their accumulated capital of experiences; and as they miss out on new experiences, they gradually become misinformed and no longer can make wise decisions. For these reasons, the role of old people is usually limited to that of advisor and counsellor rather than decision-maker. They do not share with the younger generation the fascination with risk-taking since they have become aware of the precariousness of life and of the fallacies inherent in man-made schemes. Decisions which ought to be made are left pending, and such people frequently drift into a *"laisser faire, laisser aller"* attitude. The therapy in these cases consists of incorporating the aged individual into feedback circuits in which information can be corrected, in which disordered functions like a weak memory can be compensated for by technical means such as note taking, and by involving the person in enterprises where his actions matter. As long as the individual remains involved, he will make decisions. But nobody strives to play good poker if the game is played without stakes. In this respect, retirement of employed people without transfer to other occupations and enterprises is like a death sentence. In younger people, decline of intellectual functions may be caused by a variety of diseases of the central nervous system and may bring about the same symptomatology as in older people.

Aside from scanning, comparing, selecting, and renouncing, decision-making entails an additional function. It involves knowledge of tradition, familiarity with existing standards, and judging the element of novelty that a decision might introduce against the power of existing values. Nobody changes the constitution of a nation overnight, and nobody can overrule the laws of the land with impunity. But tradition does not imply external standards only; the individual possesses his own set of internalized values which he has to abide by. Nobody can make decisions that are contrary to his internalized values unless he wishes to experience guilt or undergo the penalty of self-punishment.

The therapeutic effort to correct disturbances of decision-making, therefore, is directed first towards simplifying the problem until a choice can be made, and second to inducing the patient to make only those decisions that are in accord with his conscience and in keeping with his ideals. In the growing up process, the patient's own past experiences gradually replace those values which he took over from his elders. When an individual is capable of acting on the basis of his own past experiences, he feels internally free. Under these circumstances, he does not need to appease his feelings of guilt even if his decision is contrary to the wishes of his elders or his own conscience. A flexible moral superstructure enables an individual to resolve conflicts between his own conscience and the standards set by the group without loss of self-respect.

But how is such a flexible moral superstructure achieved without corrupting the individual? Essentially the therapist gives the patient to understand that even though no rule exists without an exception, the conscience attempts to reinforce rules at all times. The therapist conveys to the patient that we must be able to accept conflict, both intrapsychic and with the surroundings, as a natural fact of life. We also must accept the fact that conflicts should be resolved. If nobody gives in, cooperation and social life become impossible. Standards therefore have to be reinterpreted to fit the situation. They have to be modified for each occasion because in a fast changing world the standard is already antiquated by the time it gets firmly established. Somewhere between an absolutely rigid standard on the one hand and the denial of any standard on the other there exists a middle road which we have to choose. Once the individual learns to use standards as tools, he will use them judiciously.

DISTURBANCES OF MEMORY AND AWARENESS

Human awareness is limited to one subject at any one time, and if more have to be considered these have to be rotated through consciousness in succession. If memories are temporarily not available, either simultaneously or in succession, we speak of repression. This is a process that excludes unwelcome ideas from consciousness —ideas that are in conflict with other requirements of the organism (13). Repression, therefore, serves the purpose of a psychological wound-healing mechanism for unresolved conflicts. Persons with subtle repressions are usually unaware of their omissions. Repressed memories are lifted back into awareness when the conflict which necessitated the repression in the first place has dwindled or disappeared or when the individual is strong enough to cope with it. (12).

Psychogenic amnesia has to be distinguished from the organic types of retrograde and anterograde amnesia. The patient who has forgotten his address and identity is not seen as often as the person who has few or no memories for certain periods of his life. Such a patient may, for example, remember little of what happened after his father married his step-mother, or he may recall little before the family moved to a new city. Such blank periods in the memory of the patient usually indicate serious conflicts which are not embodied in a single dramatic event but rather in frequent repetition of frustrating events. The therapist works his way into these amnesias not by frontal attacks but by flanking maneuvers. To begin with, he traces the life experiences of the patient in terms of persons, places, and situations as far as possible. After remembering that which is readily recallable, the patient eventually ventures a few hesitant suggestions as to what else might have happened in that period. The utilization of dreams is extremely helpful at this point. After a varying period of time, particularly when the relationship with the therapist is satisfactory, the patient begins to open up this obscure period of his life.

Many different explanations have been offered for the phenomenon that older people tend to have difficulties in recalling recent events (27). But inability to focus attention, to retain, and to grasp do not affect old people only but also younger patients suffering from brain disease. Although it can be shown that under hypnosis the previously unavailable memories become accessible (9), on the whole the mechanism of memory disturbance is poorly understood.

In keeping with this ignorance, therapy with aged people is not particularly concerned with the memory defect but with the total level of functioning; if it can be raised, the memory defect recedes. In talking with aged patients, the doctor starts from what is remembered and continues to develop the topic until he arrives at the present situation. Following such a longitudinal approach, the memory disturbance can be minimized; but when it is tackled frontally with a direct question, it is maximized. One of the difficulties in organic disease of the brain is the integration of old with new information, and it is this central integrative factor (15) which determines the function of the memory. Repeatedly it has been observed that when adaptive demands were made upon an old man —for example, taking over his grandson's education after the death of his son—his memory function improved.

A different kind of memory disturbance exists in people who can experience and remember but cannot apply that which they have learned to another situation. Each time they approach the same problem, they treat it as if it were entirely new and they go through the same motions as they did when they met the problem for the first time. It is as if experience were isolated from action even though such a person can talk with convincing facility about his experiences. It is as if action were not synchronized with thinking and feeling —a phenomenon which is very noticeable in depressed people (29). Therapeutic communication with such desynchronized people has to occur on the action level. To talk to a depressed patient makes little sense; to listen to a depressed patient makes more sense; but to be with a depressed patient and engage in ordinary life activities makes the most sense. When action and words are desynchronized, there is little hope of utilizing words to influence action; but action can be employed to influence words.

DISTURBANCES OF EXPRESSION

Exhibitionism · Reducing intensity · The inner control of experience ·
Compensation for defects · Shifting expression to other organ systems

Expression is an organismic function which involves many components, both central and peripheral. If expression functions, the individual can relate to others and find confirmation of his own ideas and actions in the reactions of others. If he suffers from a disturbance of expression, the beneficial effects of interpersonal feedback are absent. This state of affairs has a deleterious effect upon the identity of the individual.

EXAGGERATED OR INHIBITED FORMS OF EXPRESSION

The most common disturbances of expression are found in the exhibitionist, who shows off and exaggerates, and in the inhibited person, who gets things said or done only with effort. The person who dramatizes usually goes along at an average clip until she feels that a dramatic point has to be made, whereupon she starts to mimic and enact, calling the whole body into play. The person addicted to advertising and propaganda is another type who through repetitious manipulation of props—often in a forceful and intrusive way —makes his point clear. Some of his statements are framed in such a provocative way that people are forced to pay attention.

Exaggerated communication is the result of interference with interpersonal feedback circuits. The origin of this disturbance can be observed in any family. When a boy asks his father, who is reading a newspaper, a question and does not get an answer, he will raise his voice. If he still does not obtain an answer he makes noise by banging a toy against the door. Finally, when the intensity gets unbearable, the father responds and, in effect, rewards the acting up and the exaggeration of the boy. If such an interaction is repeated hundreds of times, the boy eventually gets into the habit of using intense, misplaced, or ill-timed messages to provoke a response in the other person. The therapeutic task is simple; the relatives of the patient and the patient himself have to be induced to respond early; the patient has to be shown when and how he exaggerates and how he can be more effective if he properly places and times his messages.

In most instances, the patient's conscious expression of feelings and thoughts is accompanied by deep-seated feelings of guilt. Rather than experience these unpleasant feelings, the patient prefers to remain incommunicado. This basic conflict is worked through in several steps. First, the therapist demonstrates to the patient that he expresses himself anyway, regardless of how many controls he applies. The revelation that "everything shows" induces him to look more favorably upon conscious and goal-directed expression. In a second step, the patient's equation of communication with intrusion into the other person's privacy is explored, and possible magic connections between communication and sex are disentangled. Third, exhibitionism or exaggerated expression is distinguished from necessary expression. The patient is familiarized with the idea that exhibition constitutes a message "to whom it may concern" while purposive expression is tailor-made for a specific recipient. In a final step, the patient is made aware of the fact that he hurts others less and leads a more useful life if feeling, thought, and action work in unison.

MOTOR DEFECTS

People with peripheral nerve lesions, amputees, those afflicted by muscular disorders, the spastics, and the hemiplegics constitute a group of patients all of whom suffer from disturbances of the effector system. This group also includes patients whose motions are complicated by involuntary movements such as tremor and choreatic or athetoid disturbances and those who have difficulties with coordination and equilibrium as seen in the case of tabetics, multiple sclerotics, or people with cerebellar tumors. Last but not least, the very tense patient whose muscles are moderately contracted most of the time usually has serious difficulties with expression. The treatment of the underlying condition is the first goal of therapy; but in addition the patient has to be helped to develop compensatory means of expression. If the patient suffers from a paralysis of the seventh nerve, for example, he may be taught to use his hands for purposes of communication to compensate for the lack of expression in his face. Or if he is an amputee, he will have to learn verbal means of communication to compensate for the missing extremities (32).

The patient whose livelihood and significant human relations are mediated through the motor system experiences a severe trauma when exposed to an accident or a disease that afflicts movement. One does not need to be reminded of Lou Gehrig, Roy Campanella, or other sports greats to understand that a disease affecting the motor system hits them harder than it does the man who sits at a desk and whose hobby it is to listen to music. Whether the patient can establish new human relations and replace the motor system as a pleasure-giving system with another one—perhaps the sensory system—depends upon circumstances and age. If the patient is able to switch, let us say, to observing, he can derive gratification from a new source: formerly on the plane of movement and skill, now on the plane of observation and appreciation. But such shifts take years to accomplish. The therapist's task is not an easy one. He has to explore all significant skills the patient possesses, his knowledge, his human relations, and his ideals. From all this may emerge a picture that offers an alternate solution. But it is well to keep in mind that a significant switch in pleasure-bringing activities and human relations can only occur when it can be based upon foundations that were laid earlier. To discover these foundations is the job of the therapist.

DISTURBANCES OF ACTION

Action and experience · Initiating action · Anxiety of initiation · Inability to sustain effort · Inability to take instructions · Intolerance of success

Disturbances of action are distinguishable from disturbances of expression by the fact that expression has a symbolic function while action serves to implement biological needs. To eat, sleep, breathe, and move about are necessary activities, although if perceived by others they may have informative value for the other person. Under all circumstances, however, an action is a statement to self because in order to control action the individual has to be aware of his body and movements as he proceeds and of the outcome as he terminates. Repetition of an action leads to the acquisition of skill, which means the elimination of unnecessary movements, increased speed, improved target accuracy, and a priori knowledge of what the outcome of an action will be. Mastery of action thus involves two elements—information and skill—both of which may become disturbed. In learning through imitation (8), the process of taking over cues from the model may be defective or the rewards may not be satisfactory. Problem-solving (23) may become disturbed if the individual who struggles to discover the relevant cues himself is not given an opportunity to experiment without interference.

INITIATING, SUSTAINING, AND COMPLETING ACTION

There are some people who have difficulty in starting an enterprise in spite of the fact that they are aware of the necessity of engaging in action. To quote a patient: "I am quite aware that I should work on my thesis, but I just don't get around to it." Apparently the anxiety connected with undertaking the first step is so great that it cannot be overcome without an additional push. Such persons frequently wait until the pressure of circumstances is more unpleasant than the feelings associated with initiating action. These people are essentially motivated by different degrees of anxiety, so that all activities are somewhat unpleasant. The genesis of such difficulties may be found in the child's earlier experience that the initiation of something is met by others with so much hostility, opposition, or lethargy that he had to give up. Also the initiation of action might have forced the child into a disagreeable role within the family, with the result that he preferred not to take the first step.

The working through of these conflicts is time-consuming. First the patient has to be familiarized with the many machinations which he produces in order to get going. Insight into his troubles at first produces more passivity and wavering. Then the patient has to be weaned from his dependence upon anxiety so that natural impulses of want or desire may arise. These feeble urges are then brought to light and with the encouragement of the therapist the patient undertakes his first tentative steps. The patient who has no anxiety but lets everything slip and relies upon others has to be shown that if he is adult, others on the whole do not look out for his welfare.

There are patients who cannot keep up a sustained effort. Their flying start is not followed in the middle phase of the action by appropriate technical implementations. Once things are under way, such people get bored; and usually they abandon the enterprise before it is crowned with success. These short distance sprinters have to learn to tolerate routine. Apparently repetition without novelty and work without applause are too frustrating for them to tolerate. In many instances such a person's personality resembles that of a promoter whose task it is to bring people together, to propagandize ideas, and to get things started. Such persons are people-oriented and rarely possess technical skills or knowledge which would enable them to carry out a task in the later phase of development. The person whose dependency upon approval and stimulation prevents him from seeing a task through perhaps had parents who were satisfied with words and gestures and did not expect him to deliver any goods; or then again his parents may have been windbags who themselves did not possess skills. Be that as it may, the therapist has to guide the patient in such a way that he will acquire technical skills; otherwise, he must confine himself to promoting. And while the patient learns, the therapist can give him emotional support.

Lack of skills more often than not is the result of the patient's rebellion at taking instructions from another human being. In the past, there may have been a parent who was anxious, sadistic, or incompetent, and the child remained safer by avoiding contact with the adult. When left to his own devices, such a child may have been full of hatred, a condition which prevented him from learning by himself. In the therapeutic situation, the patient has to be shown first that he does not possess skills. Thereafter, the emotional state that prevents learning has to be exposed. Then comes a stage when instruction has to begin. If the patient and the doctor share an area of interest, the doctor may talk about the subject; if he should be a boating fan, he might discuss the merits of certain anchorages. A few sessions later, he may check with the patient and inquire into the effects this discussion has had. In so doing, he will discover the difficulties that the patient encounters. Perhaps the doctor may find that the patient is not able to take information which derives from others; or the patient may need technical supervision while carrying out the task. This latter difficulty can be remedied by asking the patient to take some lessons or to take a competent friend along. During such therapeutic discussions, the memories of earlier experiences will come back, particularly when the patient is put once more into a similar learning situation. This gives the therapist the opportunity to reconstruct the original events as well as to support the patient as he tries to master the dangerous situation anew.

The person who cannot reap the fruits of his labors usually is a masochist. He works well under adverse conditions, in opposition, or as a member of a minority. But if his labors should be crowned with success, he begins to feel guilty. Feeling basically undeserving, he is so overwhelmed at being in a position of power, wealth, or success that he abandons the enterprise, resigns, or retires. The therapist has to expose the unconscious feelings of guilt as well as the somewhat magic connections between reward and work. The therapist has to point out that reward in terms of promotions or monetary distributions are not made to the individual; they are made to the holder of a certain position within the system. And the system must have an incentive device; otherwise it does not function. Once the patient has detached the notion of reward from his level of aspiration and broken the link between material reward and measurement of achievement, he usually is capable of accepting the reward. He then considers himself as a lucky guy who happened to be around when the rewards were distributed and he does not consider them as an index of his abilities.

INABILITY TO COOPERATE

The patient learns by doing · Social intercourse as neccessity · Inability to follow instructions · Inability to sell self

In disturbances of action, whether they be brought about by insufficient or erroneous information, by lack of practice and skill, or by difficulties in initiating action or making decisions, the psychiatrist has to keep in mind that no amount of talking will remedy the situation unless the patient engages in action. The physician therefore stands by and encourages action, which is preferable to no action because without action the patient cannot learn. Only when irreversible changes are imminent should the physician interfere; bodily injury and mutilation, gross violations of the law, and large-scale indebtedness have to be avoided. But to get married to the wrong man and later to divorce is better than no marriage at all. Change of jobs is better than not working at all. Taking off for three months to see the world is better than the perennial treadmill. Living is precarious, and he who wishes to live has to engage in action, run risks, learn, and do better the next time. Otherwise he is doomed.

But in order to act, a person must be able to get along with others. In today's complex civilization, one cannot work, eat, sleep, or take a trip without the help of others. Everything is so intertwined that every person must cooperate with others if he is to survive. Perhaps this is the one feature that distinguishes our times from other historical periods; and this fact might explain the great increase in psychiatric and social aid facilities.

Some patients have difficulty in heeding warnings, reading instructions, observing traffic signals, or, in brief, in obeying verbal commands in oral or written form. This inability to follow verbal intructions begins early in life. In one family, there may exist the prevailing view that everything written should be disregarded— an attitude not infrequently found in the lower classes of the population. Or the youngster may have had a visual difficulty which, as long as it remained uncorrected, made reading unpleasant; or it may have been a lack of training in dealing with ideas that made the individual unable to stick to the meaning of the word. But by far the most frequent reason for disregarding instructions is an attitude of rebelliousness. The therapist has to work through the early circumstances that prevented the patient from taking instructions. At first, the road will be bumpy, but eventually the patient may succeed.

Although fewer in numbers every year, there are patients who cannot sell themselves. Raised within value systems where blowing one's own horn was prohibited, where social engineering was out of the question, and where all dealings with others had to have a moral tinge, these patients are at a loss to operate in our mercantile political, advertising culture. They do not appreciate the halo of others, and they cannot get others to appreciate whatever they themselves have to offer. The therapist has to help these patients abandon some of their purist values so that they are able to exist in our culture, to obtain jobs, and to be advanced. The issue of sincerity, honesty, and moral cause has to be worked through by exposing the fact that all systems without exception have insincerity, dishonesty, and immorality built into them. Only the time and place of appearance and the symbolic form vary. Under these circumstances, the patient might just as well accept the present order of things and eventually work for a better world.

References

1. Altschule, M. D.: *Roots of Modern Psychiatry.* 184 p. New York: Grune & Stratton, 1957.

2. Ames, A., Jr.: The rotating trapezoid. Pp. 65–86 in *Human Behavior from the Transactional Point of View* (Edited by F. P. Kilpatrick). Hanover, N. H.: Institute for Associated Research, 1952.

3. Barker, R. G., Wright, B. A., Meyerson, L., and Gonick, M. R.: *Adjustment to Physical Handicap and Illness: A Survey of the Social Psychology of Physique and Disability.* 440 p. New York: Soc. Sci. Res. Counc. Bull. #55 (Revised), 1953.

4. Bateson, G., Jackson, D. D., Haley, J., and Weakland, J.: Toward a theory of schizophrenia. Behavioral Sci., 1, 251–264, 1956.

5. Bleuler, E.: *Textbook of Psychiatry.* 635 p. New York: Macmillan, 1924.

6. Cantril, H.: Perception and interpersonal relations. Amer. J. Psychiat., 114, 119–126, 1957.

7. Cholden, L.: Group therapy with the blind. Group Therapy, 6, 21–29, 1953.

8. Dollard, J. and Miller, N. E.: *Personality and Psychotherapy*. 488 p. New York: McGraw-Hill, 1950.

9. Dorcus, R. M. (Editor): *Hypnosis and its Therapeutic Applications*. 1 v. (various pagings). New York: Blakiston, 1956.

10. Engel, E.: The role of content in binocular resolution. Amer. J. Psychol., 69, 87–91, 1956.

11. Farber, D. J.: Written communication in psychotherapy. Psychiatry, 16, 365–374, 1953.

12. Freud, S.: *New Introductory Lectures on Psycho-Analysis*. 257 p. New York: Norton, 1933.

13. Freud, S.: *The Problem of Anxiety*. 165 p. New York: Norton, 1936.

14. Garrett, J. F. (Editor): *Psychological Aspects of Physical Disability*. 195 p. Washington: Department of Health, Education, and Welfare; Office of Vocational Rehabilitation; Rehabilitation Service Series #210; 1953.

15. Halstead, W. C.: *Brain and Intelligence: A Quantitative Study of the Frontal Lobes*. 206 p. Chicago: University of Chicago Press, 1947.

16. Heron, W.: The pathology of boredom. Scientific American, 196: 1, 52–56, 1957.

17. Ichheiser, G.: Misunderstandings in human relations; a study in false social perception. Amer. J. Sociol., 55: 2(2), 1–70, 1949.

18. Ittelson, W. H. and Kilpatrick, F. P.: Equivalent configurations and the monocular and binocular distorted rooms. Pp. 41–55 in *Human Behavior from the Transactional Point of View* (F. P. Kilpatrick, editor). Hanover, N. H.: Institute for Associated Research, 1952.

19. Lende, H.: *Books about the Blind*. (New rev. ed.). 357 p. New York: American Foundation for the Blind, 1953.

20. Lilly, J. C.: Mental effects of reduction of ordinary levels of physical stimuli on intact, healthy persons. Pp. 1–9 in *Research Techniques in Schizophrenia*. Psychiatric Research Reports #5. Washington: American Psychiatric Association, 1956.

21. Linn, L., Kahn, R. L., Coles, R., Cohen, J., Marshall, D., and Weinstein, E. A.: Patterns of behavior disturbance following cataract extraction. Amer. J. Psychiat., 110, 281–289, 1953.

22. McCulloch, W. S. and Pitts, W.: The statistical organization of nervous activity. J. Amer. statist. Assoc., 4, 91–99, 1948.

23. Mowrer, O. H.: *Learning Theory and Personality Dynamics*. 776 p. New York: Ronald Press, 1950.

24. Nuttall, J. B.: The problem of spatial disorientation. J. Amer. Med. Assoc., 166, 431–438, 1958.

25. Preu, P. W. and Guida, F. P.: Psychoses complicating recovery from

extraction of cataract. A.M.A. Arch. Neurol. Psychiat., 38, 818–832, 1937.

26. Pribram, K.: *Conflicting Patterns of Thought.* 176 p. Washington: Public Affairs Press, 1949.

27. Rapaport, D.: *Emotions and Memory.* 282 p. Baltimore: Williams & Wilkins, 1942.

28. Rapaport, D. (Translator and Commentator): *Organization and Pathology of Thought.* 786 p. New York: Columbia University Press, 1951.

29. Ruesch, J.: Nonverbal language and therapy. Psychiatry, 18, 323–330, 1955.

30. Ruesch, J.: The tangential response. Pp. 37–48 in *Psychopathology of Communication* (P. H. Hoch and J. Zubin, editors). New York: Grune & Stratton, 1958.

31. Ruesch, J.: Values and the process of communication. Pp. 27–40 in *Symposium on Preventive and Social Psychiatry, 15–17 April, 1957.* Washington: Walter Reed Army Institute of Research, 1958.

32. Ruesch, J. and Kees, W.: *Nonverbal Communication.* 205 p. Berkeley and Los Angeles: University of California Press, 1956.

33. Sharoff, R. L.: Enforced restriction of communication, its implications for the emotional and intellectual development of the deaf child. Amer. J. Psychiat., 116, 443–446, 1959.

34. Solomon, P., Leiderman, P. H., Mendelson, J., and Wexler, D.: Sensory deprivation: A review. Amer. J. Psychiat., 114, 357–363, 1957.

35. Sullivan, H. S.: *The Interpersonal Theory of Psychiatry.* 393 p. New York: Norton, 1953.

36. West, R., Ansberry, M., and Carr, A.: *The Rehabilitation of Speech.* (3rd ed.) 688p. New York: Harper, 1957.

37. Williams, R. C. and Flank, M. D.: Therapy for the newly blinded, as practiced with veterans. J. Amer. Med. Assoc., 158, 811–818, 1955.

Chapter Seventeen

Deficiencies in Mental Capacity, Knowledge, and Skill

THE PATIENT'S inability to cope with certain life situations may be due to his inferior mental capacity. The mentally deficient, for example, even with the best of training, are unable to cope with many of the average tasks of daily life. But there are many people of ordinary or superior intelligence who by reason of character or temperament likewise are incapable of coping with certain people and situations. These emotionally disturbed people cannot learn with ease, as undisturbed people do. Although their potentiality is similar to that of normals, phenomenologically they present a picture that is similar to that of the mentally retarded. The vast group of socially inadequate people thus can be studied under three headings: deficiencies in capacity; deficiencies in knowledge and information; and, finally, deficiencies in skills.

LACK OF KNOWLEDGE

Uninformed about technical matters in line of occupation · Uninformed about matters of living and social relations · Uninformed about tradition and custom · Boot camp · Knowledge of probabilities · Eliciting favorable responses

In public life we find an ever increasing number of bureaucrats, administrators, supervisors, and directors who seem to be able to cope with the organizational aspects but not with the technical elements of their professions. In private life, we find individuals who struggle with simple tasks such as rowing a boat, starting a car, or operating a camera. Whatever they touch they seem to approach in an impractical way. Such people ride rough shod over technical details, and, because of this attitude, never learn the correct operation of technical instruments. They remain essentially unskilled throughout their lives, and often they are even incapable of holding a job in an assembly line factory. Excluding defective intelligence, the reason for such failure has to be sought in a person's attitude. In some cases, such an individual overestimates ingenuity and underestimates training. In other cases, he is aware of his shortcomings but has personal difficulties which prevent him from taking proper instruction. So he sets out on the Pacific in a small sail boat without being able to navigate, or he takes off in a plane without being able to land.

But lack of know-how may not involve technical matters alone. There are persons who do not know how to ask for information when they are lost in a strange city. There are others who are incapable of finding a telephone booth; some do not know when or how to talk to a neighbor, or how to find a restaurant in a strange town. Then there are people who do not know how to date members of the opposite sex, how to get a job, or how to say "no." These people lack intuitive knowledge of human beings and they are incapable of predicting the obvious. They do not know that people get tired after doing the same thing for a long time, that people get hungry every few hours, that they drink more fluids in summer, or that a teen-aged girl's behavior will change after she has found a steady boy-friend.

Then there are patients who seem to be partially blind to the way things are done. They are unable to take hints; they don't know rules; and they "don't play the game." They are uninformed about traditions and they don't know how to feel their way into individual situations. When they come into the doctor's office, they burst in and don't stop in the waiting room; when they park their cars, they take two parking spaces instead of one; they talk loudly where people are generally silent; and they ask for lobster Newburg at a hamburger stand. Although others label them crude, uneducated, or rude, the therapist frequently discovers that they literally have no sense of appropriacy and no appreciation of social mores.

The therapist thus has to make sure that the patient is informed about the career aspects of his occupation and that he possesses the necessary technical know-how; that he is worldly in matters of living and social relations; and that he is informed about tradition and custom. The marginal person who does a little bit of everything but is not identified with any clear-cut occupation presents a serious problem. The amateur musician who also has a hardware store and the financial counsellor who is neither broker, statistician, accountant, economist, nor banker are examples in question. Technical information is acquired in "boot camp." Any person has to accept a form of basic training and drill if he wishes to acquire some occupational skills. In one case, a patient may have to be sent to secretarial school; in another, he may have to finish college; and a third one might have to spend a year or two in an apprenticeship or training program to learn a trade or an occupation which will earn him a living. Once the patient accepts the necessity of going to boot camp and of keeping in contact with his field, he may be able to eliminate many of the occupational difficulties.

There are patients who, because of insufficient experience, underestimate or overestimate probabilities. Just because one person gets away with driving through red stop lights, it does not mean that the law of averages will not catch up with him. Such average probabilities are learned in contact with other people, through repetition of performance, and finally from books. Since occupational and professional decisions are mostly based upon correct prediction of probabilities for a given action, the therapist must help the patient to accept the fact that it takes many years to learn the art of assessing the odds.

But to assess the correct probability is not sufficient. The patient also has to learn to influence other people's selection of probabilities. This art the doctor can introduce by explaining that tradition and custom have a very essential function—namely, to stabilize and standardize behavior and to establish probabilities which help people in predicting future events. Appropriate behavior is, among other things, that kind of behavior which will elicit in the other person expectations that fit the occasion. The therapist points out time after time not only that the patient has to cue the onlooker correctly but that he has to interpret the other person's behavior in the light of average probabilities. When a person presents himself to a prospective employer, for example, he does not appear in the office as if he were a policeman with a search warrant or a beggar asking for a handout. He simply exhibits that kind of behavior which will cue the other that he is in search of a job and that he expects to be treated like a job applicant. If in the course of the interview he reveals the same features as others do under the circumstances, he is almost sure to be treated like a normal person. The therapist therefore has to train the patient to proceed from the most probable to the less probable, and this invariably elicits in the other person the impression of normalcy.

INABILITY TO ACQUIRE INFORMATION

Inability to learn from books · *Inability to learn from people* · *Inability to learn by himself*

The acquisition of information occurs in three distinctly different modes. First is the printed word, which in the form of books, periodicals, and magazines transmits a good part of the cumulative body of knowledge of mankind. A second method of acquisition of information is found in interpersonal contact, which includes long distance communication via radio and television. In the third method information is acquired by learning through trial and error. Usually the three modes have to be combined if a rounded picture is to be obtained. Patients often have preferences for or difficulties with certain kinds of learning. In part, this is determined by childhood experiences. An only child who does not play with other children may have to learn by himself; a youngest child may be taught by his siblings and may not have an opportunity to find out by himself; and a paralyzed child may have to derive his knowledge from books.

When the therapist explores the patient's ability to learn through the help of printed matter, he first has to make sure that the patient has normal vision or that refraction errors have been corrected. Secondly he has to ascertain whether the patient is able to scan efficiently. Among patients who cannot learn from books are the people who tire easily or fall asleep after two or three pages of reading. Here the difficulty is usually the patient's inability to scan. Often I have had success with these patients after having advised them to seek visual training to cope with their reading difficulties (1, 5). There are others who tend to disregard anything that is printed —particularly the small print that may contain significant clauses. They do not trust symbols and therefore cannot get themselves to utilize information. Working through of the basic conflict may improve the situation. This involves a clarification of the relation to the people who taught and rewarded reading and writing, exposure of the guilt or anxiety connected with believing "the book," and a realistic appraisal of what symbols can and cannot do. Many of the patients who have such basic attitudes do better in practical occupations, avoiding significant contact with the printed word.

Learning from people through imitation is dependent upon the availability of a human model and upon the pupil's readiness to imitate. The better the relationship and the more appropriate the reward, the faster the learning. The duration of learning thus depends upon the skill of the teacher in timing the lessons, upon the distinctiveness of the cues he uses, and upon the degree of simplification he applies. The tragedy in the upper classes of society is that children are sent out for lessons but do not learn much from their instructors because they treat them as hired servants. On the other side of the scale, we find in the lower classes of society those people who have excellent relations with their children but possess few technical skills or knowledge and therefore cannot impart much to their offspring. Both situations have undesirable consequences in that the emotionally significant person is separated from the technical model from which the cues are derived. Such separation is practical only when the child is past the age of ten or twelve and has had satisfactory and consistent experiences with one and the same person before. Only after the confusing array of things has been coordinated with the help of one and the same person can a teenager accept technical instruction from his teachers. For the patient, the therapist has to become the integrating person who was missing or did not function in the patient's early childhood. Combined with certain emotional rewards such as encouragement, therapy becomes a first experience in which cues and rewards are received from one and the same person. After a prolonged therapeutic experience, the patient then becomes able to separate the person who furnishes the cues from the person who furnishes the emotional encouragement (3).

Experimenting, testing, problem-solving, and finding out are the earmarks of an independent person. The patient therefore has to be steered in this direction. If, for example, the patient brings up the question of whether or not he should go back to the university and work for an M.A., the therapist will not make a decision for him. Instead he will raise questions such as "What are the requirements?" "How long would it take you?" "Have you talked to somebody in the field?" "What do you plan to do when you have the degree?" Each of these questions indicates to the patient that he has to prepare the ground. The therapist checks, in subsequent sessions, the answers that the patient has obtained. The therapist thus becomes an agent who, by pointing out the gaps in experience, information, and skill, induces the patient to work on the missing links, and in so doing he usually comes closer to a proper decision.

DIFFICULTIES IN OPERATING WITH INFORMATION

Inability to tolerate uncertainty · *Control of uncertainty* · *Inability to be specific or abstract* · *Inability to shift level of abstraction* · *Inability to condense, equate, and simplify*

Some patients are well read and can also gather information by talking to people; but they misuse their knowledge. These people accept only that information which supports their pet theories or proves that they are right. Existing biases can be distorted further through selective choice of information, and this eventually may lead to the development of delusions. These patients cannot tolerate the fact that we know little, that we often cannot predict the future, and that most of the time we have to take things as they come (4). An awareness of powerlessness together with a desire for control make such patients very anxious. To overcome anxiety, such a person accepts any information which promises to resolve the uncertainty, even at the cost of being wrong (6). To be wrong is more tolerable than to be uncertain.

The desire for control impels the individual towards logical extrapolations. But inasmuch as biological and social events are to a certain degree indeterminate, they cannot always be met by logical analysis and control procedures. While the animal meets such events by adaptation and analogic intuitive appreciation, the human being is tempted to use reasoning and logic which are totally inadequate to deal with the multiplicity of factors at any given moment. The ensuing failure in turn augments anxiety. Therapy in these cases is directed at making the patient relinquish his attempts to control the future and to focus upon acceptance of what is going on at the moment. As the patient begins to accept the present, anxiety diminishes and with it the need for completeness of information.

If we keep statements sufficiently abstract, they fit a multitude of situations, and if we move up the ladder of abstraction still further we finally arrive at a vocabulary that fits the whole universe. But words are useful only if they can be correlated with tangible objects and events—a process which requires some twenty years or more of formal education. Some of our patients never learned to correlate words with objects and events, and by remaining abstract and general they can hide their missing knowledge. On the other hand, there are people who talk only in concrete terms, who do not dare to transfer knowledge from one situation to the other, and who refrain from making any kind of generalization. By remaining concrete, they remain safe; but their mastery of events remains limited.

Over-specific or over-abstract behavior insures freedom from anxiety. This method is merely an exaggeration of the procedure used by normal and adaptive individuals who shift levels of abstraction when they encounter a contradiction that cannot be resolved at that particular level of abstraction. If someone makes the statement, "Cars are dangerous," and someone else confronts him with the fact that some drivers and cars have traveled over a half-million miles without accidents, he might then correct his statement to, "Automobiles traveling at a speed in excess of 50 m.p.h. are potentially dangerous." He has thus descended the scale of generalization and become specific. Conversely, if somebody says "This apple is worm-eaten" and somebody else remarks "Mine is perfect," he may reconcile these contradictions by saying "Apples picked off the ground are not always in a condition to be eaten." The shift of levels of abstraction for the management of contradictions and conflicts is learned over the years in the fold of the family. But if either abstractions or concretions were forbidden, this shift is not learned and the child remains deprived of a method of coping with contradictions. Later, in adulthood, the psychiatrist can notice the absence of such a flexible shift and the apprehension which is associated with being either abstract or specific. Therapy thus is, among other things, an exercise in shifting levels of abstraction.

The myriads of words to which we are exposed have to be sifted, selected, and organized. Events that are described in terms of one kind of vocabulary often have to be translated into another vocabulary, and what is "instinct" in one terminology is "id" in another. For this purpose, the similarities and differences between words have to be thoroughly understood. Patients of limited intelligence are unable to translate, condense, or establish correspondence of terms. Compulsive loyalty to symbols, words, or concepts is found in patients as well as in many doctors. Deep-rooted social insecurity makes such persons cling to symbolic systems rather than to objects and persons. Such difficulties are overcome if the therapist condenses events that happened at different times, if he points out analogies that exist between the patient's present behavior and past situations, and if he equates dreams with experiences that occur during the waking hours. This exercise in translation, equation, simplification, and condensation demonstrates to the patient that symbols and words are there to be experimented with until they fit the occasion. Gradually the idea seeps through that man must control symbols; that words are devices to denote or connote events, and not something anybody owes loyalty to. To make minds work better and more elastically is one of the tasks of therapy, and this is taught by demonstration.

MISSING SKILLS

Mastery as ego builder · *Unskilled in movement* · *Unskilled technically* · *Unskilled socially*

The term "information" refers to the representation of events that occur elsewhere and at a different time. The term "skill," in contrast, refers to the individual's ability to carry out specific actions. There are people who are well informed but unskilled, and there are highly skilled people who are uninformed. The acquisition of skill requires practice, and in order to find time for it the individual has to forsake universality. Commitment is hard in an age of rapid transportation and fast communication where distractions are manifold and people do not stick to one thing. But such people miss the pleasure of mastery, their self-respect suffers, and they remain in need of constant reassurance. Modern mass man, with his weak ego and even weaker superego structure, needs permanent transfusions from the outside in the form of moral and affectionate support. Through the channels of mass communication and depersonalized face-to-face encounters, this support is piped to the individual. Amidst these conditions the therapist does well to begin the strengthening of the patient by teaching him that in some area, regardless of whether it be play or work, he must become a master. Eventually the knowledge of how to become skilled can be transferred to other activities. The patient then has "learned how to learn" (2). This in itself strengthens the patient and makes him more adaptive and independent.

Particular attention has to be paid to those people who are unskilled in managing their bodies. If they are clumsy, poor in timing, use either too much or too little force, and in general do not achieve their goals, their poor coordination is more often than not related to deficient practice and exercise. If children exercise a lot, they learn the basic elements of smooth muscular operation. But without body-to-body contact, without the experience of movements that are replied to by the other person, they remain unskilled in the perception of motion and hence lag behind. The absence of inter- action with people can be detected in the angular, jerky, and un- skilled movements of shy and awkward people. The therapist has to insist that these patients engage in a pleasant physical activity. Whatever they like best serves as a starting point: swimming, tennis, boating, riding, hiking, climbing, skiing, shooting, hunting, fishing, or dancing. But in order to become a master, these activities have to be organized and carried out in pleasant company. Perhaps the family can afford a trailer or a tent and can go camping at regular intervals. The man might join a club, the family might spend the summer near a lake, the boys might built a boat, or perhaps they all live near a skating rink. The details have to be worked out depending upon location, age of the participants, and the availability of funds.

How to build a fire, how to right an overturned boat, how to re- pair a short in the electric network—these are skills which require not only skilled movement but also technical knowledge. This par- ticular combination of know-how and bodily skill is taught in most schools and therefore most children acquire a basic number of tech- nical skills such as driving a car. But scientific progress unfortunately has introduced more and more automation, and skills are conse- quently limited to push-button activities. With these modern devel- opments, the organism does not get properly exercised unless par- ents, educators, or therapists go out of their way to compensate for this deficiency. The therapist, for example, can induce the patient to engage in some activity such as woodworking, machine work, metal craft, boatbuilding, electronics, or woodcarving so that he gets in contact with materials and methods. Particularly, the desk and paper people need practical activities if they wish to keep their balance of mind in the midst of all their verbal unrealities.

Social skill consists of perception and evaluation of cues in self and others and of subsequent initiation of action. The absence of such skills is therapeutically treated in two ways: by exposing pa- tients to another person who is socially skilled and by encouraging emotional attachments so that messages become significant. The easiest way to learn consists of the pupil's surrendering himself to the teacher. He has to become the sense organs and the muscles of the other person and he has to give up his function of decision-making. If he can temporarily cease to operate as a separate social entity, he will learn easily the necessary skills. But in order to surrender, he must be a secure person—one who knows that he has an identity of his own and that he can therefore relinquish temporarily what he possesses anyway. But insecure people who constantly have doubts about their identity, who are afraid to be coerced, and who long for unity with the other person have great difficulty in surrendering. They do not adapt their muscles and sense organs to a task; they simply give up. And this the wise teacher refuses to accept. First the patient's self-respect has to be strengthened, and as the trust in the therapist increases, gradual surrender occurs. This in turn helps the patient to learn the necessary skills in an intimate two-person situation.

References

1. Bates, W. H.: *Bates Method for Better Eyesight without Glasses.* (New and rev. ed.) 200 p. New York: Holt, 1943.

2. Bateson, G.: Social planning and the concept of "deutero-learning." Pp. 81–97 in *Science, Philosophy and Religion,* 2nd Symposium. Edited by L. Bryson and L. Finkelstein. New York: Conference on Science, Philosophy, and Religion, 1942.

3. Dollard, J. and Miller, N. E.: *Personality and Psychotherapy.* 488 p. New York: McGraw-Hill, 1950.

4. Fox, R. C.: Training for uncertainty. Pp. 207–241 in *The Student-Physician.* (R. K. Merton, G. C. Reader, and P. L. Kendall, editors). Cambridge: Harvard University Press, 1957.

5. Hermann, K.: *Reading Disability.* 183 p. Springfield: Thomas, 1959.

6. Schwartz, E. K. and Wolf, A.: The quest for certainty. AMA Arch. Neurol. Psychiat., 81, 68–94, 1959.

Chapter Eighteen

Language and Speech Disorders

SPEECH DISTURBANCES

Non-technical therapy · Functional appraisal · Therapeutic classification · From the intact to the disturbed · Use of muscles · Training of relatives · Anatomical defects · Establishing nonverbal communication · Speech development · The voice of the disturbed person · Functional disorders

THE WORD "speech" refers to the production of vocal sounds. The term "language" refers to the organization of these sounds into a system of signs which have been agreed upon to represent objects, concepts, qualities, and actions. The production of meaningful sounds is mediated through nervous impulses which give rise to organized contractions of the respiratory muscles and the vocal cords. Although internal codification (nervous impulses), speech (sound of vocal muscles), and external language (printed word or recorded speech) are three distinctly different aspects of the process of communication, each of these aspects may be affected separately or in combination with the others.

The technical task of identifying the specific locus of a disturbance of speech or language is generally left to neurologists and speech experts who, with special methods, diagnose and rehabilitate patients in the technical use of speech and language functions (8). The task of therapeutic communication, then, is not to remedy the specific somatic difficulties which impede speech or interfere with language but to help the patient to communicate with others in spite of the technical obstacles. Patients who reach the psychiatrist usually have gone through the different stages of remedial measures and are faced with the task of accepting a more or less unalterable limitation in function. The threat of being disconnected from others because of a speech or language disturbance is anxiety provoking. If the anxiety concerning communicative relatedness can be handled, the patient often is capable of better mastering his own disability in the sense of accepting that which is unalterable, compensating for the existing difficulties, and improving those functions that are alterable.

APHASIA, AGNOSIA, APRAXIA

Cerebral lesions of traumatic, infectious, vascular, neoplastic, or degenerative origin may affect those parts of the brain that mediate language and speech functions. Unfortunately the finer details of the localization and classification of the various types of aphasia, apraxia, and agnosia (35) contribute little to the efficacy of rehabilitation. Most of these classifications date back to a period when scientists attempted to establish a mechanistic one-to-one relationship between disturbed functions and cerebral lesions. In most cases, several speech functions are affected simultaneously and the patient's production of speech sounds and his understanding of others are impeded by his awareness of having a disease. A cerebral lesion not only interferes with speech but may affect initiative, alertness, memory, and the readiness to engage in communicative exchange. Aphasics may vary in their responses from day to day and from person to person; and it is almost impossible to separate the somatic from the functional problem (37).

Aphasia manifests itself in two different ways: on a higher level, we find limitation in complexity, intensity, and endurance of communication; and on a lower level we find the disabilities which interfere with perception, speech production, or the interpretation of symbols. For purposes of therapy, five groups of disturbances can be distinguished (17):

–The first group comprises the typical speech disabilities such as dysarthria, motor aphasia, defective oral word formation, agrammatism or erroneous sentence formulation, difficulties in finding words, and anomia.

–The second group includes the auditory, sensory, or receptive types of agnosia and aphasia.

–The third groups is made up of the alexias, the disorders affecting reading such as reduction of the visual field, difficulties in visual recognition of forms, spatial disorientation, loss of phonetic association of visually recognized letters or words, and other reading difficulties.

–The fourth group involves agraphia and related disorders affecting writing: paralysis of the preferred hand, difficulties in formation of written words, and failure to revisualize the word.

–The fifth group includes the disorders that are characterized by difficulties with numbers.

Since many of these syndromes appear in combination, the efforts of the speech therapist are geared to the rehabilitation of three functions: the difficulties in reception, the difficulties in expression, and the difficulties with memory and recognition (27). The therapist starts with the functions that are intact and proceeds to connect these with the functions that are impaired. If visual recognition is impaired, the therapist takes auditory recognition as his healthy base function. If the printed word or number is the obstacle, then the therapist begins with the raw object. Patients with amnesic aphasia and other memory difficulties have to be induced to find associations with external stimuli that will recall the lost words. Daily, the patient is put through rehearsing those functions that he can successfully carry out; little by little, he adds exercises with functions that are more difficult. To retrain the patient in his receptive functions, the relationship between the symbol (word) and the object for which it stands has to be strengthened. Pointing, naming, tracing, and pictorial illustration serve to teach these patients, as if they were small children not familiar with words. Beginning with single-syllable words, the polysyllabic terms are added later, when the patient improves. Special exercises are devised for those patients who cannot identify the written or printed word or who have difficulties in recognizing numbers.

If the patient suffers from difficulties of expression, he has to be taught to employ his muscles. He may have to be shown how to use the muscles of his larynx, how to breathe, or how to move his lips or tongue. With the help of the mirror, simple exercises such as blowing out matches, whistling, or repeating sounds are rehearsed. Gradually simple words can be tried, particularly if the patient observes the muscles of the therapist by visual and tactile means and then attempts to use the same muscles of his own body (16, 27).

The patient with a cerebral lesion tires easily, and sessions have to be short but frequent. In a hospital setting, the nurses can do a lot to help the patient to exercise functions that are impaired. In the later phases of convalescence, the patient's relatives have to be instructed in how to help the patient. They have to be informed not to gloss over the difficulties of the patient but to rehearse the right word, not to apologise for the patient to strangers but to instruct others in what to do so that he can establish better contact (52).

ARTICULATORY DISTURBANCES

Many speech disorders manifest themselves in the inability to talk in a way that is understandable to others. In one case it may be the speed of the tongue and the laryngeal movements which handicap the child; in another, the lack of coordination. Also there may be local disturbances present in the organs of articulation. If the lips cannot move freely, if the jaws or the teeth interfere with movements, if the tongue does not move to the right place, or if the palate is deformed, speech is interfered with (51).

The predominant forms of disturbances of articulation appear as "baby talk," lisping, cluttering, and lalling (5). The baby talker is a child who, at a later age, retains or reverts to the speech of his infancy. Letters and sounds are substituted—for example, "w" for "l," "t" for "k," "r" for "s"—and audible letters and sounds take the place of inaudible ones. Very often, baby talk is reverted to in situations of stress or in order to mellow the heart of the parent who, when reminded of the time when the child was a baby, may yield. Lispers are persons who have difficulties with the enunciation of the "s"; more than ten types of defective "s" have been described by phoneticians and speech clinicians (5). The clutterer stumbles and repeats words and phrases, slurs and omits sounds and syllables while going at top speed. Cluttering is easily mistaken for stuttering, which is a somewhat different condition. The "laller" is appropriately named "the slow of tongue," and this condition is due to a relative immobilization of the tongue. Finally there are the articulatory disturbances of a neurological nature which involve paralysis of the cranial nerves. On occasion, disturbances of speech may be associated with nerve deafness. The slow development then may be due to lack of self training because the child not only is unable to hear others pronounce sounds correctly but his own exteroceptive control is impaired. And if a child has a low intelligence—a frequent occurrence in neurological conditions—it will take him a long time to learn what others master in a short time.

The communication therapist's principal task is to prepare the family for rehabilitation. While the speech therapist takes care of the technical end of training the patient, the psychiatrist works with the parents. He informs them about the technicalities of the defect, encourages them to be patient, and points out how human relatedness matters for the development of the child. It is the psychiatrist's task to see to it that the articulatory difficulties of the patient will not interfere more than is necessary with the communicative relatedness of the family. If the child talks with difficulty, others may be too impatient to listen to him. The pride of the parents may be hurt to have such a non-representative specimen as their son or daughter. Other parents may use threats or coercive measures which make those with speech disturbances even more apprehensive. The psychiatrist must see to it that the disturbance does not ruin the whole family. Instead, he has to encourage communal action and pictorial communication so that the defective speech functions carry less of an interpersonal load. If human relations and communication can be mediated through nonverbal means, the chances of recovery greatly increase.

STUTTERING

The stutterer is a person who suffers from a halting speech brought on by tonic and clonic spasm of the speech musculature.

Stuttering is characterized by a certain interruption of the normal rhythm which produces a repetition or complete blocking of the ordinary speech sounds. If the disturbance exists for some period of time, accessory movements of the shoulders, the hands, or the lips as well as facial grimaces may develop. Theories on the origin and maintenance of stuttering are so manifold that their discussion must be left to the experts (18). While technical therapy with stutterers is carried out by speech specialists (21), the psychiatrist has the task of uncovering those intrapsychic and family conflicts which cause or aggravate the stuttering (3). Since the onset of stuttering usually occurs shortly before or at the beginning of school, therapy might just as well start with the mother, include the father, and finally come to the little patient himself. In later years, the therapist can be of great help in guiding the stutterer into occupations in which his disturbance can be minimized.

DELAYED SPEECH DEVELOPMENT

Speech continues to develop well into the mature years. While at the age of eighteen the body is full grown, the cartilaginous tissues of the larynx are not as yet fully hardened. This process of growth must be slow because a number of functions must reach a satisfactory maturation stage before speech can properly develop (29). First the infant must learn to discriminate the high pitched sounds that invest speech tones with their particular characteristics. Then he has to acquire the memory for speech. Third, he has to master the movements necessary for making the speech sounds. The child must be able not only to execute specialized movements but to coordinate these specialized movements rapidly. The first sounds the infant makes employ only large muscle groups. Later, mandible, lips, tip of the tongue, soft palate, and the back of the tongue become involved (26). Sounds whose changes in pitch and intensity vary with the words or phrases are mastered first, and only later are the plosive, sibilant, and fricative noises added, giving speech its characteristic patterns. The child's first words consist of primitive interjections; then follow nouns, action verbs, and adjectives. Most children—even those who develop late—have begun to speak by the time they are three and a half years old, unless they suffer from an abnormality; and all speech sounds are normally developed by the age of seven. Language functions develop more rapidly in girls than in boys, and, strangely enough, fewer girls have speech defects (53). At the age of eight, children use language fluently and employ it for purposes of managing others (12, 38).

Delayed speech development can be related to a multitude of circumstances—mental deficiency, disturbances of memory, insufficient stimulation by parents, neurological disease, defective hearing, poor motor coordination, to mention just a few (1). The communication therapist of course encounters delayed speech development in its psychogenic and sociogenic forms. The pleasure of speaking is transmitted to the child by the adult. To listen, to imitate, to reply are natural desires of the infant, but in surroundings where people do not talk or where they use speech mainly for coercive purposes, the development of speaking, writing, or reading may be delayed. Usually we find some deviant feedback pattern. If a child does not need to speak in order to interact with his surroundings, he will show a delay in development; and if a child feels safer not to use language at all, he will also show such a delay. The art of therapy then is to make speech a pleasurable activity which is essential for all concerned. The therapy with relatives frequently involves helping them to master their anxiety about the child's slow development, to muster more strength and patience for exercise and tolerance of deviant behavior. This additional strength which the parents can muster often makes it possible for the child to eventually become adapted to his surroundings.

VOICE DISORDERS

Vocal analysis falls outside the field of the psychiatrist (36, 49). It involves the assessment of the frequency range, the resonance, the glottal stroke, respiration, pathos, speed, and many other factors (53). However, the psychiatrist has to be a keen observer of the total impact that the human voice has upon others. The healthy person usually has a self-assured voice that is sonorous and deep. Being relaxed, his diaphragm operates regularly and slowly, and he phonates upon expiration. If he is pleased, he may speed up or slow down his rate of speech, showing some changes in intensity and pitch. When he gets mad, he begins his words with a hard attack. The last syllable is strongly accented, and often too many words are crammed into one breath. When he feels defeated, he begins to speak more slowly, to articulate less clearly, to show less variation in volume, intensity, rhythm, and inflection of his voice. If he is in the mood to complain, his voice has an upward tendency, although the pitch may glide up and down over the shorter range.

In the neuroses and the psychoses, we encounter all these factors in a somewhat exaggerated form, while some additional features make their appearance (34). The undecided person has a voice that is too soft or too loud, and the last syllable is inflected upward, giving the sentence the appearance of a question; or he may lower his voice so it becomes inaudible. The voice of excitement, in contrast, shows great pitch intervals; the lower tones seem to be absent and the contraction of the pharyngeal and neck muscles gives the voice a sometimes squeaky lift. The resentful person has dry, tense vocal cords and often shows excessive pathos with sudden increases in intensity and overemphasis at an arbitrary moment. The person who is alarmed shows his alertness by a voice that fades from loud to soft and from high to low pitch. The voice of anxiety exhibits a rough, wavering tone which is brought on by respiratory pressure which is weaker than the pressure of the glottis. People then talk as if they had a frog in their throat, sometimes being out of breath, sometimes hoarse. Inspiratory phonation is not uncommon, and whispering, aphonia, or mutism may persist for some time (43). The voice of depression is characterized by uniform phonation on a narrow vocal range; the voice is monotonous and may trail off.

SPEECH REFLECTING PERSONALITY DISORDER

In addition to the technical difficulties of speech perception, interpretation, and production, we have to consider those difficulties which are the result of emotional influences and human interaction (4). Logorrhea, mutism, aphonia, falsetto voice, and similar disturbances are the result of emotional difficulties (5, 53). These may appear more or less suddenly as in hysterical disturbances; they may be based on long established habits which are present most of the time; or they may appear particularly under stress. Functional speech disorders can be as disruptive as some of the technical disturbances; and the catatonically unresponsive patient who does not speak is as much cut off from the world as the stutterer who cannot carry on a fluent conversation.

The communication therapist has no special reason to treat these patients any differently than he would treat another neurotic or psychotic person. The attitudinal disturbances of speech depend for their correction very much upon the attitude of the therapist, on how he meets the patient, what weight he attributes to the disturbance, and whether he is capable of putting up with the initial interference with the process of communication (50). The symptomatology is, as it were, designed to interfere with human relations. If the therapist succumbs, the patient does not deem him worthy of further contact. If, in contrast, he skirts the difficulty and acknowledges the patient's intent of not communicating, he may be able to establish contact. Ultimately he can ally himself with the patient's "herd instinct" and his desire to relate, which has been so deeply frustrated and hurt that he prefers to deny his innermost need.

LANGUAGE DISTURBANCES

Somatic, action, and symbolic language · Psychopathology and language · Language and identity · Experience is tied to language · Losing the compulsive drive · Difficulties with verbal logic · Analogic pursuits · Verbalization of inner experience

While the term "speech" comprises the processes of perception, comprehension, and expression of words, the term "language" encompasses the processes of codification and signification of signs and symbols. Disturbances may afflict speech and language functions in combination or separately. Those handicapped in speech suffer from nervous, muscular, bony, or emotional disorders which interfere with the sensory and motor end-organs—that is, with the mechanics of speech. Language disturbances essentially reflect human experiences which bear upon thinking, feeling, and communication—that is, the symbolic behavior of man. Very often a vicious circle is set up between speech and language functions. Specific signals which impinge upon the human being may lead to frustration. This state of alarm may interfere with speech mechanisms, and the resulting lack of communication in turn may influence symbolic behavior. Under these circumstances, the individual develops a distorted view of the situation, and eventually he uses his speech functions to communicate with others about these distorted views. As a result, communication may break down further. And so goes the vicious circle.

ABNORMAL LANGUAGE SPECTRUM

In the course of development, the child learns in succession three different ways of denotation. First, the infant's expressions are confined to intestinal, respiratory, and cardiovascular manifestations which are the result of contractions of the smooth muscles and are mediated through the autonomic nervous system. Crying and whining, which are the result of contractions of the striped muscles, have not as yet mutually agreed-upon symbolic meaning, but they do inform the bystander about the baby's condition; thus the mother learns to distinguish hunger from boredom, and cold from constipation or rage. This first method of expressing internal events to the outside world can be called "somatic language." As the central nervous system matures, contractions of the striped muscles become more prominent. Through sucking, biting, grasping, pointing, smiling, and locomotion, the child makes his wishes known. The adult interprets the actions of the infant, and this "action language" is used well into adulthood. With the second or third year of life, still another system comes into being. The child learns to make a variety of sounds and discovers that people respond to them. Eventually these sounds come to stand for other events, and this then is called "symbolic language." At a later age, then, the human being's spectrum of language is made up of three components—somatic, action, and symbolic language. The girl who blushes, for example, uses somatic language; the man who walks out of the conference room uses action language; the one who raises his eyebrows and asks a question uses symbolic language. All three forms of language are blended for purposes of daily communication; the amount of each is determined by purpose and situation.

Disturbances in somatic, action, and symbolic language are found in a variety of psychopathological conditions. The psychosomatic disturbances and some of the psychotic disorders show a preponderance of somatic language. Schizophrenic children have been known to react favorably when given baby bottles to drink from (6); and in the adult schizophrenic the stimulation of the skin through wet packs, massage, and other physical procedures has always been found in the foreground of therapy (44). Action language predominates in the rehabilitation of aggressive children and juvenile delinquents (39), and it is common experience that group activities are paramount in keeping youngsters under control. By doing things with the patient—and this applies to the schizophrenic as well—a bond can be established which cannot be produced by verbal methods of rehabilitation. Symbolic language, finally, predominates in disorders such as the psychoneuroses (42).

There are people who use an inappropriate language spectrum. A girl who unduly exposes her attractive skin while in a work situation, the man who wishes to discuss business when the other person has just become ill, and the person who presses for action when matters have first to be discussed are out of line. If patients are addicted to using the wrong kind of language, the therapist has to undertake painstaking work. To expose the history of this development, to isolate the cues that induce the patient to react erroneously, to help the patient to find gratifications under appropriate circumstances, and to expose the patient to people who react appropriately is a time-consuming but rewarding task.

CULTURE AND LANGUAGE CHANGE

Culture change from foreign to American, from the New England culture of understatement to the Hollywood culture of overstatement, from military to civilian life, from rural to urban living, or from the "wrong side of the tracks" to the "right side" entails not only a change in values but also a change in the language system used. A whole new vocabulary has to be learned, together with the rules that apply to the use of such a vocabulary (19). What can be said, when, and to whom, and on what occasion make up a social skill that can only be mastered over the years (41). Language plays an important part in the establishment of a sense of identity (54). Identification means imitation, and imitation of course involves the speech sounds (24, 51). The body of experience of people who have spent the first four years of their lives in one country, the next five in a second country, and the time thereafter in a third resembles a layer cake. Early experiences are codified in one language, later experiences in a second or third language; and most of these experiences are associated with different people. Continuity therefore is sketchy and one of the great tasks of therapy is to bridge the barriers that different codifications have created in the minds of the patients. Individuals who move from one culture into another tend to block out periods and languages unless there exists continuity in terms of contact with significant figures—parents or elders—who migrated with them (45). If the therapist encounters a functional amnesia which interferes with the sense of self and if he speaks the language of the culture in which the earlier events occurred, he can, with his linguistic talent, penetrate the patient's obscure past.

THE ANALOGICALLY HANDICAPPED PERSON

The two basic systems of codification—the analogic and the digital —are not equally developed in every human being, and this uneven distribution is sometimes so marked that one can literally speak of analogical or digital feeble-mindedness. An analogically deprived person cannot move fluently and does not see how something can be grasped, touched or adjusted. He is clumsy with his fingers and his legs, is helpless to repair little things, and does not engage in athletic sports such as riding, tennis, or swimming. A person who is impractical and has no appreciation of his own body in space cannot maintain his equilibrium under any but the most normal conditions. The person who is lacking in coordination and who personally does not get any pleasure from moving in space may also have little appreciation for color and form, for the beauty of nature or the thrill of a dance. He has little or no sense of esthetics, does not groom himself, and has no appreciation of appropriateness and elegance. The sense of fit is missing, and whatever he does seems to be based on the use of rote memory, logical deduction, or speculation. To compensate for his deficiencies, the person may talk a great deal.

The childhood experiences of such an individual were drowned in words. Mother may have responded by talking, but not by acting, playing, or exercising the child's body. If a child is prevented from playing with his age-mates and lacks personal contact, his pleasure may be concentrated on the verbal exchange with adults. The therapist of course cannot replace the missing childhood experiences—particularly not in the analogic mode. It is easier to talk about things one has experienced than about things one has not experienced, and therefore free association and talk are of little help. Such patients ought to be taken on walks to help them appreciate what is going on around them. A movement and its effects have to be interpreted; posture and other body phenomena must be observed. Of course, the best method would be to put the patient into surroundings in which people are aware of their bodies and emotions. Therefore outdoor experience, sports, dancing, and competitive or expressive games should be encouraged. And while he can sharpen his eye by engaging in ball games, he can heighten his perception of interpersonal and social events by watching the behavior of others, including the therapist. If an action sequence is subsequently discussed, the patient may become aware of all the many signals that are exchanged by the participants.

The analogically handicapped person is usually lonely and driven. He does not feel much because his propriosensory perception has never been exercised and interpersonally elaborated. But as he begins to move, he will begin to feel; and as he begins to feel he will discover that emotions are localized in the body. Anger may be felt in the pit of the stomach or in the back of the neck, and fear may be experienced in the intestinal tract or in the knees. With the opening of this world of visual, auditory, tactile, osmic, gustatory, vibratory, temperature, and pain sensations an entirely different dimension is added to experience (47). Some of the compulsive striving may be lost and life may assume a new meaning.

THE DIGITALLY HANDICAPPED PERSON

The digitally-verbally handicapped person is animal in the best sense of the word: alert, sensitive, realistic, but incapable of forming abstractions or extrapolations and of following the laws of logic. The digitally or verbally handicapped person seems to develop well until writing and reading have to be learned. Although in rare instances writing and reading difficulties of children may be due to lesions of the brain, they are as a rule functional disorders (10). Such children usually had ample contact with their mothers during their earlier years when somatic or action language predominated, but difficulties arose when the age of symbolic language arrived. To the parents of some, words did not make sense; and the children could not discuss their ideas. Or perhaps the parents helped in the homework with spelling and writing and the child sensed that words and numbers were not among their sources of pleasure. Such children, then, prefer to go outdoors and play baseball or roam around in the fields. The digitally handicapped person is essentially a much healthier individual than the analogically handicapped person because the earlier development proceeded without disturbance.

Analogically gifted people should be guided into occupations that are connected with nature and do not require much paper work. Agriculture, animal husbandry, forestry, seamanship, mountaineering, athletics, domestic occupations, and the arts are the fields of choice. Analogically gifted people often have a natural understanding of plants, animals, and children as well as of the biological needs of human beings. Their mental age scores may be lower on verbal and numerical tasks than on comparable performance tasks, and they may be lower than what one would expect in terms of their accomplishments in life. Analogically oriented children have a particularly hard time in school because our educational system is geared to the production of digital and verbal wizards; few are the nonverbal skills that can be learned in school, and the few hours devoted to music, art, and sports are but a drop in the bucket. Analogic education thus rests with the parents, and when they fail the patient will have to turn to those who specialize in rehabilitation.

Patients of this kind are often called "infantile" (40) or hysterical because they have retained the pervasive quality that surrounds all analogic codification. Although this quality is most conducive to creative work, the accompanying ideas of omnipotence often interfere with reality testing. If the therapist can add to this analogic gift the analytic and logical aspects of digital codification, he will be able to diminish the role of the omnipotent ideas while maintaining the creativity of the individual. Since the patient's proprioceptive abilities are usually well developed, the therapeutic work begins with a translation of his experiences into words. First the therapist may have to verbalize for the patient until he knows what is wanted; but soon the patient will try to translate his rich experience into words, and under the influence of encouragement and response he begins to master a new codification system.

LANGUAGE AND SPEECH DISTURBANCES IN VARIOUS PSYCHIATRIC CONDITIONS

Semantics, pragmatics, and syntactics · Dissection of language · Manic-depressive language · Schizophrenic language, movements, and nonverbal behavior · Language of brain disease · Language of psychoneurotics · Psychosomatic patients · Language of anxiety

In earlier years, words were considered representative of inner thought. Studies on the subject by Wundt (55), Kraepelin (25), Bleuler (7), and Jung (22) are too well known to be reported here. At that time, little or no distinction was made between semantics (the relationship of signs to the objects they represent), syntactics (the relationship of signs to each other), and pragmatics (the relationship of signs to their human users) (33). Only with the advent of psychoanalysis, Gestalt psychology, and general semantics did the attention shift from dictionary definition to meaning (20). The final step in this development occurred when the existentialist movement began to emphasize total human experience rather than affects, thoughts, or associations (23, 31).

Therapeutically speaking, there are no significant language disturbances which necessitate one course of treatment in preference to another. The language differences that have been described in the literature are scientific isolates, convenient to observe or measure but therapeutically insignificant. Only when the syntactic, pragmatic, and semantic functions are considered as a unit and when these expressive functions are placed side by side with the perceptive and evaluative functions do we gain an understanding of the patient's problems. While speech therapy bears upon the mechanics of speech production, language therapy is attitudinal in character. Once the likes and dislikes, resistances, and identifications have been exposed, once the experiences from various sensory modalities are welded into one, and once verbal and nonverbal and pragmatic, syntactic, and semantic aspects become fused, integrated functioning becomes possible again.

The various aspects of speech and language patterns have to be handled by the therapist so that scientific dissection does not disrupt the functioning of the patient. The manic-depressive person, for example, seems to relive earlier events, often in an emotionally prejudiced manner. To him, the world is a series of feeling states and words are used to pose rhetorical questions, to cite quotations, to name, to list, and to itemize (28). Both in flight of ideas and in psychomotor retardation we deal with an inner language disturbance, and many of the manic-depressive's difficulties may be conceived of as desynchronization of verbal and nonverbal codification. When a person speeds up, his verbal productions cannot keep up with the fast inner changes in analogic codification; when he slows down, the verbal productions are so slow that they become unintelligible or repetitious. In other words, analogic codification can proceed fast or slowly whereas verbal codification has to proceed at a uniform speed. When the person with a cycloid temperament is not psychotic, he makes ample use of analogic codifications. He is warm, interpersonal, and sometimes artistic. He frequently has well-rounded coordinated movements that in some ways express a close relationship between analogic thinking and the muscular system. Frequently one hears the comment that such-and-such a person seemed so well adjusted and his poise was so convincing that nobody would have thought he could suddenly suffer a breakdown. Once the patient is depressed, therapists often experience great difficulty in establishing rapport, and this difficulty is at times much greater than that experienced with schizophrenics (9). Therapists also are impressed by what they feel is a somewhat phony and fraudulent approach of these depressed patients (11). Some of these facts can be explained if one assumes that during a depression the synchronization between the nonverbal and the verbal systems is impaired or lost altogether. This theory seems justifiable in view of the fact that the symptomatology of depressive states can disappear in a matter of hours or days as a result of shock therapy, psychotherapy, or treatment with drugs. The effect is similar to that observed when sound track and motion picture are not synchronized; even if the scene is a powerful one, the onlooker is not moved. The defect, however, can be remedied and the proper effect produced by proper juxtaposition of picture and sound (42).

Schizophrenic patients conceive of the world as a series of processes and generalizations (13). Their language is characterized by dissociation, autistic thinking, blocking, perseveration, predicate rather than subject orientation, emphasis upon detail, and frequent use of bizarre words and neologisms (2, 7, 22). We find preference for abstract terms and compound substantives, impersonal use of pronouns—substitution of "you" or "they" for "I"—and often no reference to specific dates, names, or places. There is insufficient delineation within or between thought units. In their speech, schizophrenic children in particular show excessively high pitch levels, and where others drop their pitch, schizophrenic children do not. This gives their speech a chanting quality which produces a flat, unfinished monotone.

The early lack of appropriate and gratifying communication through action, gesture, and object is permanently imprinted on many schizophrenic patients. Their movements are characterized by angular, jerky, uncoordinated motions carried out with uneven acceleration and deceleration and at either too slow or too fast a tempo. This lack of motor agility may well be the result of insufficient practice in nonverbal interaction during infancy. There is evidence to believe that the lack of responsiveness of the parents, particularly in terms of action, led to underdevelopment of the children, and this was later compensated for by an increased perceptual sensitivity to the actions of others. Thus the role of nonparticipating observer was forced upon these patients, for the absence of appropriate responses to muscular needs prevented them from learning how to relate to others through movement and action (42).

The secret of the schizophrenic's language difficulties is found in his nonverbal behavior (32). The need for analogic, nonverbal codifications comes to the fore during psychotic episodes, at which time the patient may reproduce movements which accompanied earlier emotional experiences. In the process of recalling memories, a patient may suck his thumb or caress the arm of his chair; or he may, in the course of a verbal account, gesticulate or make shaking, pulling, or poking gestures. Even more informative are the primitive and uncoordinated movements of patients at the peak of severe functional psychoses; such movements may be viewed as attempts to re-establish the infantile system of communication through action. It is as if these patients were trying to relive the patterns of communication that were frustrating in early childhood, with the hope that this time there will be another person who will understand and reply in nonverbal terms. This thesis is supported by observations of the behavior of psychotic children who tend to play with their fingers, make grimaces, or assume bizarre body positions (48). Their movements rarely are directed at other people but rather at themselves, sometimes to the point of producing serious injuries. As therapy proceeds, interpersonal movements gradually replace the solipsistic movements, and stimulus becomes matched to response. Once these children have been satisfied in nonverbal ways, they become willing to learn verbal forms of codification and to master discursive language.

The language of patients suffering from organic syndromes is characterized by paucity of vocabulary, clumsy and inappropriate expression, circumstantiality, perseveration, stalling, and incoherence. The difficulties are primarily with the mechanics of speech, and here again we may find a disorganization of analogic and digital systems of codification. Such disorganization seems to occur under conditions of stress as well as of cerebral damage (42). Patients who have suffered a stroke with partial impairment of speech and language functions may be rehabilitated with the methods used for aphasics. If people are simply senile, they are incorporated, if possible, into an ongoing process which necessitates reality testing and moderate physical action. Contact with reality speedily brings back a resynchronization of word, image, and action.

In the psychoneurotic group we find well developed language systems, both analogic and digital. The difficulties here arise because of erroneous matching of the symbolic systems with reality. The hysterical patient in particular is likely to misuse words to relate impressions and reactions with the intent of making the listener participate. The emphasis on volubility and sensuality in preference to discourse and logic often brings about a distortion on the fantastic side. The obsessive-compulsive patient, in contrast, who emphasizes the specific and circumscribed, distorts because he is too literal. He compares, quantifies, and specifies, and his language is full of prefatory statements, repetitions, and modifying clauses (28). One gains the impression that the compulsive has a highly developed digital-verbal system to the detriment of the analogic one. The psychopathic or action person, finally, shows a preference for verbs and short sentences. To him the world is a succession of actions which words are inadequate to express.

The infantile or psychosomatic patient expresses himself in pidgin English. Short words and basic English vocabulary are preferred. He makes few references to imagination, feelings, or the inner world of experience but frequent references to somatic events and objects. He is not interested in processes or relationships, and to him the world is a succession of statements which bear upon the state of his organism (40).

These generalizations, of course, have to be taken with a grain of salt. Goldman-Eisler, for example, has shown that speech rate (15) and the sequence of activity and silence (14) are independent of role, while self reference rate depends upon the role and purpose of the speaker. Language patterns change, depending upon whether the individual is relaxed, anxious, or angry. Mahl (30) describes silence as a measure of anxiety, whereas Ruesch and Prestwood (46) elaborate upon the kind of words used. Increase in the number of words referring to feelings, personal pronouns, and subjective qualifications seems to be associated by the listener with a state of excitement. Reduction in the number of subjective qualifications and personal pronouns with simultaneous increase in the use of concrete nouns and objective qualifications, in contrast, seems to be perceived as representative of a more relaxed attitude.

References

1. Anderson, V. A.: *Improving the Child's Speech.* 333 p. New York: Oxford, 1953.

2. Arieti, S.: *Interpretation of Schizophrenia.* 522 p. New York: Brunner, 1955.

3. Barbara, D. A.: *Stuttering.* 304 p. New York: Julian Press, 1954.

4. Barbara, D. A.: *Your Speech Reveals Your Personality.* 174 p. Springfield: Thomas, 1958.

5. Berry, M. F. and Eisenson, J.: *Speech Disorders; Principles and Practices of Therapy.* 573 p. New York: Appleton, 1956.

6. Bettelheim, B.: *Love is Not Enough.* 386 p. Glencoe: Free Press, 1950.

7. Bleuler, E.: *Textbook of Psychiatry.* 635 p. New York: Macmillan, 1924.

8. Brodnitz, F. S.: *Vocal Rehabilitation.* 119 p. American Academy of Ophthalmology and Otolaryngology, 1959.

9. Bychowski, G. and Despert, J. Louise (Editors): *Specialized Techniques in Psychotherapy.* 371 p. New York: Basic Books, 1952.

10. Fernald, G. M.: *Remedial Techniques in Basic School Subjects.* 349 p. New York: McGraw-Hill, 1943.

11. Fromm-Reichmann, F.: *Psychoanalysis and Psychotherapy.* (Edited by D. M. Bullard.) 350 p. Chicago: University of Chicago Press, 1959.

12. Garrison, K. C.: *Growth and Development* (2nd ed.). 559 p. New York: Longmans Green, 1959.

13. Goldfarb, W., Braunstein, P., and Lorge, I.: A study of speech patterns in a group of schizophrenic children. Amer. J. Orthopsychiat., 26, 544–555, 1956.

14. Goldman-Eisler, F.: The measurement of time sequences in conversational behaviour. Brit. J. Psychol., 42, 355–362, 1951.

15. Goldman-Eisler, F.: A study of individual differences and of interaction in the behaviour of some aspects of language in interviews. J. ment. Sci., 100, 177–197, 1954.

16. Goldstein, K.: *Language and Language Disturbances.* 374 p. New York: Grune & Stratton, 1948.

17. Granich, L.: *Aphasia: A Guide to Retraining.* 108 p. New York: Grune & Stratton, 1947.

18. Hahn, E. F.: *Stuttering: Significant Theories and Therapies* (2nd ed., prepared by E. S. Hahn). 180 p. Stanford: Stanford University Press, 1956.

19. Hall, E. T.: *The Silent Language.* 240 p. Garden City: Doubleday, 1959.

20. Hayakawa, S. I.: Semantics. ETC., 9, 243–257, 1952.

21. Johnson, W. and Associates: *The Onset of Stuttering: Research Findings and Implications.* 519 p. Minneapolis: University of Minnesota Press, 1959.

22. Jung, C. G.: *Studies in Word Association.* (Tr. by M. D. Ede.) 575 p. New York: Moffat, Yard & Co., 1919.

23. Kahn, E.: An appraisal of existential analysis. I. Psychiat. Quart., 31, 203–227, 1957.

24. Karpf, F. B.: *The Psychology and Psychotherapy of Otto Rank.* 129 p. New York: Philosophical Library, 1953.

25. Kraepelin, E.: *Clinical Psychiatry.* (Adapted by A. R. Defendorf.) 420 p. New York: Macmillan, 1904.

26. Lewis, M. M.: *How Children Learn to Speak.* 143 p. London: Harrap, 1957.

27. Longerich, M. C. and Bordeaux, J.: *Aphasia Therapeutics.* 185 p. New York: Macmillan, 1954.

28. Lorenz, M.: Expressive behavior and language patterns. Psychiatry, 18, 353–366, 1955.

29. McCarthy, D.: Language development in children. Pp. 476–581 in *Manual of Child Psychology.* (L. Carmichael, editor). New York: Wiley, 1946.

30. Mahl, G. F.: Disturbances and silences in the patient's speech in psychotherapy. J. abnorm. soc. Psychol., 53, 1–15, 1956.

31. May, R., Angel, E., and Ellenberger, H. F. (Editors): *Existence: A New Dimension in Psychiatry and Psychology.* 445 p. New York: Basic Books, 1958.

32. Mette, A.: Contribution to the symptomatology and theory of speech disturbances in schizophrenia. J. Neuropath. & Psychiat., 55, No. 11, Moscow, 1955.

33. Morris, C. W.: *Signs, Language, and Behavior.* 365 p. New York: Prentice-Hall, 1946.

34. Moses, P. J.: *The Voice of Neurosis.* 131 p. New York: Grune & Stratton, 1954.

35. Nielsen, J. M.: *Agnosia, Apraxia, Aphasia.* (2nd ed.) 292 p. New York: Hoeber, 1946.

36. Ostwald, P. F.: Visual denotation of human sounds. Arch. gen. Psychiat., 3, 117–121, 1960.

37. Penfield, W. and Roberts, L.: *Speech and Brain-Mechanisms.* 286 p. Princeton: Princeton University Press, 1959.

38. Piaget, J.: *The Language and Thought of the Child.* (2nd ed.) 246 p. London: Kegan Paul, Trench, Trubner; 1932.

39. Redl, F. and Wineman, D.: *Controls from Within.* 332 p. Glencoe: Free Press, 1952.

40. Ruesch, J.: The infantile personality: the core problem of psychosomatic medicine. Psychosom. Med., 10, 134–144, 1948.

41. Ruesch, J.: Social factors in therapy. Pp. 59–93 in *Psychiatric Treatment* (ARNMD #31). Baltimore: Williams & Wilkins, 1953.

42. Ruesch, J.: Nonverbal language and therapy. Psychiatry, 18, 323–330, 1955.

43. Ruesch, J.: *Disturbed Communication.* 337 p. New York: Norton, 1957.

44. Ruesch, J.: The schizophrenic patient's ways of communication. Pp. 198–207 in *Congress Report* (1957), *Vol. 4.* Zurich: IInd International Congress for Psychiatry, 1959.

45. Ruesch, J., Jacobson, A., and Loeb, M. B.: Acculturation and illness. Psychol. Monogr. 62(5), 1–40, 1948.

46. Ruesch, J. and Prestwood, A. R.: Anxiety, its initiation, communication, and interpersonal management. A.M.A. Arch. Neurol. Psychiat., 62, 527–550, 1949.

47. Ruesch, J. and Kees, W.: *Nonverbal Communication.* 205 p. Berkeley and Los Angeles: University of California Press, 1956.

48. Ruesch, J., and Kees, W.: Children in Groups. 16 mm film. Running time, 25 min. The Langley Porter Institute, San Francisco, 1954.

49. Starkweather, J. A.: Vocal communication of personality and human feelings. J. Communication, 11, 63–72, 1961.

50. Travis, E. L. (Editor): *Handbook of Speech Pathology.* 1088 p. New York: Appleton-Century-Crofts, 1957.

51. Van Riper, C.: *Speech Correction: Principles and Methods.* (2nd ed.) New York: Prentice-Hall, 1947.

52. Wepman, J. M.: *Recovery from Aphasia*. 276 p. New York: Ronald Press, 1951.
53. West, R., Ansberry, M., and Carr, A.: *The Rehabilitation of Speech*. (3rd ed.) 688 p. New York: Harper, 1957.
54. Wheelis, A.: *The Quest for Identity*. 250 p. New York: Norton, 1958.
55. Wundt, W.: *Völkerpsychologie*. (2nd ed.) 4 v. Leipzig: Engelmann, 1904.

Chapter Nineteen

The Disabled

WHEN, in the absence of trauma or disease, behavior patterns are non-adaptive, we commonly label the condition a neurosis or a psychosis. However, the same picture of non-adaptive, disruptive behavior can also be produced by illness of the central or peripheral nervous system. Brain disease may afflict the organs of communication directly or an amputation of the arm may interfere with expression. The task of rehabilitation then is to restore the functions of the afflicted organ system or, if this is impossible, to have the patient compensate in the best way he can for his disability.

THE PERSON WITH A BRAIN LESION

Localization of lesion · Reversible and irreversible lesions · Rehabilitation and care · The anxiety of invalidism · Mental defectives

Degenerative, inflammatory, toxic, neoplastic, infectious, and traumatic lesions of the brain may damage the organs of perception, evaluation, and transmission. Attempts to establish a one-to-one relation between brain lesions and communicative patterns have failed because in a function as complex as communication many areas of the brain are involved. This is clearly shown in the study of aphasia, agnosia, and apraxia, where in the past investigators labeled syndrome after syndrome, only to discover that these rarely occurred in isolation from each other and that often the lesion assigned to a particular area in the brain could not be verified at autopsy (6). The data brought forth by experimental methods were equally disappointing inasmuch as it was practically impossible to set a circumscribed traumatic lesion, regardless of how carefully planted, without affecting the neighboring structures. Modern microchemical methods may be able to clear up some of these questionable points (25). But what we can conclude is that the brain operates as a whole, and a focal lesion is disruptive not only because of the deficit it creates but also because of its inhibitory influence upon other parts of the brain (7).

From the standpoint of communication, therefore, it is wise to assume that a brain lesion has a variety of effects: directly, through destruction; indirectly, through vascular and chemical influences upon neighboring areas; and functionally, through the disruption of a pathway which may necessitate a rerouting of network functions. Usually it holds that the more extensive and diffuse a lesion is, the more likely it is to affect brain functioning, although this principle will not hold up in all cases. A prognosis of the patient's condition can be arrived at by taking an inventory of the functions that are irreversibly disturbed and by deciding whether the area involved is highly specialized. For example, if the optic nerve has been severed on both sides, vision will not return; but if an occlusion of the middle cerebral artery has affected speech functions in the left temporal region, there still exists the possibility that the patient might relearn some of the lost functions. Whether this is possible because of use of the contralateral hemisphere or because the lesion is reversible is often difficult to determine. In considering the prognosis, the therapist has to estimate whether rehabilitation can occur within the period of time in which the patient will live. Vascular lesions may or may not affect the longevity of the patient, while rapidly growing, space-consuming lesions which cannot be checked inevitably lead to an early death.

The rehabilitation of patients suffering from aphasia, agnosia, or apraxia (28) and from sensory and motor disturbances (20) of a non-progressive type takes patience and involves a relearning process. Such a patient should be referred to the appropriate specialist (9). Diffuse and progressive lesions as they occur in encephalitis or in the various kinds of degenerative conditions usually lead to a gradual deterioration of the communicative patterns of the individual. New information cannot be absorbed, and old information may be blocked and rendered inaccessible. The extensive interpersonal feedback circuits—those that lead to the correction of information with the help of others—gradually deteriorate; and as the disorder progresses, the intraorganismic feedback circuits also become more involved. Thinking and feeling get progressively so disturbed that the individual cannot even attend to routine functions. The art here is to confine the patient's activities to situations he is familiar with, to provide him with familiar tasks, and to expose him to familiar patterns of communication. As long as his adaptive reserves are not taxed, his lesion will show less.

On the whole, the therapist should not be too impressed with the localizable pathology of the disorder. The patient is sick; he is upset about not being able to function; the ensuing anxiety disorganizes him further. The therapist's task therefore is to support the patient, to alleviate his anxiety, and to guide him into the appropriate rehabilitation channels. The patient may need physical therapy, speech therapy, or psychotherapy. While the technical aspects of rehabilitation can be delegated to specialists, the patient's emotional development and the strategic decisions concerning the reorganization of his life have to be discussed with the psychiatrist or the family physician. Too often the patient is treated as a technical problem, and the fact that the integrative aspects of existence are likewise disturbed is forgotten. This is where therapeutic communication comes into its own.

A special case of brain injury, disease, or malformation occurs in the mentally defective. For purposes of rehabilitation, it makes little difference whether mental retardation occurs with or without a demonstrable brain lesion. The methodology remains the same. Although a good deal is known about the neuropathology and the ensuing functional difficulties of the mentally retarded (10, 26), the development of psychotherapeutic procedures is still in its infancy (8, 24). The reason for this difficulty is found in the underdeveloped language and communication system of the patients. The feebleminded have unusual difficulties with words and numbers and their education has to be geared to doing, and to analogic appreciation of events. To teach them to read and to write is often a waste of time; but to train them to cope with a limited, practical situation is rather rewarding. In the good old days when writing and arithmetic were a monopoly for the few and education was confined to the performance of practical tasks, the mentally retarded had a better time. Anybody who deals with feeble-minded people should have the patience of an animal trainer, who knows exactly what to demand, when to reward, and when to stop. We have to give up trying to educate the mentally retarded as we do normal people; and once our ambition as doctors is lowered, we begin to make headway with these less fortunate people. Even so, many of them do not as yet receive the attention given to dogs in an average home, not to speak of the care that a performing monkey or a circus horse receives.

THE INVALID

He leads a special life · The first step: Acceptance · Second step: Practical considerations · Third step: Social reorientation · Fourth step: Prevention of doom · Fifth step: Childhood conflicts and invalidism

The blind, the deaf, the amputee, the spastic person, or the one suffering from paralysis due to disease or injury is a person who must face more or less permanent invalidism (5). Not being able to look forward to recovery, this person must accept his invalidism and find a way of living which may differ from that of his fellow citizens. If his handicap has existed since birth, he has never known anything else. He has probably attended special schools and training centers. and has been given the opportunity to avail himself of the body of knowledge that the rehabilitation centers have accumulated. But the one who acquires a handicap in middle life has to readjust his way of living so radically that often a psychotherapist has to help him to overcome anxiety and depression before he can avail himself of technical help (2).

The first step in the rehabilitation of an invalid is directed at making him accept invalidism and relinquish his secret belief that things will get better. This does not mean he should give up hope for the future, but it means that he must act realistically on the merits of the situation at the moment. If the psychotherapist treats the deaf patient as a deaf person, it will help the patient to accept his deafness. There is no more tragic sight than to see a deaf person behave as if he were hearing. Because he understands only a few words out of every sentence, he cannot give adequate replies; and as time goes on he is progressively excluded from human intercourse.

Once the patient has accepted the status quo, the time has come to review the social consequences of his invalidism. For a polio victim, it may mean that somebody has to drive him to and from work; or it may involve a different plan for living—perhaps the wife has to go to work or the whole family has to move in with the in-laws. Once the patient has faced his social reality (14, 15), he has to be familiarized with the government agencies, hospitals, and private organizations that specialize in the technicalities of mastering his specific disability (9). Referral to the proper agency will help the patient to get started. Blind people will have to learn Braille, be trained in special occupations, or be taught to use a guide dog. Deaf people will have to learn lip-reading; amputees will have to be familiarized with the use of prostheses (21).

In a third phase, the patient has to readjust to new ways of communication. If a person's pride was lodged in bodily coordination, sportsmanship, and physical mobility, and he is incapacitated by a physical disease, not only his motility but his whole pride, the way he related to others, and his social and recreational life will suffer. The person who sits behind a desk and is a bookworm will suffer less by a paralysis of the legs than a person who was a professional baseball player. In order to acquire a new form of self-respect, the invalid has to learn new ways of expression and perception, to build his pleasure around new pursuits, and to associate with different people.

In phase four, then, therapy is designed to prevent neurotic exploitation of both the patient and his relatives. The patient has to learn not to be a tyrant and not to advance his disability to make others suffer. The family members have to be taught not to take pity on the patient but to treat him realistically for what he is. Allowances have to be made for deficient functions, but self pity must be avoided. This procedure requires interviews with the various family members, employers, and even friends. The therapist must work with each and every one of them to adapt expectations to a realistic level and to prevent the patient from involving the others in his actual or potential neurosis.

People who have a personality disorder and are also afflicted with a handicap present a special problem. They begin, as it were, with a learning difficulty, and when maximal demands are made in terms of adaptation and learning, they cannot mobilize their resources. In this situation, the psychiatrist determines first whether the disability has a special meaning within the framework of neurosis. Thus the therapist has to explore whether earlier experiences shaped the patient's attitude towards his handicap; and if the answer is affirmative, the patient has to work through his earlier conflicts before he can deal with the present situation. There are, of course, many neurotic persons whose handicap did not trigger earlier conflicts, and there are a number of cases in which the disability improved the neurosis.

THE PERSON WITH A CHRONIC DISEASE

Living with a disease · The first step: Acceptance · Second step: Adaptation · Third step: Understanding · Fourth step: Emergency help · Fifth step: Enjoy life as long as you can · Sixth step: Information and education

People suffering from arthritis, diabetes, tuberculosis, bronchial asthma, hypertension, colitis, ulcers, multiple sclerosis, or heart disease are faced with at least a partial disability (27). There is uncertainty as to the outcome: they may get worse or they may improve. It is this uncertainty which is difficult for the patient to tolerate. Among the chronic diseases, some improve with age and some get worse. Some conditions can be held under control if the patient lives carefully—if he does not overexert himself, does not indulge in excesses, takes certain precautions, observes diets, or takes medicines. In other words, when people with chronic diseases learn to nurse their diseases, they may be able to survive. But this is not without danger. To make health one's sole concern is all right during the acute phase of a disease, but during the chronic phase it interferes with human relations, with activity, and with learning. The patient therefore has to find a compromise solution, and here the psychotherapist can be of help. The disease that afflicts the patient is often the result of, or is aggravated by, certain personality features (19). Thus the angry and aggressive person may be accident prone, while the fearful person may have to please and may be unable to assert himself.

The first phase of therapy is geared to the acceptance of the disease and the restrictions, special measures, and medications that it imposes. The patient has to learn to live with his disease (12), and the therapist has to help him to accept the chronic nature of his condition so that he will not assume that the precautions have to be observed only for a matter of days. If a statistic shows that the patient has a thirty per cent five year survival chance, the patient has to be taught to disregard statistical evidence and live as usual.

In the second phase of therapy, the patient is urged to return to his previous occupation if possible or to modify his occupation so that it will become compatible with his disease. The style of living has to be adapted to the patient's health, and some work with relatives, who may have to prepare special diets, move to different climates, or reduce their standard of living, may have to be undertaken. Also, a decision has to be made as to who carries out physical treatment, if any, and whether periodic checks are needed.

In the third phase, the relationship between personality and the disease is tackled. The patient's basic intrapsychic conflicts and his ways of resolving them, the influence of the disease upon human relations, the chances of recurrence or acute exacerbations, and the avoidance of certain situations which are dangerous for him have to be discussed with the patient (13).

The fourth phase, which may be rather protracted, is characterized by minor relapses and by the patient's resentment against his disease. The psychotherapist must be ready to help whenever the patient runs into trouble. In this phase, therapy may be intermittent: active—that is, frequent interviews—when there is trouble; inactive —that is, vacation from therapy—when the patient proceeds according to plan (1).

In phase five, the patient has to decide whether he will cease to treat himself like an invalid and whether he desires to live reasonably as other people do, pursuing his interests, social life, and occupational duties. Since he is not going to live forever, he might as well enjoy life while it lasts. Taking care of emergencies, living reasonably, but forgetting about the disease seems to benefit the patient most.

A certain amount of information can be conveyed to the patient by lectures and group discussion (17). This information bears upon the way the disease can be managed, the dangers that have to be avoided, and the medical goals towards which the patient should strive (18). In almost all periods of history the prevailing opinions about disease have been shaped by healthy outsiders, and isolation of tuberculous, syphilitic, and leprous patients was the result. In modern medicine we do not leave the development of opinion about disease to chance. With the insight gained into the role of psychological and social factors, we make the patient consciously participate in the shaping of the disease image, rather than to leave it to advertisers. We physicians, in turn, try to participate in such a way that patients and the community can benefit maximally. Undoubtedly, open discussion of secret apprehensions, sharing of concerns with others, and acquisition of factual information go a long way to help the patient. Concretely, this is achieved by having diabetics eat at diabetic tables and amputees trained by other amputees; the blind and the deaf convene in their own circles; and even the relatives of the mentally retarded or schizophrenics meet in groups to discuss their problems (5). Last but not least, the patients can join organizations that will protect their interests.

THE PERSON WITH AN INCURABLE DISEASE

Death is inevitable · *The role of the psychiatrist* · *Relatives* · *Reading*

An individual with cancer, leukemia, a neurological disorder such as amyotrophic lateral sclerosis, an inoperable brain tumor, or malignant hypertension presents a special problem (3). The patient is faced with uncertainties of a grim nature (22), and he asks himself when death will occur or how long it can be postponed. While the healthy person is actually faced with the same proposition, he is not reminded of illness and death every hour and every day. Once the patient has weathered the initial shock and has learned of his poor prognosis, he begins to adapt to the inevitable (4). Talks with a wise and perhaps elderly person, a minister or priest, or with people who have suffered a great deal may be very helpful. Once the patient has accepted the idea of an early death and knows that his hour may come at any time, his ability to enjoy life returns (23). Like the soldier who knows that sooner or later he will be killed in battle, he begins to live for the moment and therefore becomes more realistic. He is freed of many irrelevant preoccupations—concern with status, promotion, and loss of property—and in his last years of life he often is capable of making great strides towards maturity and self-realization.

If the patient seeks the counsel of a psychiatrist, he first is helped to bring his affairs in order. This involves making a lot of decisions concerning work, place of residence, disposition of property, and the making of a will. New enterprises which require a lot of commitments in terms of energy and money should be avoided. Once all these practical arrangements have been made, the patient has to live as if he didn't have a disease, not waiting for the inevitable but enjoying himself, being creative if possible, educating his children if he has any, and being a useful member of his family (29). The therapist helps the patient to live like an ordinary person without bemoaning his forthcoming death. Sometimes patients tend to deny their forthcoming death, although on another level of consciousness they know that the inevitable will come, and then the therapist may indicate that he knows of this dual attitude. While all this goes on, the therapist makes an attempt to hold the patient to his usual way of life, proceeding on the assumption that he will live for a long time. He should be encouraged to complete the things he started, integrating his experiences and arriving at a more rounded philosophy of life. If the patient is young, he will compress much of his development into the remaining months or years. If he is old, he usually reviews his life. During this period the dying patient may or may not express some of his anxiety. On such occasions, the psychiatrist may be able to show him that much of his anxiety is not related to death. At this point, anxiety usually is connected with the patient's problems of living, with the many things he left uncompleted, and the things he did that were wrong (11).

The relatives are often a bigger problem than the patient himself. Many of the relatives impatiently wait for the patient to die because they cannot tolerate uncertainty. Others wish him to die because he has become a burden, whereupon they begin to feel guilty. Again other relatives are afraid of being left behind, and they have to be supported and consoled. Anxiety, anger, and guilt of the relatives and all the defenses against these unpleasant sensations often make life for the dying patient intolerable. The psychiatrist can do much to bring honesty into the situation, helping all to face the inevitable, helping them to enjoy life, and realistically planning for the future.

As for the patient himself, reading will be his principal solace (16). Great thinkers and essayists will have more to say on many of the subjects that the patient is struggling with than other mortals who are still concerned with riding the merry-go-round of happy expectations. The patient who is faced with an incurable disease will have to acquire depth rather than power, and communication with those who have left shallowness behind is an exhilarating experience.

References

1. Alexander, F.: *Psychosomatic Medicine—Its Principles and Applications*. 300 p. New York: Norton, 1950.

2. Apton, A. A.: *Your Mind and Appearance*. 212 p. New York: Citadel, 1951.

3. Eissler, K. R.: *The Psychiatrist and the Dying Patient*. 338 p. New York: International Universities Press, 1955.

4. Feifel, H. (Editor): *The Meaning of Death*. 351 p. New York: McGraw-Hill, 1959.

5. Garrett, J. F. (Editor): *Psychological Aspects of Physical Disability*. 195 p. Washington: Department of Health, Education, and Welfare; Office of Vocational Rehabilitation; Rehabilitation Service Series #210; 1953.

6. Goldstein, K.: *Aftereffects of Brain Injuries in War*. 244 p. New York: Grune & Stratton, 1942.

7. Hebb, D. O.: *The Organization of Behavior*. 335 p. New York: Wiley, 1949.

8. Hutt, M. L. and Gibby, R. G.: *The Mentally Retarded Child*. 334 p. Boston: Allyn and Bacon, 1958.

9. Kessler, H. H. and others: *The Principles and Practices of Rehabilitation*. 448 p. Philadelphia: Lea & Felbiger, 1950.

10. Kugelmass, I. N.: *The Management of Mental Deficiency in Children*. 312 p. New York: Grune & Stratton, 1954.

11. LeShan, L. L. and Gassmann, M. L.: Some observations on psychotherapy with patients suffering from neoplastic disease. Amer. J. Psychother, 12, 723–734, 1958.

12. Levine, M.: *Psychotherapy in Medical Practice*. 320 p. New York: Macmillan, 1948.

13. Margolin, S. G.: Psychotherapeutic principles in psychosomatic practice. Pp. 134–153 in *Recent Developments in Psychosomatic Medicine* (Edited by E. D. Wittkower and R. A. Cleghorn). Philadelphia and Montreal: Lippincott, 1954.

14. Michal-Smith, H. (Editor): *Pediatric Problems in Clinical Practice*. 310 p. New York: Grune & Stratton, 1954.

15. Michal-Smith, H. (Editor): *Management of the Handicapped Child*. 276 p. New York: Grune & Stratton, 1957.

16. Moore, T. V.: Bibliotherapy in psychiatric practice. Pp. 132–153 in *Current Therapies of Personality Disorders* (Edited by B. Glueck). New York: Grune & Stratton, 1946.

17. Pratt, J. H.: The group method in the treatment of psychosomatic

disorders. Pp. 85–93 in *Group Psychotherapy: A Symposium*. New York: Beacon House, 1945.

18. Rennie, T. A. C., Burling, T., and Woodward, L. E.: *Vocational Rehabilitation of Psychiatric Patients*. 133 p. New York: Commonwealth Fund, 1950.

19. Ruesch, J., Harris, R. E., Loeb, M. B., Christiansen, C., Dewees, S., Heller, S. H., and Jacobson, A.: *Chronic Disease and Psychological Invalidism*. 191 p. New York: Amer. Soc. Res. Psychosom. Probl., 1946. 2nd printing, Berkeley and Los Angeles: University of California Press, 1951.

20. Rusk, H. A. and Taylor, E. J.: A program for the paralyzed: rehabilitation of neurological patients. Pp. 148–171 in *New Hope for the Handicapped*. New York: Harper, 1949.

21. Rusk, H. A. and Taylor, E. J.: *Living with a Disability*. 207 p. Garden City: Blakiston, 1953.

22. Schwartz, E. K. and Wolf, A.: The quest for certainty. AMA Arch. Neurol. Psychiat., 81, 68–94, 1959.

23. Sheps, J.: Management of fear of death in chronic disease. J. Amer. Geriat. Soc., 5, 793–797, 1957.

24. Stacey, C. L. and DeMartino, M. F. (Editors): *Counseling and Psychotherapy with the Mentally Retarded*. 478 p. Glencoe: Free Press, 1957.

25. *Symposium on Chemical Concepts of Psychosis, Zurich, 1957*. (Edited by M. Rinkel). 485 p. New York: McDowell, Obolensky, 1958.

26. Tredgold, R. F. and Soddy, K.: *A Textbook of Mental Deficiency* (9th ed.). 480 p. Baltimore: Williams & Wilkins, 1956.

27. Weiss, E. and English, O. S.: *Psychosomatic Medicine; A Clinical Study of Psychophysiologic Reactions*. (3rd ed.) 557 p. Philadelphia: Saunders, 1957.

28. Wepman, J. M.: *Recovery from Aphasia*. 276 p. New York: Ronald Press, 1951.

29. Worcester, A.: *The Care of the Aged, the Dying, and the Dead* (2nd ed.) 77 p. Springfield: Thomas, 1940.

Chapter Twenty

Emergencies

RESTITUTION IN ACUTE DISTURBANCES

Quantitative deviations · Individual crises · Group crises · Adaptation of the organism to quantitative deviations · Regulating input and output · Regressive disorganization of communication · Protective and preventive interference

A SIGNAL becomes a sign when it impinges upon earlier impressions. But the quality of a signal—let us say the sound of a voice—is only recognizable and comparable to earlier experiences when it has the same quantitative proportions. Meaning, therefore, is intimately tied to quantitative considerations. The further we move from the optimum in perception, evaluation, and transmission, the more disturbing the performance becomes; either overload or underload in perception, evaluation, or transmission can produce a breakdown of the whole system of communication. When signal input and output exceed the capacity of the system—that is, fall below the threshold or above the tolerance limits—then we deal with a quantitatively defined deviation of communication. Such a definition includes not only the magnitude of input or output but also time characteristics. Complete absence of stimulation, as in sensory deprivation, has an effect that is about as disturbing as excessive stimulation (12). What happens inside the organism is difficult to envisage; tentatively we might say that in maximal stimulation a large number of neurons are fired which with normal stimulation are not excited (6). This overstimulation produces a jamming of the networks; the previously established order, in terms of the number of neurons fired and in terms of the sequence of firing, falls by the wayside. We must also assume that there exists in the central nervous system something analogous to fuses. When the excitation exceeds the tolerance limits or falls below the threshold, habitually functioning circuits cease to function and new circuits come into being. What the human being responds to, therefore, is the deviation from the usual input-output ratio.

The straw that broke the camel's back can be identified in most crises. All the physician has to do is to examine both the patient and his surroundings and to decide how the previously established balance was upset. In lay language, the term "pressure" is usually used to refer to those processes which are believed to have contributed towards the breakdown. These so-called pressures can be observed in both individuals and groups.

Individual crises usually develop around some quantitative alterations which affect the individual's relation to his surroundings.

Input crises occur:
–With overstimulation consisting of rapid bombardment without pause or with intense stimulation which exceeds the tolerance limits of the individual—e.g., torture, combat fatigue (7).
–With understimulation consisting of voluntary or forced sensory deprivation, as in prisoners kept in solitary confinement (28).
–With stimuli that are inappropriate for the moment—e.g., offering of food to a person who is nauseated (20).

Anticipation and recollection crises occur:
–When statements are shown to be at variance with the actual events (20)—e.g., faulty reconstruction from memory.
–When ideals or hopes collapse, anticipation of future states is no longer possible, and the individual is depressed and loses the will to live (14).
–When repressed memories emerge, flood the awareness, and change the outlook of the individual (5)—e.g., sudden insight.

Decision-making crises (20) occur:
–If the decisions do not solve the problem.

–If the situation changes so rapidly that decisions come too late.

–If the decision-making process is difficult because of some personality problem—for example,

> If a cautious person has to make decisions on the basis of incomplete information
>
> If an impulsive person is required to wait for complete information before reaching a decision
>
> If a rigid person has to change his decisions
>
> If a flexible person has to stick by his decisions

Output crises occur:

–With overactivity in terms of insufficient rest, as in physical exhaustion (17) or sleep deprivation (1).

–With underactivity, lack of exercise, and absence of meaningful tasks, leading to boredom and breakdown of morale (25)—e.g., inactive military units.

–With inappropriate activity in which a chosen implementation does not achieve the desired purpose—e.g., the person who tries to put out a brush fire with a bucket (20).

Group crises develop when either communication within the group or communication with other groups is disturbed.

–With *changes in the composition of the group*—when persons are added to or removed from the group through birth, marriage, divorce, separation, reassignment, or death (22, 23).

–With *changes in the mutual relationship*—when prestige, role, or age brings about changes that force a mutual readaptation.

–With *reorganization* of military units, civilian government agencies, private corporations, or teaching institutions which suddenly forces people together or separates them; when new rules are introduced, new positions are created, and old positions are removed (35).

–With *changes in the symbolic and value systems*—voluntarily through migration, occupational change, or change of religion; forced, through economic reverses or conquest (19, 21).

–With *interruption of the flow of messages* (20): when telephone messages do not reach their destination or letters are lost; when a station cannot be contacted—e.g., trying to reach police, fire department, or doctor.

–In *contact with disturbed people,* when anxious and panicky people transmit their apprehensions to others (24) or when people threaten life, welfare, or property as in riots, revolutions, and wars (13).

–With *catastrophic situations* or changes in the physical surroundings such as hurricanes, earthquakes, floods, fires, explosions (31), drought or damage to crops, or contamination of food and water supply (2).

The organism is usually able to correct some of the naturally occurring quantitative deviations. In depression, the thoughts of an individual become restricted to a few sometimes unessential ideas; this impoverishment in the range of thought reduces the number of choices, obviates decisions, and distracts the individual from remembering painful experiences. Fear leads to a flight reaction which separates the individual from the assumed or real dangers. In acute anxiety, the internal disorganization leads the individual to seek others who in turn become infected with this anxiety, but eventually it wears itself out. In most of the acute disturbances, the progressive physical exhaustion has its beneficial effects, provided the patient survives. Sleep induced by exhaustion restores the physical health and increases the repressive forces of the individual. Most parents know these laws of nature and when their children get over-excited they send them to bed.

The task of therapeutic communication in acute disorders is one of regulating the intensity and timing of the flow of messages. It can be summarized as follows:

–In acute anxiety and panic, the knowledge that other persons are not disorganized, are not infected by the presence of the anxious or panicky, and are capable of making sensible decisions reduces, through negative feedback, the anxiety of the anxious patient. Communication, and sharing of information pertaining to the source of the anxiety, help to reorganize disturbed behavior. In such situations, the healthy person acts as the brain for the other person, or the group, until such time as the sick can again make their own decisions. Temporarily a symbiotic relationship is established which resembles the early mother-child relationship and which, in all probability, enables the individual to repress disconcerting thoughts.

—In acute fear which originates in the patient himself, the therapist's acceptance of the fear reduces the flight tendencies of the patient who, if he can communicate his fear and finds an understanding ally, gains a feeling of protection. Though cognitively the fear remains, the acute alarm subsides and projection of causes is avoided.

—In acute excitement, the lack of enthusiasm on the part of others acts, through negative feedback, to quiet the patient down.

—In acute depression, the removal of decisions and possible choices from the patient acts beneficially. The patient follows willingly the decisions made by others; or, if he opposes them, the idea of opposition has an integrating effect upon him. Moderate opposition is provoked by the slightly aggressive therapist who enables the patient to turn anger away from self and against an outside object.

—Comparison of actual observations with anticipations can create disruption. The infantile symbiotic person, for example, dreams of unity with another person but develops anxiety when facing the fact that such unity cannot be established. Conversely, the schizophrenic expects to be different from others, and the observation that he is not disturbs him. Therefore, those processes which within the individual reduce the gap between anticipation and observation become therapeutic. Reassurance of the dependent person and non-reassurance of the schizophrenic are of the essence.

Disruption of the communication system occurs in several steps. The individual tends to withdraw—first from societal, then from group, and eventually from interpersonal networks. Disease and trauma finally disrupt the organism and the network within until death has occurred. This hierarchical regression order can be utilized therapeutically. Schizophrenics who in their minds are concerned with impersonal and suprapersonal matters temporarily improve in the face of a physical disease when they are forced to concern themselves with practical issues. Pain, disability, and other discomforts force them to accept help from others and improve the relationship to other people. Most quantitative deviations are managed today by means of drugs, removal from the noxious environment, and group activities. The tranquilizers and energizers (4, 30) have given the physician a tool to control the quantitative deviations until such time as the patient can be approached by ordinary communicative means. Any of the modern drugs may be used to stabilize the patient, to keep him out of the hospital, and to make him accessible for psychotherapy. Removal of the patient from his ordinary environment may become necessary when he cannot take care of himself, when he is dangerous to others or to himself, or when nursing becomes a technical problem which cannot be carried out at home. In these instances, removal of the patient to a psychiatric hospital is indicated.

Although not all quantitative deviations in behavior constitute an emergency, they do so if they are associated with exhaustion, sleep deprivation, disturbances in nutrition, exposure to cold or heat, or injury to self or others. Quantitative deviations in behavior usually require protective and preventive interference on the part of the therapist in order to safeguard both the patient and the people surrounding him (16). If somebody shows unusually aggressive behavior, perhaps with threats to life and limb of others, the physician and sometimes the police have to act. If a patient refuses to eat, goes on a hunger strike, becomes anorexic, or exhausts himself through constant pacing of the floor, the doctor has to feed or isolate or sedate the patient. Many times the psychiatrist is called upon to deal with an emergency that is situationally determined. Migration, retirement, death of a relative, sudden financial reverses (32), or overwork may be cited as examples. Although past experiences of the patient may sensitize him to certain situational stimuli, the trigger factor is always found in the present situation. The expectations of the individual, the support given by the group, and his physical state determine the resistance to stress. A conflict that is impossible to manage in a state of exhaustion and without the moral support of others can often be easily resolved after sleep, food, and strengthening of the group bonds have restored the individual to his habitual level of functioning.

Protective and preventive interference is therefore indicated whenever a quantitative deviation of behavior is encountered. This may be due to actual situational stress or to presumed dangers arising from within (29). Just as the flight surgeon keeps an eye on pilots subjected to stress, the physician has to keep an eye on these patients who may be wearing themselves out in the fight with daily routine or with unusual circumstances. Psychotherapy in these instances is often directed at making the individual aware of the stress to which he exposes himself. And if the patient persists in his activities, the psychiatrist has to take things in hand. He may do so by interfering in three different places: with the stimuli that bombard the individual from the outside; with the organism that has to resist this bombardment; and with the group ties that bind the individual to his peers.

THE NEW PATIENT AS AN EMERGENCY

Panic and shock in disaster   ·   Anxiety attack of the neurotic patient   · Tranquilizers · 24-hour supervision · The assaultive patient · The agitated patient · The diagnostic value of disturbed consciousness · Examination of semiconscious patients   ·   Management of confused patients   · Detection of suicidal intent · Suicide precautions

A distinction should be made between patients who initially present an acute condition and those who require emergency measures in the course of psychotherapeutic treatment. If the patient is under treatment when the emergency occurs, the doctor usually has some information about the circumstances that surround the incident; but with a new patient, the doctor usually has to make a number of assumptions since the sick individual is rarely capable of reporting in a coherent manner. The doctor's first task here is to safeguard the patient and the people around him.

THE MANAGEMENT OF ANXIOUS OR EXCITED PATIENTS

Acute anxiety attacks may develop when external stimulation exceeds the tolerance limits of the individual. Thus when physical or psychological danger threatens the individual and when fatigue and exhaustion lower his tolerance limits, behavior may become disorganized. Such behavior has been observed in people exposed to natural catastrophes such as earthquakes, floods, fires, railway accidents, bombings, and plane crashes. Panic spreads easily and may produce regressive behavior in whole groups of people. Under stress, the clinical picture of anxiety and fear predominates. Alarmed at approaching dangers, people are tense and silent; they sweat, feel weak in their knees, and tight around the collar; they may have the typical butterfly sensation in their stomachs, may have urinary frequency and diarrhea, or may sigh and hyperventilate. Once the danger is imminent or present, a person may look pale, feel unable to talk, tremble, or perhaps repeat the same words over and over again. While fear is communicated to others through facial expression, the rest of the body may appear corpse-like. Paralysis can quickly change into excitation and violence. The urge to do something then grips the individual. He may begin to run or wander about aimlessly; he may use emergency devices such as calling the police or the fire department; he may crowd into a lifeboat on a ship or push towards an exit in a theatre; he may attack others; or, if he has a gun, he may start shooting. Then again he may beat his fists against a wall, shout, or show signs of a temper tantrum.

The management of a situation in which panic develops is dependent upon the emergence of a leader (33). The doctor is rarely if ever called upon to cope with the situation, but he is expected to deal with the casualties. The first step consists of separating the patient from other panicky people. A protective, supportive, consoling attitude on the part of the doctor, who should have his own anxiety well under control, here is absolutely essential. Inquiry and questions should be avoided, but offerings of hot coffee, tea, soup, cigarettes, or food are in place. The treatment of such emergencies has perhaps been best formulated by the military (8), who have concluded that food, drink, bath, sleep, company, and catharsis are remedies that, in less than a week, are usually capable of returning young people to duty. These oral gratifications are more efficient than narcotics, barbiturates, or alcohol. They can be supplemented by moderate skin stimulation. Patients with fear or anxiety suffer from peripheral vasoconstriction as evidenced by their moist and cold skin. Mountain guides slap the faces of people who panic, or rub their skin with snow; blankets, a warm footbath, or sponge bath, or a sniff of ammonia salts may contribute towards the well-being of the patient. In brief, the treatment does not differ markedly from the management of a patient in shock.

After the shock phase has been successfully handled—and this includes the calming down of excited patients—catharsis may be tried. The panicky person is helped to elaborate upon the fright just experienced. Fear has a kind of incubation period, and its full impact may be felt only after all danger is over. In acute anxiety states, the patient will readily talk without the help of sodium amytal. He is made to lie down in a semi-dark room. After the talk, it is suggested that sleep will restore the patient to health, and here a hypnotic, a tranquilizer, or a placebo may be in place.

The management of acute anxiety attacks in daily life is similar to that of catastrophic reactions except that in the case of mental disease more individual care can be given to the patient. Almost all patients get better when they receive friendly, non-coercive attention; often it is sufficient to have another person sit in the room, or to take the arm of the patient and walk up and down the hall, to sit with the patient when he eats, to help him dress and undress, or to assist him when he goes to bed or gets up. If the patient is allowed to lean upon others and the doctor acts in a parental capacity, the patient will improve, even without awareness of the specific conflicts that generated the anxiety (15).

In some instances, a stimulus may not have a mass effect but may selectively impinge upon earlier memories. This phenomenon is not only present in psychoneuroses but may operate in almost any major psychiatric disturbance. Thus, out of the blue, the patient may complain about manifestations of respiratory alkalosis due to rapid, shallow breathing and increased respiratory volume. Dizziness, faintness, and sensations of pins and needles in the extremities will quickly disappear if the patient is instructed to hold his breath when these sensations appear (11). Since acute anxiety can hide almost any disease, a physical examination and diagnostic studies are indispensable. When physical causes have been excluded, the anxiety state can be treated as a psychiatric condition.

At the present time, the best treatment of acute anxiety is medication with tranquilizers. These fall into four groups: the phenothiazine derivatives, the rauwolfia alkaloids, the diphenylmethane derivatives, and the propanediol dicarbamates. Best known among the drugs of the first group are Thorazine, Stelazine, and Pacatal; of the second group, Serpasil; of the third, Frenquel; and of the fourth, Miltown and Equanil (3). As soon as medication, sleep, food, and fluids have restored the patient to a more nearly normal condition— requiring a period of from two to five days—psychological exploration of the causes of the anxiety gradually will replace medication.

ACUTE CATATONIC SYNDROMES

The common clinical picture of catatonic schizophrenia is characterized by catalepsy, stupor, hyperkinesis, stereotyped movements or posture, mannerisms, negativism, or automatisms of various kinds. At the onset of a schizophrenic episode and intermittently during the chronic phase, symptoms of acute catatonic excitement may develop. These are characterized by increasing emotional tension with outbursts of rage, assaultiveness, destruction of objects, self-inflicted injuries, smearing of urine or feces, and increased hallucinatory experiences. The patient may sing, scream, somersault, laugh, cry, spit, or engage in other violent activities. Catatonic excitement thus is characterized either by unorganized random motor activity and incoherence of speech and thought or by impulsive, aggressive acts. The management of these conditions consists of:

–Immediate hospitalization and isolation of the patient in a seclusion room, or 24-hour watch by experienced attendant in the home of the patient.

–Regulation of fluid and food intake, inasmuch as such patients tend to become dehydrated and neglect to eat and drink.

–Medication with tranquilizers to control psychomotor agitation.

–As soon as the patient has quieted down, he should be allowed to mingle with others; psychotherapy and emotional support are at this time of crucial importance.

MANIC STATES AND AGITATED DEPRESSIONS

In the hypomanic state, the patient is outgoing, affable, boisterous, and unconventional; he spends his money, is full of schemes, and tends to exaggerate. He blurts out what he wishes to say and often becomes argumentative. Being unaware of the cyclic nature of manic depressive psychosis, most lay people consider hypomanic moods and activities as normal variations of human temperament. But once the patient becomes manic, the abnormality of the situation is usually recognized. The patient's tempo is fast, his mood is exalted, he has ideas of grandeur and delusions of wealth and power. He is loquacious and overactive, sleeps little, often loses all modesty, and cannot focus his attention on the same activity for any length of time.

A truly manic patient has to be hospitalized early. In his management, the following points are to be kept in mind: avoidance of dehydration; treatment of minor infections of the skin which the patient acquires when he hurts himself; restraining the patient from bothering others; keeping all stimulation such as TV, radio, or visitors away in order to avoid further excitement. Some patients have to be kept in isolation, and many lose weight because of their overactivity. Intercurrent diseases, infections, nutritional deficiencies, or degenerative conditions tend to be overlooked because the patient does not seem to complain of any symptoms. Tranquilizers represent the treatment of choice.

When the manic condition subsides, the patient may recover a balanced state of mind or he may become depressive. Among the various forms of depression, the agitated depression represents a particular problem inasmuch as the patient exhibits incessant motor activity instead of reduction of activity. He paces the floor, rubs his hands, does not sleep, is on his feet for hours at a time without sitting down. The agitation is associated with apprehension, anxiety, and fear. Frequently he expresses the idea that he, together with his beloved ones, is going to suffer severely. Agitated depressions are treated like other depressions, the patient usually reacting favorably to electroshock therapy (10). However, care has to be taken to supply food and fluids, to avoid dehydration, and to forestall loss of weight due to the overactivity.

CONFUSED PATIENTS

There exists a sliding scale of disturbances of consciousness which vary from simple intellectual impairment to coma:

–Simple intellectual impairment consists of disturbances of memory and sometimes poor judgment, while orientation is undisturbed and hallucinations or illusions are absent. Intellectual impairment occurs predominantly in the age groups above fifty. It is a sign of a brain disorder.

–Intellectual and personality changes combined indicate a more severe condition. In addition to the abnormalities mentioned above, recent difficulties in interpersonal relationships or changes of attitude, ideas of reference, delusions, or mood swings may be observed.

–Confusion refers to a condition in which there is disturbed orientation as well as intellectual impairment. The condition usually requires hospitalization and is indicative of central nervous system disease.

–Delirium is a state of confusion complicated by marked restlessness and hallucinations. The majority of deliria last only for a few days or weeks and require immediate hospitalization, possibly in a psychiatric hospital.

–Drowsiness is a state of impaired responsiveness which affects mostly young people and children.

–Fluctuating levels of consciousness can be observed when a patient varies at short intervals between alertness and drowsiness.

–Stupor encompasses all conditions with apathy and lack of interest in the surroundings. It is an intermediate state between drowsiness and semicoma and is clinically characterized by the patient's ability to keep the body position although verbal responses may be inadequate.

–Semicoma and coma are states of irresponsiveness in which the sensory processes are seriously disturbed and the condition is associated with changes in respiration, pulse, and blood pressure.

The examination begins with the question of whether or not the patient is capable of cooperating. If he is, the doctor ascertains whether impairment of the higher intellectual functions exists (34). If the picture is accompanied by disorientation, the doctor is faced with a confusional state. In conditions labeled "drowsiness," "somnolence," and "stupor," the higher reflexes are usually affected, and in semicoma and coma the elementary reflexes are disturbed or extinguished (18).

From the examination, some diagnostic conclusions can be made. In catatonic stupor, the higher and elementary reflexes are not disturbed; the person perceives everything but does not respond voluntarily. Stuporous, comatose, delirious, or confused patients with disturbances of higher reflexes can be presumed to suffer from a brain disorder. This may be temporary and reversible or progressive and irreversible. To be considered are:

–Brain disease: senile dementia, Pick's disease, Alzheimer's disease, epilepsy.
–Cerebral vascular accident: embolism, thrombosis, rupture of an aneurysm.
–Brain injury: concussion, contusion, subarachnoid and subdural hematoma, gunshot wound, and fracture of the skull.
–Space-consuming lesions: brain tumors.
–Infectious conditions: encephalitis, meningitis, brain abscess.
–Toxic influences upon the brain: carbon monoxide and other gasses; lead, barbiturate, and morphine poisoning; alcohol intoxication.

–Metabolic influences upon the brain: diabetes, uremia, pellagra.

In addition to etiological considerations, the physician usually ventures a guess as to the extent of the damage. A localized cerebral lesion that causes aphasia or agnosia may mimic confusion because the patient has lost the ability to perceive or to express himself. Initially most cerebral vascular accidents are accompanied by disturbances of consciousness and aphasia.

The specific orders for the care of patients suffering from disturbances of consciousness are:

–Physical protection from injury through falling out of bed; from strangulation with bedsheets; from aspiration of food, fluids, and mucous.

–Constant surveillance of patient: check pulse, respiration, blood pressure, pupils, body temperature, corneal and tendon reflexes; lucid moments to be used to ascertain history which might lead to diagnosis.

–Catheterization of patient and exact measurement of fluid intake and output.

–No drugs before positive diagnosis has been made.

–Aspiration of mucous from airways.

–Oral or nasal oxygen, by catheter if necessary.

Isolation is the best remedy for restlessness and agitation. However, this has to be done in a room where the patient cannot hurt himself and where the temperature is controlled. Restraint of the patient has to be avoided inasmuch as he usually becomes more combative, and it is preferable, if adequate nursing care is not available, to lock him in an escape-proof room. This room should be well-lighted, and extraneous noises, odors, and unknown people should be kept out since confused and delirious persons tend to misinterpret stimuli. If in a general hospital such a room is not available, it is advisable to transfer the patient to a psychiatric institution rather than to subject him to drug treatment which may interfere with the already disturbed cerebral functioning.

THE MANAGEMENT OF DEPRESSED PATIENTS

The picture of depression is too well known to be described here, but any patient who feels he can't go on, that he "ought to end it all," that there is no future, or who has "the blues" is in a more acute depression than the person who feels lifeless and empty and who has ceased to care for the things he used to be concerned with. Such a patient may well lighten up when in company and not give the picture of a depressed person; but anxiety at night and hate for self are signs which have to be taken seriously. The diagnosis of a depression can only be established by knowing more about the course of the disease. Repeated self-destructive acts, self-deprecia-tion, self-blame, feelings of being unworthy, and lack of self-respect have to be interpreted as warning signals. Also, the physician will note a relative absence of initiative on the part of the patient and an absence of emotional contact with the therapist. The patient's report of improvement following a depression has to be taken as a warning signal, as patients tend to commit suicide when they come out of a depression. Every depressed patient represents a potential suicide risk (27).

Four principal categories of suicidal thoughts and behavior may be differentiated:

–Suicidal thoughts or ideas of a transient and ephemeral char-acter.
–Regular suicidal ruminations in obsessional states.
–Suicidal gestures and suicide attempts as symbolic and manipula-tive devices.
–Near successful suicide attempts of the person who, realistically speaking, has nothing to look forward to.

Immature, infantile persons—particularly women—are apt to be melodramatic, histrionic, and unsuccessful in their suicidal attempts (26). A striking feature of such cases is the dominant motivation to take revenge, to gain attention, to force sympathy, and to retain affection. The attempt is impulsive and may follow a lovers' quarrel or a domestic row. The act itself, the turmoil which follows, the anxiety aroused in everyone, and the attention gained serve to relieve the emotional tension of the patient at least temporarily. Prolonged hospitalization is generally not indicated inasmuch as this only tends to increase the already excessive dependency needs of the patient. Occasionally a schizophrenic patient may indulge in a sudden impulsive suicidal attempt, especially when subjected to threatening hallucinatory experiences or the realization of passivity and impotence vis-à-vis external control. An acutely intoxicated patient whose inhibitions have been reduced and who is somewhat depressive may attempt suicide; and delirious patients may react to frightening hallucinatory experiences by throwing themselves from a window or a balcony in order to escape. When fear overwhelms good judgment and self-control, patients may attempt suicide, especially when in a so-called homosexual panic. Patients with brain disease, as in general paresis, senility, and cerebral arteriosclerosis, may develop serious depressive states with suicidal intent. All of these patients, as well as the neurotic, involutional, and manic-depressive depressions, can at times become suicidal risks (9).

If the physician has established that the patient is a suicidal risk, the following safety precautions have to be taken. If the patient is carried as an ambulatory patient, adequate provisions have to be made so that he is not left alone at any time during the day or night. Many suicides have been committed when it was quiet in the house or when a relative went away for a week-end. The patient should be seen repeatedly by the therapist—often as much as twice a day, even if it is for a few minutes only. It is important to inform the relatives that they probably cannot prevent the patient from jumping out of a window or stepping in front of a car if he has so decided. But others have the indirect power to prevent suicide; as long as somebody is around and has time to spend with the patient, he usually does not make the final decision to commit suicide. If the patient lives alone, there is frequently no other alternative but hospitalization. But hospitalization for depression is usually protracted and therefore expensive. In order to enable the patient to rest at night, hypnotics and sedatives are prescribed; however, drugs should be dispensed in small quantities only, and the relatives must be warned that hoarding may occur. If the patient is hospitalized, shock therapy may be indicated; and if the patient is restless, some of the modern tranquilizing drugs have been used with success. The effect of energizers (4) has not been conclusively evaluated, but initial experiences have not been spectacular.

EMERGENCIES WITH PATIENTS IN TREATMENT

Traumatic events · *Breakdown of defenses* · *Self-destructive ideas* · *Intercurrent disease* · *Personal problems of the therapist*

At any one time, it is possible that patients in treatment may experience sudden and unplanned emotional traumata. The person that they hate most may suddenly die; the income may suddenly be interrupted; the person they are most attached to may get sick. Such extracurricular accidents may complicate therapy to the point of provoking an acute psychosis, and under these circumstances the patient has to be treated as if he were acutely sick. The therapist then has to stand by, to support the patient, to offer advice, to go out of his way to help the patient overcome the emergency. If the patient feels that he really has somebody he can rely upon, his relationship to the therapist will improve to such an extent that later therapy will progress more rapidly. It goes without saying that the underpinnings of a person's psychological structure cannot be tackled at times when the external reality requires his undivided attention. Once the situation is stabilized, the events which precipitated the emergency can be discussed in all their ramifications.

In addition to external interferences, there may develop emergencies which are the result of the patient's internal conflicts. Whenever the defenses that control anger, fear, shame, guilt, and depression break down, an emergency may arise. The patient's ordinary behavior patterns usually are insufficient to manage the situation. In the first place, he consulted a psychiatrist because his defenses did not work; and in the second place, the rearrangement of behavior patterns that occurs in therapy may leave the patient temporarily unprotected. When the patient feels vulnerable and misunderstood, he may begin to act out. Instead of discussing what bothers him, the patient engages directly in action—often with destructive results. One of the common forms of acting out is to stay away from therapy. At such times, the therapist has to use all his personal resources; he has to call the patient; he has to go after him; he has to contact relatives if necessary. The patient usually responds when the therapist decides to react and to meet action with action.

At any one point during therapy the patient may say that he has lost pleasure in living. Statements of planned suicide have to be handled within the therapeutic situation as symptoms of a disturbed interpersonal relationship. Suicide may be used as blackmail, to force signs of friendliness on the part of the therapist, or to evoke guilt feelings in others. The assumption that the announced suicidal intent is a message to the therapist does not reflect upon the etiology of a depression. Obviously the lowered self-respect and the unexpressed anger of the patient may have little if anything to do with the therapist. But if the therapist openly verbalizes this state of affairs he is likely to accentuate the depression. Treating the whole episode as if it could be improved by focusing upon the relationship to the therapist reintegrates the patient into the community of living people. The therapist must be strict and at the same time supportive—a task which is difficult to accomplish. He has to appeal to that part of the patient's personality which the patient himself disapproves of. If the secret is shared, the sense of unworthiness tends to disappear. If the depression is the result of actual insight into a hopeless situation—for example, the presence of an incurable disease—the absence of repressive tendencies in the patient cannot be modified by discussion of the problem. By simply supporting the patient and by gratifying his wishes as much as possible, the therapist may give him a new lease on life.

Curable physical disease of either the patient or the therapist also may interrupt therapy. If the therapist is incapacitated by illness for a prolonged period of time, he should give the patient the choice of going to somebody else or of awaiting his return. If disease incapacitates the patient, the doctor may see him in the hospital or at home. If the disease is an acute one, therapy becomes supportive.

If the patient changes his residence because he has been transferred, the therapist should recommend a therapist at the new place of domicile. If the patient's economic situation changes so that he can no longer afford therapy, special arrangements have to be entered into. The doctor may see the patient over his difficulties and consider this a loan to be repaid at a later date.

Occasionally the psychiatrist's personal problems will interfere with the progress of therapy. A member of his family may be sick or may die; he may experience a serious disagreement with his wife; or an expected honor or promotion in his professional career may not have materialized. Any of these or other circumstances may make him angry, anxious, sad, guilty, or preoccupied. In such circumstances, he does well to openly admit his preoccupation to the patient; or he may cancel the interview without giving the reason. He may simply state, "I am unable to keep my appointment and I shall expect to see you on such and such a date." Or if he has to see the patient because the patient is very sick, he should remain rather passive and not participate much. Under no circumstances should he interpret the patient's behavior, lest his own emotions obscure his vision.

References

1. Bliss, E. L., Clark, L. D., and West, C. D.: Studies of sleep deprivation. Arch. Neurol. Psychiat., 81, 348–359, 1959.
2. Bowers, W. F. and Hughes, C. W.: *Surgical Philosophy in Mass Casualty Management.* 204 p. Springfield: Thomas, 1960.
3. Cattell, J. P. and Malitz, S.: Revised survey of selected pharmacological agents. Amer. J. Psychiat., 117, 449–453, 1960.
4. Featherstone, R. M. and Simon, A. (Editors): *A Pharmacologic Approach to the Study of the Mind.* 384 p. Springfield: Thomas, 1959.
5. Freud, S.: *New Introductory Lectures on Psycho-Analysis.* 257 p. New York: Norton, 1933.
6. Gerard, R. W.: Some of the problems concerning digital motions in the central nervous system. Pp. 11–57 in *Cybernetics,* Trans. 7th Conference. New York: Josiah Macy, Jr. Foundation, 1951.
7. Glass, A. J.: The problem of stress in the combat zone. Pp. 90–102 in

Symposium on Stress (16–18 March, 1953). Washington: Army Medical Service Graduate School, 1953.

8. Glass, A. J.: Psychiatry in the Korean campaign: a historical review. U.S. Armed Forces med. J., 4, 1387–1401 and 1563–1583, 1953.

9. Henry, A. F. and Short, J. F., Jr.: *Suicide and Homicide*. 214 p. Glencoe: Free Press, 1954.

10. Kalinowsky, L. B. and Hoch, P. H.: *Somatic Treatments in Psychiatry*. 413 p. New York: Grune & Stratton, 1961.

11. Kerr, W. J., Dalton, J. W., and Gliebe, P. A.: Some physical phenomena associated with the anxiety states and their relation to hyperventilation. Ann. int. Med., 11, 961–992, 1937.

12. Lilly, J. C.: Mental effects of reduction of ordinary levels of physical stimuli on intact, healthy persons. Pp. 1–9 in *Research Techniques in Schizophrenia*. Psychiatric Research Reports #5. Washington: American Psychiatric Association, 1956.

13. Meerloo, J. A. M.: Mental contagion. Amer. J. Psychother., 13, 66–82, 1959.

14. Menninger, K.: Hope. Amer. J. Psychiat., 116, 481–491, 1959.

15. Querido, A.: Early diagnosis and treatment services. Pp. 158–169 in *The Elements of a Community Mental Health Program*. New York: Milbank Memorial Fund, 1956.

16. Redl, F. and Wineman, D.: *The Aggressive Child*. 575 p. Glencoe: Free Press, 1957.

17. Ross, W. D.: *Practical Psychiatry for Industrial Physicians*. 401 p. Springfield: Thomas, 1956.

18. Ruesch, J.: The diagnostic value of disturbances of consciousness. Dis. nerv. Syst., 5, 69–83, 1944.

19. Ruesch, J.: Social factors in therapy. Pp. 59–93 in *Psychiatric Treatment* (ARNMD #31). Baltimore: Williams & Wilkins, 1953.

20. Ruesch, J.: *Disturbed Communication*. 337 p. New York: Norton, 1957.

21. Ruesch, J.: Values and the process of communication. Pp. 27–40 in *Symposium on Preventive and Social Psychiatry*. Washington: Walter Reed Army Institute of Research, 1958.

22. Ruesch, J., Harris, R. E., Christiansen, C., Loeb, M. B., Dewees, S., and Jacobson, A.: *Duodenal Ulcer*. 118 p. Berkeley and Los Angeles: University of California Press, 1948.

23. Ruesch, J., Harris, R. E., Loeb, M. B., Christiansen, C., Dewees, S., Heller, S. H., and Jacobson, A.: *Chronic Disease and Psychological Invalidism*. 191 p. New York: Amer. Soc. Res. Psychosom. Probl., 1946. 2nd printing, Berkeley and Los Angeles: University of California Press, 1951.

24. Ruesch, J. and Prestwood, A. R.: Anxiety, its initiation, communi-

cation, and interpersonal management. Arch. Neurol. Psychiat., 62, 527–550, 1949.

25. Sargant, W.: *Battle for the Mind.* 263 p. New York: Doubleday, 1957.

26. Shneidman, E. S., and Farberow, N. L. (Editors): *Clues to Suicide.* 227 p. New York: McGraw-Hill, 1957.

27. Simon, A.: The diagnosis and management of the depressed patient. California-Western Academy Monthly, 9–13, July, 1953.

28. Solomon, P., Leiderman, P. H., Mendelson, J., and Wexler, D.: Sensory deprivation: A review. Amer. J. Psychiat., 114, 357–363, 1957.

29. Standal, S. W. and Corsini, R. J. (Editors): *Critical Incidents in Psychotherapy.* 396 p. Englewood Cliffs, N.J.: Prentice-Hall, 1959.

30. *Symposium on Chemical Concepts of Psychosis, Zurich, 1957.* (Edited by M. Rinkel.) 485 p. New York: McDowell, Obolensky; 1958.

31. *Symposium on Stress (16–18 March, 1953).* 332 p. Washington: Army Medical Service Graduate School, 1953.

32. Tyhurst, J. S.: The role of transition states—including disasters—in mental illness. Pp. 149–169 in *Symposium on Preventive and Social Psychiatry.* Washington: Walter Reed Army Institute of Research, 1958.

33. Tyhurst, J. S.: Problems of leadership: In the disaster situation and in the clinical team. Pp. 329–335 in *Symposium on Preventive and Social Psychiatry.* Washington: Walter Reed Army Institute of Research, 1958.

34. Wells, F. L. and Ruesch, J.: *Mental Examiners' Handbook* (2nd ed.). 211 p. New York: The Psychological Corporation, 1945.

35. Whyte, W. H., Jr.: *The Organization Man.* 429 p. New York: Simon & Schuster, 1956.

Part Six

The Disturbed Individual and
His Surroundings

Chapter Twenty-one

The Individual in a Defective Network

INADEQUATE NETWORKS

Overload · Lack of collateral connections · Misplacement of human talent · Incompatible tasks at the same station

IN SOME organizational systems the networks of communication are arranged in such a way that they cannot function properly. The most frequent functional defect is the overloading of central stations with incoming messages and with decision-making which could very well be relegated to subordinate stations. Although complicated organizational charts contain descriptions of who is responsible to whom and for what, these schemes often do not indicate what kind of a load a specific person can handle during his working hours and how time-consuming his task is.

The second most frequent disturbance arises when the principal avenue of communication in an organization is blocked and no collateral networks have been established. Just as traffic is rerouted if a main artery is closed, so communications have to be rerouted in case an individual is temporarily disabled. This rerouting is often dependent upon the ingenuity of those who take over and establish informal networks to maintain the flow of messages. Such is the case when the head man has a personality disorder which prevents him from making decisions, when he is frequently away hunting and golfing and not on the job, or when his subordinates isolate him from the public.

A third kind of disturbance occurs when an individual is shifted to a position for which he is not suited. A scientist, for example, should hold a position near the decision-making center but should not be placed in the line of command. The pursuit of truth and the art of making workable decisions often are mutually incompatible. Likewise, a decision-maker should not be placed in an advisory capacity or a staff position. The underloading or misplacing of a talented individual is damaging to him as well as to the network.

In examining a network, it may turn out that the tasks carried out by various stations are done satisfactorily; but in modern communication systems the implementation of a task—let us say, the job of the doctor in the hospital—is not the only duty to be attended to. The maintenance of the network makes demands in itself. Reports to superiors and inferiors and the paper work involved in bureaucratic practices of local, state, and federal government, of labor unions and associations, and of other groups may require far more effort than is needed for the direct completion of the task. In some networks the reading of memos, the filling out of reports, and the attending of meetings are delegated to a special task force. But in less well organized groups the professionals have to do these chores themselves. The result is that they cannot carry out the tasks for which they were chosen. This "beaureaucratic snafu" inevitably leads to a breakdown in communication. When a person finds himself in such a vulnerable position in a communication network, no amount of personal skill, talent, or devotion will help him remedy the situation. Instead he has to obtain a different position altogether. On occasions, an individual is not aware that he is a victim of circumstance and is not aware of the defects in the organizational plan. In such cases, if the psychiatrist is consulted, he has to analyze the situation and help the patient to change positions. A malfunctioning organization usually has to break down before it is reorganized, and in the course of this process the chances are that the personnel will be replaced anyway. To take a temporary demotion and join another organization therefore is the lesser evil for the individual who is caught in such an impasse.

UNSUITABLE VALUES

Overruled values   ·   Opposition to the majority   ·   Finding compatible groups

Acceptance of an official position in an organization necessitates that the individual abide by the principles upon which the organization is built. The officers in an army of occupation, for example, may find that people of the underground resistance have raided the munitions depot and their leaders may be captured. The commanding officer then is put into a position of having to punish or execute the leaders because those are the army regulations, although his personal feelings may be in favor of setting them free. This situation occurred countless times during World War II, and only those persons were considered fit for command who could abide by the rules without letting their own judgment and feelings interfere. On the other hand, commanders who are merely robots who comply without thinking are also undesirable. Thus a difficult problem arises—when to follow established rules and when to disregard them.

There are many patients who cannot abide by the values that have been established. Their non-acceptance may be soundly based and their rebellion may be in good faith, but because of their non-conformance they get into conflict with the group, which then resorts to sanctions. Such conflicts were clearly revealed at the Nuremberg trials (6). Repeatedly the question was raised whether or not an individual could resist the rules of the existing regime. That the judges and prosecutors expected to find a solution to this problem became obvious as the trials progressed. But it became equally clear that a single individual could not oppose the whole system without losing freedom or life; and a mass exodus was equally impractical because the other natives would have restrained those fleeing and because other nations would not have accepted them. What, then, is the solution to such a problem? The answer has never been given.

Fortunately in peace time the patient does not have to face such monumental questions, and in most instances he can work out a satisfactory solution. The therapist has to help the patient to clarify this matter of values. First, the values of the patient have to be pinpointed and their origins traced to specific practices of father, mother, grandparents, and the groups to which they belong. Next the patient has to analyze the values of the groups to which he belongs. It follows that he should only join organizations and seek positions which are governed by rules and values with which he can agree in principle. In one case, this may entail a move from one part of the United States to another; in another it may mean a change of employment; then again it may involve a change of occupations, a change of friends, and sometimes even divorce. The therapist must impress upon the patient that no price is really too high if the result enables the individual to live with a group whose values he can abide by.

DIFFICULT POSITIONS

Poorly conceived positions · Persons not qualified for the position · Internal conflicts and position

A distinction has to be made between functions that are difficult to fulfill because of the way they have been set up and functions that are difficult to fulfill because of the individual's personality. In the present era of "organization man" (13), when planners sit at a desk and create a new position instead of letting it evolve, it happens rather frequently that such a position contains mutually contradictory elements. A man cannot be prosecutor, supervisor, judge, counsellor, father confessor, and propagandist all in one. Human functions group or cluster around certain central features to the exclusion of others: a good salesman usually makes a poor researcher; a decision-maker is not a pure technician. In recognition of these facts, government is traditionally separated into the judicial, legislative, and executive branches. Similarly, in corporations the sales, production, research, personnel, and administrative branches form separate divisions. In most nations of the world—the United States excepted—the head of state and the head of government are not the same person; and in corporate life, the chairman of the board and the president are not the same person. If the therapist encounters a patient who holds an organizationally ill-conceived role or position, he has to help the patient to quit such a job. Unless the individual is very powerful and carries a lot of prestige, he is unable to change his duties. If he wishes to survive, he should quit, even if this means a financial sacrifice, and seek a position that does not have built-in contradictions.

In their occupational lives, there are occasions when people cannot fulfill the tasks that have been assigned to them. An individual, for example, may be called upon to mediate between rival parties, but he may be unable to handle hostility and competition. Or he may be assigned the task of drumming up ideas, but he may not be equipped with a productive fantasy. People thus are propelled into positions which require personality features and skills which they do not possess. In a civilization like ours, where money and prestige matter more than individual satisfaction, such temptations are rather commonplace. Later on, then, the individual discovers that he really does not like the work he is doing but he feels reluctant to undertake steps to correct the situation. The title of a job or the nominal aspects of a position often do not betray the qualifications needed. In military life, for example, the commander of a unit may have to be, in one case, a stern disciplinarian, in the next an organizer, and in the third an unorthodox, adaptive, courageous man; but the rank, pay, privileges, and paper qualifications may all be the same. With the help of the therapist, the patient may proceed with an operational analysis of the position and a review of his personal assets. A careful study of the life history of the patient, the kind of work he has done, and the kind of roles he has occupied will reveal his basic qualifications (10). If these do not fit the job or the position in question, a transfer is in order.

The problem grows more involved when the patient has internal conflicts he is unable to resolve. A doctor who would enter the academic career also would like the financial rewards that derive from private practice. An engineer who aspires to hold an administrative position also would like to work in the laboratory. The resolution of these internal conflicts follows along established lines of procedure. However, the therapist can rely upon one device which usually speeds things along. If the patient has the courage to try both alternatives, he may discover that he wants neither. Once he has tried what he dreamed about and discovers that a compensatory fantasy is not designed to be implemented in reality, he may need assistance in finding a third solution which lies outside the reach of his conflict.

NOMINAL RELATIONS

Formal relations · *Reconditioning non-functional relationships*

The psychiatrist frequently encounters persons who have a lot of friends and relatives, but whose relationships to these people are inoperative. A patient may have a father, but he has not seen him for many years; he has a mother, but she works at night and on weekends. He belongs to clubs, but he never visits the premises; he has close friends, but they live in another part of the country. Such a person fools himself into believing that he belongs, but actually he is worse off than the unattached ones. The mother of a family may satisfy her conscience by feeding and clothing her children and sending them to good schools; but her financial sacrifices do not provide for shared experiences, participation in action, or emotional warmth. Technically, the family does not exclude such a mother and the formal aspects of the various relationships are meticulously maintained; but operationally the relationships are not providing the needed satisfactions.

The psychiatrist's task is a subtle one. Social operations, not the roles and actions that people tend to cite in their place, determine human relations. When a patient says "I am married," the question arises as to what he does with his wife and what he does and does not talk about with her. Often the psychiatrist will discover that invoking a role or relationship is a substitute for meaningful action with that same person. To name, to cite, or to refer to becomes a magic act which the patient hopes will lead to wish fulfillment. A careful evaluation of nominal relationships may begin with the patient's wife or husband, father, mother, brother, or sister, and then proceed to the more casual associations. And once the patient has solved in his own mind what kind of living relationships he can maintain, he may be ready to drop his fictitious memberships and seek new acquaintances and connections. People with nominal relations have to be prevented from becoming unattached people. Groups seem to exclude people who are disturbing or aloof, and the patient must be made aware of his ambivalence. In active participation, such a patient may reveal that he does not get along with people. Because of his past experiences, he even may be trying to undermine the group that he endeavors to join. Therapy therefore has to expose the difficulties of interaction and sometimes, indeed, nominal relations have to be accepted as the solution to the patient's problems.

THERAPEUTIC COMMUNICATION WITH SEVERAL MEMBERS OF THE SAME GROUP

One therapist · Multiple therapists for one patient · Collaborative treatment · Separate treatment · Family therapy · Individual and group therapy

Pathology due to a faulty organization of the network usually can be approached only if several or all participants undergo treatment. In the military situation, a unit with low morale is usually broken up. In civilian life, this is more difficult to effectuate and therefore treatment of all members is preferable to breaking up the unit (1). These are the possibilities that present themselves:

1. One person alone is in therapy with one therapist. The advantages here are in the lower cost and the greater prospects for improvement of the patient. Therapy with one person is suitable if the individual wishes to leave the family or the group, the mate, or whatever other people he is connected with, and if he tries to seek a new and independent existence. It is also suitable for those patients who have been hospitalized and do not wish to return to the family fold (4).

2. One person is in therapy with two therapists. These thera-

pists can be seen in succession, alternately, or simultaneously at the same session (12). Although simultaneous therapy with different therapists interferes with the identification of the patient, successive therapists offer great advantages. The usefulness of any one therapist is probably exhausted after several hundred hours, and the patient will profit more from a fresh therapist. This is particularly true of the end phases of therapy. There are, for example, certain problems, particularly in young people, that the patient may work out better with a therapist of the other sex. After all, every person has two parents, and the problems with each are quite different in nature.

3. Several members of a family or group are in therapy with different therapists who meet regularly to discuss the therapeutic problems of the family. This method, which is frequently used in clinics and hospitals for children, is perhaps the most efficient but also the most costly. Those therapists who deal with children directly may have a different training and background than the therapists who deal with the parents. One member may be in psychoanalysis, another may be seen only occasionally, and the child may be in an institution. The treatment reviews insure that the problems common to all are put into the foreground and that all the therapists are informed about what goes on with each member (11).

4. Several members of the same family or group are in therapy with different therapists who do not review the treatment together (3). In this instance, father, mother, and perhaps one or two children each has a different therapist (9). On the whole, this method is contraindicated inasmuch as the family is treated as if it consisted of separate individuals; the common themes are neglected, and as a result the family usually falls apart. The only circumstances where such procedure seems to be permissible is when the family has very loose connections, the children are grown, and the parents do not intend to stay together.

5. Several members of the same family or group are successively or simultaneously in therapy with the same therapist. This method, which is perhaps the least costly, is at the same time perhaps the most integrative one (7). If there is only one therapist, he has an

undisputed advantage in that he recognizes the effects that the behavior of one person has upon another. This is particularly true of emergencies or acute crises in family life: a husband who is morbidly jealous, a mother who is extremely punitive, or a homosexual team that is devouring itself by means of sadistic-masochistic games. In all of these instances, it is useful to see both members of the team simultaneously. Once the emergency has subsided, one member can be taken into treatment until his character problems have been handled, and then the other member can follow later (2).

6. One or two members of the same family are in individual therapy with one or different therapists while the other members are in group therapy (8). This method is particularly useful where the group therapeutic discussion deals with the relatives of the patients. The mothers of schizophrenics; the husbands of expectant mothers; the family members of amputees, diabetics, arthritics, the blind, and the deaf—all of whom have to be informed as to how a disease or a disability affects a patient (5).

References

1. Academy of Psychoanalysis: *Science and Psychoanalysis: Vol. 2. Individual and Familial Dynamics* (J. Masserman, editor). 218 p. New York: Grune & Stratton, 1959.

2. Ackerman, N. W.: *The Psychodynamics of Family Life.* 379 p. New York: Basic Books, 1958.

3. Eisenstein, V. W. (Editor): *Neurotic Interaction in Marriage.* 352 p. New York: Basic Books, 1956.

4. Fromm-Reichmann, F.: *Principles of Intensive Psychotherapy.* 246 p. Chicago: University of Chicago Press, 1950.

5. Garrett, J. F. (Editor): *Psychological Aspects of Physical Disability.* 195 p. Washington: Department of Health, Education, and Welfare; Office of Vocational Rehabilitation; Rehabilitation Service Series #210; 1953.

6. Gilbert, G. M.: *Nuremberg Diary.* 471 p. New York: Farrar, Straus: 1947.

7. Grotjahn, M.: *Psychoanalysis and the Family Neurosis.* 320 p. New York: Norton, 1960.

8. Kahn, S. W. and Prestwood, A. R.: Group therapy of parents as an

adjunct to the treatment of schizophrenic patients. Psychiatry, 17, 177–185, 1954.

9. Midelfort, C. F.: *The Family in Psychotherapy*. 203 p. New York: Blakiston, 1957.

10. Spiegel, J. P.: The social roles of doctor and patient in psychoanalysis and psychotherapy. Psychiatry, 17, 369–376, 1954.

11. Szurek, S. A.: *The Roots of Psychoanalysis and Psychotherapy*. 134 p. Springfield: Thomas, 1958.

12. Whitaker, C. A., Malone, T. P., and Warkentin, J.: Multiple therapy and psychotherapy. Pp. 210–216 in *Progress in Psychotherapy*. (F. Fromm-Reichmann and J. L. Moreno, editors). New York: Grune & Stratton, 1956.

13. Whyte, W. H., Jr.: *The Organization Man*. 429 p. New York: Simon & Schuster, 1956.

Chapter Twenty-two

Confused Metacommunication

THE PREFIX "meta-" derives from the Greek and indicates "along with" or "after." Metalanguage thus refers to events that go along with language—specifically, a device which the speaker uses to instruct the receiver and which the latter uses to interpret a statement. These communications about communication may be embodied in a twinkle in the eye that changes the perhaps somewhat threatening statement into a joke, or in the uniform of a policeman, which changes his pleasant "Move on, move on" into a command (1). Metacommunication shapes the general meaning of words into specific statements made by a well-defined speaker and addressed to a specific receiver, nailing down the time and the place of the statement and its range of application. Since metalanguage is far more complicated and complex than language itself, only experience can teach the mastery of the unwritten rules which govern its use. Metacommunicative practices vary somewhat with each group and each locale, and newcomers, even if they speak the same language, often take years to learn local meanings (4). This happens regularly to Englishmen and Irishmen who come to America and usually require several months to discover that they do not understand, and that they are misunderstood; then they need several years to learn how to remedy the situation, if they do so at all (8). The majority of psychiatric patients have serious difficulties with metacommunication, primarily because metacommunication is learned only through consistent contact with one and the same group. Interrupted, discontinuous, or non-existent human relations thus prevent the mastery of metacommunication. This state of affairs in turn seriously interferes with the social processes that connect the patient with his surroundings.

DIFFICULTIES WITH INSTRUCTIONS

Implicit and explicit instructions   ·   Inability to give or receive instructions · Clues for the therapist · Difficulties of appeal · The person blind to context · Training for appropriacy

Instructions may be explicit or implicit. A doorknocker at the front entrance, chairs located in the waiting room, an ash tray on the side table—all contain self-evident instructions (10). When a man rings the doorbell, he may introduce himself as the insurance appraiser or the Fuller brush man. He may then add his name and specify his functions in greater detail so that the housewife is clear what the meeting is about. Introductions often are obviated through uniforms, as in the case of the mail carrier, the policeman, the fireman, the grocer, or the barber. The uniformed person relies upon the fact that the other has understood the context in which he is operating. But things get more complicated when there are frameworks within frameworks. A mail carrier may talk to a receiver of mail about postage due, but in parentheses, as it were, he may add that the swallows are late this year—a remark that is addressed to a fellow bird-fancier and not to the recipient of the mail.

The schizophrenic patient, notably, has difficulties with instructions. Personally, he does not care to instruct, and often he disregards the instructions of others. The self-centered, neurotic person expects other people not only to appreciate his instructions but to comply with them as well. In therapy, then, a good deal of time is devoted to the decoding of secret instructions. A patient who comments, "I have nothing to say today," and rubs her hands nervously while clutching a handkerchief to wipe her wet hands makes a clear statement: "Verbally I have nothing to say, but I am extremely anxious and tense." With his knowledge of nonverbal communication, the therapist often reacts to metalanguage more than to ordinary language. This is particularly true when metalanguage and language are not coordinated (6). If covert and overt meaning do not coincide, the therapist does well to neglect the dictionary meaning of words and to clarify the instructions first. Or, to put it more precisely, only when metalanguage and language fit together can the therapist consider the content of what is said. Thus when a schizophrenic girl berated her therapist for not understanding and called him all sorts of names, he replied, "You ask for my permission to use vile language and you have it, but I may add that I don't like it"; whereupon she replied, "I didn't think you would," and for the rest of the interview no further insults were thrown at him.

The interpretation of the patient's metalanguage may meet with difficulties if the channels and modalities which carry the main message and those that carry the instructions are not well defined. The patient may say something through his movements and use words as instructions, or he may take the context of a situation as an instruction for the words he utters. A schizophrenic patient once verbalized to the therapist: "How can I trust you? You are not my friend . . . (long pause) . . . You are paid to help me." Thereupon the therapist replied, "I see that you do not trust anybody, but those who are paid you trust a bit more than those who are not." Then the patient smiled. It was the long pause that disconnected the last part of the statement from the first that contained the clue—some sort of attenuating modification of the principal message. In order to detect significant clues the therapist at all times has to ask himself the question, "What does the patient want to say and what are his instructions?" If the therapist does not understand, he had better continue to explore; and this he can do by patiently commenting on his own actions. He may say, "When I didn't reply a moment ago, I wondered whether you would add anything else." By directly illustrating his own use of pauses, the doctor conveys to the patient the secrets of his metacommunication. After such demonstration, the patient in turn may eventually be able to phrase his own bizarre statements in a more comprehensible way.

It is difficult for psychiatric patients to silently appeal and to set the other person's expectations. For example, a hysterical girl may not be able to decline the advances of a man until the moment he embraces her, or a schizophrenic boy cannot appeal to the adult for affection which he so much desires. Then there is the dependent patient whose life is based solely on appeal and salesmanship, who appeals to the wrong person in the wrong way at the wrong time. He pretends pseudo-intimacy where distance is more suitable, and by using the tricks of parapsychological communication he often repels more than he attracts (5). The psychiatrist here has the arduous task of bringing the patient back to the social reality of the situation. The patient's actions in the therapeutic hour can be used for sharpening behavior; the therapist teaches the patient that before as well as after a statement has been made he is responsible for its correct interpretation by the other person. And this takes preparation, skill in delivery, and care in follow-up.

A particular form of metacommunicative disability is found with the person who does not understand the context of a situation. Someone who insists upon having a long telephone conversation with a doctor who is just seeing another patient is obviously out of order, as is a person who bursts into another's office although he sees that a conference is going on. Such intrusive behavior could be attenuated with a remark such as "I see you are busy; I will come back later." But in the absence of such an apology, people usually react rather sourly. Or when all stalls are full, there will always be a joker who puts his car into the driveway of the parking lot so that nobody can get out. Although it is common practice to interpret such behavior as aggressive or hostile, more often than not one will discover that such people just cannot read the clues embedded in the material environment. They seem to be incapable of reading the arrangement of objects or the disposition of furniture or the clustering of people. They sing at funerals, they transact business when others play, or they ask for advice when the other person is practically asleep.

The therapist can sharpen the patient's awareness by focusing on the occurrences in the office. Suitable for this purpose is the greeting or leave-taking ceremony. Usually the patient has to be trained to depart on time without starting on a new topic at the doorway; sometimes he has to be reminded to be on time—neither too early nor too late. If the therapist has to answer the telephone in the presence of the patient, he may say, "Please forgive me for the interruption; this was an emergency." In this way the patient understands that the therapeutic interview is not habitually used for carrying on long-winded telephone conversations. On another occasion, the therapist may remark, "You know, you don't come here to pay me a social call." Then again he may discuss with the patient his manner of sitting in a chair, or lying on the couch or dressing, as being appropriate or inappropriate for the situation. Later on, as the patient becomes more aware, situations and contexts outside the therapist's office can be discussed. In all of these talks, the patient has to become aware of the physical limitations of the situation, the conventions that govern it, and the built-in leeway for individual variation.

CONFUSION OF RULES

The social game · Teaching the interpretation of rules · The rule stickler · The rebel against rules

Customs and traditions can best be understood if one conceives of behavior as a social game which is governed by rules that define who can talk to whom, when, where, for how long, on what subject matter, and how (9). Rules differ from instructions in that the participants are supposed to know the rules before they begin the interaction. Disturbances of communication may arise when the participants do not abide by the traditional or agreed-upon rules and do not know how much leeway they have in the interpretation of rules. People who have difficulties with rules fall into three distinct groups:

–Those who are unable to abide by explicit rules are the rebellious, delinquent, or criminal people.

–Those who are unable to observe implicit rules are the nonconformists.

–Those who are unable to improvise rules if the situation demands it and who stick to the letter of the law are the obsessive-compulsives.

The normal person keeps it in mind that rules are devices which under the best of circumstances can only describe a general orientation. He sees in the rule a crude generalization of what goes on, and therefore he sees fit to alter, exaggerate, or stretch one aspect or the other to make it fit the specific circumstances. The normal mind always seeks the agreement of others and so modifies the rules that living can proceed under as favorable conditions as possible. Patients, in contrast, attempt to subordinate living to rules; apparently they have not discovered that rules are abstractions that have all the shortcomings inherent in a generalization. The patient therefore has to become aware that all symbols are man-made and cannot be better than the man who made them; no symbol can ever adequately represent the original event. Rules exist to facilitate man-made order; and order is conceived in the brains of people. As long as people agree to abide by rules, such order is maintained; once they do not agree, such order cannot be retained. The patient thus has to learn to abide by agreements but at the same time never to overlook the exception that proves the rule. Again the therapeutic situation is the prime occasion for teaching the patient by example how the rules of therapy are handled, observed, and modified.

Rules are defined in terms of words or numbers, and whoever wishes to abide by or use rules must interpret them first. The ones that stick literally to the letter of the law often defeat the goals for which the rules were set up in the first place. These people tend to omit the pragmatic aspects of symbol interpretation—the relationship of sign to bearer—and concentrate entirely upon the semantic aspects—the relationship of the sign to what it stands for. While a rule stickler is commonly referred to as a compulsive personality, he has, in communication terms, a specific deficiency of understanding. He does not realize that words and numbers stand for something else and that one cannot use words or numbers without interpreting their significance. And he does not allow for the fact that a number of additional factors outside of meaning have to be considered (7). With the patient who lives by rules, laws, and regulations—and this includes all the logically and scientifically minded people—the therapist has to avoid any intellectual argument (3). Instead, the therapist has to gently point out the defective understanding in the patient's procedure. The whole problem of why the patient is afraid to take personal responsibility, why he defers to the impersonal authority of the rule, and why he sets symbols above human beings has to be carefully worked through. He has to realize that symbols are man-made for the consumption of other people and that unless the intention of the legislators of rules is understood, people cannot function properly.

The rebel who flouts rules laid down by a person or an organization is defying authority; instead of challenging somebody personally he does it indirectly by breaking the rules. In order to defy rules, he must of course know them. Among criminals are many who know the rules so well that they can take advantage of them. Rebels usually can be controlled by personalized authority; the impersonal rule is the thing that gets them. They are at war with symbolic behavior but respect action and understand any person who will use action language. Rebels are persons with whom it is difficult to make verbal agreements, although they are willing to respect silent agreements entered into during action. The therapeutic endeavor in the case of the rebel is directed at making him aware of his addiction to action language and his enmity toward the symbolic system. Thus when the patient improves he will begin to seek personal contact and perhaps personal fights, which later may give way to cooperation with people. A somewhat immature person sees in rules mainly an instrument of coercion used by those in authority to satisfy their whims. He does not understand the significance of the assumptions one has to make in order to communicate or the rules one has to abide by if one wishes to reach agreements. He believes that people in authority follow one rule one day and another rule another day, not recognizing that he projects upon them his own instability. Such arbitrariness develops when the patient is exposed to one or two parents who apply different rules to old and young, to rich and poor, to men and women. Arbitrary persons can only be helped through a protracted human experience with one and the same person so that the more permanent rules of conduct can be worked out.

INAPPROPRIATE ROLES

Rigidity and flexibility · *Misinterpretation of roles* · *Ambivalent roles* ·
Multiple roles · *Therapy of role confusion*

Roles define mutual relationships. They indicate the identity of the other person with regard to oneself and the identity of self with regard to the other person. Roles define, of course, modes of action and communication. Family roles such as father and son, and occupational roles such as doctor and patient, are known to most people and serve as guideposts in social situations. Disturbances arise when people either persevere in their roles irrespective of the situation or switch roles too rapidly. For example, when a father insists upon the prerogatives of being a father when he visits his married daughter, he may be heading for trouble. Excessive flexibility in role adaptation is likewise a source of confusion, and murder and spy stories abound with such entanglements. In human interaction, roles may quickly change, and it is the art of following these changes appropriately which distinguishes the healthy from the sick person. A person may talk in one capacity without perceiving that the other has in the course of the conversation modified the initial relationship; a conversation may shift in its role aspects from a colleague-colleague relationship to a golfer-golfer, gourmet-anorexic, smoker-nonsmoker, paternal-filial combination all in a matter of minutes; and unless both are capable of following these modifications, misunderstandings are likely to develop.

There are people who project their own expectations upon a situation and mistake these for first-hand observations; others who perceive correctly may misinterpret the situation. For example, a friendly greeting to a girl swimming at the beach may be interpreted as a come-on; or courtesy in letting somebody get into a parking space may be taken as an indication of weakness. Such misinterpretations may come about when people belong to different castes, classes, or national or regional cultures and are unfamiliar with a situation. Finally there are those whose systematic blindness for certain cues is due to their neurotic conflicts. A man with feelings of inferiority must ignore the attractiveness of a girl; or the childless woman must declare that all children are a nuisance. Neither of these individuals can accept the role that touches upon his central conflict.

People may be ambivalent about their roles. They start out being somebody for an hour or two and then get fed up with it. They like to play mother, but after a while the children bore them. They like to go to a dinner, but after three-quarters of an hour they would like to leave. Such people cannot sustain an activity or a relationship and cannot commit themselves for a longer period of time. Their well-developed anticipatory behavior makes an imagined role more attractive than the one they possess. Not living in the present but in the future, they are tempted to give up what they hold at the moment.

There are patients who pride themselves in being everything. A girl may boast, "I am mother, lover, friend, and child to my husband, all in one." But these overadaptable people often discover that they do not accomplish these functions with any degree of perfection. The bearer of multiple roles is usually a non-committed and unidentified individual who senses intuitively what kind of role he or she can assume in order to obtain gratification from the other person. These people specialize in rendering service for the sake of approval, but eventually they resent the contortions they have to go through to achieve their ends.

Confusion with roles has to be handled in four ways: Training social perception, adapting outer role to inner need, teaching the patient to abandon his stereotyped roles, and helping the patient to overcome excessive fluidity of adaptation. Training for social perception is not a role specific problem but a task which is practiced in acquiring social maturity. The adaptation of the role to feeling and thought, to personal needs and identity is a foremost goal of therapy. The patient must be taught to reject those roles that violate his sense of integrity. The elimination of stereotyped roles is a more difficult problem to cope with. The principle here is to throw the patient into the water and let him swim. Trained from early childhood to avoid situations which force role adaptation, the patient has to be encouraged to seek social contexts with which he is unfamiliar. For such a person, all the principles pertaining to stability of behavior have to be modified; for him it is good experience to hold a job for one month and then change, to visit people, to travel, to date different girls, and to try different sports. The therapist faces quite a different task with the over-adapter who is capable of getting along by subordinating himself to the needs of the other person. Inasmuch as such adaptation is only achieved at the price of self denial, such a patient has to be helped to express himself rather than to please the therapist. Eventually he may come to recognize that he gets just as much approval and affection for genuine expression as he did for adaptive action. The therapist has to convey to him that other people are as eager to adapt to him as he is to adapt to others. Gradually, as the patient gets the courage to be himself, he may relinquish the role of chameleon, restricting himself to those roles which he can successfully fill.

DEVIANT SOCIAL TECHNIQUES

The three phases of human relations · The object-oriented patient · The person-oriented patient · The vertical communicator · The patient who imitates the therapist

Communication is invariably adapted to the social situations in which it occurs. But whenever one person meets another, regardless of whether he be familiar or unfamiliar, distant or close, superior or inferior, similar or different, he goes through three phases of human relations. A person who wishes to approach another informs, attracts, proposes, or, under certain circumstances, rejects the other person. Then follows a phase in which the established relationship is maintained; this involves satisfaction of the other person's needs and acknowledgment and understanding of his messages. But inasmuch as all human relationships are temporary and eventually outlive their usefulness, there also comes a time for separation. This may be achieved by detachment or by frustrating the other person's needs so that he will begin to withdraw. In some instances, there may be symbolic or actual attempts made to annihilate the other person.

In therapeutic practice, the doctor frequently meets the kind of patient who is overly formal and distant. As a result, the doctor feels in himself a sensation of coolness, aloofness, and lack of interest. The patient who attempts to become prematurely familiar produces in the doctor feelings of being hemmed in, monopolized, and coerced. These patients all have a deficient sense of timing. Instead of being distant at the beginning and more intimate in the course of time, the patient avoids this gradual move and remains familiar or distant all of the time. In communication, the overly distant person avoids statements about self, about the other, and about feelings; and therapy therefore is directed at luring the patient away from his object orientation. This the therapist achieves by interjecting comments about himself, about the patient, and about feelings and thoughts that are subjective, and above all by working through the doctor-patient relationship. This repeated emphasis upon the subjective and the human may eventually loosen the patient's rigid impersonal attitude.

The overly familiar person at first enthusiastically accepts everything and then feels the need to reject it. To use a bodily analogy, one might say that such an incorporative patient eats too much too fast and as a result has to spit out the undigested food. Everybody can use only a certain amount of information from others, and the overly familiar person does not select, digest, and integrate but takes over without discrimination. Eventually such a person gets loaded down with things he cannot use; and there is always a danger that he will leave therapy in disgust, only to repeat the same cycle elsewhere. This breakdown of therapy can be prevented by the therapist's firm attitude. When the patient comments on the therapist's good taste in decorating his office, he may comment "Does this really make any difference?" When the patient adoringly comments on the therapist's charming personality, he may say, "Perhaps you should take a second look." These somewhat critical and chilling remarks are designed to lessen the appetite of the patient. In response, the

patient will feel rejected and the therapist may warn, "You are resentful, and I think we should talk about it." With such a patient, the
early regulation of the rate of incorporation is paramount. This the
doctor achieves by calling attention to pieces of information which
the patient has accepted uncritically and by exposing his anger and
resentment which are the result of over-compliance.

The patient who looks up to the therapist as if he were a deity
and the patient who belittles the therapist as if he were his lackey
represent another kind of orientation. By putting the therapist on
a pedestal, the patient provides for himself an association with an
all-powerful person; as a result, he feels safe and there is no reason
for him to test reality. Almost the reverse occurs in the case of the
patient who is afflicted with a sense of superiority. By belittling the
other, or by labeling his statements as superfluous, illogical, and
irrelevant, he can retain his views, does not have to adapt, and
does not need to face the reasons for the disagreement. There are
several ways of coping with this kind of patient. It is possible to
undermine what one might call "vertical communication" by constant
rectification of the assumed differences in status, power, and position.
To the inferior patient, the therapist points out that he really possesses
more power and skill than he is giving himself credit for; and to
the superior-minded patient, he points out that the others are not
really so stupid as he makes them out to be. Once this has been
brought into the open, he can discuss the vulnerability of the patient
in situations of equality.

There are patients who are quite resistant to slow debunking, and
here the therapist has to resort to provocation. The inferior kind
of patient can be moved by the human qualities of the therapist;
therefore the therapist reveals himself as a human being who is
subject to all the doubts, hopes, and disappointments the patient
has had. This exposure lessens the patient's belief in the godlike
qualities of the therapist. With the superior patient, a frontal attack
upon his almost delusional attitude often serves the purpose. The
patient may be reminded that he is not of noble birth, has no
money or position of influence, and has no creative contributions
to point to or any other kind of success to his credit. If he really

is such a great intellectual, why didn't he have a brilliant career? If he has a knack for business, why hasn't he amassed a fortune? And why is he in therapy? The therapist explores the patient's past experiences and pinpoints the fact that his significant human relations were associated with marked status awareness. A discussion of the protective qualities of his air of superiority may give the patient the needed insight to work on the conflict that underlies his behavior. However, the therapist has to keep in mind that the therapeutic situation itself favors vertical communication, and he must take care not to fall into this pattern.

Patients who identify with the therapist—usually out of fear— may outwardly adopt his mannerisms and interests; and those who are afraid of him frequently make a point of the fact that they do everything differently. In either case, the patient's attention has to be called to the problem of similarities and differences. The over-identifying patient first is allowed to accept some of the external characteristics of the therapist because often such acceptance serves as a learning experience. This is particularly true in the case of younger colleagues who at first may assume an attitude which is alien to them, but eventually discover their own true feelings. The therapist can speed up this process by scrutinizing some of the features that the patient has imitated. Just because the therapist has a sailboat, it does not mean that sailing is the patient's choice of recreation. On the contrary, after an ill-fated adventure with boating, he may discover that he is much more inclined to putter in his own garden because it makes more sense in terms of his past experiences. Conversely, the patient who underscores the dissimilarities with the therapist has to be helped to understand that this is a technique which serves the purpose of delineating his own identity (2). A person with a weak identity may arbitrarily over-emphasize the differences from others, very much like an adolescent who rebukes his elders in an attempt to undertake independent steps of his own. Often the patient is afraid of being overwhelmed by the therapist, whom he knows as a skilled and perceptive individual. After the therapist has tactfully exposed the weakness in the identity structure (11), the patient is usually ready to begin reality testing and experimentation. He has to learn that anything said or done by the therapist has to be re-examined by the patient; if it is useful, he can incorporate it into his knowledge; and if it does not make sense he should discard it. Gradually then we see a shift from imitative or oppositional behavior to a behavior of discrimination. In the later stages of therapy, the patient at one moment will imitate and accept, at other times will oppose, and then again he may discard or ignore, depending on whether or not the action or information fits into his pattern of living.

References

1. Feldman, S. S.: *Mannerisms of Speech and Gestures in Everyday Life*. 301 p. New York: International Universities Press, 1959.

2. Freud, A.: *The Ego and the Mechanisms of Defense*. 196 p. London: Hogarth Press, 1942.

3. Gitelson, M.: Intellectuality in the defense transference. Psychiatry, 7, 73–86, 1944.

4. Hall, E. T.: *The Silent Language*. 240 p. Garden City: Doubleday, 1959.

5. Horton, D. and Wohl, R. R.: Mass communication and para-social interaction. Psychiatry, 19, 215–229, 1956.

6. Lennard, H. L. and Bernstein, A.: *The Anatomy of Psychotherapy*. 209 p. New York: Columbia University Press, 1960.

7. Morris, C. W.: *Signs, Language, and Behavior*. 365 p. New York: Prentice-Hall, 1946.

8. Orsler, M. and Bradbury, M.: Department of amplification. The New Yorker, 36, 58–62, July 2, 1960.

9. Ruesch, J. and Prestwood, A. R.: Interaction processes and personal codification. J. Personality, 18, 391–430, 1950.

10. Ruesch, J. and Kees, W.: *Nonverbal Communication*. 205 p. Berkeley and Los Angeles: University of California Press, 1956.

11. Wheelis, A.: *The Quest for Identity*. 250 p. New York: Norton, 1958.

Chapter Twenty-three

Disturbances in Correction, Feedback, and Reply

THERE are two kinds of feedback which maintain pathology. The first kind involves circuits which are largely limited to the organism; it occurs in phenomena such as stuttering, diarrhea, urinary frequency, or hallucinations. The second type consists of feedback circuits which include other persons; dependency, acting out, and antisocial behavior fall into this category. Although, in many instances, the two types are intimately interwoven, the distinction is significant for therapeutic purposes. In cases where the intrapsychic mechanisms have to be influenced, the psychiatrist has only indirect means of therapy available. He has to rely upon the slow introjection of recent experiences which are then superimposed on the older ones. But where other people are involved in the maintenance of pathology, the social forms of therapy are effective.

MISMANAGEMENT OF ENERGY HOUSEHOLD

Apportioning energy · Difficulties with timing · Appropriacy of energy output · Maximum effort and relaxation · Learning energy dissipation · The pressurized person

The wisdom of the organism is such that every animal and every human being in his natural state will apportion his energies in a way that will ensure his survival. Depending upon the situation, the organism will respond with a casual effort, a sustained effort, or a maximum effort. But there are people and animals who cannot adapt optimally to the occasion and who, for a variety of reasons, respond unselectively with little or maximal effort to all situations. These people become our patients.

To time action correctly, to allot the necessary time for completion of the action, and to apply the appropriate rate and speed are features that are learned in sports, at school, and in one's occupation. But there are patients who have perennial feuds with timing, and this is not because they lack intelligence or training but because they suffer from an emotional block. Perhaps they are regularly late for work because they leave home ten minutes before check-in time, although they know that it takes them about thirty minutes to get there. Upon closer analysis, the psychiatrist will discover that such a patient does not really accept the fact that it takes thirty minutes to get there. He cherishes the magic belief that he can compress thirty minutes into ten. In therapy, then, the patient is confronted with the need to properly time his arrival and departure, to meet deadlines, and to fulfill obligations. The magic thought of mastery over time—the only really scarce commodity in the human being's life—has to be properly explored. Time is perhaps the only feature in life that requires a complete and relentless adaptation on the part of the individual.

If left to himself, a child will move about when rested and sleep when tired. But in our civilization the situation is not so simple. People move and sleep according to schedule, and children are put to bed for the afternoon nap not so much because they need it as to give mother a rest. We demand that our children be quiet and restrained. They have to be toilet trained before they enter nursery school, and they are not allowed to run across the street. Under such serious limitations, the development of the motor system suffers and the child can be compared to a dog that is constantly chained down. Such a dog either sleeps or runs wild when let loose. The clock and other people control the expenditure of energy more than the proprioceptive devices which tell an individual about his state of relaxation or fatigue.

Ideally speaking, the organism adapts its dissipation of energy from minute to minute. But a neurotic patient may create imaginary emergencies or disregard serious situations completely, with the result that he may find himself in a continuous state of tension or suffer from uninterrupted weakness. The continuously tense patient uses too much energy for the little affairs of daily life and is incapable of making an effort when effort is needed. The lethargic, apathetic person does not get aroused by emergencies. If maximum effort has been suppressed, it usually can be traced to the fact that in the childhood of the patient his outbursts of temper were severely punished. A permissive and kind attitude of the therapist eventually tends to resuscitate the old temper, and after a period of testing in which the patient discovers that anger and temper are not punished but constitute reactions which can be used and developed, the patient eventually improves.

The therapist can cope with such uneven expenditures of energy right in the interview. He can point to the patient-created emergencies—those patterns which require support, sympathy, and affection, and the little scenes and complications—which to the patient are the spice of life and to the doctor are a nuisance because they interfere with progress. The even behavior of the therapist eventually rubs off on the patient and he learns from example to do without maximum effort for meaningless occasions. Above and beyond what happens in the therapeutic hour, the therapist has to enlist outside help so that the patient may learn about energy control. The therapist has to find out in which physical activity he could interest the patient, because no person will enjoy golf if he is not also interested in the landscape and no person will enjoy swimming if he is afraid of the water. Also, it is easier to learn energy control together with another significant person. Sex activities, of course, belong in the same category. A person who can experience satisfactory orgasms will create fewer emergencies than the person who has to experience maximum effort by creating a scene.

There are people who can function only under pressure. They begin to work shortly before the deadline; they pay their bills when the collection agency knocks at the door; they never have time to leisurely think or do anything; and their life proceeds from one emergency to another. Such persons have to keep up a certain anxiety level in order to function, and when left without pressure they feel that they cannot act. The parents of such patients usually are impatient, and instead of giving the youngster time to learn they pressurize him into premature activity. Gradually this becomes a habit, and the child's disgust, reluctance, and lack of mastery are overcome by artificially created tension which spurs him into activity. The therapist's first step usually consists of eliminating the emergency. This is done by reacting with placidity to the excitement of the patient. Gradually the patient discovers the role of anxiety in his own motivation; and once given time in terms of years, he realizes his lack of mastery. Under the benign guidance of the therapist, the patient learns—at first slowly and clumsily and later more proficiently —to perform. And as skill and knowledge increase, he may be able to use less effort in getting the necessary things done.

UNSKILLED IN THE FUNDAMENTALS OF COMMUNICATION

The basic types of reply · Diagnostic categories and failure to communicate · Understanding · Acknowledgment · Agreement

Communication cannot occur without understanding. Understanding is reached if the listener can connect a more recent experience with his older body of knowledge. Once a person has reached a state of understanding, it becomes his task to acknowledge that which he believes to have been understood. This involves first a statement that the other person's intent to communicate has been perceived and, thereafter, that the content of the message has been properly appreciated. But unfortunately not all people attribute the same referential properties to the symbols used. One person may say, "I saw a large animal," referring to a dog standing about twenty inches high; and the next one, upon hearing these words, believes that the speaker refers to a horse standing about seventeen hands high. The art of understanding therefore is based upon the detection of what the other person really means. Therefore, after a message has been perceived and properly acknowledged, a third step has to be taken—namely, the reaching of an agreement. Agreeing differs from acknowledging in that it involves the active commitment of both participants. Agreement is always limited to a certain situation, topic, or action and does not encompass the whole existence of the participants (6).

Phenomenologically speaking, patients who do not understand usually fall into the organic, the feeble-minded, or the exceedingly narcissistic group. Patients who do not acknowledge or who acknowledge only in rudimentary fashion usually are schizophrenics, depressives, or compulsive personalities. By failing to acknowledge, some of these patients hope to induce others to renew their efforts. The self-centered people who do not acknowledge messages, however, are most eager to have their own messages responded to. Patients who cannot reach agreements or who cannot stick to them comprise the group of psychopathic personalities, the ambulatory schizophrenics, the floaters and drifters, the non-conformists, and the rebellious and marginal people.

In therapy, a clear distinction has to be made among the three phenomena—understanding, acknowledgment, and agreement. Understanding is taught to the patient by the example set by the therapist. The doctor demonstrates to the patient how pieces of information, recollections of the past, or previously unconscious fantasies can be connected with current experiences. The views of the patient can be compared with the knowledge of the therapist, and thus the patient receives a lesson in the operational approach to understanding. He learns what it means to ascertain facts, to connect them, and to establish a small-scale model of the situation at hand.

The process of acknowledgment is taught to the patient in action. By acknowledging a facial gesture of the patient, a faint blush, or an abortive attempt to say something, the doctor teaches the patient to react. By focusing upon the intention of the patient, by acknowledging his wish to communicate, by replying to the content of his message, the doctor strengthens the patient's desire to communicate and also increases his pleasure. Acknowledgment thus is the principal tool by which the therapist exerts leverage upon the patient in order to motivate him to seek further improvement. The patient has to be trained to acknowledge in turn the messages of the therapist, and in an atmosphere of mutual respect the more difficult task of outlining the areas of agreement and disagreement can be tackled.

The final step is taken when doctor and patient attempt to reach a state of agreement concerning an isolated topic such as the payment of a bill. Agreement implies understanding and acknowledgment and adds the ingredient of commitment. Agreements are reached with the patient in matters such as appointments, payments, vacations, permission to talk to relatives, and other matters which involve a plan of action.

DIFFICULTIES WITH GOAL-ORIENTED BEHAVIOR

Goal-seeking behavior · Goal-changing

If a person wishes to accomplish a task, all those activities that further the task have to be encouraged and all those that interfere have to be minimized. But inasmuch as the human being cannot strive towards a long-term task twenty-four hours a day, his pursuits have to be intermittent. Furthermore, if a young man wishes to attend to his studies or if a young woman wishes to catch her man, all those wishes and desires that interfere have to be suppressed and all those implementations that are not appropriate have to be eliminated. In the pursuit of short-term goals, the individual must be capable of minimizing long-term considerations which might interfere with short-term success. And while engaged in the pursuit of long-term goals, the individual must be capable of discarding short-term considerations.

If the overtly stated and conscious goals do not coincide with the covert and unconscious goals, behavior becomes conflictive. Like Penelope, who undid at night all the weaving she had done during the day, the neurotic patient goes on undoing what was done before, careful not to reach the stated goal. Therapy with such patients is geared to detecting those processes that interfere with goal-seeking behavior. First the therapist has to uncover the unconscious goals—those that have actually been sought throughout a lifetime.

Then he has to unmask the apparent goals—those to which the patient has paid lip service. After exposure of the conflict, the therapist has to pinpoint those procedures which the patient undertakes which interfere with the realization of both the conscious and the unconscious goals. The therapist tries to help the patient readjust his unconscious goals until they become attainable.

Goal-changing behavior comes about when negative feedback alters the nature of the ongoing activity, its direction, or its intensity. Change has to occur when the original goal cannot be attained, when the situation has changed and the goal has been obviated, or when a vastly more promising goal appears on the horizon. Phobic and compulsive people tend to stick to the same goals, even if these are hopeless ones, while unstable persons change goals so rapidly that they never can harvest the fruits of their labors. Therapeutically, therefore, the task appears as follows: With the person who is incapable of changing goals, the therapist does well to go along with the old scheme. Often the patient knows that a change would bring about a depression, and only after years of work, when new human relations have been established, does he feel strong enough to change his ways. With the goal changer, the procedure is somewhat different. The therapist's first step is to inquire whether the individual's goal-changing behavior is real or apparent. Many a drifter's goal is to be free of responsibility, unattached, and uncoerced, and what appeared as goal-changing was really goal-seeking in the first place. The therapist's second step consists of exploring whether patients such as the psychopath, the adventurer, or the incorporative character possess satisfactory techniques for seeking a goal over the longer term. In these cases, the therapist has to cope early with the patient's boredom, resentment, and anger before he can expect him to pursue a task for any length of time. In the later phases of therapy, finally, the patient learns to change goals rationally; after careful consideration of his needs, the opportunities, and the circumstances, he may initiate a change even at an advanced age.

CHANGE OF ENVIRONMENT

Choice of environment · Culture change · Therapy with immigrants ·
Ecological change · Personal change · Ill health and aging

Understanding, acknowledging, reaching agreements, and pursuing and changing goals can be accomplished if the intra- and extra-organismic organization is optimal. There are people who are fortunate enough to be born into a favorable environment, and there are others who have the knack of selecting an environment with optimal characteristics. But then there are others—mostly those who later become psychiatric patients—who select for themselves an environment which is far from optimal. An adventurer, for example, may do very well in the French Foreign Legion, but he may do very poorly in an office. The relationship to men, the authoritarian characteristics of a military organization, and the presence of emergencies may suit him better than a life of perennial routine. Artists may do well when they live with other artists in bohemian quarters; and mathematicians thrive when they are left in peace on a university campus. Age, sex, occupation, health, religion, social class, and temperament all are significant determinants in the choice of an environment.

People who, because of inner conflict, are incapable of selecting suitable surroundings and those who, because of external circumstances, are forced into unsuitable surroundings present similar problems. Migration, economic reverses, change from military to civilian life, imprisonment, hospitalization, or interracial marriage all contribute to this particular kind of stress. Under these circumstances, the individual is unfamiliar with values, language, custom, and tradition as well as practical implementations of daily life. If he is young, he is likely to learn about the assumptions and interpretations required in his new surroundings, but if he is old he may not have the flexibility to change. The individual who was compelled by circumstances to move into a new culture is more likely to adapt to the new system than the person who moved voluntarily. The voluntary migrant usually is a person with serious personality conflicts who already was maladjusted in the old culture (5).

Therapy with persons undergoing culture change is twofold. It is concerned on the one hand with the patient's identity, and on the other with the acquisition of new values. While the first part is standard therapeutic procedure (7), the second taxes the ingenuity of the therapist. He has to induce the patient to seek social situations in which he can learn the prevailing habits and customs. He can send the patient to language classes; he can encourage him to accept social invitations and to mingle at dances, cocktail parties, and other occasions; he can induce him to work, either free or for compensation, always with the idea of learning the ways of others. And when the patient is full of frustration and disappointment, the doctor can perhaps clear up some of the misinterpretations he is likely to make.

When an individual moves his residence from country to city, he changes his way of life in various ways. He alters his habits of nutrition; he exposes himself to noise and random stimulation; his closeness to nature becomes disrupted; he has far more frequent contact with people, although each contact is emotionally less significant. Most people are capable of taking these and other changes in their stride, but occasionally an individual makes a wrong choice. Although the pay scales are higher in the city, it does not mean that the individual chose the best possible environment for himself. The psychiatrist has to explore the reasons for ecological change; and if it was undertaken voluntarily he may discover that the patient is running away from something (2).

A family faces serious problems of adaptation when one of its members marries, separates, or divorces; when a child leaves his parental home or when a baby is born into the family; when in-laws move in or move away; when death takes its toll; when one of the marital partners acquires a mistress or a lover; when there is serious illness in the family; or when there occurs a radical change in economic situation or occupation. The addition or removal of people in a well-established circle involves a change in the group structure, a redistribution of roles, and a reformulation of the rules of interaction. A widow may need to support herself, or a teen-ager may have to look after her younger siblings. A family consisting of a mother and three daughters may have to be completely restructured when the mother remarries. A woman who devoted her life to the care of her children has to readjust when the last of the youngsters has left for boarding school or college. In these situations, the therapist first and above all has to help the individual to cope with the immediate hurdles. The individual has to learn to satisfactorily adapt to whatever will occur the same afternoon or the next morning. There is no sense in studying the reasons that induced the change or to fix the blame on external circumstances. Occasionally overt conflicts can be discussed and misunderstandings can be cleared up. The patient needs encouragement, advice, and frequent contact with the therapist until the situational stress has disappeared. Only after the patient has regained a semblance of equilibrium does the time come to discuss conflicts, motivations, and interests which will determine future plans of living.

People may be forced to change their material style of living because of physical illness or disability. One person may be tied to a wheel chair; another may be dependent upon a seeing-eye dog; and a third may need a particular diet. These changes in physical health usually are accompanied by ecological changes. The man who is paralyzed has to take an apartment on the first floor or live in a house with an elevator. The recently blinded person may require a seeing-eye dog. An individual who has serious diabetes may not only have to eat at a diabetics' table but also have to change his patterns of physical exercise. The therapist does well to confront the patient with the fact that an irreversible change has occurred and that the patient has to undertake the necessary steps to compensate for the disability. It is obvious that this involves not only walking on crutches, the use of prostheses, the employment of hearing aids, lip reading, or similar devices but also a change in ecology, patterns of living, and social relations (3). New friends, altered relations to family members, perhaps a different occupation and hobbies are inevitable. In helping the patient through the period of adaptational stress, the psychiatrist does not commiserate with him but, like an engineer, tries to help to solve practical problems. A patient may be reluctant to abandon his beautiful house for one that conforms more to his state of health, or he may prefer isolation to company. The psychiatrist's role is to gauge physical and mental exercise to the strength of the patient and to adapt the surroundings to the needs of the patient. Gently, the psychiatrist reminds the patient of the actually prevailing circumstances and presents the advantages of adaptation, pointing out the realistic rewards inherent in what is possible rather than supporting the patient's wishful thinking about that which is impossible. All of these processes are of course studied by the new social discipline of geriatrics, which is vitally concerned with the ecology of an aging population (1, 4).

References

1. *Handbook of Aging and the Individual.* (J. E. Birren, editor.) 939 p. Chicago: University of Chicago Press, 1959.

2. Malzberg, B. and Lee, E. S.: *Migration and Mental Disease.* 142 p. New York: Soc. Sci. Res. Council, 1956.

3. Piddington, R. A.: *The Limits of Mankind.* 153 p. Bristol: John Wright & Sons Ltd., 1956.

4. Pressey, S. L. and Kuhlen, R. G.: *Psychological Development through the Life Span.* 654 p. New York: Harper, 1957.

5. Ruesch, J.: Social factors in therapy. Pp. 59–93 in *Psychiatric Treatment* (ARNMD #31). Baltimore: Williams & Wilkins, 1953.

6. Ruesch, J.: *Disturbed Communication.* 337 p. New York: Norton, 1957.

7. Seward, G.: *Psychotherapy and Culture Conflict.* 299 p. New York: Ronald Press, 1956.

Part Seven

Summary

Chapter Twenty-four

Principles of Communication: A Summary

THERAPEUTIC communication makes use of all the ways of communication that human beings are capable of. The description of such behavior would be a monumental task of dubious value—first, because it would duplicate what poets, writers, and philosophers have said over the centuries; and second, because no shorthand language has as yet been devised to reproduce successfully the complexity of human communication. But this in no way prevents a short recapitulation of the principles that govern human communication, including, of course, the endeavors of the therapist.

The principles set forth in this chapter are intended as a sketch of a theory of human communication as it applies to the problems of therapy. This outline has three aims:

–To contribute towards a unified theory of human behavior.
–To conceive of psychopathology and social pathology as disturbed communication.
–To view human communication as a therapeutic tool.

By eliminating the dichotomy between normal and abnormal behavior, deviant communication is viewed as a special case of ordinary communication—that is, distorted through erroneous timing, deviations in intensity, and inappropriacy of messages (7). The various methods of psychiatric therapy in turn can be viewed as efforts at improving either the organ systems or the functions of communication of man. In subsequent paragraphs, a few of the basic principles of human communication in general (8) and of therapeutic communication in particular are outlined.

PRINCIPLES OF HUMAN COMMUNICATION

DEFINITION OF COMMUNICATION

"The word 'communication' will be used here in a very broad sense to include all of the procedures by which one mind may affect another. This, of course, involves not only written and oral speech, but also music, the pictorial arts, the theatre, the ballet, and in fact, all human behavior" (Warren Weaver, in 12).

GENERAL CHARACTERISTICS OF COMMUNICATION SYSTEMS

Biological and social entities are characterized by:

a) The existence of boundaries.
b) An internal structure and function of the organization that is surrounded by a boundary.
c) Maintenance processes involving reversible changes in support of the existing structures and functions.
d) Irreversible changes which alter existing structures.
e) Growth and evolution in time.
f) Relationship of the existing system to other systems of the same order.
g) Relationship of system to systems of a different order.

Any properties attributed to a naturally existing system stand in a relation of complementarity to the properties attributed to the human observer. The more that is known about the one, the less is known about the other (6).

THE HUMAN OBSERVER

Without a human observer there can be no scientific information. In any scientific communication, therefore, the properties of the observer have to be made explicit (6). The report of the observer is determined by:

a) The position of the observer in the system.

b) The time and space scales of the observer relative to the scales of the system.

c) The theoretical system of the observer.

d) The methods and instruments of the observer.

e) The purpose of the observer.

f) The bias of the observer.

THE PROCESSES OF COMMUNICATION HAVE TO BE CONCEIVED OF IN CIRCULAR TERMS

Human communication processes are characterized by goal-seeking, goal-changing, and corrective behavior whereby the maximization or minimization of certain features may lead to the creation or maintenance of a steady state at a fairly high level of orderliness. In human communication, part functions are always functions of the system as a whole and the chains of causation are at least circular, if not more complex (9).

SIGNAL, SIGN, AND SYMBOL

A signal is an impulse in transit regardless of whether it circulates inside or outside a human organism. A sign constitutes a circumscribed part of an action or event which either by force of its own structure or because of attention paid to it possesses for an observer problem-solving properties or cue values. A symbol is an extra-organismic device which has been agreed upon to refer in a condensed way to a series of actions or events; it is used for coding purposes in order to transmit messages (4).

SEMIOTIC PROCESSES

The field of semiosis is concerned with sign processes (4). It includes:

a) Syntactics, or the relationship of symbols to other symbols;

b) Semantics, or the relationship of signs to the events or objects they purport to designate;

c) Pragmatics, or the relation of signs to their interpreters.

COMMUNICATIVE BEHAVIOR AS A BASIC CHARACTERISTIC OF BIOLOGICAL ORGANIZATION

When a biological or social entity is equipped to register the impact of signals, to react selectively, and to emit signals, it is prepared to enter into communication with other entities. Under these conditions, the processes of communication exert an organizing influence upon the constituent parts and weld them into a larger system (9).

DELINEATION OF COMMUNICATION SYSTEM

In human communication, the unit of study is the total communication system and not any single person, organ system, or part function. A communication system is not determined by morphological criteria. Instead, the system is defined by that sector of the universe which is occupied by a network of communication. It does not matter whether, within such a system, signals originate from a pamphlet distributed by a governmental agency, from a human voice addressing another person, from the cerebral cortex firing efferent neurons to move a muscle, or from the adrenal cortex to pour out adrenalin. What matters is the perception of signals by another station of the network and its responses to the signal, regardless of how many stations participate and how much of the network is involved. For practical reasons, however, the study of the network may be confined to a social situation, to an association, or to the intrapsychic events of an individual (6).

MESSAGE

The purposive expression of internal events with the intent to convey information to other persons is called a statement. A statement becomes a message when it has been perceived and interpreted by another person (10).

PERSONAL OR INTRAPSYCHIC COMMUNICATION

Communication within the self is a special case of interpersonal communication. When traces of past experiences are organized into entities—ideals, images, fantasies, or sentiments—the internal organization of the individual is experienced as consisting of several components. The communication carried on between these various entities is referred to as thinking and feeling (9).

INTERPERSONAL COMMUNICATION

Interpersonal communication (9) is characterized by:

a) The presence of expressive action on the part of one or more persons;

b) Conscious or unconscious perception of such expressive action by other persons;

c) The observation that such expressive action was perceived by others (perception of perception).

GROUP COMMUNICATION

Communication within a group (9) or between groups may be structured as follows:

a) Communication of one to many.

b) Communication of many to one.

c) Communication of many to many.

In the one-to-many communication, the flow of messages is centrifugal, towards the periphery; the recipients usually are unable to reply immediately, and feedback is slow. In the communication of many to one, the flow is centripetal and the messages have to be abstracted and condensed in order to be manageable by the recipient. Through abstraction, distortions are introduced which in turn influence the feedback circuit. In communication of many to many, the messages of the individuals are condensed into communiqués which are issued by committees or spokesmen and are interpreted by committees or delegates of the other group. The speed of communication is slow, and response is delayed.

COMMUNICATION APPARATUS

The communication apparatus of man (9) is composed of:

a) His sense organs, the receiver;
b) His effector organs, the sender;
c) His evaluative apparatus, including the functions of scanning, memory, and decision-making;
d) His body, the shelter of the communication apparatus.

CAPACITY OF SYSTEM

The capacity of man's communication system is limited. The number of incoming and outgoing signals and signals in transit which can be handled by the organism, or by a group, is determined by anatomical and physiological considerations and the skill with which certain functions are used. If a network is taxed above its capacity, it tends to disintegrate; if it is not used at all, it atrophies (7).

In order to avoid overloading of channels and in order to speed up feedback, short-circuits are established. In the armed forces, it is the chaplain who reaches the commanding officer and represents the plight of the soldier in an emergency. Likewise, government officials make use of laymen to obtain uncondensed, first-hand information. If the same information were transmitted through channels, it would have to be abstracted and hence distorted.

STATIONS OF TRANSFORMATION

Sensory endorgans are stations of signal transformation. Phylogenetically old are the chemical and mechanical endorgans which serve as primary receivers. Phylogenetically younger are the more complex distance receivers found in visual and auditory endorgans. The proximity receivers serve as both exteroceptors and proprioceptors, while the distance receivers can function as exteroceptors only. Transformations also occur within the organism, particularly when central nervous system impulses are transformed into muscular contractions. Stations of transformation thus are located at the boundaries of organisms; their signals are decoded and encoded for transmission through different media and channels (6).

CODIFICATION

The technical process of representing signals is referred to as codification. Inside the organism, events are signaled by means of nervous and humoral impulses; outside the organism, any muscular contraction—be it verbal or nonverbal—or its traces can be used for purposes of codification. Analogic codification makes use of continuous representation whereby the signs and symbols used are, in their principal proportions and relations, similar to the things, ideas, or events for which they stand. Digital codification, in contrast, is based upon discontinuous representation of events in which the continuity of nature is sliced into discrete steps. As in the case of numbers or words, these discrete elements are put together by man-made rules which are based upon previous agreement (9).

LANGUAGE

Language is composed of a plurality of signs or symbols, the significance of which must be known to a number of interpreters. These signs must be of such a nature that they can be produced by human beings and will retain the same significance in different situations (3). These requirements usually necessitate that a method be available to arrange the signs in more complex patterns (2).

INFORMATION

Information controls all action and refers to the knowledge of relationships. It is available in coded form inside of human organisms and is made accessible to other persons by means of speech, writing, or demonstration. Information can best be compared to a small-scale model of self and of the world which enables a person to predict events, to correct his own behavior, and to partially alter the shape of the environment (1, 5).

SOURCES OF INFORMATION

Exteroception informs the individual or the group about events occurring outside of the boundaries of the organism, proprioception about events occurring inside the boundaries. Emotions and feelings are terms which refer to the state of the organism proprioceptively evaluated from an inside observation point. Thinking is a term which refers to exteroceptively evaluated matters seen from an outside observation point. The two phenomena are complementary to each other (7).

MATURATION

Man is born of a mother. After birth, certain death would embrace the infant unless it was fed, clothed, and sheltered. Progressive maturation following birth consists of achieving a relative degree of independence, the first step of which is the severing of the umbilical cord. Initially, the infant relies upon the protective actions of others; but gradually, with the accumulation of knowledge and social learning, communication and cooperation with contemporaries replaces the dependence upon physical and emotional assistance from elders. The acquisition of information and its periodical renewal and correction thus become essential for proper functioning and survival (7).

CONTENT

When two or more interpreters of signs can agree with each other as to the events to which the exchange of signals refers, the message can be said to have content. Because content is dependent upon exchange of messages, any shift in content is usually accompanied by a change in feedback and language characteristics (6).

MEMORY AND CONSCIOUS INSPECTION

Experiences which have been intraorganismically codified and retained later become accessible in terms of skills, emotional states, and knowledge. Conscious inspection of past events has to be conceived of as a special intraorganismic feedback device in which certain pieces of information which are earmarked by specific emotional concomitants are selected for focusing. Experiences which can be easily integrated tend to escape conscious inspection, while those which are discordant in any respect are subjected to special inspection (6).

INSTRUCTION

When people communicate with each other, they break up their statements into two parts: content and instruction. The latter consists of statements which refer to the communication process itself and includes references about when, where, and how a statement ought to be interpreted. Some of the statements about communication are explicit; some remain implicit (9).

SOCIAL SITUATIONS, RULES, AND ROLES

Since all social encounters eventually become structured, the participants apply or evolve rules which regulate who can talk to whom, when, for how long, in what manner, or on which subject. In order to choose the right set of rules, individuals have to be capable of recognizing a social situation and attaching to it an identifying label. Finer discrimination is achieved by studying the roles of the participants, which serve as keys to the interpretation of messages; the direction, origin, and destination of certain actions; and finally the arrangement of the material environment (11).

FEEDBACK AND CORRECTION

Control of action through incorporation of information about its effects is referred to as feedback (13). The control function thus is not localizable in any particular spot of the network but is dependent upon circular relay of messages. These in effect steer the behavior of organisms and organizations and regulate the performance of machines (14). While the process of negative feedback stabilizes the status quo and creates an apparent steady state, positive feedback maximizes the existing tendencies of the system and may introduce irreversible changes.

RESPONSE

A person or a group cannot gauge the effects produced upon others who do not respond to action in a perceivable way. The correction of any performance thus is dependent upon the reaction of others, which fact offers opportunities for influencing and steering the behavior of individuals and groups. In order to be effective, a response has to be properly timed and economically formulated, and it must be appropriate to the situation. Individually, a response that fits the initial statement as a key fits into a keyhole is experienced as a great pleasure (7).

SUCCESSFUL AND UNSUCCESSFUL COMMUNICATION

Successful communication can be conceived of as the establishment of concordant information, unsuccessful communication as the establishment of discordant information in various participants. Obviously such correspondence has to be limited in subject matter and time, as no two individuals can be expected to possess identical information in all matters at all times (7).

GRATIFYING AND FRUSTRATING COMMUNICATION

The pleasure that individuals derive from well-functioning communication constitutes the driving force which induces them to seek human relations. Frustrating communication, in contrast, manifests itself by increasing symptom formation, and it tends to make individuals withdraw from ill-functioning networks. Gratifying communication is the keynote of mental health (7).

PRINCIPLES OF THERAPEUTIC COMMUNICATION

DEFINITION OF THERAPEUTIC COMMUNICATION

Therapeutic communication differs from ordinary communication in that the intention of one or more of the participants is clearly directed at bringing about a change in the system and manner of communication. For simplicity's sake, the persons in charge of bringing about such a change are called therapists; the others are called patients. The therapist steers communication in such a way that the patient is exposed to situations and message exchanges which eventually will bring about more gratifying social relations. The procedures used to initiate such beneficial changes do not differ qualitatively from the methods of communication used in daily life. Special methods such as free association and hypnosis, which require a more rigorous control of the situation, are used only in special cases.

DISTURBANCES OF COMMUNICATION

Disturbances of communication arise when messages are too intense or too weak, when they arrive too early or too late, or when they are inappropriate to the situation. Any disturbance of intensity, timing, or appropriacy may interfere with the feedback mechanisms and their regulatory effects. When these wider social feedback circuits fail to function, the individual replaces them with intra-organismic and solipsistic feedback devices (7).

The individual as the seat of disturbed communication: Illness which affects the individual communicator can be caused by:

–Disease, trauma, or malformation of the organs of communication, in which case the functions of perception, evaluation, and expression will be affected.
–Insufficient mastery of nonverbal or verbal denotation and language, in which case the sign processes will suffer.
–Insufficient or erroneous information about self and about others, in which case erroneous action will be the result.
–Insufficient mastery of metacommunicative devices—both instructive and interpretative—so that an individual's actions are misinterpreted and he in turn misinterprets the behavior of others.
–Inability to correct information because of inadequate skill in the utilization of feedback circuits, both intraorganismic and interpersonal.

The multiperson situation as a cause of disturbed communication: Even though all members participating in a social network may be healthy and free from intraorganismic pathology, there exist other conditions which are conducive to the development of disturbances of communication:

–If the communications of one person or group are not responded to by the communications of another person or group, the two social entities do not join in a common feedback circuit. In the absence of self-steering properties, disturbances of communication are the result.

–If the feedback devices in a large network do not work properly, a coalition of people may set up a separate network within the larger system. Thus a new sub-system with different rules, feedback circuits, and codifications is established which may be tolerated or excluded by the people who form the larger system. But in any case, it brings about difficulties of communication.

THE GROUP AS SUBJECT OF THERAPEUTIC COMMUNICATION

The presence of another person who understands, acknowledges, and responds to the patient is a prerequisite for therapeutic communication. This person may be a doctor, nurse, relative, or friend. Most patients live either with their families or with friends, and these persons form an integral part of the patient's communication network. If feedback is relied upon to have a corrective effect, it is necessary that the therapist steer the communications not only of the patient but also of the network as a whole. For this purpose, the therapist may at any one time designate one person as the principal patient and have the others stand by as auxiliary patients. Later on, the roles may be reversed. In this manner the responsibility for illness is carried by the group rather than by the individual, and exclusion for illness is prevented. Also, the pathologic ways of communication are counteracted not only by the therapist but by the other participants in the network as well.

INDICATIONS FOR THERAPEUTIC COMMUNICATION

If his condition is related to an inner conflict which is evidenced by guilt, shame, fear, anger, or depression, communication can help the patient to relive past experiences, to gain insight into his present circumstances, and to adopt a behavior which is favorable for the gradual reduction of the conflict. Working through of the resistances against unconscious conflict here is the method of choice.

If his condition is brought about by, or is related to, isolation, misunderstandings, disagreements, or social conflict, mastery of communication may help the patient to correct erroneous information, to associate productively with people, and to eliminate disturbances as they arise.

If the patient has an infantile personality, utilizes naive ways of communication, or lacks knowledge of people and situations, contact with an experienced therapist may help him to grow. As a teacher, the therapist may map out a course of informal education which enhances the patient's chances to achieve maturity.

If his condition is related to the experience of anxiety in the face of unalterable somatic, physical, or social circumstances, communication with the patient may help to reduce his apprehension and fear. In communicating with the patient, the therapist may help to clarify contradictory issues and lend moral and emotional support so that the patient is better capable of struggling with his problems and may learn to accept the unalterable.

ACUTE CONDITIONS

To an acutely sick patient, the therapist lends support; by being there, he alleviates anxiety, initiates medical or surgical measures, communicates with relatives, and if necessary makes temporary decisions until the patient can resume his social functions. In acute conditions, correction of communication, uncovering of unconscious conflicts, and confrontation with the facts of reality are avoided. The patient in his helpless state is treated much like an infant, whereby others attempt to take over the deficient functions as much as possible.

CHRONIC CONDITIONS

The difficulties of communication of a patient whose condition is stable are worked through in an intimate patient-doctor relationship. The patient thus has an opportunity to experience, through the corrective replies of the therapist, his distortions of reality and his deficiencies of communication. Only when the processes of communication are operating satisfactorily can the unconscious conflicts be worked through in a satisfactory manner.

CRISIS AND ENVIRONMENTAL STRESS

Unusual stimulation, separation from habitual surroundings, specific danger to life and limb, threats to the offspring or to the group, war, famine, pestilence, opportunities for action, and new social contacts all present instances of intense experience when behavior may change spontaneously. The therapist makes use of these naturally occurring crises to help the patient to readjust his life in a new direction.

EXPERIENCE IS THE SUBJECT OF STUDY

Ability to respond, mastery of language, flexibility in the assumption of roles, appropriate knowledge, and awareness of self and others are prerequisites for satisfactory human experience. It is not in the past nor in the future, but in the present that the individual experiences the self and his surroundings as one. Boundary lines are dropped, artificial linguistic distinctions are abandoned, and feeling, thinking, and doing cease to be separate. Such a state of mind is achieved through satisfactory communication and exposure to a variety of life experiences. The patient has to test his ability to experience while he still has the support of the therapist. The interview or hospital situation is but a laboratory or classroom where the patient learns what he has to try out on his own in private life. If nothing happens in the patient's life, therapy may come to a complete standstill.

ANTICIPATORY BEHAVIOR AND MOMENTARY ADAPTATION

Although the anticipatory behavior of man may block his adjustment to existing realities, it is, on the other hand, the most powerful tool of survival. Commitment to the task at hand, anticipation of needs to come, foresight, looking towards a brighter future, and belief in the less or least probable of possibilities can keep a man alive in the face of unfavorable odds. Anticipatory behavior is one of the powerful motivations which induce people to tolerate the frustrations experienced, including those imposed by therapy. A complex and optimal relationship between anticipation and adaptation to the needs of the moment is achieved by the mature individual. For the patient, this often remains an unattainable goal.

THERAPEUTIC COMMUNICATION AND SPONTANEITY

Therapeutic communication can occur anywhere—in the office, at the bedside, on the street, or at work. Scheduled and planned interviews may alternate with field visits in the home of the patient or at the place of work. The frequency of sessions depends upon the condition of the patient. In an acute psychosis, the patient may be seen several times a day. Later on, the number of meetings can be reduced to two or three a week, then to once a week or even less. A flexible schedule whereby the patient comes frequently when things are happening in his life and infrequently when life has settled into a routine proves a happy solution. No steadfast rules as to place, time, or frequency of the meetings, therefore, can be given.

THE THERAPIST WITHOUT A MASK

Therapeutic communication is an art which depends upon the therapist's ability to communicate, his understanding of people and situations, his personal experience with pathology and therapy, and his willingness to help other people learn to communicate. In contact with patients, the therapist behaves like an ordinary human being, in as natural a way as possible. He does not hide himself from view, he does not use a special language, he does not employ gadgets; he simply tries to communicate as efficiently as possible with the patient. Rather than living up to the stereotyped image of a doctor, a psychologist, or a psychoanalyst, the therapist is himself. As a result, the therapist's personality is not a tabooed subject but becomes part of the discussion. Just as the doctor learns to address himself to the patient's particular ways of responding, the patient learns to reply to the expressions of the therapist. Instead of deferring to an impersonal method, the therapist conveys to the patient that no two people communicate in the same way and that the patient will have to put up with some of the doctor's idiosyncrasies, no matter whom he works with. The therapist's courage to be himself and to reveal himself induces the patient to do the same.

THE LEVERAGE OF THE THERAPIST

In addition to the motivation of the patient to gain or regain a state of well-being, the therapist can exert leverage through three fundamental processes: understanding, acknowledging, and agreeing.

Understanding involves the establishment of an accurate idea or model of the patient's behavior in the therapist's mind. Acknowledging refers to the specific response of the therapist to the patient's purposive or involuntary messages. Agreeing implies the isolation of certain aspects in the world of human experience and establishing correspondence of views or opinions. All three of these processes are pleasurable. Once the patient has experienced the pleasure of these processes of communication, he will seek more of them and hence learn to communicate better. This in turn puts him into a position of solving his own problems.

WORKING THROUGH

At the beginning of therapeutic communication, the patient can only relate to others with the means he brings with him, and this often involves a distortion of persons or situations. This initial distortion, which is commonly referred to as transference, may later develop into a transference neurosis, indicating that the expressions of inner disturbances have been replaced by a variety of feelings towards the therapist. These can then be worked through by focusing upon the preconscious and unconscious behavior of the patient as revealed through dreams, daily life mistakes, and his metacommunicative devices. Free association, a time-consuming device requiring an extraordinary degree of strength and health, is usually not resorted to in therapeutic communication.

In face-to-face communication, the antithesis between conscious and unconscious is minimized. The patient is helped to experience the unconscious aspects of his behavior as much as he is helped to repress elements which interfere with purposive behavior. His insights are the result of improvement and not its cause. When people have learned to correct their performance and information, when they begin to experience more fully and cease to be afraid of others and of themselves, they will try to connect events which they previously were forced to keep separate.

TERMINATION OF THERAPEUTIC COMMUNICATION

Therapeutic communication differs from ordinary communication in that the therapist's gratification does not derive from the pleasure of communication with the patient but from the satisfaction inherent in earning a living and in the practicing of his skills. Therefore, when the patient has become capable of communicating successfully and the human network in which he operates shows signs of corrective feedback, the patient can be trusted to solve his own difficulties. This point can be detected when, after a time, both therapist and patient experience pleasure in communicating with each other. This pleasure is an indication that the time for termination of therapy has come. Apparently the patient has learned to communicate satisfactorily with his therapist, and therefore there is little sense in continuing treatment.

References

1. Cherry, C.: *On Human Communication*. 333 p. New York: Wiley, 1957.
2. Hayakawa, S. I.: *Language in Thought and Action* (2nd ed.). 307 p. New York: Harcourt Brace, 1949.
3. Miller, G. A.: *Language and Communication*. 298 p. New York: McGraw-Hill, 1951.
4. Morris, C. W.: *Signs, Language, and Behavior*. 365 p. New York: Prentice-Hall, 1946.
5. Quastler, H. (Editor): *Information Theory in Psychology*. 436 p. Glencoe: Free Press, 1955.

6. Ruesch, J.: The Observer and the observed. Pp. 36–54, 303–304, and 340–361 in *Toward a Unified Theory of Human Behavior* (Edited by R. R. Grinker). New York: Basic Books, 1956.

7. Ruesch, J.: *Disturbed Communication*. 337 p. New York: Norton, 1957.

8. Ruesch, J.: Principles of human communication. Dialectica, 11, 154–165, 1957.

9. Ruesch, J. and Bateson, G.: *Communication: The Social Matrix of Psychiatry*. 314 p. New York: Norton, 1951.

10. Ruesch, J. and Kees, W.: *Nonverbal Communication*. 205 p. Berkeley and Los Angeles: University of California Press, 1956.

11. Ruesch, J. and Prestwood, A. R.: Interaction processes and personal codification. J. Personality, 18, 391–430, 1950.

12. Shannon, C. A. and Weaver, W.: *The Mathematical Theory of Communication*. 117 p. Urbana: University of Illinois Press, 1949.

13. Wiener, N.: *Cybernetics, or Control and Communication in the Animal and the Machine*. 194 p. New York: Wiley, 1948.

14. Wiener, N.: *The Human Use of Human Beings—Cybernetics and Society*. 241 p. Boston: Houghton Mifflin, 1950.

Index

Where authors are cited on a text page, even though not mentioned by name, they are indexed to that page number.